CONVERTING THE ROSEBUD

THE CIVILIZATION OF THE AMERICAN INDIAN SERIES

CONVERTING THE ROSEBUD

Catholic Mission and the

LAKOTAS

1886–1916

Harvey Markowitz

UNIVERSITY OF OKLAHOMA PRESS : NORMAN

Library of Congress Cataloging-in-Publication Data

Name: Markowitz, Harvey, author.
Title: Converting the Rosebud : Catholic mission and the Lakotas, 1886–1916 / Harvey
    Markowitz.
Other titles: Catholic mission and the Lakotas, 1886–1916
Description: Norman, OK : University of Oklahoma Press, [2018] | Series: Civilization of
    the American Indian series volume 277 | Includes bibliographical references and index.
Identifiers: LCCN 2017033952 | ISBN 978-0-8061-5985-0 (hardcover : alk. paper)
Subjects: LCSH: Lakota Indians—Missions. | St. Francis Catholic Indian Mission (Rosebud
    Indian Reservation, S.D.) | Lakota Indians—Religion. | Lakota Indians—History. |
    Jesuits—Missions—South Dakota—Rosebud Indian Reservation—History. | Rosebud
    Indian Reservation (S.D.)—History—Sources.
Classification: LCC E99.T34 M355 2018 | DDC 299.7/85244—dc23 LC record available
    at https://lccn.loc.gov/2017033952

Converting the Rosebud: Catholic Mission and the Lakotas, 1886–1916 is Volume 277 in The
Civilization of the American Indian Series.

The paper in this book meets the guidelines for permanence and durability of the Committee
on Production Guidelines for Book Longevity of the Council on Library Resources, Inc. ∞

1 2 3 4 5 6 7 8 9 10

To my parents, Mitch and Gert,
and Ate George Horselooking

Contents

Illustrations

Map

Preface

This study examines the origins and early history of Saint Francis Indian Mission on the Rosebud Sioux Reservation within the overlapping contexts of nineteenth-century federal Indian reform, Catholic mission policy, and pre- and post-reservation Lakota culture. I arrived in the town of Saint Francis in 1975 prepared to write an ethnography on contemporary Lakota ethics. However, my exposure to the diaries of several of the mission's original company of Jesuit priests soon led me to set aside that topic for an investigation of the challenges that the mission faced during its first thirty years—from its founding in 1886 to 1916 when a fire reduced it to ashes. It is this latter study on which the present book is based.

Not long after beginning my research, I realized that these three decades of mission history could not be studied as an isolate but needed to be framed by a narrative of the battles waged on a national level between the Catholic Church and federal and Protestant organizations that often opposed its agenda for American Indian conversion and education. The outcomes of these contests conducted on high held very real repercussions for Saint Francis, sometimes calling for its missionaries to modify or abandon preferred methods of evangelization and classroom teaching or, at their most extreme, threatening the mission with financial collapse. Because a majority of these religious were émigrés from the anti-Catholic policies of German Chancellor

Otto von Bismarck's Kulturkampf, such crises could not help but remind them of their recent confrontation with religious persecution and color their day-to-day relationships with the Rosebud's Protestant missionaries and local representatives of the Office of Indian Affairs.

Like so many other Indian missions that originated in the latter nineteenth century, Saint Francis owed its existence to the reforms in Indian policy of that time, when the federal government requested the assistance of mainline Christian denominations to help solve the "Indian problem." As chapter 1 explains, the roots of this long era of federal-Indian relations, lasting approximately from 1867 to the early 1930s, can be traced to the failure of Andrew Jackson's policy of Indian removal. In the aftermath of removal's collapse, two successive Indian commissioners of the late antebellum, Orlando Brown and Luke Lea, promoted a unique combination of Indian removal and assimilation as offering the best chance for "saving" the Indians. A key element in their plan was for the government to create reservations where it could resettle Indians and systematically transform them from savage heathens into Christianized U.S. citizens. Chapter 1 also examines the changes that occurred in Brown and Lea's original program for reservation-based Indian assimilation once it was absorbed into post–Civil War Indian reform policy. This examination takes special note of a well-heeled group of Protestant reformers (the self-designated "Friends of the Indians") whose reconciliation of their liberal version of salvation history with the Indian Office's normative view of social development became the essential element in linking the goals of Indian "civilization and Christianization."

Chapter 2 investigates the reasons for the Catholic Church's decision to participate in Ulysses S. Grant's flagship of Indian reform, the "Peace Policy," and the subsequent controversies with the Indian Office that its participation spawned. Of particular interest are disputes concerning the continued use of Indian reservations as a tool of assimilation and whether the government's support of church-operated reservation boarding schools breached the constitutional wall separating church and state. Believing that an anti-Catholic animus lay behind such controversies, Catholic Church officials quickly took steps to protect the interests of their Indian missions and educational institutions. Among their most important measures was to establish the Bureau of Catholic Indian Missions in Washington, D.C., to serve as an intermediary and lobbying agency for its personnel and converts. Although the extent to which "anti-Romanism" was responsible for the difficulties that beset Catholics during the reform era is open to debate, there is no question that Catholic assessment of the methods that best served the goals of Indian assimilation and salvation differed significantly enough from those of Protestant reformers to generate a great deal of rancor.

Chapter 3 describes the federal government's relentless attempts through warfare and diplomacy to conquer and colonize the Lakota tribes. It then examines the effects of reform Indian policy on the Sicangu Lakotas, especially their transformation from a politically and culturally sovereign people into government wards designated the "Rosebud Sioux."

The book's next two chapters detail events that led to the inception and growth of Catholic missionary work among the Rosebud's Lakotas. Chapter 4 details Martin Marty's elevation from abbot of Saint Meinrad Benedictine archabbey in Indiana to bishop of Dakota Territory, highlighting his increasing contact with Lakota tribes and his work to establish missions among them. The next chapter portrays Rosebud's first, trouble-plagued Catholic mission, focusing on the battles of one of its priests—Fr. Francis Craft—with Rosebud agent George Wright.

Chapter 6 begins with an overview of German Chancellor Otto von Bismarck's anti-Catholic Kulturkampf during the late nineteenth century and the emigration to the United States of large numbers of Jesuit and Franciscan religious that it spawned. It next identifies the circumstances that led Bishop Marty to select some of these émigrés to staff the newly established Saint Francis Mission and boarding school on the Rosebud Reservation.

Chapter 7 first describes the various difficulties Catholics encountered in constructing and opening Saint Francis Mission. Some of these problems were a consequence of the reservation agent's transparent antipathy toward the Catholic Church, but others stemmed from unfortunate choices concerning the mission's location and architectural design. The chapter next recounts the Jesuits' and Franciscans' initial meeting with the Sicangus, spotlighting the welcoming meal that the missionaries hosted for the Indians who had gathered to greet them. It ends with a survey of the growth of the mission's physical plant, staff, and school enrollment between 1886 and 1916.

The paradigm of late-nineteenth and early twentieth-century missionization at Saint Francis is the subject of chapter 8, which first describes the methods the religious employed to "civilize and Christianize" the students at their boarding school and then examines the missionaries' efforts to convert and assimilate adult Sicangus.

The next two chapters consider the obstacles to which missionaries attributed the slow progress of their work among the Sicangus. Chapter 9 explores those impediments that they attributed to Indian sources, including Lakota psychology, culture, and religion, and chapter 10 considers those obstructions that they considered of non-Sicangu origin, including the antipathy of Protestant missionaries, local Indian Office personnel, federal Indian policies, and natural disasters such as hailstorms and fires, which missionaries often attributed to the devil.

Sicangu responses to Catholic missionary work are the subject of chapters 11–13. Chapter 11 identifies elements of an indigenous Lakota missiology that may have prepared them for their initial encounters with Pierre-Jean De Smet and other early Catholic missionaries. Chapter 12 recounts how the great Sicangu leader Spotted Tail, among other Sicangus, attempted to utilize the Catholic Church to achieve social and political ends, including the struggle to remain on the Rosebud and to choose where and by whom their children should be educated. The thirteenth chapter considers the Sicangus' appropriation of selected Catholic doctrines and ceremonies, placing particular emphasis on how their traditional concept of sacred power entered into this process. It also presents some of the ways in which Catholic Sicangus and other western Sioux shaped elements of their yearly Catholic Sioux Indian Congress to reflect aspects of traditional Lakota ceremonies, especially the Sun Dance.

The book's conclusion explores the devastating fire of 1916 that destroyed most of the mission's buildings, along with the subsequent investigation into its causes. It then turns to the missionaries' decision on whether to continue with their Sicangu mission.[1]

A Note on Language

The designation "Sioux" is still commonly employed to refer to Dakota, Nakota, and Lakota tribes and even remains a part of some of their official tribal designations. Nevertheless, its pejorative etymology has made its continued use increasingly controversial.[2] Many have found the indigenous term "Oceti Sakowin" ("Seven Council Fires"), which includes all Dakota, Nakota, and Lakota peoples, a more acceptable alternative. In the following pages I employ "Sioux" only when using an alternative term would compromise the taken-for-granted usages of federal agents, missionaries, and other non-Lakotas of the period. In most other contexts, especially those of ethnological nature, I employ the terms "Sicangu" or "Lakota" where appropriate.

Acknowledgments

This book owes its existence to the intellectual and moral support of teachers, peers, coworkers, family, and friends. Since my debts are legion, the following paragraphs can present only a partial roll of individuals to whom I am indebted.

Heading this list are Drs. Martin E. Marty, Frederick E. Hoxie, David Tracey, and Craig Howe, for whose wisdom, nurture, and patience I will always be grateful.

I would also like to extend my appreciation to the staff of the Newberry Library, whose D'Arcy McNickle Center for American Indian History was my home for many years. I am especially indebted to the late Helen Tanner, John Aubrey, Fr. Peter Powell, Ruth Hamilton, Susan Rosa, Jay Miller, Hjordis Halvorson, Raymond Fogelson, Peter Iverson, R. David Edmunds, Gary and Emily Bevington, James Grossman, and members of the library's Special Collections and Technical Services departments.

From 1999 to 2002, my colleagues at the Smithsonian Institution's National Museum of the American Indian were unstinting in their encouragement and support. These include Ann McMullen, Casey Macpherson, Cecile Ganteaume, Emil Her Many Horses, Mary Jane Lenz, Emily Kaplan, Truman Lowe, Jennifer Shannon, Teresa Tate, Heidi McKinnon, Carmen and Gabriela Arenallo, Romero Mateos, Veronica Harrell, and Rebecca Graham.

I am grateful to Raymond J. DeMallie of Indiana University, who first suggested and arranged for my fieldwork on the Rosebud. Special thanks are additionally due to Phillip Bantin, formerly of the Marquette University archives, and Mark Thiel, now head archivist at Marquette, for their decades of assistance and friendship. I am also thankful to Sr. Mary Serbacki, archivist for and a member of the Eastern Province of the Franciscan Sisters of Penance and Christian Chairty at Stella-Niagra, N.Y., for her considerable help in locating important documents used in this work. I am greatly indebted as well to Marie Kills in Sight, director of the Buechel Memorial Museum, my friends and colleagues O. Kendal White, Dick Grefe, Elizabeth Teaff, and Laura Hewitt of Washington and Lee University for their much sought after and appreciated help with this book's final draft, George and Rhea Kosovic, David Colin Carr, and Alessandra Tamulevich, John Thomas, Sarah Smith, and Emily Schuster of the University of Oklahoma Press for their suggestions, encouragement, and support.

Finally, it would be unconscionable to omit acknowledging my indebtedness to the two communities whose intertwined histories are the subject of this book. One group is the Saint Francis Mission pastoral staff who invited me to join their company as a researcher and friend from 1975 to 1985 and once more from 1988 to 1990. I am especially grateful for the understanding and support of the following Jesuit priests, Franciscan sisters, Jesuit and Xaverian brothers, and former mission volunteers: Frs. Robert Hilbert, Bernard Fagan, Harry Zerner, Richard Jones, Joseph Gill, Jim Egan, Kenneth Walleman, Roc O'Connor, and Raymond Bucko; Srs. Helen Borszich, Candace Tucci, Genevieve Cuny, Bernadette Clifford, Marie Therese Archambault, and Mary Francis Hilbert; Brs. Joseph Schwartzler, John Carr, Bede Benn, and Dan Lynch; Linda, David, and Beth O'Donnell, Hal Dessel, John Melcher, Jim Green, Georgia Hackett, Marge Werner, Pat Simonik, Alice and Ray Culligan, and Harold and Marjorie Moore.

Composing the second community are the Sicangu Lakotas, whose wisdom, humor, deep-seated spirituality, and love for their language and traditions have been a constant source of empowerment and inspiration. From my arrival on the Rosebud, I was the undeserving benefactor of the generosity of one family in particular—the Horselookings—whose patriarchs, George and Henry, conducted their lives in accordance with the values and traditions that make the Lakotas a great people. In addition to teaching me Lakota language and customs, they presented me with the most precious gift a Lakota can give to another person: a family. *Wopila tanka eciciyapelo.*

CONVERTING THE ROSEBUD

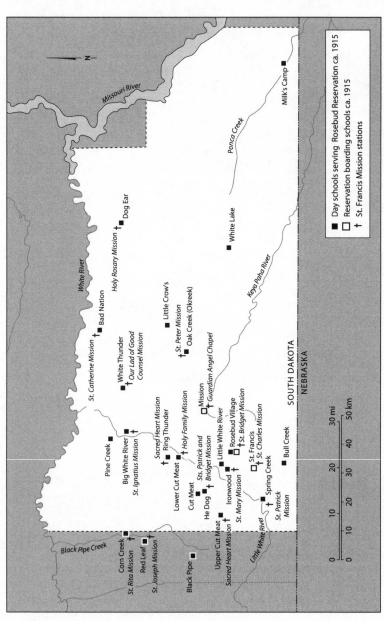

Day schools, boarding schools, and Catholic Mission stations serving the Rosebud Sioux Reservation, ca. 1915. The reservation borders depicted here approximate the legal boundaries set forth in the Sioux Agreement of 1889 until they were radically diminished by the 1977 U.S. Supreme Court decision of *Rosebud Sioux Tribe v. Kneip* (430 U.S. 584). *Map by Bill Nelson. Copyright © 2018, University of Oklahoma Press.*

CHAPTER ONE

The Road to Reform
in Federal Indian Policy

From 1789 to 1829, U.S. Indian policy remained wedded to modes of thought and action largely inherited from the nation's colonial past. Among this legacy's most important concerns was to steer the country away from conflict with its often stronger neighboring tribes by establishing a twofold approach to Indian affairs. One of these tactics entailed negotiating treaties through which Indian communities agreed, for stipulated considerations, to cede portions of their homelands that loomed as flash points for conflicts with whites (removal); the other operation called for the use of friendly persuasion to convince Indian tribes to abandon their traditional beliefs and practices for those of Euro-American culture in order one day to assimilate them within the general population (assimilation or "civilization"). Although during this period the comparative importance of each of these measures experienced both minor and major fluctuations, there was never a time when one or the other totally dominated the discourse and practice of federal Indian affairs.

Jacksonian Indian Removal

The first significant break from dualistic Indian policy arrived on the heels of Andrew Jackson's presidential inauguration. In his first message to Congress, delivered on December 8, 1829, Jackson characterized all previous Indian policy as a failure, citing as its chief weakness the inability of its framers to

recognize the essential antagonism existing between removal and assimilation. Summing up this myopia, he noted that it had "long been the policy
of Government to introduce among [the Indians] the arts of civilization,
in hope of gradually reclaiming them from a wandering life." However, he
continued, this policy "has been coupled with another wholly incompatible
with its success. Professing a desire to civilize and settle them, we have
at the same time lost no opportunity to purchase their lands and thrust
them farther into the wilderness." Through this misguided combination of
antithetical strategies, the Indians "have not only been kept in a wandering
state, but been led to look upon us as unjust and indifferent to their fate
[while the] Government has constantly defeated its own policy, and the
Indians in general, receding farther and farther to the west, have retained
their savage habits."[1]

To correct this shortcoming Jackson called upon Congress to grant a
divorce between the two processes and to award sole custody of Indian
policy to removal. He also appealed to lawmakers to provide a large quantity
of land west of the Mississippi (later to be called Indian Territory) that the
federal government could apportion among the removed tribes and upon
which each would continue to exercise its sovereignty, limited only by U.S.
intervention to safeguard the peace. All efforts toward civilizing tribes, he
underscored, would be transferred from the government to humanitarian
organizations and would proceed only with the permission of tribe or tribes
involved. Jackson's plan called for congressional approval to grant tribes the
right to swap their treaty-recognized lands in the East for new territories in
the West. The Indian Removal Act of 1830, which authorized the deportation of thousands of southeastern natives west to Indian "Country" or
"Territory," most fully expressed the presuppositions informing Jacksonian
Indian removal.[2]

There is good reason to question whether Jackson sincerely believed that
removed tribes would be able to retain claims to their lands in perpetuity.[3]
Wherever the truth on this matter may lie, by his second term in office it
was becoming clear that his removal policy could no more guarantee the
permanence of Indian claims to their territories than the dualistic policy it
had superseded. Thus, for example, the ink was still wet on the 1834 Trade
and Intercourse Act's delineation of Indian Territory's official borders when
the erosion of the lands contained therein commenced.

From Removal to Reform in Indian Policy

With no end to the reduction of native lands in sight, in 1850 Indian commissioner Orlando Brown devised a new approach to pre-Jackson Indian policy that he believed would set the nation on the road to solving its "Indian problem." His central innovation was to establish "reservations" where Indian tribes could be removed and confined so that the government could begin carefully orchestrating their transformation from savage collectivism to civilized individualism.

Brown's approach represented nothing less than a "turning turtle" of Jacksonian removal. Not only did it once again plunge the federal Indian Office into the business of administering Indian lands, but it also saddled it with responsibility for funding and directing programs to assimilate the tribes settled upon them. From Jacksonian segregation the nation had thus taken its first steps toward reservation Indian policy in which removal and assimilation would presumably work together in perfect harmony.

Brown's successor, Luke Lea, was so strongly committed to the former's assimilationist policy that he dedicated much of his first report as Indian commissioner (1850) to its hypothetical application to the Chippewa (Anishinaabe) and Sioux (Dakota) tribes. Lea's plan first called for the removal of these traditional enemies to clearly demarcated reservations in order to reduce the frequency with which they encountered one another, other tribes, and non-Indians. After being confined to their respective lands, he argued, it would only be a matter of time until they had hunted out the available game. At this point they would have little choice other than to accept a federal program in agricultural training in order to keep from starving. Once they were transformed into sedentary farmers, Lea concluded, it would be possible to build schools, churches, and other instruments of civilization among them.[4]

Brown and Lea's antebellum revival of Indian assimilation was largely a response to demographic pressures—most important, the ever-increasing westward expansion of the country's white population into and through Indian lands, and the clashes between the two populations to which these movements invariably led. By the end of the 1840s this expansion, nourished by European immigration, territorial acquisitions from the Mexican-American War, and the California Gold Rush, had already spread well beyond the borders of Indian Territory and was making a "fact" of the credo of manifest destiny.

From the early 1850s through the Civil War, reservation Indian policy had evolved into the taken-for-granted approach to U.S.-Indian relations. But behind this facade of "business as usual" lay one of the federal government's worst-kept dirty little secrets. The public had long been aware that many Indian Office employees were political appointees who, though demonstrating little acumen in running Indian affairs, were incredibly adept at enjoying lives of luxury in spite of their meager wages. Such glaring disparities between their salaries and "take-home pay" were equally common among the Office's reservation employees and those residing in Washington, D.C.

In response to these scandals, on March 3, 1865, Congress approved the formation of a joint special committee to investigate the social and economic conditions of Indian peoples, as well as the civilian and military conduct of Indian affairs.[5] The data for the committee's findings were to be gathered from questionnaires and interviews with Indian agents, military personnel, missionaries, and others persons with firsthand knowledge of native communities.

Almost two years in the making, the so-called Doolittle Committee (named after the committee chair, Wisconsin senator James Rood Doolittle) sent its report to Congress in January 1867.[6] Included among its findings were statistics on tribal populations and their dynamics, Indian mortality and morbidity rates, and the prevalence of alcoholism, prostitution, and other "social diseases" on reservations. The report also contained respondents' descriptions and opinions on such topics as the suitability of reservation locations, individual and tribal land ownership, the amount of Indian farming under way, the quality of schools, and the quality of missionary work.

In spite of the time and labor the committee had lavished on its survey, Doolittle had severe misgivings about much of the information it contained, and not without reason.[7] Not only did some of its data prove to be unreliable, but the narrative also contained unsubstantiated, inflammatory accusations that impugned the integrity of civilian and military personnel. Not the least of those whose reputations suffered a severe drubbing was the Indian commissioner himself, William P. Dole. Doolittle delayed releasing the report until he could investigate some of the more provocative accusations. In spite of this precaution, a portion of the unredacted document wound up in the hands of one of the Indian commissioner's political enemies. A reporter at the *Cincinnati Gazette* then made much of its contents public. Given the negative publicity that these leaks provoked, Doolittle had little choice but to release the report.

For all its shortcomings, the Doolittle investigation led to some significant changes both in the handling of Indian affairs and in the public's perceptions of Indians. It helped to settle, at least temporarily, the debate over whether civilians or the military should be in charge of managing Indian affairs. Siding with the commission's recommendation, Congress voted to continue civilian oversight of the Indian Office. As well, the investigation portrayed Indians in a highly sympathetic light as the victims of white treachery and greed. Speaking for the commission, Doolittle wrote that the abject condition of American Indians was yet another outcome of "the irrepressible conflict between a superior and an inferior race when brought in the presence of each other. Upon this subject all the testimony agrees"[8] Finally, it elicited demand for an end to the abuses of public monies and trust that had become synonymous with the management of Indian affairs. What was needed was reform.

Among the Doolittle Report's most avid readers were members of an alliance of politically connected Protestant philanthropists and reformers who were prepared to dedicate their influence to cleaning up the Indian Office. Referring to themselves as the "Friends of the Indians," these religiously credentialed pillars of society were precisely the bedfellows President Ulysses S. Grant, whose administration had inherited the scandal-riddled Indian Office from its predecessors, needed to restore public trust in his administration's handling of Indian affairs. Although the Friends' power over Indian affairs was safely limited to an advisory capacity, their deeply rooted commitment to church-based social reform and to a broadly shared philosophy of human social development worked to reshape reservation-based Indian policy.

Evangelical Protestantism, Christian Civilization, and the "Friends of the Indians"

For most of America's post–Civil War Protestant establishment, the proper practice of Christianity rested on the customary principles of Calvinism and Puritanism as they had been mediated during the eighteenth and early nineteenth centuries by the religious pietism and awakenings of John Wesley and George Whitefield. Although American Protestants remained committed to the fundamental doctrines of the Reformed Church, a personalist fervor radiated from their stress on the experience of conversion. This emphasis on the individual, in combination with the Enlightenment principles found in American democracy and the voluntary nature of American church affiliation, shaped the web of meanings through which they interpreted that experience. An optimistic understanding of salvation, stressing the importance of individual volition and cooperation, thus gradually eclipsed the more somber doctrines of total depravity and double predestination.

The evangelical tendencies of antebellum Protestantism continued to hold sway after the Civil War, preparing the way during the rest of the century for a renewed emphasis on revivalism as a means of propagating the faith. Of equal significance to its function in church recruitment, however, revivalism promoted theological accord among the many Protestant denominations. Describing revivals as a "mighty engine of doctrinal destruction," Sydney Ahlstrom explained that, "because revivalists so often addressed inter-denominational audiences . . . a kind of unwritten consensus [gradually] emerged, its cardinal articles being the infallibility of the Scriptures, the divinity of Christ, and man's duty to be converted from sin to a life guided by a pietistic code of morals."[9]

A major prescription of this homogenized moral code was the duty of those graced by salvation to find appropriate avenues for translating their spiritual transformation into acts of Christian *caritas*. Denominational and interdenominational organizations committed to philanthropic projects and social amelioration provided ready-made structures for church members to channel their righteousness. Thus, just as many reform-minded Protestants in the antebellum North had contributed their money and efforts to organizations dedicated to the abolition of slavery, so in the years following the Civil War evangelicals throughout the nation participated in groups committed to improving the social and religious lot of their fellow humans. Among the primary objectives of these collective endeavors were the prohibition of alcohol and gambling, Sabbatarianism, and prison reform. Mission associations directed toward the propagation of the faith both at home and abroad also experienced a dramatic upswing in their recruits and supporters.

Because of the emphasis that evangelical Protestants placed on individual salvation, one might suspect that the goal of Christianizing society was merely tangential to their religious agenda. In fact, however, evangelicals remained committed to Calvin's ideal of a "holy commonwealth," though refashioning its contours and substance to accord with the principles of republican government. "The assumption that Christianity was the only basis for a healthy civilization," George Marsden observed, "was basic to evangelical thinking—as essential as the belief that souls must be saved for the life to come. Virtue among the citizenry . . . was the foundation of successful civilization, especially republican civilization. Religion was the basis for true virtue; the purer the religion the higher the morality. Christianity was the highest religion."[10]

By transforming America into what Martin E. Marty has termed a "Righteous Empire" or "a kind of public and semi-public counterpart to . . . the religious ideal of the Kingdom of God," Protestants believed that they could help lay the foundations for Christ's second coming.[11] That their image of this empire was essentially a glorified version of America's political economy is significant, though not particularly surprising. Sidney Mead long ago commented on the proclivity of America's churches to lend "themselves to the sanctification of current existing expressions of the American way of life," adding that during the nineteenth century the ability of the denominations to launch a cogent criticism of their culture "was almost nonexistent."[12]

Although Christianizing America emerged as a key element in the evangelicals' sacred history, they also believed that it constituted only a small portion of their role in God's plan. Taken in its totality this role entailed nothing less than harvesting all of humanity for Christ.[13] God, they assumed, had favored America with wealth, power, and piety so that Protestant churches could spearhead the conversion of the world. The light emanating from American religious, economic, and political institutions, they reasoned, should serve as a beacon illuminating the way for less fortunate nations.

Mission, as William R. Hutchison has stated, "urged within a thoroughly affirmative depiction of the millennial role assigned to a Protestant society and culture," constituted the primary response to this calling.[14] Between 1815 and 1914—the period that Kenneth Latourette has termed "the great century" of modern Christianity—the Protestant churches of America created scores of denominational and interdenominational missionary boards, societies, and movements from which issued a virtually endless stream of Christian soldiers.[15] Until the turn of the twentieth century, the mood among the majority of these legions was one of confidence. And although shortly thereafter murmurs could be heard concerning a "crisis in mission," missionary literature and conferences continued to provide predominantly ebullient depictions of the work and accomplishments of the evangelical outreach. The publication, in 1900, of John R. Mott's crusading work, *The Evangelization of the World in This Generation*, simultaneously stirred and reflected the optimism that pulsated throughout the missionary movement.[16] William E. Dodge likewise stoked and echoed this confidence when he observed at the Ecumenical Missionary Conference held in New York that same year, "We are going into a century more full of hope, and promise, and opportunity than any period in the world's history."[17]

Social Development and "Christian Civilization"

If the crusade to missionize the world stemmed from concepts central to evangelical and revivalist Protestantism of eighteenth- and nineteenth-century America, it is nevertheless true that these ideas do not alone fully account for the methodology and goals characteristic of Protestant missionary work of that period. Instead, they were additionally dependent on the assumptions of a popularly espoused philosophy of history sometimes referred to as "social evolution" but more appropriately labeled "social development."[18] When properly "baptized," these assumptions furnished Protestant missionaries and reformers, such as the Friends of the Indians, with a doctrine of "civilization" that was a worthy companion to their ambition of making disciples of all nations.

One of these assumptions was that human society displayed a pattern of growth as clearly articulated and ordered as the ontogenetic structure associated with any particular species. Just as the development of a normal man or woman conforms to a sequence of childhood, adolescence, and adulthood, it was held that the institutions of a typical human community would pass through a series of predetermined stages during the course of its history. Commencing in a state of collective infancy, referred to as "savagery," a society would pass through a stage of youth, or "barbarism," before reaching maturity, or "civilization."

Behind social development's empirical claim that all societies shared a pattern of collective growth lay a number of metaphysical assumptions that transformed it into a philosophy of human progress. One of the most important of these assumptions was that human nature was simultaneously unchanging and dynamic. The observation that societies at all stages of development possess some form of government, law, marriage, religion, and economy both supported and was explained by the metaphysical thesis of the "psychic unity" of humanity. At the same time the structured growth assigned these institutions was linked to stages of development within the human psyche. Whereas the lifeways of savages were believed to reflect the operations of a primitive mentality, those found among civilized peoples were considered the product of complex and sophisticated thought. Rather than being essentially different, the savage and civilized minds were thought to reveal two aspects of the same unfolding reality. The analogy with ontogenesis may again be put to good service, for just as we assume that an individual as a child and as an adult is essentially the same person, the nature of savage and civilized human beings was assumed to be one.

If the thesis of "constancy-in-change" transformed social development from an empirical generalization concerning the universal pattern of human history into a philosophical treatise on the dynamics of human nature, it had yet to account for value-laden nature of this philosophy. The source of its normative character was rather to be found in the identity that nineteenth-century thought posited between social development and progress. By conflating the descriptive thesis that human social history proceeded according to the same stages with the normative thesis that this transformation was progressive in nature, social development was transformed into a theory of social advancement. This prescriptive character is best observed in the polysemy characterizing the term "civilization," which was commonly employed to signify both the final stage of sociocultural growth and the entire process of development. In both cases, however, the significance is predominantly normative, expressing the belief that civilization represents a fundamental good through which human collective life achieves its telos.

For Protestant reformers this "telos" was the millennium, which they believed would occur after they had "harvested" the world for Christ. It was therefore contingent upon them to conform their efforts to the demands of God's providentially arranged sacred history by transmitting the social and religious truths of Christian civilization to all nations ignorant of them. The "Christianization" and "civilization" of the American Indians was one important division of this worldwide mission needed to bring about the return of Christ.

Although the concept of "Christian civilization" helped liberal Protestant reformers and missionaries of this era understand the importance of the cooperative, intertwined nature of civilizing and Christianizing non-Western peoples, they nonetheless maintained a theological distinction between these two processes. In agreement with the popular social thought of their day, they considered the transformation from savagery to civilization to be one of progressive development. Accordingly, they conceived their role as civilizers to involve devising and applying techniques that would foster this growth. Yet the Christianization of peoples, though correlative, was an essentially different project. Whereas the missionaries believed that most of the variations among societies were a consequence of their respective degrees of development, the contrasts between Christianity and non-Western religions constituted differences of kind. Only through Christ's sacrifice had God thrown open the gates of salvation to humanity. Other religions, by contrast, not only lacked the supernatural graces necessary for redemption but also served to blind their adherents to the one and only path to salvation. The idea that heathenism and Christianity were phases of a single process of religious growth—like that of Judaism and Christianity—would have been anathema to Protestant missionaries. Conversion represented a revolution, not development, in religion. As such, it required that all converts forever abandon their non-Christian beliefs and practices.

The "Indian Problem" and Christian Reform

The interests of evangelical Protestants in missionary work and moral reform dovetailed, during the final third of the nineteenth century, with the desire finally to solve the "Indian problem." In view of the Indians' domestic status and the many injustices to which they had been and were subject, the Friends of the Indians and other Protestant reformers believed that native peoples were deserving of special consideration in the agenda of worldwide Christianization and civilization. They nevertheless insisted that their ministry await fundamental reforms in Indian-white relations as urged in the Doolittle report.

For many of the Friends, a major precondition for reform lay in arresting the mounting violence between Indians and settlers in the Northeast Woodlands and Great Plains. Although the attention of most Americans in the early 1860s was primarily focused on the Civil War, they were also aware of conflicts with the country's Indian population, including the "uprising" of Minnesota Dakotas, Col. John M. Chivington's massacre of peaceful Southern Cheyennes at Sand Creek, and Lakota raids along the Oregon and Bozeman trails.

Like the Doolittle commissioners, Christian reformers attributed these outbreaks primarily to the predatory actions of whites. Though ranking encroachments on Indian lands as the primary cause of violence, they considered the morally bankrupt policies and behavior of federal Indian Office personnel as running a close second. After the Civil War, some of the higher-profile Friends, such as Episcopal bishop Henry B. Whipple of Minnesota and Philadelphia philanthropist William Welsh, began pressuring Congress to take measures that would protect the lives and rights of American Indians.

The first important fruit of their lobbying was the creation of the United States Peace Commission in June 1867, six months after the release of the Doolittle report. Among the chief tasks that Congress assigned to the Christian reformers and military officers on the new board was to convince the hostile tribes of the northern and southern plains to settle on reservations. They argued that, once tribes were confined to these areas, the government could more easily protect them from unscrupulous whites and teach them the benefits of civilization and Christianity. It should not pass unnoted, however, that most of the proposed reservation sites lay at great distances from the pathway selected for the Union Pacific Railroad. Aside from humanitarian motivations, there were also keen economic incentives fueling the desire to seal Indians away on isolated pockets of land.

In addition to authorizing the commission to negotiate treaties, Congress charged its members (as it had those on Doolittle's committee) to investigate the causes of Indian depredations and submit recommendations for resolving them. In their report the commissioners cited white Americans' "uniformly unjust" treatment of Indians as the chief reason for the hostilities. They singled out for particular scourging those unscrupulous employees in the Indian Office who "have pocketed the funds appropriated by the government and driven the Indians to starvation." To rectify this situation, the commissioners advised Congress to set a date for all superintendents, agents, and special agents to resign their posts so that only those who had proven themselves "competent and faithful" would be retained. Rejecting the growing sentiment that Congress return the Indian Office to the Department of War, they argued that, although the military was well suited to handle tribes that were "continually hostile or unmanageable . . . we are satisfied that not one in a thousand would like to teach Indian children to read and write, or Indian men to sow and reap."[19]

No less than Indian commissioner Nathaniel G. Taylor threw his weight behind these reforms. In his annual report for 1868, "Shall Our Indians be

Civilized? And How," Taylor dedicated several paragraphs to enumerating the great advances that the Five Civilized Tribes had achieved in Christianity and civilization under the guidance of missionaries. "Now, if the laws of God are immutable," he reasoned, "the application of similar causes to each of the other tribes under our jurisdiction must produce a like effect upon each. If the Cherokees, Choctaws, Chickasaws, Creeks, and Seminoles are civilized and advancing in development," the commissioner continued, "so will be the Cheyennes, Arapahos, Apaches, Kiowas, Comanches, Sioux, and all our other tribes, if we will only use the means in their cases that have been so wonderfully successful in the first named tribe."[20]

The conviction that missionaries and church-affiliated philanthropists should play a more active role in federal-Indian relations was approaching its apogee in 1868, just as Ulysses S. Grant entered office as U.S. president. Working in collaboration with a coalition of Episcopal and Quaker reformers, Grant authorized the formation of the Board of Indian Commissioners, composed of ten unpaid persons selected "from men eminent for their intelligence and philanthropy" and empowered to act as advisors to the commissioner of Indian affairs and the secretary of the interior on matters concerning Indian policy and service.[21]

The Board of Indian Commissioners constituted the first of two major elements in the radical restructuring of Indian affairs that came to be known as the Grant "Peace Policy." The second element authorized the Indian commissioners to distribute the seventy-one Indian reservations among mainstream Christian denominations—an experiment which, as the president explained in his second annual message to Congress on December 5, 1870, "was tried with a few agencies given to the denomination of Friends, and has been found to work most advantageously." Upon receiving its share of reserves, each church nominated agents who would assume full responsibility for the Christianization and civilization on their respective tribes. One of the powers conferred on these agents was the right to expel members of other denominations discovered proselytizing on their assigned reservations.[22]

A major springboard by which the proponents of the Peace Policy sought to catapult Indians from savagery to civilization was the on-reservation boarding school. They believed that such self-contained environments would seal children off from the primitive conditions of their home camps and allow them to be tutored systematically in the habits of civilized society. The Indian Office therefore drew up plans to build, furnish, and operate a number of boarding school facilities. As well, from 1869 until the last decade of the nineteenth century, the Office encouraged Christian denominations to establish and maintain such schools. As an incentive the government agreed to furnish churches with food, clothing, and tuition for each student under their care.

At first glance, there appears to be nothing markedly new with the Peace Policy's invitation to the churches to take up the burden of Indian education. Under the "Indian Civilization Fund" Congress had been awarding churches small stipends to sponsor mission schools in American Indian communities since 1819. With reform Indian policy, however, Indian education was for the first time integrated into a systematic approach to native civilization and Christianization that was rooted, at least theoretically, in Christian humanitarianism. This transformation would lead in the early twentieth century to a crisis in church-state relations and a Supreme Court test for the constitutionality of federal support for sectarian education, most notably for our interests the Saint Francis Mission boarding school on the Rosebud Reservation. Yet, as Grant unveiled his policy in 1870, many of the president's supporters, and especially the Friends of the Indians, believed that America was finally on the way to solving its "Indian problem."

CHAPTER TWO

The Catholic Church
and American Indian Policy

A mong the denominations invited to participate in Grant's Peace Policy was the Roman Catholic Church.[1] Although wary of involvement with the Protestant-dominated Indian Office, the Roman hierarchy quickly accepted the offer to work with the agency's assimilationist agenda. Several factors lay behind the church's positive response. Its leaders considered the government's offer to underwrite the educational work of participating denominations with student tuitions and treaty rations and clothing "gift horses" that they could ill afford to look in the mouth. In addition, most of the executors of Catholic-Indian affairs shared an understanding of church history that was commensurate with the developmentalist assumptions of assimilationist policy and that suggested a pivotal role for Catholics in the Americanization of the Indian. They saw no reason why the church could not repeat its success in civilizing and Christianizing the savages and barbarians of Europe with the New World's primitives. Finally, and perhaps most important, the hierarchy deemed the methods and goals of the Peace Policy to be consistent with some of the basic assumptions of Catholicism's missiology. Adopting the Thomist credo that "faith builds upon nature," they regarded "civilized" forms of social life to supply the temporal substratum necessary for spiritual truths to take root. They accordingly viewed the government's agenda of reservation-based assimilationism as a natural means for achieving the supernatural goals of saving Indian souls and developing self-supporting Indian parishes that would propagate the church. Once tribes adopted "civilized" lifeways, they believed that suitable *natural* ground would exist in which to plant the *supernatural* truths of Catholicism. In reciprocal fashion, the hierarchy deemed Catholic principles of faith and morals to be "indispensable" factors in the effort to elevate less advanced "races," first, by "subduing [their] fierce nature by the softening influences of . . . holy religion,"[2] and, second, by lending "motive and permanence to . . . civilization."[3]

Catholic Objections to the Peace Policy

After initially supporting Grant's initiative, it did not take long for Catholic officials to begin vociferously denouncing both the theory and the practice of church-administered Indian affairs. Their strongest objection concerned the manner in which the Indian Office had distributed the reservations. They complained that the Protestant-controlled Board of Indian Commissioners had shortchanged the Catholic Church of its rightful share of reserves, awarding it only seven of the forty agencies to which they believed it was entitled. They also objected to that portion of the policy that granted an agent the authority to exclude and expel interlopers from churches different from the one assigned to that reservation. These officials observed that it was the duty of their church to minister to Catholic Indians wherever they might live. They therefore held that for the government to prevent their church members, Indian or white, from receiving the sacraments constituted a grievous violation of their religious freedom. Additionally, Catholic leaders believed that it was immoral to deprive heathens or Protestant Indians of the opportunity to embrace Catholicism merely because the Indian Office had opted to administer Indian missionization by comity. As heirs to revivalism's spirit of interdenominational cooperation, most Protestant denominations found that dividing the reservations among churches was both sound and practical. For Catholics, though, who contrasted the truth of their teachings with "sectarian" (i.e., Protestant) error, this "solution" smacked of indifferentism—the idea that one religion was just as good as another—and were wholly opposed to it.

In the article "Our New Indian Policy and Religious Liberty," which appeared in the October 1877 issue of *Catholic World*, P. Girard bluntly summarized Catholic objections to the Peace Policy. He aimed his heaviest fire at the members of the Board of Indian Commissioners—"gentlemen" whom he described as "quite free from any predilection in favor of Catholicity." Girard went on to assert that owing to the Board's intolerance, "sectarian fanaticism, Protestant bigotry, and anti-Christian hatred have been called into play, and the arm of the government has been made to be the instrument for the restriction, and even the abolition, of religious freedom among many of the Indian tribes." As for President Grant, who had established the Board and under whose watch its reputed misdeeds had occurred, Girard insisted that there was no reason to question the "purity and kindness" of his motives. However, at "the time of its inauguration . . . he was surrounded by influences decidedly hostile to the Catholic Church; and it is probable that from the beginning the men 'behind the throne' had a clear conception of the manner in which the new policy could be worked for the benefit of the sects."[4]

Perceptions of anti-Catholic bias in federal Indian policy spurred J. Roosevelt Bayley, archbishop of Baltimore, to appoint Charles Ewing as Catholic Indian commissioner for the bishops and to agitate for the formation of the Bureau of Catholic Indian Missions (BCIM) for "the protection and promotion of Catholic Indian mission interests in the United States of America in 1874."[5] Located in Washington, D.C., this office functioned both as a lobby on behalf of Catholic missionaries, reservation personnel, and Indians and as an official intermediary between individual missions and the federal government. Bayley and other Catholic Church officials were convinced that, lacking such an agency, their missions would be at the mercy of the Protestant bigots whom they believed controlled federal Indian affairs.[6]

Catholics were far from alone in their opposition to the Peace Policy and, in 1883, after more than a decade of interdenominational rancor, the Indian Office finally pulled the plug on Grant's noble experiment. Still, the reform principle of Christianization and civilization continued to serve as the theoretical centerpiece of Indian policy. Thus, although the churches lost much of their authority as overseers of reservation affairs, the federal government continued to finance sectarian-operated Indian schools and other programs directed toward the cultural and religious assimilation of native peoples. The Board of Indian Commissioners also continued as the investigatory and advisory arm of the Indian Office, functions that it maintained until 1934.

The Push to Abolish Indian Reservations

The two decades following the repeal of the Grant Peace Policy marked an era of generally amicable relations between the Catholic Church and the federal government. During this period the BCIM successfully secured government support to build and staff reservation boarding schools among groups that had formerly known only Protestant missionaries and teachers. This included the Saint Francis boarding school on the Rosebud Reservation.

Yet, even as Catholic Indian education was enjoying this dramatic expansion, transformations were occurring in Indian policy that would soon threaten its very existence. These changes were primarily the result of the frustrations experienced by many powerful Protestant reformers over the slow pace of Indian advancement. Most of the advocates of reform policy saw no reason why, given suitable methods and efforts, Indians could not be civilized and Christianized within one generation. Nevertheless, as the decades sped by and the new century approached, they found it increasingly difficult to maintain their original optimistic prognosis.

In searching for the origins of this failure, Christian reformers quickly zeroed in on the reservation system. They now concluded that segregating Indians from the rest of American society had not only proven to be an ineffective means of protecting them from unscrupulous whites but had also deprived them of salutary and civilizing contact with the nation's virtuous citizenry. Reformers additionally argued that the existence of tribally "owned" reservations had allowed the government to continue dealing with Indian groups as domestic "nations" instead of individualizing its relationship with them. This practice, reformers complained, kept alive the outmoded notion that Indians shared a "special relationship" with the U.S. government. As well, they argued that by continuing the distribution of treaty-stipulated rations and annuities the reservation system undermined attempts by agents and missionaries to transform Indians into self-sufficient and responsible citizens.

It would be difficult to find a more scathing indictment of reservation policy than the following passage taken from a letter by anthropologist Alice C. Fletcher. Writing to the participants at the Eighth Lake Mohonk Conference, a convention for the Friends of the Indians that met annually in upstate New York from 1881 to 1916, Fletcher asserted that, "if the Indian is to be saved as a man, the reservations must be broken up, and civilization be allowed to enter in among the people. Even the rude form found in the sparsely settled West," she continued, "is better than the stagnation of mind and labor caused by barren, profitless acres and the arbitrary methods which necessarily belong to the agency system."[7]

During the 1880s, reformers set to work developing strategies that they believed would both counteract the deleterious effects of reservation life and finally get Indians on the road to civilization. One approach involved sending children to schools located far from their agencies, such as the Carlisle Indian Training Institute in Pennsylvania. Reformers maintained that these schools provided the double advantage of removing students from the primitive conditions of reservation life and situating them close to white populations where they could be "outed," that is, placed in "civilized" homes as domestics and laborers of various kinds.[8]

The most ambitious attempt to dismantle the reservation system, however, came with congressional passage of the Dawes Severalty, or General Allotment, Act in 1887. This measure called for the division of tribal lands into plots of sufficient acreage to sustain family farms. Reformers were confident that, once assigned to their individual homesteads, Indians would rapidly develop an appreciation for private property, take up the plow, and eventually appropriate manners of life and behavior indistinguishable from their non-Indian neighbors. The act also provided a "trust" period of twenty-five years during which allottees would remain wards of the government with title to their lands held under the protection of the Office of Indian Affairs. At the end of this period, at least in theory, these "wards" would be sufficiently civilized to both receive the patents to their homesteads in fee simple and gain U.S. citizenship.

The Dawes Act passage reignited hope among many reformers that the end of the "Indian problem" was finally at hand. In an address inaugurating the Eighteenth Lake Mohonk Conference in 1900, Merrill E. Gates, president of the Board of Indian Commissioners, observed that the "supreme significance of this law [the Dawes Act] in marking a new era in dealing with the Indian problem lies in the fact that [it] is a mighty pulverizing engine for breaking up the tribal mass." Freed from the deadening weight of communal life and customs, individual Indians would finally be at liberty to experience the edifying effects of "civilization, education, and Christianity. . . . We have learned that education and example, and preeminently, the force of Christian life and Christian faith in the heart, can do in one generation most of that which evolution takes centuries to do."[9]

As the new century progressed, however, the enthusiasm about the speed at which Indians could be civilized again began to fade and became increasingly mixed with negative assessments of the many barriers blocking their social and religious progress. Only three years after Gates's heartening address, Fr. H. G. Ganss, president of the Marquette Missionary Extension Society, commented on the "tone of doubt and uncertainty, not to say, pessimism," he detected in many of the discussions at Lake Mohonk. "Are we not painting the difficulties in too vivid colors, and not making due allowance for the limitations that handicap the Indian? We cannot expect to accomplish in civilizing the Indian in one or two generations what took the Anglo-Saxon and Teuton centuries."[10]

In underscoring the necessarily gradual pace of Indian civilization and Christianization, Ganss was merely espousing the conventional wisdom of Catholic missiology that held that although savage peoples were susceptible to a certain amount of cultural advancement they could achieve civilized lifeways only in slow increments. Eight years later William Hughes, field lecturer of the BCIM, would make the same point at Lake Mohonk in order to highlight an important difference between Protestant and Catholic missiology: "In general I should say that the Catholic missionary sets a later term than is popularly set down as the term of the Indian's education . . . for complete citizenship as opposed to all wardship." Illustrating the long established nature of this difference, Hughes noted, "The early California missionaries more than a century ago were accused by civil and military officers of wishing to keep the Indians under tutelage too long. The missionaries pleaded the long period of barbarism and the short time of preparation for active citizenship that had elapsed. In spite of their protestations the process was hurried. . . . And even today there is grave question whether [the Indians of California] are ready to be entirely released from wardship."[11]

Of particular concern to Catholic missionaries and their supporters were adult Indians who had lived, until recently, exclusively according to the traditions and standards of tribal society. Teaching such persons the rudiments of Christianity and civilization was a necessarily protracted process that would more often than not bear negligible results. Others offered an even more pessimistic reading, assessing the potential of adult Indians to be so low as to warrant hardly any effort at all. In his essay "A Glance at the Indian

Question," E. Butler thus warned the readers of *Catholic World,* "There is no use in trying to make the adult Indian of today an agriculturalist, or to take him far out of the sphere in which he was brought up. . . . It is folly to attempt it. You cannot reconcile to our nineteenth century civilization those who have grown up to maturity with the ideas, manners, and morals of the heroic ages. You can no more expect Crazy Horse to use a shovel and the hoe than you could Achilles and Tydides Diomed to plant melons or beans."[12]

From the Catholics' perspective, the existence of a large and virtually uneducable population of adult Indians made Protestant talk of terminating reservations appear both naive and dangerous. Nor, according to Catholic critics, did the folly end there. Given the relaxed pace of civilization, the prospects of successfully preparing the children or even the grandchildren of these adults for assimilation seemed to them little more than a pipe dream. Facing this issue head on, Martin Marty, bishop apostolic of Dakota Territory, stated, "The same law of development which history shows in the gradual civilization of other nations can be clearly traced in our experience among the Indians. We must be satisfied to bring our pupils to a stage within their reach, whilst we see their children will doubtless be able and willing to go higher and traverse other regions of science, art, and culture."[13] As for the claims of Protestant reformers that Indian children could be quickly civilized in such off-reservation schools as Carlisle, Catholics pointed to the high percentage of students from such institutions who reverted to savagery once back on their reservations. Regarding this recidivism, Fr. William Ketcham, director of the BCIM from 1901 to 1921, observed, "[We] carry them into the full glare of our enlightenment and then seem to think it strange that the poor creatures are dazzled and bewildered and that they feel more content in the simple life of the wigwam than in our complex mode of existence. . . . We forget that we have reached our present harbor only after sailing over the turbulent and bloody seas of the Middle Ages."[14]

It is important to note that Catholic missionaries were no less cognizant of the shortcomings of the reservation system than were their Protestant counterparts. They wrote eloquently and often of the difficulties that these isolated environments posed to eradicating savagery and paganism. Nevertheless, Catholic officials continued to maintain that reservation policy offered the best hope for civilizing and Christianizing Indians. The basic problem with the reservation system in their estimation did not lie in its theory but with federal Indian Office personnel who either were derelict in working for the progress of their charges or had alienated them through their incompetence, graft, or brutality. They saw no reason why, once corrected of these abuses, reservation policy should not succeed in fostering the *gradual* advancement of Indian peoples. In 1907, Father Ganss forcefully expressed this viewpoint when he insisted that "there remains no doubt, that in [the reservation's] preliminary conception, it harbored the elements of beneficence and practicality." Moreover, he argued, "under proper discharge of its functions it would have been comparatively successful, not only in shielding the Indian from fraudulent adventurers, but in advancing him by progressive stages to civilization." Identifying the idea as a "Catholic one" that the Franciscans had applied effectively in the American Southwest and the Jesuits had employed to civilize and Christianize natives of South America, Ganss argued that, in common with contagious diseases, "segregation with aboriginal people . . . means salvation; dispersion means disorder and anarchy." As if to remind reservation critics of the preverbal danger of disposing of baby and bathwash, Ganss concluded, "Of course it could work two ways. Under the control of arbitrary and tyrannous agents it could create the greatest hardship and lay the seeds of fatal demoralization; under the influence of upright and practical supervisors it could become the vehicle of an incalculable amount of good."[15]

Whether reservations should remain the centerpiece of reform policy emerged as the major theoretical dispute between Catholic and Protestant Indian missionaries at the end of the nineteenth century. Riding on its coattails was a debate concerning the constitutionality of federal support for church-operated reservation boarding schools. And, in fact, it was this latter contest that reignited the battle between the Catholic Church and the Indian Office.

Since the inauguration of the Peace Policy, the Catholic hierarchy had invested sizeable amounts of capital and labor in constructing mission complexes whose structure and operation revolved around boarding schools. Writing in the early 1900s of the importance of reservation boarding schools, Director Ketcham asserted that they have "proved to be the most effective, if not the only effective means of weaning [the Indian] from paganism, thoroughly instructing them in Christianity, and habituating them to civilized customs." He went on to state, "As the mission work progressed, these schools became numerous. They became the kernel of the work, centers of activity, homes of missionaries, places where Indians congregated and to which they looked for help and guidance. The schools did not comprise all that there was of mission work, but it is safe to say that they were the major part of it, and that they afforded much of the inspiration that made the Catholic Indian Missions successful in a remarkable degree."[16]

We examine Father Ketcham's claims regarding the "remarkable" success of the Catholic Indian mission in more depth when we consider its results among the Sicangu Lakotas of the Rosebud (see chapters 9 and 10). But note here that the astounding growth of the Indian Office's support for Catholic Indian education during the late nineteenth century testifies to the accuracy of his evaluation of the importance of schools to these missions. In 1884 the Catholic Church received $65,220 in federal contracts. During the next five years the annual amount grew to $347,672, about three-fifths of the total amount budgeted for contract schools and more than eight times the stipends awarded to its nearest Protestant competitor, the Presbyterians.[17] By 1893 the Catholic schools were receiving $389,745 from the government, with the aggregate for the decade 1884–94 at $2,882,540.[18]

This lopsided allocation of government monies leads us to a second reason for the transformation of federal-Indian relations in the post–Peace Policy era of Indian reform. The success of the Catholic Church in tapping funds to support its Indian schools added fuel to the flame of Protestant reformers' hostility toward reservations. It also served to reinforce the nativist sentiments of those Protestants who were already alarmed by the steady waves of Catholic immigrants and the rising political fortunes of urban Irish Catholics toward the end of the nineteenth century.[19] As was the case with other perceived attacks on Protestant sociopolitical hegemony, the American Protective Association (APA)—the mouthpiece of nativism and heir to the "Know-Nothings" of the earlier part of the century—succeeded in strategically placing one of its sympathizers to challenge the interlopers. As the result of the APA's intense lobbying, president-elect Benjamin Harrison nominated Thomas Jefferson Morgan for commissioner of Indian affairs in 1889.[20]

Morgan's reputation as a Civil War general and subsequent career as a Baptist minister conferred upon him the proper military and religious credentials to command a Protestant offensive against the Catholic contract schools.[21] But it was his renown as a leader in the National Education Association and as an advocate for the "common" or public school system that brought him to the attention of the APA. Like many other APA sympathizers, Morgan had interpreted the proliferation of Catholic parochial schools in the 1880s as a papist plot to destroy public education by establishing a rival, clergy-controlled system that would then demand a major portion of the public school funds. For Morgan, the foreshadowing of this plot was detectable in the field of Indian education, where Catholics received more than three-fifths of the monies allotted for contract schools.[22]

Working in close consultation with his superintendent of Indian schools, Daniel Dorchester (who was also a minister, though in the Methodist Church), Morgan quickly drew up a blueprint to replace all sectarian contract schools with government-owned and -administered facilities.[23] In addition to building new day and boarding schools as needed, he proposed that the federal Indian Office purchase the campuses and equipment belonging to denominations that were vacating the field. Although this portion of his plan endorsed continued federal support of camp and agency schools, its ultimate goal was to develop a "non-partisan, non-sectarian" Indian common-school system that would "seek the disintegration of the tribes, and not their segregation." In accord with this goal, he proposed that the government construct large industrial high schools, on the model of Carlisle and Hampton, "located in the midst of a farming community, remote from reservations, and in the vicinity of railroads and some thriving village or city . . . [where] students would . . . be free from the pull of the camp, and be able to mingle with the civilized people that surround them, and to participate in their civilization." He recommended that these schools "bring together . . . members of as many different tribes as possible, in order to destroy the tribal antagonism, and to generate in them a feeling of common brotherhood and mutual respect." Here In dian students would also be exposed to a curriculum "saturated" with lessons of the superiority of Christian civilization and morals: "fear of God and respect for the rights of others; love of truth and fidelity to duty; personal purity, philanthropy, and patriotism." They would, in addition, be taught that in "the sweat of their faces must they eat bread . . . [that] nothing can save them from the necessity of toil."[24]

Many Protestant mission boards and associations that shared Morgan's anti-reservation philosophy and viewed his plan as a way of diminishing Catholic influence among American Indians quickly threw their support behind the proposal.[25] Officials in charge of the Catholic Indian missions, not surprisingly, were far from pleased and immediately attacked the commissioner's plan. Like their Protestant brethren, they recognized it as a thinly veiled ploy to eradicate their reservation churches and schools. They rejected the commissioner's hostility toward the reservation system and his enthusiasm for carting Indian children off to schools located near centers of Western civilization. Furthermore, given Morgan's ties to the APA, they found it impossible to credit his claims that the schools under his management would be "non-partisan and non-sectarian." In an interview with the *Philadelphia Press,* Archbishop John Ireland publicly aired his suspicions concerning the commissioner and his plan: "The administration of the Indian Department has been decidedly anti-Catholic. General Morgan was for a time a Baptist preacher and president of a Baptist college. Mr. Dorchester, the superintendent of Indian Schools, is a Methodist minister, and shortly before his elevation to this office published one of these vile and slanderous anti-Catholic books, filled with historic falsehood and misconstruction of Catholic teachings."[26]

Morgan's reign as Indian commissioner ended with Grover Cleveland's defeat of Harrison in the presidential race of 1892. Evidence abounds that the Catholic Church was both instrumental and delighted in this change of administration. If this is true, Catholic support for the new president proved to be short-lived. On December 21, 1894, BCIM director J. A. Stephan wrote the bureau's consultants, "Not any preceding administration has been so actively and persistently bitter in antagonism to Catholicism, and the persecution of Catholics, as the present one; and in this policy the President, his Cabinet and all the chief influences of the party in power appear to be acting as a unit." Stephan fingered Cleveland's secretary of the interior, Hoke Smith, who "was, at his home in Georgia, known as a prominent Sunday-school teacher, and as being closely identified with elements of organized . . . prejudice and enmity against Catholicism." The director went on to relate that "on assuming office [Smith] at once conferred with Ex-Commissioner Morgan, Herbert Welsh, Painter and others of like character, [and] with their advice he selected as Superintendent of Indian Schools, one William N. Hailmann, a Hebrew, I am told, from LaPorte, Indiana, and a notoriously bitter enemy of our faith. With such a fitting tool, this combination of all the bigotry and malice . . . I felt and feel confident of their ability to drive us soon and finally out of the field of Indian work."[27]

Following Morgan's lead, Smith called for a completely federalized system of Indian schools. This carry-over from the former commissioner's agenda caused Stephan to lament that Morgan's "malign influence [had] survived his retirement."[28] The mechanisms Smith and his associates adopted to accomplish their goal were both familiar and innovative. The interior secretary first requested that Congress provide the funds needed to build government schools in sufficient numbers to accommodate all Indian scholars. Second, he recommended that congressional appropriations to contract schools be reduced 20 percent per annum. Third, again paralleling Morgan's agenda, he proposed that the federal government purchase sectarian campuses and equipment for its own system. Finally, in 1896, Smith's commissioner of Indian affairs, Daniel M. Browning, issued an order granting government schools priority over contract schools in filling their classrooms, regardless of parental wishes or consent. This order, soon known as the "Browning Ruling," would stay on the books for nearly six years until the McKinley administration abrogated it on January 18, 1902.[29]

In 1896 the House Committee on Indian Affairs began its deliberation of Smith's five-year phase-out of government support for sectarian Indian schools. By then the overriding question before the committee had changed from how best to educate Indian children to the larger constitutional issue of whether the government's allocation of public monies to support church-run Indian schools compromised the separation of church and state. Fearing that federal financing of these institutions did pose a danger to this constitutional principle, the members of the committee voted to recommend congressional passage of Smith's proposal.

In a desperate attempt to forestall Secretary Smith's plan, Father Stephan on February 3, 1896, addressed a letter of protest to Rep. James S. Sheridan, chair of the Indian Committee. After briefly rehearsing the history of the Catholic Indian schools, Stephan cited statistics from the previous year's report of the Indian commissioner demonstrating that, even counting the rolls of church-operated facilities, 40 percent of Indian children went unschooled. According to his calculations, the cuts planned for 1896 would add another six hundred to this number, for "it must be understood," he warned, "that the Catholic schools cannot, because of lack of means, continue, as they have been doing the past year, to support and care for pupils for which no compensation is allowed." Addressing the issue of the government's subsidies for Catholic Indian schools, Stephan insisted that, since government had not awarded this money for religious purposes but "to pay for services rendered by the schools in furnishing care and tuition to the Indian pupils entrusted to their care," it did not violate the Constitution. He went on to cite former

Indian commissioner Francis A. Walker's argument that, although it would be wrong "to appropriate public moneys for establishing and maintain sectarian schools, for the sake of having sectarian schools . . . [to] make use of good schools already existing and partly maintained by private contributions, even though under sectarian control, involves no departure from sound principle, if the sole object in doing so is the good of the Indians themselves." Stephan observed that, since there "can be no question that the Government sends the Indian children to the contract schools not for the benefit of the denominations maintaining them, but solely for the good of the children . . . as Gen. Walker states, no objection to the nature of a principle applies in this case."[30]

Stephan's arguments failed to move the members of the committee to reconsider their actions. On June 7, 1897, Congress enacted a law stating:

> it is hereby declared to be the settled policy of the Government to hereafter make no appropriation whatever for education in any sectarian school. Provided: That the Secretary of the Interior may make contracts with contract schools apportioning as near as may be the amount so contracted among schools of various denominations for the education of Indian pupils during the fiscal year 1898, but shall only make such contracts at places where nonsectarian schools can not be provided for such Indian children and to an amount not exceeding 40 per centum of the amount so used for the fiscal year 1895.[31]

During the following two years, Congress ordered similar reductions that finally left the Catholic Indian schools nearly totally divested of government support by 1901.

Despite Stephan's warning to the Senate committee, Indian schools had become so important to Catholic missionary efforts among American Indians that the church could ill afford to abandon them completely. Speaking of the "dreadful crisis" through which the mission schools were passing, Cardinal James Gibbons stated that, "deprived of Government help, which they had a right to expect, the numerous schools, nurseries of Catholicity and civilization, which were flourishing among the tribes, are on the verge of destruction. When we abandon the Indian schools we virtually abandon the Indian Mission. . . . Hence we take from the Indian the Holy Mass, the blessed Sacrament, and all the Sacraments."[32]

To make already critical matters worse, in 1901 the Indian Office ceased furnishing those Indian mission schools located on "ration-agencies" with the treaty-stipulated food and clothing that their students would receive if living at home.[33] BCIM director Ketcham estimated that this withdrawal represented a loss to the Catholic mission schools of more than $25,000 a year. After failing to win concessions from Indian commissioner William A. Jones, Ketcham presented his case directly to President Roosevelt. In a strongly worded letter to the president, he protested that the "objectionable order of the Commissioner of Indian Affairs has injuriously affected a number of mission schools, both Catholic and Protestant, and is a decided injustice to the Indian children attending those schools, and it is earnestly desired that it should be revoked, and the old order of affairs restored." To underscore the reasonableness of his demand he added that it was "of interest to note that the Indian Rights Association was in full agreement with the BCIM's protest over the withdrawal of rations, making it one of the extremely rare instances when Catholics and Protestants joined forces in battling the Indian Office."[34]

With the demise of the Indian missions looming before them, Gibbons and his fellow officers at the BCIM began an urgent search for alternative means to support Indian education. One method they devised was to request that the bishops of large cities preach and lecture on the Indian problem in order to increase the amount normally collected from their annual Lenten appeal for the Indian missions. The officers also encouraged reservation priests to visit wealthy eastern parishes on so-called begging tours.[35]

Another means for filling the Indian schools' coffers was through the creation of missionary extension societies, most notably the BCIM's own Society for the Preservation of the Faith among Indian Children. Incorporated in 1902, the Society sought to gather financial and spiritual support for the Indian schools and missions through the formation and activities of parish chapters. In recognition of their efforts, the organization's local "promoters" received certificates, badges, and the opportunity to win a Navajo blanket. Meanwhile, an annual fee of 25 cents entitled each chapter recruit to a certificate of membership (available in English, German, Polish, Czech, French, Spanish, Italian, Hungarian, and Sioux), occasional circulars on matters of import to the Indian missions and schools, and a copy of the Society's feature-filled journal, *The Indian Sentinel*. Members also received the opportunity to secure a plenary indulgence during the Feast of the Epiphany and an indulgence of one hundred days by reciting a specified prayer. By using these and other material and spiritual incentives, Gibbons hoped to secure the 400,000 sustaining members that he estimated were needed to fund the schools.

Without doubt, the most important patron of the missions during this critical period was Mother Katherine Drexel, founder of the Sisters of the Blessed Sacrament for Indians and Colored People and a scion to the fortune of Philadelphia banking magnate Francis Martin Drexel. As a young woman, Katherine had developed a keen interest in the Indian missions through discussions with her family pastor and friend, Fr. James O'Connor (later, bishop of Omaha). Her first encounter with Americans Indians was also the result of her association with O'Connor, occurring when several Sioux from the cast of Buffalo Bill's Wild West Show attended one of his masses. In 1885 she memorialized her recently deceased father by financing the construction of the Saint Francis Mission and school on the Rosebud Sioux Reservation, and two years later she funded the Holy Rosary Mission among the Pine Ridge Sioux.

Soon afterward, while young Katherine was visiting Rome, Pope Leo XIII granted her an audience during which she inquired how she might best propagate the faith among Negroes and Indians. He replied that she should give herself, becoming a missionary to them. Taking the holy father at his word, she entered the Sisters of Mercy in 1889 and two years later received permission to found the Sisters of the Blessed Sacrament for Indians and Colored People. As part of her ministry, Mother Katherine continued to sponsor the building of Catholic Indian schools. She also contributed money from her inheritance that allowed these schools to educate and care for children in excess of the number paid for by the government. Moreover, when the government temporarily ceased its funding of Catholic Indian schools, she donated sufficient funds to keep them afloat through the crisis.

While the members of the BCIM board were struggling to devise means to cover the shortfall created by the termination of federal contracts and rations, they continued to seek the reinstatement of government support for some of their Indian schools. Since the beginning of the crisis they had insisted on the need to distinguish between those contract schools that were maintained by "gratuities," or public moneys appropriated by Congress, and those subsidized by trust funds or other remunerations that were due to tribes as a result of treaty stipulations and were disbursed for their benefit by the secretary of the interior.[36] They maintained that under the latter dispensation Indians should be allowed "to use their own money, in educating their own children in the schools of their choice."[37]

At the center of this contest were the eight boarding schools that the Catholic Church operated among the Menominee, Osage, Sioux, Northern Cheyenne, and Quapaw tribes. Still, the apparently few institutions in question should not cloak the magnitude of their importance, for numbered among them were Saint Francis and Holy Rosary, two of the largest facilities in the Catholic contract school system. What is more, together the schools boasted an enrollment of almost nine hundred students with contracts worth nearly $100,000.[38]

Ketcham reported that after "fortifying" the Catholic position with "legal authorities of the first order" he petitioned the secretary of the interior, Cornelius N. Bliss, to recommence awarding contracts to those Catholic schools that previously had been financed from tribal funds. Failing to win Bliss's cooperation, he decided to try once again with the latter's successor, Ethan A. Hitchcock. When Hitchcock failed to issue a ruling, either in favor or against his appeal, Ketcham again approached Theodore Roosevelt.[39] Although sympathetic with Ketcham's arguments, Roosevelt consulted his attorney general, Philander C. Knox, regarding their legality. Upon receiving Knox's approval, the president issued an executive order in 1904 restoring the distribution of Indian trust funds to sectarian schools.[40] In conformity with the individualistic bent of reform policy, the order required that the dispersal of these funds henceforth be contingent on gathering sufficient petitions from the adult males of each tribe who agreed to consign their shares of the trust and treaty moneys to support sectarian schools.

The matter, however, was far from settled. In 1907, Reuben Quick Bear, a Rosebud Lakota representing the Indian Rights Association (IRA), challenged Roosevelt's order on the grounds that it licensed the government to act in a "sectarian manner." The legal case that ensued eventually found its way to the Supreme Court, which in 1908 confirmed the right of the government to allocate Indian trust funds for sectarian education.[41]

While the BCIM was locked in battle with the IRA over the right of Catholic Indian schools to tribal funds, Ketcham received heartening news concerning his earlier petition for the restoration of rations and clothing to children attending mission schools. As part of the Indian Appropriation Act of 1907, Congress declared, "Mission schools on an Indian reservation may, under rules and regulations prescribed by the Commissioner of Indian Affairs, receive for such Indians duly enrolled therein the rations of food and clothing to which said children would be entitled under treaty stipulations if such children were living with their parents."[42]

During the next two decades the proprietors of the Catholic Indian schools and missions continued to experience upheavals in their relationship with the Indian Office and Congress.[43] With just cause or not, they invariably detected Protestant bigotry at the root of these crises. Thus, for example, when Indian commissioner Robert G. Valentine issued a ruling barring the use or display of religiously distinctive "garb" and "insignias" by teachers in federal Indian schools in 1912, Father Ketcham merely took for granted that this order was a "pretext to the opposing of the employing of Catholic religious and, in the last analysis, of Catholics in Government Indian schools."[44] These battles waged on high were mirrored on a local, reservation level in countless brushfire wars in which Catholic religious accused agents and school superintendents of bigotry against their church. Large or small, such skirmishes served to fuel persistent rumors that Protestants in Congress and in the Indian Office were searching for ways to reinstate the ban on the support of sectarian schools with trust fund moneys. Nevertheless, with the restoration of rations and a portion, if not all, of government contracts, the Catholic Church had survived the main assault of reform policy on its missions.

CHAPTER THREE

The Lakotas and "The Peace"

Early in the spring of 1868, the eight members of the United States Peace Commission arrived at Fort Laramie to reopen treaty negotiations with the Lakota and Arapaho nations.[1] Haunted by their aborted efforts during the previous two years, and pressured by the need to clear Indians from the worksites of the Union Pacific Railroad, the commissioners had come armed with concessions that they hoped would finally induce the tribal delegates to "touch the pen."

From the Lakotas' perspective, Fort Laramie was more than a convenient place to bargain for peace. Rather, its history captured in miniature their changing relationship with white America.[2] During the earliest phase of this history, from 1834 to 1848, the post operated as a trading depot primarily under the auspices of the American Fur Company.[3] Here Lakota bands would frequently converge, bearing buffalo hides and deer skins to exchange for the weapons, metal tools, and other items of Western manufacture on which they were becoming increasingly dependent.

Then, in 1849, the Lakotas watched with concern as the army purchased the fort from the American Fur Company (for $4,000) and converted it into a military post. Almost instantly, what had been a marketplace for amicable Indian-white trade was transformed into an armed fortress to protect the increasing number of pioneers who traveled the Oregon Trail through the western portion of Lakota territory.[4] Although Lakota bands continued to visit the fort, with the so-called Laramie Loafers even settling at its gates, they could not help but view it as a provocative symbol of foreign occupation and of the militarization of their relationship with the U.S. government.[5]

In an abrupt reversal from this militaristic posture, in 1851 the Indian Office invited the Lakotas to participate in a "grand council" at Fort Laramie with the Crows, Cheyennes, Assiniboines, Shoshones, Arikaras, Gros Ventres, Mandans, and Arapahos. Before the negotiations had gotten under way, however, the horses belonging to the estimated 10,000 Indians and three hundred whites present had devoured the grasslands surrounding the post. The government's primary representative, Col. David D. Mitchell, superintendent for western Indian Country, quickly selected Horse Creek, thirty-five miles to the southeast of the fort, as the new venue for the proceedings. After a mass exodus from the devastated campgrounds, the council was finally convened on September 8, 1851.

Despite the animosity that existed among many of the tribes and the absence of the Crows during the first session of the talks, a treaty acceptable to both Indians and whites was negotiated and signed in just over two weeks. As their part of this pact, the Lakotas agreed to refrain from molesting whites traveling along the Platte River. They also consented to reside peacefully within the great territory the government assigned them and to respect the borders of those areas allotted to the other tribes attending the council.[6] As recompense for these concessions, the United States pledged to protect the Lakotas and the other Indian signatories from depredations committed by its citizens. It additionally promised to pay them $50,000 per annum "in provisions, merchandise, domestic animals, and agricultural implements" for a period of not less than ten years in "consideration of the treaty stipulations, and for the damages which have or may occur by reason thereof the Indian nations, parties hereto, and for their maintenance and the improvement of their moral and social customs."[7]

For three years after the treaty at Horse Creek, both the Lakotas and the government generally abided by its terms. However, on August 17, 1854, an incident occurred which, although ludicrous in itself, precipitated the first phase in a twenty-four-year conflict that has come to be known as the "Sioux Wars." Once again, Fort Laramie figured prominently in this turning point in Lakota-white relations.

The episode began benignly enough when a cow belonging to a member of a Mormon wagon train wandered into Brave Bear's Lakota camp, one of the many villages constituting the Sicangu division of Lakota people.[8] Rather than enter the camp himself to retrieve the animal, its owner reported it as stolen when he reached the fort. Upon hearing a biased report of the event, Lt. John L. Grattan requested and received permission to proceed to the Sicangu village with a company of soldiers and interpreter (who was drunk at the time) to recover the cow and to apprehend its rustler. Eager to avoid bloodshed, Brave Bear was willing to overlook Grattan's belligerent manner and his interpreter's garbled translations of the soldiers' mission. The Sicangu leader was, however, in no position to comply with either of the lieutenant's demands since the beast had already been butchered by High Forehead, who as a Miniconjou Lakota visitor to the camp was under no obligation to comply with Brave Bear's appeal that he turn himself in. Squeezed from both sides, the headman offered to reimburse the Mormon for his loss. Nevertheless the lieutenant, who appears to have been uninterested in compromise, ordered his men to take High Forehead by force. This ill-conceived action triggered a melee that cost the lives of Brave Bear, Grattan, and the entire detachment of soldiers.

Seething with indignation over High Bear's murder, Sicangu warriors staged raids along the Oregon Trail into the following spring. In one of the most publicized of these attacks, Spotted Tail, Red Leaf, and Long Chin raided a mail coach in which two drivers and a passenger were killed and $20,000 stolen.

In retaliation for the "Grattan Massacre" and mail coach murders, on September 3, 1855, Gen. William (The Wasp) Harney unleashed a six-hundred-man offensive on Little Thunder's Sicangu camp at Ash Hollow that took the lives of eighty-five of the band's estimated 250 members.[9] After this attack, the general ordered his soldiers to conduct seventy of the camp's women and children to Fort Laramie to serve as bargaining chips in apprehending the ringleaders of the recent Sicangu hostilities. And there the hostages remained until September 18, when Spotted Tail, Red Leaf, and Long Chin arrived at the fort to turn themselves in in exchange for the release of the others. Soon thereafter, the three prisoners-of-war were transferred to Fort Leavenworth, where it was generally assumed they would be executed. However, the following fall, they all received presidential pardons. As for High Forehead, the now infamous butcher of the Mormon cow, in spring 1856 he journeyed to Fort Pierre with the leader of his *tiyospaye* (extended family), where he presented himself for arrest. Evidently appeased by this display of submission, Harney granted him absolution.

As hostilities temporarily abated farther west, tensions continued to mount between whites and the Santee Sioux of Minnesota.[10] At the root of the rising agitation was the federal government's failure to fulfill its part of agreements it had struck at the treaty councils at Traverse des Sioux and Mendota in 1851. According to these pacts, the Santees had extinguished their claims to nearly twenty-four million acres of land in exchange for approximately $3 million, annuity goods, and the Yellow Medicine and Redwood agencies that were located along the Minnesota River. Resentment soon swelled among many of the Dakota bands concerning the location and size of the reserves as well as the government's duplicity in distributing the promised money and goods. In August 1862 bitterness flared into open revolt when the Santees, on the verge of starvation, failed to receive their treaty-stipulated rations. Under the leadership of Little Crow, warriors primarily from Redwood's Mdewakantowan and Wahpekute bands attempted to recapture their former lands in southern Minnesota. By the time federal and territorial troops managed to quell the "uprising," approximately five hundred settlers and soldiers had been killed. A military commission appointed in September 1862 condemned 303 Indians to the gallows.[11] After personally reviewing the tribunal's judgments, President Abraham Lincoln commuted the sentences of 265 of the prisoners. The remaining thirty-eight were hanged on December 26 at Mankato, and members of the bands that white Minnesotans identified as hostile were banished from the state and relocated to the Santee Reservation in Nebraska and the Sisseton-Wahpeton Reserve in present-day South Dakota.

In an attempt to evade the advancing white forces, many of the Santees fled west to Dakota Territory. This strategy, however, afforded them only temporary protection and resulted in drawing several Lakota bands into the conflict. In July 1863 troops under the command of Gen. Henry Sibley engaged and defeated allied Dakota and Lakota war parties at Big Mound, Dead Buffalo Lake, and Stoney Lake, and one year later units led by Gen. Alfred Sully overpowered allied Dakota and Lakota forces at Killdeer Mountain.

At the same time that fallout from the Minnesota uprising was reigniting hostilities between Lakotas and whites, events on the southern plains conspired to broaden the conflict. As part of a general campaign to expel Cheyennes and Arapahos from their hunting grounds in Colorado and Kansas, on November 29, 1864, John M. Chivington's volunteer company from the Third Colorado Cavalry massacred two hundred members of Black

Kettle's peaceful band of Southern Cheyennes at Sand Creek.[12] News of the savagery of Chivington's attack eventually resulted in a congressional investigation and the colonel's forced resignation.

Whatever its utility in allaying white guilt over the massacre, Chivington's unceremonious retirement failed to satisfy Indian demands for justice.[13] Upon learning of the atrocity, Indian peoples on the northern and southern plains, including the Lakotas, took to the warpath, attacking white travelers, army detachments, and settlements. In January 1865, Sicangus joined forces with Cheyenne and Arapaho warriors in an attack on the town of Julesburg, Colorado, and that summer Lakotas, Cheyennes, and Arapahos overwhelmed a division of horse soldiers during the battle of Platte Bridge.

Despite these outbreaks, the federal government pressed forward its plans to build army posts along the Bozeman Trail. First charted by John B. Bozeman in 1862, the trail turned north just past Fort Laramie on the Oregon Trail and then veered west to the gold fields near the present-day Montana-Idaho border. Although offering prospectors the most direct route to potential fortune, it posed the very serious drawback of leading them through the Powder River country of the Lakotas, Cheyennes, Arapahos, and Crows. In an effort to avert trouble, the Peace Commission invited these Indian nations to a council at Fort Laramie in June 1866. Although most of the Lakota tribes saw these talks through to their conclusion, the Oglala bands associated with Red Cloud stormed out of the gathering once they learned of the government's desire to establish forts in the area. The second phase of the "Sioux," or Red Cloud, Wars was thus under way.[14]

Among the Oglalas' first targets were detachments of Col. Henry B. Carrington, who had been delegated the unenviable assignment of building the new Bozeman Trail forts.[15] Then, on December 21, 1866, Lakotas, Cheyennes, and Arapahos led by Crazy Horse succeeded in baiting Lt. William J. Fetterman and eighty of his men away from the recently completed Fort Phil Kearny in northern Wyoming by staging a sham raid on a wood train. As the lieutenant's command galloped to the rescue, 1,500 Indians who had been lying in wait swept down upon them.[16]

The Peace Commission, the Lakotas, and the Treaty of 1868

Reeling from the news of the Fetterman massacre, the federal government determined to seek a peaceful resolution to the "Sioux Wars." In April 1868 the Peace Commission was once again dispatched to Fort Laramie in an attempt to restore peace to the northern plains. Officials in Washington were especially concerned that the commissioners secure an Indian-free environment to safeguard the crews laying tracks for the Union Pacific. In fact, their determination to achieve this end extended so far as to agree to abandon the newly constructed forts along the Bozeman Trail for its sake.

From the Lakotas' viewpoint, the commissioners' agenda for the 1868 negotiations was markedly similar to that guiding the 1851 Fort Laramie council. Once again, representatives of Tunkasila, the "Great Father," in Washington had journeyed to the heart of the northern plains seeking peace. And just as before, they offered the gathered Indians rations and other material incentives for agreeing to stay within the boundaries of a region reserved for their exclusive occupation and protected from the trespass and mischief of "bad men among the whites, or among other people subject to the authority of the United States." The treaty included provisions for agriculture, animal husbandry, and general "social improvement"—things that the Lakotas knew were important, for some mysterious reason, to whites but that held negligible value to themselves.[17]

The area set aside for the Lakotas, soon referred to as the "Great Sioux Reservation," was smaller than the homeland that the government had assigned to them in 1851. It remained, however, a majestic territory, comprising nearly 34,000,000 acres and encompassing all of what is today western South Dakota. In addition to the promise of a vast homeland, the treaty guaranteed the Lakotas the right to hunt outside the reserve on any lands north of the North Platte and the Republican Fork of the Smoky River, "so long as the buffalo . . . range[d] thereon in such numbers as to justify the chase." It also designated as "non-ceded Indian land" the area near the Bozeman Trail from which, in accord with the desires of Red Cloud and other more militant Lakota leaders, the government agreed to withdraw its soldiers.

The minimal impact that the 1851 Fort Laramie treaty had exercised over the Lakotas' daily lives may well have shaped their understanding of the new agreement.[18] Nevertheless, despite the council's familiar surroundings and seemingly similar agenda, Indian policy had sufficiently changed over the intervening seventeen years to create radical differences between the two pacts. The greatest of these departures was white America's commitment, under the influence of Christian reformers, to assimilate Indians into the social mainstream by force. Thus, in addition to the 1851 treaty's goal of making the plains safe for white travel and habitation, the new agreement sought to compel the Lakotas to "cast off their blankets" and commence the process of becoming civilized citizens of the United States. This difference is nowhere more apparent than in the sections of the two treaties dealing with "civilization": by 1868 the brief and rather airy allusions to agriculture and social "improvement" contained in the agreement of 1851 had taken the form of a carefully articulated "strategy" for transforming hunters and gatherers into yeoman farmers.

The first step in this program was to induce the nomadic Lakotas to settle in one place. To this end, the treaty called for the construction of an agency headquarters located on the Missouri River near which the Lakota tribes were required to live. Here, at least in theory, they would be exposed to the skills and civilizing influences of carpenters, farmers, blacksmiths, millers, engineers, teachers, and missionaries. These emissaries of civilized life were also jointly ascribed the task of encouraging Lakota males over eighteen to select tracts of land so that they could "commence cultivating the soil for a living." To entice them to the plow, the treaty authorized the agent to divide an annual prize of $500 among the ten individuals whom he judged grew "the most valuable crops."

While Lakota men were exchanging their instruments of the hunt and warfare for plowshares (the treaty, incidentally, says nothing concerning the training of adult women), the agent was to establish a system of compulsory education for their children. The United States agreed to furnish the Lakotas a schoolhouse and teacher "competent to teach the elementary branches of an English education . . . who will reside among them" for every thirty children between the ages of six and sixteen.

When reading the text of the 1868 Fort Laramie treaty, one cannot help but be struck by its conflicting goals of "pacifying" and "civilizing" the Lakotas. In its attempt to bring tranquility to the plains, the Peace Commission was prepared to promise the Lakotas the three things that they most desired: a spacious, protected homeland with guaranteed access to those traditional hunting grounds that technically fell outside its boundaries; the removal of army troops from along the Bozeman Trail; and frequent distributions of clothing and other goods from the government's larder. Running headlong into the first and third concessions, however, was the commissioners' reformist aspirations of making the Lakotas into self-sufficient farmers and, ultimately, Christian citizens. Thus, although the treaty accorded the Lakotas their "Great Reservation" and permission to frequent their customary hunting sites, the majority of its provisions were oriented toward settling the Lakota communities in a specific location. What is more, as reformers would later complain, the distribution of government goods undermined the efforts of agents and missionaries to make Indians self-reliant. Judging from the fact that the majority of Lakota bands proceeded directly to their spring hunting grounds after the conclusion of the council, there is good reason to suspect that they either failed to comprehend or attached no great significance to the treaty's requirement that they settle along the Missouri and learn to farm. Though the federal government would soon add sticks to its carrots, for a few remaining months the Lakotas were free to follow those customs that had traditionally infused their existence with meaning and value.

From Sicangu to Rosebud Sioux

After the conclusion of the 1868 Fort Laramie council, the Sicangu bands commenced the long journey toward their customary hunting territories near the fork of the Republican River in present-day Nebraska. It was to this area several months later that government couriers brought orders that they immediately strike their camps and move to the newly established agency at Whetstone Creek near the Missouri River. This directive must have seemed at once preposterous and shocking to the Sicangus, who were by then in the midst of their summer buffalo chase. It was undoubtedly a staggering embarrassment for their principal leader, Spotted Tail (Sinte Gleska), who, as the government appointed head chief, had been vocal in his support of the Peace Commission since its first meeting at Fort Laramie in 1866.

Spotted Tail's blessings did not derive from any lack of mettle. His bravery as a warrior, including the self-sacrifice he had displayed by surrendering himself to General Harney, flies in the face of any such conclusion. Rather, they stemmed from a familiarity with Anglo-American society that far surpassed most of his contemporaries. During his journeys to and from confinement at Fort Leavenworth in 1855 and 1856, he had quickly grasped that the whites were far too numerous and powerful for Lakotas to defeat in war. At that point, Spotted Tail had determined that the best chance for his people's survival rested primarily upon maintaining a cordial relationship with the federal government.

A major component of Spotted Tail's strategy was to convince his fellow Sicangus to abstain from actions that would lead to confrontations with the U.S. Army. He constantly admonished the younger members in his camps to direct their horse stealing raids against the Pawnees, Poncas, and other Indian enemies while scrupulously avoiding clashes with whites. To be sure, external events sometimes conspired to upend this policy, as, for example, the Sicangus' retaliatory attack on Julesburg in which Spotted Tail himself had participated. For the most part, however, during the 1860s the Sicangus managed to maintain a comfortable distance from whites and, by so doing, were able to avoid the tragedy of another Ash Hollow.

Spotted Tail's blueprint for coexistence entailed not only segregation but also constructive engagement with whites. This positive aspect of his policy primarily took place at the negotiating table and was directed toward the goal of resisting federal attempts to strip the Sicangus of their customary lifeways. In his dickering with government agents both before and after 1868, Spotted Tail learned the value of reasoned compromise, prioritizing matters that he deemed of vital importance over those he considered of less urgency. He also discovered that coating his demands with diplomacy and wit often wrung more concessions from the government than threats and intimidation. Whatever formal agreements emerged from such talks, Spotted Tail found that in practice there were usually ways of resisting or circumventing those not to his liking. These methods included detecting loopholes in the wording of treaties, manipulating structural flaws in the theory and operation of Indian policy, and manipulating those individuals assigned to oversee or carry out the accords.

In addition to Spotted Tail's general openness to negotiations, there remains another reason why he was prepared to meet with the members of the Peace Commission in 1866, even after the Lakotas had discovered that the government planned to build forts along the Bozeman Trail. As George Hyde long ago noted, these forts were of little consequence to the Sicangus, since they were planned for an area of the Powder River country where they seldom ventured. Spotted Tail was much more concerned with defending a treaty provision that guaranteed the Sicangus' right to continue their hunts near the Republican River.[19]

The attitude of the Oglalas and the northern divisions of Lakotas, whose prime hunting grounds lay around the planned forts, was understandably quite different. The prospect of increasing numbers of white invaders depleting their game was vexing enough without the added irritant of the army building forts to protect these trespassers. They therefore stormed out of the negotiations and, under the lead of Red Cloud, took to the warpath.

In the short term, Red Cloud's aggressive strategy paid off. Loathe to initiate a costly conflict on the plains, yet in need of reestablishing peace with hostile tribes, the government blinked and dispatched the Peace Commission back west with word that it would dismantle the Bozeman Trail forts. Even after news of this concession had reached Red Cloud, he was in no particular hurry to settle the matter. In early November, several months after the Commission had returned to Washington, he and his forces finally arrived at Fort Laramie to touch the pen to the treaty.

In the final analysis, Red Cloud's triumph was little more than a hollow victory. At the end of the day his militancy could no more redirect the government's objective of containing the Lakota tribes on reservations than Spotted Tail's policy of accommodation. The fact that the Fort Laramie treaty awarded the Lakotas a massive homeland and made provisions for them to continue their hunts was little more than a smokescreen cloaking the government's assimilationist intentions.

It thus counted for little that the army's order for the Sicangus to vacate the Republican Valley was in direct violation of the recently signed agreement. Fully aware that ignoring the directive could open them up to military assaults, Spotted Tail's camps reluctantly began the long journey from the Beaver to Whetstone Creek, arriving at the agency late in the summer of 1868. Or, to be more precise, they arrived in the vicinity of the agency. Aware that the river-bottom lands of Whetstone Creek were abundant in both diseases and whiskey traders, Spotted Tail's people refused to establish their camps any closer than forty miles from the agency. By keeping their distance, they also avoided contact with agency personnel whose job it was to turn them into farmers and Christians.

It is important to stress that not all Lakotas assigned to Whetstone were opposed to settling near the agency. Among these were the members of Oglala chief Big Mouth's Loafer band. After years of camping on the outskirts of Fort Laramie, the Loafers were perfectly content to have the agency's personnel as their neighbors. The members of the Corn band, led by chiefs Swift Bear and Standing Elk, were of a similar mind. As their name suggests, the Lakotas of this band—or at least its women—had previously planted crops and were not opposed to taking up farming again.

With their estimated four hundred lodges, however, Spotted Tail's camps constituted the largest segment of Whetstone's population. The fact that they were settled so distant from the Missouri and reservation headquarters presented Whetstone agent Dewitt C. Poole with monumental problems. In the first place, supplies and annuities brought up to the agency by riverboat had to be hauled to them overland, a particularly onerous and expensive undertaking during the winter. And, as previously observed, the great distance that separated the agency from the camps made it difficult for Poole to press forward the government's civilizing programs.

The distance of the Sicangus' camps from "civilizing" forces was not the only obstacle to their progress along the white man's road. Agent Poole also had to contend with the brute fact that most of his charges were perfectly content to adhere to their Lakota lifeways. Their resistance to the government's attempts at directed change took interesting and varied forms. In one episode from his account of his eighteen months as Whetstone agent, he burlesqued with vinegar with the Sicangus' reaction to an uninvited and unannounced government shipment of "civilized dress." When the clothing (repurposed soldiers' uniforms) arrived, the gathered Sicangus immediately attempted to improve upon their stylishness and utility. "The legs of the pants were cut off, making rather poor leggins, and the whole upper part discarded. The overcoats were ripped up and appropriated by the women for making skirts. . . . The hats were thrown away." Poole concluded that "this plan of immediate civilization failed; and many good men, who believed that it was not necessary to plod through a generation or two of these people to change their mode of dress to that of their enlightened benefactors, were doomed to disappointment. The experiment cost more than twenty-five thousand dollars, and was for the time perhaps a misdirected expenditure."[20]

Although Poole intended his account to lampoon the naive optimism of most reformers, his description is equally noteworthy for presenting an eyewitness description of what the Sicangus, quite literally, made of this apparel. Not yet under the full yoke of reservation policy, they recapitulated the time-honored process by which Lakota bands rendered the customs and material products of alien nations suitable for adoption. The Sicangus, if not the reformers, thus considered the distribution of clothing on the Whetstone a rousing success. They may not have requested the avalanche of army surplus that fell upon their camps, but once delivered they certainly knew what to do with it.

Federal efforts to Christianize and civilize the Sicangus were further frustrated by their constant transfer from one reservation to another. In the decade following the 1868 treaty they were uprooted and replanted no fewer than five times and barely managed to escape removal to Oklahoma. When one considers that a major goal of reservation policy was to transform the Lakotas and other Plains tribes from hunters and gatherers into sedentary farmers, such government-sponsored nomadism can only be deemed ironic. Years ago George Hyde demonstrated how Spotted Tail was able to manipulate the government's waffling on where to locate the band in order to frustrate attempts at civilization as well as to lobby for his own choice of homeland. However, it is not less true that, exasperated by the number of these disloca- tions, Spotted Tail is reported to have remarked: "I think you had better put the Sioux on wheels and then you can run them about whenever you wish."[21]

This "running about" finally came to an end in 1878 with the establish- ment of the Rosebud Reservation, located in the south-central portion of present-day South Dakota.[22] With the creation of a permanent reserve, the Indian Office recommenced its efforts to civilize Sicangu institutions and dress. Yet, federal pressures and sanctions notwithstanding, most Sicangus failed to "cast off the blanket" with the rapidity that some of the leading framers of reservation policy had originally prophesied.

Several factors account for the lackluster results. For one, the great majority of Sicangus experienced no desire to abandon the ways of their ancestors. This individual proclivity toward conservatism was given collective force by the Sicangus' continued preference for residing in *tiyospaye* camps. Not only did the traditionalist sentiment saturating these settlements serve to reinforce customary lifeways, but it also kept under control the few persons wishing to assimilate. Furthermore, the distance separating camps, as well as their isolation from the agency, prevented the pro-assimilationist forces from forging an effective coalition.

In addition to Sicangu conservatism, Spotted Tail's continuing domina- tion of the tribe's political landscape acted to undermine the impact of assimilationist policy further. Until Crow Dog assassinated him in 1881, the great Sicangu head chief remained virtually unchallenged. Unmolested by internal constraints, he was free to deploy a subtle blend of passive and active resistance to frustrate all government attempts at civilization. In one particularly bold display of political éclat, he succeeded in coercing a particularly weak agent into sending invitations to Lakotas on other reserva- tions to attend his great Sun Dance in 1880.

It is undeniably the case that no amount of traditionalist sentiment could permanently stymie the countervailing forces compelling Sicangus to bend to the material, social, and spiritual conditions of their new reservation environment. Yet it must be recognized that most Sicangus did not passively submit to the ideals of government-designed change. Rather, with Spotted Tail in the lead, they continued—where feasible—to adapt foreign materials and ideas to Lakota templates, just like they had done with the clothes they received at Whetstone. Another illustration of their creative resistance can be found in their reworking of the government's distribution of cattle so that it resembled the traditional *wanaspi*, or buffalo hunt. Perfecting this adaptation shortly after their confinement at Whetstone, they continued its practice after their relocation to the Rosebud. Henry Pancoast of the Indian Rights Association described such an "issue day":

> About ten o'clock the Indians began to assemble on their ponies, armed with pistols and short rifles, and very soon the hills were bright with gay groups of horsemen. Suddenly there is a scattering among the riders, and over the sharp edge of the hill, plunging down the slope in a wild, irregular gallop, come the cattle, fierce Texas steers with huge horns. With remarkable precision each Indian selects his victim and separates it from the throng. . . . Every few minutes comes a puff of smoke and the sharp crack of a rifle . . . some heavy beast thunders on, staggers, stumbles, and his great bulk tumbles in a convulsive heap. After it is overcome the squaws, like the stragglers on the field after a battle, knock those that are yet alive on the head with a tomahawk, and cut up the slain for their expectant families.[23]

In the years after Spotted Tail's murder, the political and cultural landscape of the Rosebud slowly evolved in ways that reflected both his passing and the continuing pressures of reservation policy. Among the most important of these changes was the emergence of three sociopolitical divisions. At one extreme were the Sicangu conservatives who continued, to the extent that confinement on the reservation allowed, to live and dress in traditional Lakota fashion. Government officials labeled such individuals with the unflattering sobriquet "blanket Indians." At the other extreme were the so-called progressives, those individuals who had committed themselves to becoming Christianized and civilized.

Although official reports generally dichotomized the population of the Rosebud—as well as other reservations—into "blanket" and "progressive" Indians, evidence indicates that the majority of the population fell somewhere in between. I refer to this majority, for lack of a better term, as "moderates." Because of their outward conformity to Western standards of appearance and behavior, government officials and missionaries tended to identify these individuals as progressives. This "official" interpretation notwithstanding, there is little evidence that such individuals endorsed the ideological subtext of the reform policy. Rather, their attitude appears to have been based on a pragmatic evaluation of Euro-American lifeways within the wider contexts of reservation life.

Such pragmatism is significant for at least two reasons. For one thing, it allowed the development of distinct cultural spaces in which Lakota and Western forms of behavior and dress could coexist. Thus, although many moderates sported Western attire on most occasions, they also found or created fissures in the federal prescriptions on the use of civilized clothing that allowed them to wear customary Lakota garb. Such venues included federally sanctioned celebrations and community dances and surreptitiously conducted curing ceremonies and Sun Dances.

Additionally, this pragmatic spirit afforded Sicangus a certain amount of flexibility with regard to which elements of Western dress and adornment to embrace or reject. For example, despite the constant harangues by agents and missionaries, photographs and documentary sources suggest the reluctance of many Sicangu men and women to cut off their braids. Although the cultural conditions underlying their resistance are too complex and varied to enumerate here, it is important to note that one potent factor was the Sicangus' traditional use of hair cutting to express grief.

These two responses formed the psycho-cultural foundations for a period of adjustment during which many Sicangus imbued selective institutions and materials of Western culture with meanings and values, simultaneously, continuous with and divergent from those of pre-reservation days. This transitional period, in which lie the roots of contemporary Sicangu reservation culture and identity, was already under way in the early 1880s when the first Catholic missionaries arrived on the Rosebud. And it was these moderates who were to constitute the majority of their flock.

CHAPTER FOUR

Catholic Dakota, Nakota, and Lakota Mission and the Grant Peace Policy, 1869–1886

The proprietors of Catholic Indian affairs were enraged over the manner in which the Board of Indian Commissioners had apportioned the seventy-one reservations among the denominations participating in President Grant's Peace Policy. They believed that the seven agencies assigned to their church constituted a fraction of the forty to which it was entitled. Although they continued to participate in the Peace Policy, their assumption that Protestant bigotry was responsible for this shortfall led them to institute measures—including the formation of a Catholic Indian bureau—that they hoped would protect the interests of their church and its Indian members in all future dealings with the federal government. Meanwhile, the Catholic press launched a vigorous campaign, decrying the nativism and religious intolerance that made a mockery of Grant's well-intentioned, if flawed, experiment.

Of the seven reservations that the Catholics acquired in 1870, two—Devil's Lake and Grand River—had mixed populations of Dakotas, Nakotas, and Lakotas. Located in the northern portion of Dakota Territory, the Devil's Lake Agency was established in 1869 for the divisions of Santee (Dakota) and Yanktonnai (Nakota) who had previously been attached to the Sisseton Agency. For four years after the designation of Devil's Lake as a Catholic reservation, the BCIM struggled without success to recruit missionaries to serve there. Throughout this time, religious instruction and care were inconsistent. During the winters of 1871 and 1872, Father Reville of the Dominican order celebrated Mass twice each Sunday before ill health forced him to resign his post. Between 1872 and 1874 an oblate priest, J. B. M. Genin, occasionally entered the reservation to perform Mass and other sacraments. Finally, on the advice of Standing Rock's agent, William Henry Forbes, BCIM treasurer and general-director Fr. J. B. A. Brouillet appealed to the Grey Nuns of Montreal to supply the reservation with teachers and nurses. On November 2, 1874, four members of that order arrived at the agency to take charge of the recently constructed school. In their company was Fr. Louis Bonin, a parish priest from Montreal, to act as mission chaplain.[1]

Located at the confluence of the Grand and Missouri Rivers, the Grand River Agency proved even more difficult to staff than Devil's Lake. There were glimmerings that personnel would soon be on the way when in 1871 the governing board of the Jesuits' Missouri Province at Florissant dispatched Frs. Francis Kuppens and Peter De Meester to investigate the potential for evangelizing the agency's Lakota and Yanktonnai residents.[2] But the conditions they encountered so discouraged the priests that, upon their recommendation, the board withdrew its plans to establish a mission. One of the leading causes for the board's change of heart was the hostility that many of the Indians had expressed toward becoming Christian citizens.[3] Among the most resolute of these opponents was the Hunkpapa leader Sitting Bull in whose camp the Jesuits had lodged for a portion of their stay.

Martin Marty and the Lakota Missions

In July 1873 the administrative center of the Grand River Agency was moved fifty miles upstream from its original site to Standing Rock, and on December 22, 1874, the reserve was officially renamed to reflect this change. What had not changed since the creation of the reservation in 1869 was the inability of the BCIM to recruit church personnel to civilize and Christianize its residents. When by June 1875 this problem had not been solved, the reservation's exasperated agent, John Burke, wrote to BCIM Catholic Indian commissioner Charles Ewing to complain, "I find that little or no attention has been paid to the religious education of the Indians for a length of time, no Church, or any other necessary arrangements to carry out an agent's or Indians' wishes in this respect."[4]

What makes Burke's outburst both surprising and significant is that he was a Catholic. This strong rebuke by a member of the fold may have awakened the BCIM to the potential danger of losing the agency, for by autumn Ewing had nearly completed negotiations with the Indian Office to build a school at the agency. On November 11 he informed Indian commissioner Edward P. Smith that upon the construction of a suitable building for a boarding school the Catholic Church would provide it with four teachers for $2,400 a year, including room and board.[5]

It was, of course, one thing for Brouillet to promise teachers and missionaries to serve at Standing Rock, but quite another thing for him to deliver them. Growing increasingly desperate to find the necessary personnel, he decided to follow up on a report by Mrs. Ellen E. Sherman, head of the Catholic Indian Mission Association and wife of General Sherman, that Martin Marty, abbot of the Benedictine monastery of Saint Meinrad in Indiana, had expressed an interest in working with American Indians.[6] This inquiry bore fruit. After an exchange of letters in May 1876, the abbot informed Brouillet that he would leave for Standing Rock in early July to investigate the prospects for establishing a mission.[7] Waiting until the eleventh hour to advise the Benedictines at Saint Meinrad of his departure, Marty accepted the offers of two members of the community, Fr. Chrysostom Offa and Br. Giles Laurel, to join him in Dakota when he deemed fit.

Marty entered the reservation on July 31, slightly more than a month after Custer's defeat at the Little Big Horn. Despite his seemingly inauspicious arrival, and contrary to the experience of Kuppens and De Meester, the abbot reported that he found the chiefs receptive to the founding of a mission. Still, after only one week on the reservation he had identified three obstacles that "might defeat [his] best efforts." One of these barriers was a disagreement raging between Agent Burke and the military commander, Colonel Poland, for which he acknowledged "there is no remedy." A second concern centered on Poland's orders to arrest, dismount, and disarm Indians returning from the warpath—an action which, Marty feared, would trigger "a general stampede of both peaceable and hostiles, and might even lead to open conflict and bloodshed." A third and "lasting obstacle" was the barrenness of the Dakota landscape, which "frustrated year after year all attempts at agriculture." According to Marty, everyone he consulted agreed "that the first condition required to make these Indians self-supporting is to remove them to a country where the field they cultivate will bring them a fair return from their labor."[8]

Marty's goal of transforming Lakota nomads into farmers was consistent with the mandate of both reform and Catholic Indian policy of his time, but his rank as an abbot in the Order of Saint Benedict influenced the manner in which he understood and sought to execute this edict. Writing to Fr. Frowin Conrad, prior of Conception Monastery in northwestern Missouri, he observed that the "education of several generations is unthinkable with out stability, and the family life of a genuine Benedictine family, embracing the material as well as the spiritual progress, is the exemplar and ideal of the Christian family life, upon which the welfare of the individual and of society rests. The *ora* and *labora* is today still the only remedy for healing the children of Adam and neither the one nor the other can be taught in words alone."[9]

For Marty the central doctrine of Benedictine monasticism, *ora et labora* (prayer and work), constituted the irreducible formula for Christianizing and civilizing all savages, including the Lakotas. However, because he identified *labora* with farming, he almost immediately despaired of establishing a monastery on the Standing Rock. He observed that the "greater part of the soil within this reservation is only adapted to grazing, the climate excludes cereals and most vegetables, and the grasshoppers invariably eat whatever is planted." The abbot therefore concluded that the "Ora and Labora of the Benedictine can never take root in this soil." "I could perhaps," he continued, "maintain a missionary station here, but shall never be able to establish here a Benedictine monastery, such as they have been of old."[10]

Given the bleak prospects for "Benedictizing" Indians, Marty was delighted when he learned that the government was preparing to remove the inhabitants of Standing Rock, the Spotted Tail Agency, and other Dakota reservations to Indian Territory. Writing to the BCIM he stated, "Col. Poland, who has been in the Indian Territory thinks that it would be a good home for the Sioux and that now we have the most favorable moment to move them: whilst the agent and myself have no doubt, but that we could persuade them to go there with us." In fact, so confident was Marty that the Lakotas could be convinced to relocate that he went on to declare that "under these circumstances I shall not think of building church or school house now, but I will use my time here in studying the Sioux language and extending my acquaintance with the different bands of the tribe."[11]

Marty's predilections notwithstanding, the Lakotas protested and success-fully staved off plans for their removal. In the fall of 1878 the abbot made a tour of several Dakota camps and agencies to determine the prospects for missionary work among them. On October 9 he wrote Ewing an enthusiastic report on the results of his investigation: "I have found the entire nation anxious to have Catholic missionaries, churches and schools. Had I the men and means, it would not be a long and difficult task to make them Christians." Concerning the method of mission he suggested, "At every agency there are from two to four villages, camps or settlements; if there was a resident priest in each of them he could regulate their whole life. The Indians, young and old, would assemble in the chapel morning and evening; they would work willingly under the direction of the man of God; two or three Sisters might take charge of the school, and in a few years Christian faith and life would grow into all of them."[12]

Marty was aware that the success of his program depended on access to a pool of specially trained and dedicated personnel. Although he had despaired of establishing a Benedictine monastery to serve as the heart of missionary work at Standing Rock, the abbot now believed that such an establishment could train and sustain priests and brothers of sufficient "virtue and heroism" to Christianize Lakota Indians. He therefore proposed to Ewing that the BCIM construct "at some favorable point in the Dakota or Sioux country a Benedictine Monastery, built after the same plan, if not of the same dimensions, as the abbeys erected a thousand years ago in the wilderness among the barbarous nations of Europe." He believed that such a spiritual center would meet several critical needs, including helping to secure divine blessing for the Dakota mission; serving as a retreat center for "bodily and spiritual restoration"; and as regards the surrounding Indian population "of hitherto untutored savages . . . exhibiting a bright model of Christian life, in its liturgical, moral and social aspect, where they could learn how to work and pray, how to cultivate their soil and their souls."[13]

Among the Lakota groups that Marty hoped eventually to supply with Benedictine religious were the Sicangus, whom he had first visited in December 1877 on the Spotted Tail Agency near Niobrara, Nebraska, and again in October 1878, soon after their transfer to the Rosebud. The first of these visits closely followed major events in the lives of both Marty and Spotted Tail. In May 1877 the abbot had made an unsuccessful bid to convince Sitting Bull to return to the United States from Canada, where he and most of his band had fled after the battle of the Little Big Horn. In a description of this meeting that appeared in *Annals of the Catholic Indian Missions of America* of 1878, Marty quoted the Hunkpapa chief as having declared that "he was in a better country now than to one he had left, and that not only the country was better, but that the people and the Government also were better. He liked the English because they had not interfered with him, while the Americans had never allowed him or his people to have peace."[14]

Late in the summer of 1877, Spotted Tail had traveled to Washington, D.C., as part of a delegation of Lakotas and Arapahos who met with President Rutherford B. Hayes. During one of his speeches the Sicangu leader had asked the president to replace the Episcopal missionaries serving the Sicangus with Sina Sapa ("Blackrobes"), the Lakota term for Catholic priests. In the official transcript from these proceedings, Spotted Tail's request appears sincere but pragmatic. He expressed no interest whatever in the religious objectives of the Catholic missionization. Rather, he desired Blackrobes to teach the children of his camps how to read and write English, something that the Episcopal ministers had failed to accomplish.[15] Contrary to this transcript, the BCIM's report on the delegation portrayed Spotted Tail and Red Cloud as having issued "urgent appeals" for Catholic missionaries and schools.[16]

It was these "appeals" that brought Marty to the Spotted Tail Agency in 1877. On November 17 he concluded a brief stay at Saint Meinrad and returned to the Dakotas. Before meeting with Spotted Tail and Red Cloud, he stopped in Omaha to consult with Bishop James O'Connor, whose expansive see included all of Dakota Territory. During this meeting, the bishop appointed Marty as vicar general for that area of the Dakotas inhabited by the Lakotas.

Soon after Marty's arrival on the reservation, the acting agent, Lt. Jesse M. Lee, escorted him to the major Sicangu camps. In a letter to Brouillet dated December 28, the abbot stated that the Indians gave him a hearty welcome. Three weeks later, after touring the Red Cloud Agency and before departing for Saint Meinrad, he briefly returned to the Spotted Tail Agency, where he again wrote to Brouillet. After commenting on the cordial reception that the Lakotas on the agencies he met had accorded him, he noted, "I am also informed that the Sioux of the other agencies along the Missouri River are fully as anxious to have Catholic priests and teachers." He immediately added, however, that "unhappily we have neither men nor means to provide for those who are already under our care, and while there is the brightest prospect possible for us on the side of the Indians, there is a dark outlook concerning this on our side."[17]

Despite this bleak prognosis, a secular priest entered the Spotted Tail Agency shortly after Marty's departure for Indiana. On March 15, 1878, this priest, Fr. A. H. Frederick, wrote to Bishop O'Connor concerning the implication of recent and impending events on the reservation for missionizing the Sicangus. He first described a council that had been held the previous day. Frederick wrote that Spotted Tail again expressed his desire for a Catholic priest and school, quoting the Sicangu chief as follows: "I and my people are very glad to see that a catholic priest has arrived amongst us, and I want the government to erect two larger buildings, so that the Father can teach my children." According to Frederick the chief then pointed to him and continued, "This is the man we want with us, this man with the long black dress we want to reside with us and nobody else. I don't want the other church (meaning the Episc. Church) amongst us and when we move away from here, I do not want the church to move along with us, only the Father with the long black dress shall go along with us."[18]

Frederick went on to discuss the Sicangus' imminent departure for their new reservation: "The time is drawing near, when the Indians will move to their new home and it is therefore of the utmost importance to do the best we can to hold what we have. I do not think that the government will dare to prevent me from going with the Indians, it would wound them to the quick, and I am positive they will rise to a man to oppose all steps that may be taken to drive me away from amongst them."[19]

Indeed, when the Sicangus removed to the Rosebud in August 1878 they invited Frederick to accompany them, at the same time barring the Episcopal clergyman from making the journey.[20] Frederick's popularity with the Indians was not, however, shared by his superiors, and when Abbot Martin visited the new agency a few months later he made it part of his duties to dismiss him on the grounds of misconduct.[21] During his discussions with members of Spotted Tail's camp, Marty vowed to send new missionaries the following spring, a pledge he would also make to the Oglalas, who were now living on the Pine Ridge. According to Marty's report, his promise of Blackrobes prompted Spotted Tail to declare, "The priest you see here has promised that he will come to us next spring with other religious men and women to teach us and our children. The Black Gown is the kind of teacher we want and no other." Red Cloud and the other Oglala headmen echoed Spotted Tail's sentiments, according to Marty: "The chiefs came to tell me how glad they were to see I would not abandon them, but would open the school, and be with them next spring." With the endorsements of the Sicangu and Oglala leaders still fresh in his memory, Marty wrote a letter cautioning Brouillet that, "if the Indians do not become Catholic soon, the fault is not theirs."[22]

The Sicangus on the Eve of Catholic Missionization

Despite Marty's pledge to supply the new Sicangu and Oglala reservations with Catholic missionaries, it was by no means certain that the federal government would permit him to fulfill his promise. From the beginning of the Peace Policy, the responsibility for civilizing and Christianizing both Sicangus and Oglalas had been delegated to the Episcopal Church. Nonetheless, as the time approached for relocating these tribes to the Rosebud and Pine Ridge, Marty had reason to believe that both groups would be placed under Catholic control.[23]

An important reason for Marty's optimism came from information he had gleaned about the official response to Spotted Tail and Red Cloud's insistence that their people be sent Blackrobes. Not only were the two chiefs under the impression that President Hayes had bowed to their demand for Catholic priests, but Agent Lee of the Spotted Tail Agency was of this opinion as well. Lee informed Marty that during a visit to Washington he had been told that Hayes had promised Spotted Tail Catholic priests.[24] Even more significant, this was also the understanding of Gen. John H. Hammond, superintendent of the Indian agencies for Dakota, who notified the abbot that the new agencies were to be placed under Catholic control.[25]

Enthused by these reports, Marty pledged to supply Rosebud and Pine Ridge with Catholic missionaries, and the following spring he authorized Fr. Meinrad McCarthy of his abbey to take up residence among the Oglalas. Although Red Cloud received the priest warmly, when Indian commissioner Ezra Hayt learned of his presence he ordered agent Valentine T. McGillycuddy to expel him from the reservation. To avoid the demeaning spectacle of a forced eviction, McCarthy voluntarily vacated Pine Ridge, relocating two miles south of its border near Camp Sheridan. There he waited while Marty, O'Connor, and the Catholic Bureau struggled to gain permission for him to teach and evangelize the Oglalas. After four months, all concerned had lost hope that such permission would ever be granted, and the priest returned to Saint Meinrad.

Father McCarthy's plight not only dealt a blow to Marty's aspirations to found Catholic missions on the Pine Ridge and Rosebud reservations but confirmed his fears that the Hayes administration would continue the policy of denominational exclusivism. While McCarthy was biding his time at Fort Sheridan, the abbot wrote him: "From what I heard when in Washington, 26–28 July, we need not expect that President Hayes will change the policy of President Grant with regard to the Indians. Our only hope is that Congress in the next session will by a special bill grant religious liberty to the Aborigines remaining in the land of the brave and the home of the free."[26]

Contrary to McCarthy's expectations, events were unfolding at Marty's Dakota base of Standing Rock that would finally bring denominational control on reservations to an end.[27] Ironically, it was the Protestants who were the handmaidens of this change. In 1878, Congregational minister Daniel Renville and several coworkers requested permission from Standing Rock's Catholic agent, James McLaughlin, to establish a church on the reservation. In sharp contrast to Agent McGillycuddy's actions, McLaughlin not only approved their petition but the next year applied for government rations to aid them in their work. It was at this point that Commissioner Hayt discovered the existence of a Protestant beachhead on a Catholic reservation. Consistent with his actions on Pine Ridge, Hayt issued an order to McLaughlin to expel Renville and his company from Standing Rock. Infuriated by the commissioner's ruling, Stephen Riggs and other American Board missionaries launched a vigorous campaign to revoke the proprietary rights of particular churches on reservations. In 1881, secretary of the interior Carl Schurz capitulated to the mounting pressure and allowed the participating denominations to determine the fate of Indian mission by comity. By mid-February most of the churches had voted to end restrictions on reservation missionary work and, in March, the Indian Office ruled that, "except where the presence of rival religious organizations would manifestly be perilous to peace and good order, Indian reservations shall be open to all religious denominations providing that no existing treaty stipulations would be violated thereby."[28] In 1883, Indian commissioner Hiram Price gave this ruling a broader interpretation by granting permission to religious societies to engage in missionary work on all reservations "provided they do not interfere with the conduct of agency matters."[29]

    With the abrogation of Indian mission by comity, the path was finally cleared for the Catholic Church to enter reservations from which it had been barred for a decade. By spring 1885, Marty would recruit Blackrobes to work on the Rosebud, and by 1886, much to the dismay of the reservation's Episcopal establishment, a Catholic mission and boarding school would begin the work of "Christianizing and civilizing" the Sicangu Lakotas.

CHAPTER FIVE

The Beginnings of
Rosebud Catholic Mission, 1878–1886

After volunteering his services as an Indian missionary in 1876, Abbot Marty found it necessary to spend extended periods away from Saint Meinrad. His first visit to Dakota Territory lasted thirteen months, during which time daily life at the monastery fell under the direction of its prior, Fintan Mundwiler. This arrangement was evidently not to the liking of many of the abbey's monks, for upon Marty's return to Indiana in August 1877 several of his confreres leaped at the opportunity to inform him of the toll that his missionary work was taking on the community's operation and morale.[1]

Marty's ability to juggle the offices of abbot and missionary grew even more precarious when he accepted the appointment as Bishop O'Connor's vicar general for Indian missions in November 1877. By assuming this office, he committed himself to the time-consuming task of recruiting qualified personnel to evangelize the Lakotas of Dakota. Additionally, in August 1879 he undertook a second journey to Canada to persuade Sitting Bull and his followers to end their self-imposed exile from the United States. Some historians have credited the abbot's visit as the primary reason for the Indians' return, but Robert F. Karolevitz is probably closer to the mark in suggesting that their decision was prompted by their growing disaffection with the Canadian government and dwindling food stores.[2]

Bishop Marty and the Origins of the Rosebud Mission

Around the time that Marty was preparing for his second rendezvous with Sitting Bull, events were transpiring in Rome that would ultimately compel him to choose between his vocations as abbot and Indian missionary. Upon the recommendation of Bishop O'Connor, on August 5 Pope Leo XIII issued a bull appointing Marty titular bishop of Tiberias. The next week the pope published another pronouncement that named him vicar apostolic (missionary bishop) of the newly established vicariate in Dakota Territory.[3] Knowing full well of Marty's passion for Indian missions, most of the monks at Saint Meinrad assumed that he would immediately accede to this elevation. The abbot, however, apparently struggled with his decision, waiting until December 1879 to notify the community that he had accepted the post. On February 1, 1880, he was consecrated bishop at the parish church at Ferdinand, Indiana.[4]

By placing the duties of abbot behind him, Marty was not thereby free to devote exclusive attention to spreading Catholicism among the tribes of his vicariate. By becoming bishop he had exchanged his spiritual oversight of the monks of Saint Meinrad for that of the ever-increasing population of white Catholics in Dakota Territory. He consequently spent much of his first years in office visiting the see's non-Indian parishes, as well as enlisting priests and sisters to staff their churches and schools.[5] Additionally, at the time of his elevation to bishop, Protestant denominations still exercised exclusive control over the Dakota reservations that had been assigned them by the Peace Policy. Marty thus lacked the legal authority to send missionaries to Indian agencies in his diocese other than those that the government had allotted to the Catholic Church.

As support for the Peace Policy crumbled between 1880 and 1883, Marty began visiting Protestant Lakota agencies in his missionary rounds. In autumn 1882 he returned to the Rosebud for the first time since his illegal stop there four years earlier when he had met with Spotted Tail and other Sicangu chiefs about their reported desire for a Blackrobe school. He spent most of his five-day stay informing reservation officials and Indian headmen of his intention to honor his earlier commitment to send priests.[6]

Marty's trip to the Sicangus quickly bore fruit. In April 1883 he commissioned Fr. Francis Craft, a Presbyterian convert whom he had recently ordained at Conception Abbey, Missouri, to inaugurate a Catholic mission on the Rosebud. Shortly thereafter he appointed two additional secular priests, Frs. Caspar A. Hospenthal and Joseph A. Bushman, to assist Craft on the reservation.[7]

Father Francis Craft and the Sicangus

Despite all of Marty's efforts, the fledgling mission was soon engulfed in controversies that jeopardized its survival. At the center of the turmoil was Father Craft, whose relationship with Rosebud's agent, James George Wright, had degenerated to the point of manifest hostility by autumn 1883.

Wright's animosity toward Craft is readily observed in the section of his 1883 report to the Indian commissioner describing missionary work on the Rosebud. Focusing first on the labors of Episcopal minister William J. Cleveland, the agent wrote enthusiastically, "No agency could be better, more ably, or more acceptably cared for in Mission work, than this one. . . . No more earnest Christian and more highly respected gentleman can be found among missionaries, to do the work of his Lord and Master in a more conscientious manner. Indians recognize him as their friend and appeal to him on many occasions." Yet the ink from Wright's pen suddenly ran cold when he turned to the subject of Catholic missionary work: "The Revd. Francis of the Roman Catholic Church came here as missionary this last spring. He claims many of the Indians to be of his faith and persuasion, and is endeavoring to build a Church and School. With what success, I am not advised." Although Wright went on to describe Craft as "active and zealous in his calling, ministering to the ailments of soul and body," his addition of the following admonition left no doubt concerning his feelings about the priest and his activities: "The Christianizing of the Indians is a large field to work in, where any and all, so disposed, can do good, and after doing all they can, there will be room for others. If ministers or laymen would work for this," he continued, "there is not any reason why Indian reservations should not be open to all, but if those, permitted to come, and in their mistaken idea of religion and the service of the 'Great Spirit' try to undermine what little faith has been planted in the benighted hearts, by persuading them, that what they have been taught to believe, is error, they should be denied access to reservations and Indians." Wright concluded his counsel with this ominous warning: "If they teach, or try to teach these people, that they should look to them, before the law, Agent, or other authority, it is better they should be denied the privilege of an Indian reservation, before discontent and trouble is generated."[8]

The first record of overt conflict between Craft and Wright is found in a letter dated November 3, 1883, in which the priest advised BCIM director J. A. Brouillet to expect a message from the agent containing complaints against him "for attending a council of the Indians, and dissuading them from sending their children to Carlisle Pa. School." Craft admitted that he had participated in the meeting, noting, "I cannot find in the U.S. Statutes relating to Indian affairs anything by which a missionary is prohibited from attending meetings of the Indians especially as their instructor and the one to whom they look for advice." He likewise confessed to having criticized the sanitary and educational conditions at Carlisle. The priest, however, maintained that he merely had told the Indians what they already knew and what he "had heard from them." Moreover, he insisted that he had urged the Indian parents to send their children "away to school, and if at Carlisle or any other school they could live and study [he] would be pleased." Notwithstanding his endorsements, Craft stated, "Maj. Wright now tells me that I made myself answerable to the law by attending an Indian council and interfering in temporal matters."[9]

Whatever actually transpired at the meeting, Craft's behavior so incensed Wright that he wrote to the district court of Dakota Territory, not to Brouillet, seeking advice on how to remove the meddlesome priest from the reservation. The response from district court clerk A. R. Z. Dawson must have profoundly disappointed Wright, for it informed the agent that, although he had "no reason to doubt [Craft] seriously disturb[ed] the proper administration of affairs at the agency and ought to be removed," he was without authority to do so. He nonetheless advised Wright that, "if the facts were stated to the Commissioner of Indian Affairs . . . he would act promptly in the matter." Dawson went on to note, "In the meantime I would forbid his [Craft's] attending any more council and if he disobeys your orders, put him off the reservation or in the guard house."[10]

During the next two months relations between the missionary and agent steadily deteriorated. Finally, on January 16, 1884, Wright sent a blistering letter to Indian commissioner Hiram Price that contained a litany of new allegations against Craft. The agent first recounted that the preceding November the priest had, without Wright's knowledge or consent, conducted a crew of Indians to the white community of Valentine, Nebraska, to haul lumber that he had purchased for his church and school. In addition, Wright alleged that while the party waited for the lumber to arrive they "danced the Omaha dance in the public street where there are liquor saloons on all sides [and] that the Priest took off his own hat to receive contributions which he solicited." The agent complained that the episode violated his "instructions that no Indian shall remain in Valentine over night [and] under no circumstances to have or engage in any dances there."[11]

Wright then turned to an infraction so severe that it had overridden his normal repugnance "to complain of or take action against any minister of the Gospel." This transgression once again involved Craft's reputed interference with recruiting Rosebud children for an off-reservation school, this time at Genoa, Nebraska. Wright explained that he had invited the priest and Genoa's superintendent, Col. S. Tappan, to attend a meeting that he had called to remind Rosebud parents of the requirement to send their children to school. According to the agent, he had told those at the meeting—whom he "afterwards learned . . . were the Omaha dancing club of which . . . [he was] informed Revd. Craft [was] a member, has worn the insignia, and eagle feather in his hat"—that he "would be satisfied with whatever school the children should attend, the Priests['], the Agency, or to any away from the Agency, but the children must go to school, or [he] should suspend their rations, according to their treaty agreement." He had made a special point, however, of noting the advantages of the Genoa school, stressing that "it was the urgent wishes of the President, the Honr. Secretary of the Interior, the Honr. Commissioner and [his] own, that their children should go there, that it was a new building, prepared expressly for them."

Wright charged that when Craft took the floor he announced that "he did not *care* for the wishes of the President, Secretary, or Agent, he was not under any man's authority, but only that of *God*, that when it was shown to him that the President located a school in the proper place, such as *he* could approve, where the children could go and *live* and *not die*, he would tell them of it and would advise them to send their children, as it was good for them to send their children among the Whites to learn their ways." Wright stated that as a result of Craft's criticisms the Indians proclaimed that they would not send their children to Genoa and "unceremoniously" left the room. He further noted that the majority of Indians and whites on Rosebud concurred that the priest had "set at defiance all law and authority [and] if allowed to pass unnoticed it must in effect undermine the Agent[']s control and authority, leading the Indians to look to the Priest as their law giver, and leaving the Agent but a nonentity." Echoing the sentiments contained in his 1883 report to the commissioner, Wright observed that, although he believed that there was "room for all" religious denominations on Rosebud, he could not "believe it advisable or prudent for any Priest or Minister to assume or set at defiance the constituted authority of the Agent, when by so doing the Indians are taught to disregard such authority, and may at any time, more easily be led into mutiny, then be retained under proper control."

On January 24, 1884, Commissioner Price notified Wright that he had informed secretary of the interior Henry M. Teller of the havoc Craft was raising with educational work on the Rosebud. "I infer," Price wrote, "that Mr. Craft not content with influencing the Indians against sending their children to Genoa prevents children from going whose parents desire to send them. This must not be tolerated." Six days later Price followed up this stern warning with a letter informing Wright that Teller had granted him the "authority for the removal from the Sioux reservation of Father Crafts, who is charged with exerting a pernicious influence over the Indians."[12] On February 20, Wright enforced the commissioner's directive, notifying the priest that he was to "depart *without delay*."[13]

Craft quickly complied with the commissioner's orders, withdrawing from the Rosebud and relocating to Bishop Marty's residence at Yankton in southeastern Dakota Territory.[14] He did so despite the fact that no Indian Office official had informed him of the charges against him or given him the opportunity to appeal Teller's decision. However, once the initial shock of being cast off the reservation had begun to abate, he sought avenues of redress for his unfair treatment. On March 12, 1884, Craft wrote to BCIM secretary Charles Lusk asking him to deliver a letter to Senator James Kenna of West Virginia requesting that he be allowed to tell the Indian Office his side of the story. He complained to Lusk, "At all times, and in all places, men accused, no matter of what crime, have been allowed to hear the charges against them, and have had the chance to defend themselves. In my case . . . I have been accused, condemned, and banished, without hearing the charges against me or having the opportunity to answer them." Having vented his anger against the Indian Office, Craft went on to accuse BCIM director Brouillet of sharing much of the responsibility for his plight: "When I found that I had been reported to the Secy. of the Interior by Capt. Pratt in November last, I wrote at once to Rev. Brouillet, explaining the matter, and asking him to represent it properly to the Department. If he had done so, the trouble would have ended then and there." Craft closed by underscoring his desire to return to his ministry on the Rosebud as soon as possible: "Just as you would object strongly to being driven from your home and your children, so I object to being driven from my Indians."[15]

Sensing that Craft's grievances might have some merit, on May 24, 1884, Lusk wrote Price for permission to examine the correspondence relating to the priest's expulsion and "to make copies of each paper as are necessary for our intelligent understanding of the case by this Bureau."[16] Three weeks later he sent Craft duplicates of the complaints with a letter stressing the necessity of supplying the BCIM with a detailed account of his version of the debacle. By June 23, the priest had completed his defense. In the note that accompanied his statement, he advised Lusk, "The only thing the Department can decently do is to permit me to return to Rosebud Agency. If the Bishop wishes to remove me from one Agency to another, I have nothing to say, but I decidedly object to being driven from my mission to gratify the malice of a bigoted Protestant."[17]

Addressing Wright's accusations point by point, Craft first presented his version of the controversial trip to Valentine. Far from being a radical departure from the norm, he informed the commissioner that the "Indians have been in the habit of going to Valentine to bring freight for the stores and for others, and I never heard that any permission from the Agent was required, or asked for, and from what I know of the matter, I do not believe that the Agent ever gave any instructions to the contrary. If I had any idea that permission was necessary I would have asked it." As for his having encouraged and profited from the Omaha dance, Craft notified Price that he had made the Indians promise that they would stay in their camp on the outskirts of Valentine. He stated, "While near the depot, I heard the drum, and saw the Indians coming towards the town. I went to stop them, and reached them just as they were beginning a dance at the first corner of the town. I kept them from coming any further, and scolded them for breaking their promise. . . . The whites threw money to the Indians to get them to continue the dance. As for my 'passing round a hat,' and soliciting contributions, it is simply *false*."[18]

Craft next contested Wright's charge that he was a member of a "dancing club" and had "worn its insignia." He adamantly denied the existence of any such organization, although he acknowledged being a member of the "Grass Society," whose activities centered on cutting hay and building houses. Craft claimed that he had joined the society "to encourage and teach the young men to work." The priest did confess to having worn an eagle feather. However, as with his membership in the Grass Society, Craft insisted that he had worn the feather to promote the Sicangus' civilization. He wrote:

> The Indians gave me an eagle's feather, and told me they wished to consider the "Black Robe" as one of their people. I put the feather in my hat and told them that as they gave me a right, as one of their nation, to say something about their customs, they must aid me in doing away with whatever was displeasing to God, and injurious to themselves. On several occasions, when I wished to put a stop to bad practices, such as polygamy, gambling, superstition, etc., I have silenced opposition by reminding them that they themselves gave me a right to interfere with their customs. In this way I certainly did "wear an eagle feather," though not as a member of any "club" and not at all times, as Maj. Wright's accusation would seem to imply.

Having dealt with the "lesser" charges against him, Craft turned to Wright's accusation that he had used the agent's meeting to encourage Sicangu parents to boycott the Genoa boarding school. He informed Price that during the meeting Wright kept "directing angry and contemptuous looks and gestures" toward him and referring to the "priest" and "priest's school" in a bitter tone that angered the Indians. Craft wrote, "I said once or twice, 'Major, this is doing no good; to speak plainly, you are cutting your own throat. I came here to help you, and you are exasperating the Indians, and preventing me from doing anything.'"

Craft's account of his speech at the council, as one might expect, differed markedly from that Wright had presented. The missionary informed Price that he had begun by asking the agent why he had invited him to the meeting if he believed him to be opposed to his policies. Alluding to their earlier battle over the Carlisle boarding school, he reminded Wright, "Once before you sent, or caused to be sent by others, to the Department reports misrepresenting what I said and did while Capt. Pratt was here, and you also had a meeting here in this council room, before the Indians, and took statements, and sent them to Deadwood, and tried to get a warrant for my arrest."

Craft insisted that he used the rest of his talk to coax the Indians to cooperate with Wright. He wrote that when he had finished he turned to Tappan, who "seemed very much pleased." Before either one could continue, a Sicangu leader named Turning Bear commenced a very boisterous speech. "There was something in the Agent's speech he didn't like and he wanted to answer it. He seemed to be the mouthpiece of those who did not wish to give their children. They applauded him, and the others, upon whom we relied to help us, remained silent. He concluded by saying that his people did not want to send their children away, and then turned and left the room followed by all the others."[19]

In the remaining portion of his letter, Craft responded to the several additional complaints against him. In each case he declared his innocence, claiming that he had never knowingly acted to undermine the agent's authority. With regard to the source of the agent's hostility toward him, Craft stated, "The chief cause of Maj. Wright's opposition to me, is his bigotry and hatred of the Catholic Church. When I had been only a short time on the Agency," the priest continued, "he began to find fault . . . because I said that there was but one true Church—the Catholic Church. . . . He positively forbade me to administer the Sacrament of Matrimony to any whom he had married. . . . I told him that if he found me interfering with his affairs, or with his authority as Agent, I would thank him if would tell me of it, but I would not tolerate the slightest interference, on his part, with my religious duties."[20]

On July 28, Lusk forwarded Craft's rebuttal to Secretary Teller. In a letter to Commissioner Price informing him of this action, the BCIM secretary petitioned the Indian Office to rescind Craft's expulsion from Indian Country. He argued that, in addition to the reasons given in the priest's response, "Rt. Rev. M. Marty . . . desires to place him at the Catholic Mission at Standing Rock and for that reason I would again fervently request that said order to be revoked, assuring you that it is not the intention or desire of either Bishop Marty or this Bureau to send Father Craft to Rosebud Agency, believing, as we do, without regard to the truth or falsity of the charges made against him, that his return to that Agency would be productive of no good, and might result in trouble and discord."[21]

Lusk's diplomatic efforts on Craft's behalf were a resounding success. In autumn 1884, Commissioner Price repealed his order forbidding the priest from working on Indian reservations. Honoring the BCIM secretary's promise to Price, Marty reassigned Craft to Standing Rock, leaving the less controversial Bushman and Hospenthal to minister to the Sicangus. Dropping his earlier demand that he be returned to Rosebud, Craft not only accepted the compromise but also thanked Lusk for his efforts on his behalf. On October 14 he informed the BCIM secretary that, "as the order has been revoked leaving everything in the hands of the Bishop, I am perfectly satisfied. . . . I hardly know how to express my thanks for your kindness in arranging everything for me."[22] Concerning his sentiments toward Director Brouillet, the priest remained silent.

Although it removed the major thorn in the relationship between the government and Catholic Church on Rosebud, Marty's decision to relocate Craft apparently did little to improve conditions for the agency's remaining priests. Early in spring 1885, Father Hospenthal wrote to BCIM director J. A. Stephan denouncing "Wright's bigotry" and implored him to use his influence to replace the agent with a Catholic "in order to insure justice to the Indians and freedom to ourselves." In a tone reminiscent of Craft's complaints against Brouillet, Hospenthal bitterly observed that although he had sent Bishop Marty "an almost complete statement of all [Wright's] bigoted actions . . . he scarcely gave them passing notice." The priest lamented that the "Indians befriending us are refused everything and we are kicked, ridiculed and scoffed as though we were dogs." Wright's unrelenting aggression had "thoroughly disheartened" Hospenthal and the Indians. "I really feel ashamed of our abortive attempt on a protestant agency," he confessed. "Our advent only excited the Epis church to wonderful and *very extensive* building and now they are laughing at us making promises but to be broken. I trust that God in His divine Providence will even ordain otherwise and that the dawn of our success may soon appear."[23]

For his part, Wright sought to maintain the appearance of ecumenical cooperation with his Catholic brethren. The agent's evaluation of Bushman's work contained in his 1885 report to the commissioner provides a fascinating case in point: "Rev. J. A. Bushman pursues the even tenor of his way and works among the Indians in an energetic, quiet, and faithful manner. While no particulars of his work are furnished me, I am convinced he is not neglectful of the spiritual wants of his people."[24] Wright's flowery prose cannot hide the fact that he had nothing of substance to report on Catholic missionary work among the Sicangus, the outcome of a breakdown in communication more in keeping with the hostile relations described by the priest than the agent's hollow paeans.

Hospenthal remained with the Sicangus until December 1885, outlasting Bushman, who had been transferred from the reservation the preceding fall.

In his book *My People the Sioux*, Luther Standing Bear briefly described what became of the Catholic mission as Hospenthal prepared to leave Rosebud. He recalled, "One evening when I returned from school, my father told me that the 'black-dress man' (Catholic priest) wanted to sell his house, which stood about fifty yards from the dwelling the Government had erected for Chief Spotted Tail. My father thought it would be a good buy," Standing Bear continued, "and specified the amount which the priest asked for it; so I told him to buy it. He made the purchase in part cash and the balance in spotted horses and cattle. The priest who had been occupying it then packed up all his belonging and moved away."[25]

The convulsive beginnings of Catholicism on the Rosebud were consistent with the adversarial relationship between Protestants and Catholics permeating the entire system of government-sponsored Indian work. Although Protestants and Catholics were equally committed to the goals of Indian civilization and Christianization and shared most assumptions concerning Indian anthropology and social history, religious and ethnic intolerance (e.g., nativism) both highlighted the real differences between them (e.g., the need for reservations and reservation-based boarding schools) and made cooperative efforts nearly impossible in areas where no opposition existed. Whether valid or not, Craft's claim that Wright's antagonism toward him stemmed from his bigotry against Catholics made both cultural and psychological sense given the mutual hostility and suspicion that existed between Protestant and Catholics working in the field. Moreover, as we see in later chapters, Craft's accusations would be repeated time and again concerning other agents and federal employees by the first generation of Saint Francis religious.

CHAPTER SIX

Otto von Bismarck, the Jesuits' Buffalo Province, and the Franciscan Sisters of Penance and Christian Charity

In spite of Catholicism's troubled first years on the Rosebud, Marty remained committed to a Sicangu mission and continued to seek the necessary material and human resources to work toward establishing a permanent church among them. This search would ultimately lead him to a wealthy patroness and representatives from two European religious orders who had sought asylum in the United States from Otto von Bismarck's Kulturkampf.

Bismarck's Kulturkampf against the Catholics

In a manifesto delivered before the Prussian Landtag on January 17, 1873, Rudolf Virchow proclaimed that Germany was in the throes of a grave crisis that daily took on "the character of a great struggle for civilization [Kulturkampf] in the interest of humanity." Virchow, a renowned pathologist who was also a leading spokesman for Prussia's Fortschrittspartei, the radical liberal party, ascribed the crisis to the proclivity of the country's Catholics to place their fidelity in the conservative policies of Pope Pius IX and his council above their loyalty to the state. These ultramontanist tendencies, Virchow and the liberals complained, not only frustrated national development but also spawned legitimate apprehensions on the part of non-Catholics concerning the patriotism of Germany's Catholic citizenry.

Virchow's depiction of a "civilized" Prussia at war with Catholic sedition and priestcraft so resonated with the fears of the state's non-Catholic majority that the latter quickly adopted his militarist neologism, Kulturkampf, as the catchphrase for their struggle. It remained the work of Otto von Bismarck, a royalist with little affection for either liberal or confessional agendas, to transform political rhetoric into action. The origins of this transformation can be found during the period 1862–71, when Bismarck used his authority as prime minister to orchestrate Germany's evolution from a *Staatesbund*, or loose federation of states, to an empire.[1]

From its beginning, German Catholics strenuously opposed Bismarck's empire building. Having periodically been the target of religious persecution, they preferred to be citizens of a confederation in which power was diffused among several semiautonomous leaders rather than of an empire with authority concentrated in the hands of the Protestant Wilhelm I. Catholics also objected to Bismarck's plans to block Austria's admission to the new empire. Excluding Austria, the sole stronghold of Catholic power, ensured that Bismarck's own state—the overwhelmingly Protestant Prussia—would dominate the country's political life. Also objectionable, Bismarck's nationalistic theory of church-state relations reduced Germany's Christian denominations to little more than handmaidens of the emperor. Bismarck's position was therefore diametrically opposed to the doctrine of papal primacy championed by Pius and his cardinals.

Through a skillful deployment of realpolitik during the 1860s and early 1870s, Bismarck managed to defuse Catholic opposition to his program. One of his most effective stratagems was to use Catholic resistance to his policies to rouse suspicions regarding their allegiance to the state. His most valuable ally in this effort was, ironically, Pope Pius himself, whose attempts to rejuvenate the papacy at the expense of the growing sovereignty of Europe's nation-states enraged Germany's non-Catholic citizens. The pope's 1864 "Syllabus of Errors," which denounced modernism and laissez-faire economics, outraged liberals. Six years later the Vatican Council infuriated liberals and conservatives alike with its decrees on papal infallibility.

To counter the Vatican's growing influence over German Catholics, in 1867 the Reichstag approved a new constitution that called for sweeping secularization of the nation's institutions. One of the legislation's immediate goals was to eliminate the influence that both the Protestant and Catholic churches had traditionally exercised over the operation of Germany's schools. To this end it granted individual states exclusive control of the administration of the educational institutions within their borders.

Catholics did not acquiesce silently to these measures. In 1870 they established the Center Party (RCC), through which they hoped to maintain some control over their social and religious affairs, above all the power to select and accredit individuals teaching in their schools. Their "confessional party," however, only spurred liberal legislators to push for stronger measures to secularize German society.

Although Bismarck was primarily concerned with promoting the interests of the emperor and nobility, he quickly perceived the advantage of joining the liberals in their war against the Catholics. As the empire's new chancellor and recently invested prince, he entered into this alliance reluctantly, and only after having first unsuccessfully appealed to the pope to reign in the more extreme members of the RCC. On July 8, 1871, he delighted liberals by dissolving the Catholic division of the Prussian ministry of education and public worship, an event that many historians cite as the commencement of the Kulturkampf. Four months later the Reichstag enacted the Kanzelparagraph, or Pulpit Law, which imposed severe penalties on priests and ministers who used their office to criticize the state.

In January 1872, Bismarck appointed Adalbert Falk as Prussia's minister of culture, to accelerate the pace of his anticlerical program. By March 11, Falk had won the Prussian Landtag's endorsement of a measure that required all public and private schools to adopt secular curricula and submit to state inspections. This law reversed a long-standing policy that allowed denominational schools the right to establish their own educational programs and to play a major role in the inspection process. The minister followed this initiative in May 1873 with a legislative onslaught that soon became known as the "May Laws." One of these statutes, "A Law Governing the Training and Appointment of Clergy," required that all candidates to the priesthood and ministry receive their academic training in state high schools and universities. To further increase state control over these candidates, the law additionally required that they pass government-administered examinations in philosophy, history, and German literature. Other laws granted the government unprecedented powers over church life, including the modes and exercise of church discipline and the procedures by which parishioners could separate themselves from their churches.

The May Laws were followed in 1874 by an "expatriation" statute that permitted states to banish clerics who had been deprived of their offices. The attack continued into the next year, first with a law that made civil marriage obligatory throughout Germany, and then with a measure that authorized the establishment of church vestries, or boards of lay trustees, to oversee church property.

With his patience for Bismarck's usurpation of church powers finally exhausted, on February 5, 1875, Pope Pius issued an encyclical that threatened any Prussian Catholic who submitted to state regulations with excommunication. The resulting war between the pope and the state quickly exacted a heavy toll on Prussia's episcopate. By 1876 all of that state's bishops had been either arrested or forced into exile. The turmoil proved equally disastrous for Prussia's 4,600 parish priests, whose number had dwindled by more than a quarter by 1877.

The primary targets of the expatriation and other laws were the Catholic religious orders, with the Society of Jesus heading the list. With Bismarck's encouragement, on July 4, 1872, the Bundesrat enacted a law that prohibited the Society from establishing new institutions on German soil while compelling them to shutter many of their older houses and schools. Other provisions of the law restricted the areas where Jesuits could travel and reside, granted states the right to deport members of the order living within their borders, and virtually banned immigration and visits by nonnative Jesuits.

Despite the considerable energy and political capital Bismarck poured into crushing "political Catholicism," by 1878 he was ready to concede that the Kulturkampf was a failure. Instead of intimidating Catholics into submission to the state, religious persecution had only galvanized their support for their clergy and pope. Thus, for example, by 1874 Catholic representatives had won control of twice as many seats in Germany's parliament as they held at the time of the formation of the Center Party. Changes in Germany's political environment provided additional incentives for Bismarck to abandon his war with the Catholics. Among the most important of these changes was the rise of socialism, whose radical agenda made it the common enemy of the German aristocracy, liberals, and Catholics. Finally, the election of the politically moderate Pope Leo XIII after Pius's death in 1878 convinced the prime minister it was time to bring his assault on Catholicism to an end.

Notwithstanding its eventual collapse, the Kulturkampf was of sufficient severity and duration to deal a severe blow to Germany's Catholic religious orders. These measures exacted their greatest toll on the Society of Jesus. During the 1870s thousands of deported or emigrating Jesuits booked passage on ships destined for the United States. The initial destination for the majority of these emigrants was the so-called German Province of Buffalo, New York, but after a sometimes very brief period of cultural acclimation many of them were assigned to provinces and ministries in other parts of the country. Among these were several members of the first generation of Jesuit religious assigned to Saint Francis Mission.

The "German Province" and the Buffalo Mission

The emigration of large numbers of Jesuits to the United States in the late nineteenth century was not without precedent.[2] As a result of anti-Jesuit sentiments during the revolutions in Switzerland, Germany, and Austria in 1847 and 1848, many of the order's priests and brothers from those areas had sought refuge in America. By the end of 1848, eighty-eight, or more than a third of its members in these countries, were scattered among various missions and provinces in North America. Although the Jesuits' German provincial, Anthony Minoux, had charged these exiles with founding a college, by 1850 the political climate in Europe had sufficiently improved for him to commence their recall. Within ten years, all but a few had returned to their respective communities in Europe.[3]

Although this first emigration of Jesuits had been relatively short-lived, it laid the foundation for an official North American headquarters to welcome future waves of Jesuit religious from German-speaking lands. In fewer than twenty years, the growth in the number of immigrants from Germany to the northeastern United States gave rise to a renewed call for the services of German priests and brothers. Early in 1868, Jesuit general Peter Beckx gave his provisional endorsement to a request by James Perron of the Society's New York–Canada mission to make Buffalo the site of a new mission for German Jesuits in North America. Before the end of 1869 this mission was in full operation with a staff of thirteen priests and five brothers from the German Province. By 1871 their number had grown to thirty-three.[4]

The work of the first members of the Buffalo mission, like that of their New York–Canadian predecessors, was focused on the city's parishes. In 1874, however, the mission accepted a proposal by Bishop Grace of Minnesota to take charge of a parish at Mankato. Three years later, the mission responded to an invitation from the bishop of Dubuque to supervise the Saint John's Church in Burlington, Iowa.[5]

In addition to widening the geographic scope of their parish work, the Jesuits of the Buffalo mission diversified their ministerial activities. Among the most successful of these new vocations was in the field of higher education. In 1870 the mission founded Canisius College in Buffalo. This was followed by the College of the Sacred Heart at Prairie du Chien, Wisconsin (1880), a high school and Saint Ignatius College in Cleveland (1886), and Saint John's University in Toledo (1898).[6]

The growth in the number of priests and brothers attached to the Buffalo mission made it possible to staff these schools. After 1888, seminarians from the mission's novitiate at Prairie du Chien supplied much of the additional manpower. During the preceding decade, however—especially between 1872 and 1878—the increase was largely the result of emigrant Jesuits who had joined the community to escape the Kulturkampf.[7]

Aside from parish and educational ministries, the Buffalo Jesuits were increasingly drawn to missionary work among the western Indians. The priests and brothers who chose this ministry were aware of the contributions of their Jesuit forbears to Indian missions, especially those of Pierre-Jean De Smet, whose accounts provided them with both inspiration and instruction. Before the end of the century some of them would be given the opportunity of fulfilling De Smet's goal of founding a mission among the Lakotas.

The Franciscan Sisters of Penance and Christian Charity

The Jesuits' reputation for political intrigue made them a favorite target of German nationalists, but the Kulturkampf's anticlerical legislations proved calamitous for all Catholic religious. This was especially true for teaching orders of sisters that were scattered throughout Germany.

Among these congregations was the Sisters of Saint Francis of Penance and Christian Charity, which was established in 1835 at Heythuizen in Dutch Limburg.[8] Its foundress, Catherine Daemen, was born in Laek, Holland, on November 19, 1787. At about the age of eighteen she walked to the nearby town of Maeseyk, where she found employment as a housekeeper for the parish. On the advice of Peter Leonardus, a local Capuchin friar who served as her spiritual director, Catherine joined a small community of Franciscan tertiaries. In 1825 she decided to accept a request by Peter Van der Zandt, the parish priest of Heythuizen, for members of the community to help him teach catechism and to care for the church. During the next three years several young women joined Catherine in her work. Following her lead, on November 8, 1828, the trio made their profession in the Third Order of Saint Francis. Seven years later Father Van der Zandt invested the members of the community with a Franciscan habit and religious names. Foundress Daemen, now Mary Magdalen, was appointed the congregation's first superior and served in that capacity until 1840.

Under the leadership of Magdalen and her successor, Mother General Theresa (1840–46), the order grew slowly and remained largely confined to Holland. However, during the tenure of the next superior, Mother Bernadine (1846–59), the order founded an additional twenty-two convents. The tremendous strain that these new houses placed on the congregation's human and financial resources was the source of considerable tension within the community. The fact that thirteen of the new convents were located in Germany generated particular controversy. As a native of Westphalia, Bernadine left herself open to the charge that she had allowed chauvinism to cloud her judgment in determining where to establish the new houses.

The order's German convents also occasioned an international crisis that remained for Bernadine's successor, Mother Aloysia (1859–76), to resolve. During the 1870s the animosity and mistrust directed against Germany's Catholics fell even heavier on members of religious communities whose administrative centers lay outside of the empire. Aware of the danger, Mother Aloysia undertook a series of preemptive steps to deal with the problem. First, she successfully petitioned to change her citizenship from Dutch to German. She also sought permission from Rome to transfer the order's administrative seat from Holland to Capellen, Germany. Finally, she temporarily consigned title to the congregation's German property to a Catholic layperson.[9]

It was largely due to Aloysia's efforts that none of the order's German sisters were expelled during the Kulturkampf. Nevertheless, she was powerless to shield many of the congregation's schools and educational activities from the reforms contained in the May Laws and other legislation.[10]

With the outlook for the order's German houses growing increasingly bleak under the Kulturkampf, in 1874 Aloysia decided to investigate the prospects for inaugurating a mission in the United States. Several sisters from the order had been working as missionaries in the Dutch West Indies since 1869 and in Brazil since 1872. There thus existed a precedent within the congregation for committing personnel to a missionary apostolate. Aloysia had received several letters from Fr. Henry Behrens, the superior of the Buffalo Province, assuring her that sisters from her congregation were needed to serve Buffalo's large number of German Catholics.

Despite these promising signs, the congregation's consulters proved resistant to Aloysia's plans. The German representatives voiced the strongest opposition, arguing that the Kulturkampf was a passing phase and that prematurely draining the country of its younger sisters for missionary work would eventually prove disastrous for their houses and schools. In May 1874, Aloysia nevertheless booked passage from Antwerp to New York for herself and three volunteers for the Buffalo mission. After more than two weeks at sea their boat docked in New York on June 5. The following day Father Behrens greeted them with some disturbing news. Having encouraged them to make the long journey, Behrens now informed them that Msgr. Stephen Ryan, the bishop of Buffalo, had decided against them establishing a convent and school in his diocese.

Instead of immediately returning to Europe, Mother Aloysia and her companions extended their stay in New York for one month to see whether the bishop would change his mind. When July arrived and Father Ryan remained unwavering in his opposition, Aloysia decided to accept the invitation of Bishop Sylvester Rosencrans of Columbus, Ohio, to open an orphanage in that city. Then, almost immediately after notifying Rosencrans of her decision, she received a letter from Behrens stating that Fr. Wilhelm Becker of Saint Michael's Church had been able to win Father Ryan's approval for her sisters to teach classes there and at Saint Anne's parochial schools. Now faced with two options, Aloysia followed the counsel of Father Becker to accept the positions in Buffalo schools and notify Bishop Rosencrans that she would have to delay opening the orphanage in Columbus until additional personnel arrived from Europe. By the beginning of 1875, there were sufficient sisters to care for the children at the orphanage.

Under the direction of Aloysia and her successor, Mother General Alphonsa, the order established six foundations staffed by forty-six sisters between 1874 and 1885. The duties of these American apostolates located in the eastern and midwestern United States replicated those of the German sisters prior to the Kulturkampf, including operating boarding and day schools and orphanages. "Foundations seven and eight broke with these traditions. They were fields of service with no precedent in the Congregation, either in Europe or in America [including] . . . a readiness to cross a vast expanse of the continent to the Great Plains into territory not yet admitted to statehood."[11] This distant territory was that of Dakota, where they were to work with the Rosebud and Pine Ridge Lakotas.

Top: Father Francis Craft, one of the trio of priests whom Bishop Martin Marty assigned to the Rosebud Reservation in 1883. Indian commissioner Hiram Price expelled Craft from Rosebud at the urging of its agent, James G. Wright. *Courtesy Red Cloud Indian School and Marquette University. Holy Rosary Mission—Red Cloud Indian School Records, ID no. HRM-RCISs06-1B03-33.*

Bottom: An early photograph of Saint Francis Mission, probably taken around the turn of the twentieth century. With the closest flowing water five miles from the mission, maintaining the well and water tank was of high priority. *Author's collection.*

Top: Jesuit priests and brothers from Saint Francis Mission, ca. 1900–1910. While the priests spent most of their time visiting Sicangu camps, the brothers constructed and repaired mission buildings and trained the mission's older boys for various vocations. *Courtesy Red Cloud Indian School and Marquette University. St. Francis Mission Records, SFM_6-01-07.*

Bottom: Sisters of Saint Francis of Penance and Christian Charity stationed at Saint Francis Mission, ca. 1915–25. In addition to teaching most of the academic and catechetical classes, the sisters offered vocational training to the older girls. *Courtesy Department of Special Collections and Archives, Marquette University Libraries. St. Francis Mission Records, SFM_6-6_0934.*

Top: Thomas J. Morgan, commissioner of Indian affairs, introduced a plan for federalizing the entire system of Indian education in 1889, thereby hoping to end the need for denominational contract schools such as Saint Francis. *Marquette University Archives, Bureau of Catholic Indian Missions Records, Francis Paul Prucha, S.J., Papers.*

Bottom: Reverend Joseph A. Stephan, the second director of the Bureau of Catholic Indian Missions. The BCIM served as a buffer between the individual missions and the U.S. Indian Office. *Courtesy Department of Special Collections and Archives, Marquette University Libraries. Bureau of Catholic Indian Mission Records, 01603.*

Father Francis Digmann, S.J., probably taken in the early 1920s. Before his hair turned gray, Sicangus gave him the Lakota name Puthin Sapa (Black Beard). *Courtesy Red Cloud Indian School and Marquette University. Holy Rosary Mission—Red Cloud Indian School Records, HRM-RCISs06-1B03-33.*

LITTLE BOY'S SCHOOL

ST. FRANCIS MISSION, S. DAK. 1917.

Sleeping in beds was a novelty for most of the students who enrolled in the Saint Francis Mission school. Here girls collect corn husks for the students' mattresses. *Courtesy St. Francis Mission and Marquette University. St. Francis Mission Records, SFM_6-6_0052.*

Opposite, top: A classroom of the mission's young boys. When students were sufficiently matured, the sisters and brothers would begin to teach them vocational skills deemed appropriate to their gender. *Courtesy Department of Special Collections and Archives, Marquette University Libraries. St. Francis Mission Records, SFM_6-6_00769.*

Opposite, bottom: Brother Henry Rupp (*far right*) instructs Sicangu school boys on shoemaking in the mission's cobbler shop. *Courtesy Department of Special Collections and Archives, Marquette University Libraries. St. Francis Mission Records, SFM_6-6_0638.*

The women of the Saint Mary Society watch as the men of the Saint Joseph Society proceed to the Catholic Sioux Indian Congress arbor during one of the gathering's opening rituals. *Courtesy Department of Special Collections and Archives, Marquette University Libraries. Bureau of Catholic Indian Mission Records, 01897.*

Opposite, top: Catechists photographed at the 1911 Catholic Sioux Indian Congress on the Pine Ridge Reservation, South Dakota. The famous Lakota holy man and catechist Nicholas Black Elk is pictured sixth from the left. *Courtesy Department of Special Collections and Archives, Marquette University Libraries. Bureau of Catholic Indian Mission Records, 00669.*

Opposite, bottom: The goal of the mission's curriculum was to expose its students to the virtues of being loyal Catholics and patriotic Americans. *Courtesy Department of Special Collections and Archives, Marquette University Libraries. St. Francis Mission Records, SFM_6-6_07593.*

A scene from the nativity as depicted in one of the mission's Christmas pageants. Christmastime was one of the few opportunities during the school year when parents were able to visit with their children. *Department of Special Collections and Archives, Marquette University Libraries. Bureau of Catholic Indian Mission Records, 01379.*

Opposite, top: The remnants of Saint Francis Mission after a fire that started in the girls' dormitory attic on the morning of January 20, 1916, destroyed all but a few of its buildings. *Courtesy Department of Special Collections and Archives, Marquette University Libraries. St. Francis Mission Records, SFM_6-6_0047.*

Opposite, bottom: After 1916's disastrous fire, the Jesuits and Franciscans received permission from their religious orders to continue their Sicangu mission. Cement buildings replaced the wooden structures that formerly constituted most of the mission's campus. *Courtesy Department of Special Collections and Archives, Marquette University Libraries. St. Francis Mission Records, SFM_6-6_1236.*

REBUILDING ST. FRANCES MISSION, S.D.
AUG. 28

CHAPTER SEVEN

The Founding and Evolution of Saint Francis Mission, 1886–1916

The ordeals of the Kulturkampf left a psychological scar on the German- and Austrian-born Jesuits and Franciscans who were to serve at Saint Francis Mission. It was not difficult for them to draw parallels between the policies of Thomas J. Morgan and other Indian commissioners and the repressive educational and religious reforms that had forced them to flee Bismarck's Germany. Like the directors of the BCIM, the Saint Francis staff developed a pragmatic program of accommodation that allowed them to work within the guidelines of federal Indian policy while remaining vigilant against actions on the part of local government officials that they perceived as anti-Catholic or as jeopardizing their work on the Rosebud. With few exceptions their battles with these officials centered on the spiritual welfare of the Lakotas as determined by the theological and social assumptions of their paradigm of missionization.

The "Drexel" Mission

As the original company of priests withdrew from the Rosebud, Bishop Marty began searching for religious orders from outside his diocese to assume the role of missionizing the Sicangus. By early 1885 his investigations had led him to the communities of German Jesuits and Franciscans living in Buffalo. The bishop harbored strong hopes that these refuge houses would accept this assignment. He knew that both communities were open, even eager, to pursue missionary work, demonstrated by their recent agreement with his former superior and friend, Bishop James O'Connor, to direct a mission for the Arapahos and Shoshones on Wyoming's Wind River Reservation. He was also aware that obstacles blocking the progress of that mission would probably soon force these religious to withdraw from their contract with O'Connor and thus liberate them for work on the Rosebud.

Marty lost no time contacting the superiors of both houses to explore their willingness to provide missionaries for the Sicangus. In a turn of events that must have surpassed his most optimistic expectations, by midsummer 1885 both houses had committed themselves to the enterprise. With preparations for the mission having taken a sudden leap forward, the bishop visited Buffalo that fall to confer in person with the communities. In December, Fr. John Jutz, who had directed the short-lived mission on the Wind River, called on the Franciscans to provide them with some background on Lakota history and lifeways and to show them some examples of Lakota beadwork. As far as the records indicate, Jutz's brief show-and-tell served as the sisters' sole introduction to the Sicangus.

In addition to helping Marty staff his mission, Bishop O'Connor also served as his conduit to the bounteous coffers of Katherine Drexel. In October 1885 he convinced Marty and BCIM director Fr. Joseph Stephan to visit the young Katherine and appeal to her for funds to build the Rosebud mission and boarding school. As a result of that meeting, the heiress agreed to contribute $12,000 on the condition that the mission be named after her father, Francis. The decision to name the mission Saint Francis after Saint Francis of Assisi not only fulfilled Katherine's stipulation but must also have been especially pleasing to the Franciscan sisters.

At approximately the same time Marty was completing his negotiations to staff and fund Saint Francis, the Indian Office was processing the bishop's application for land on which to build a boarding school. On October 9, 1885, acting Indian Office commissioner A. B. Upshaw informed the Rosebud's agent, Maj. James Wright, that the Office had approved this petition and directed him "to permit the Catholic Church authorities of the Territory of Dakota, to select a suitable tract of unoccupied land, not exceeding 160 acres in extent . . . for the establishment of an Indian school thereon, with the understanding, however, that no rights should vest in the said church or anyone else, to said lands . . . other than the right of temporary occupancy for the purpose above stated."[1]

Anticipating Upshaw's directive by several months, Stephan had journeyed to the Rosebud during spring 1885 to select a suitable location for the mission. In consultation with Father Bushman and some Sicangus, he settled on a site near the Indian encampment of Owl Feather War Bonnet, eight miles south of the agency and ten miles north of the Nebraska line.[2] In his 1885 report to the commissioner, Agent Wright briefly commented on the anticipated opening of a Catholic boarding school, which, he wrote, "is represented by the plans as intended to be a finely finished and complete building, estimated to cost $12,000, and is expected to be ready for occupancy about October next."[3]

Despite the enthusiastic tone of Wright's published report, he apparently harbored grave misgivings about both the school's location and design. On January 11, 1886, he wrote Upshaw complaining that the "Catholic school site has neither wood, water or good land; an injudicious location, so represented to the authority by me, before the erection of the building." Of the school building itself he stated that, although it was "good, plain and substantial," it was nevertheless "not so well planned or arranged" as the one the Episcopals had built."[4]

Given the animosity that the Craft affair had aroused between Wright and the Catholic Church, it would be imprudent to take any of the agent's criticisms of Catholic missionary work on the Rosebud at face value. On this occasion, however, his critique appears to have been without prejudice, for it paralleled that of Father Jutz, who took possession of the mission on January 1, 1886. In a published reminiscence written over thirty years after his arrival at Saint Francis, Jutz described his first impressions of the mission:

> As soon as I saw the building, I thought it would make quite a satisfactory villa for scholastics or boarders to spend their vacation in for several weeks; but it would be most impracticable and unsatisfactory as a boarding school for boys and girls, and a residence for the fathers, brothers and sisters. It seemed to me, therefore, that it was entirely unsuited for the purpose for which it had been built. Another requisite too, and one of vital importance, had been overlooked. There was no water on the place. The brook in the ravine which the Indians frequented was the nearest water supply.[5]

About two weeks after Jutz's arrival at Saint Francis, his former confrere on the Wind River, Br. Ursus Nunlist, joined him. The two Jesuits placed top priority on digging a well that would supply the mission with a reliable and convenient source of water. Jutz had set out for the Rosebud with the understanding that Stephan had contracted a local work crew to dig a well on the site of a spring-fed pool near where the mission would stand. He soon discovered, however, that the supposed pool was nothing more than a buffalo wallow that the crew had abandoned after failing to strike water. Instead of selecting a new site for the well, Jutz and Nunlist continued to dig where their predecessors had left off.

> We set up three strong beams over the opening, secured them tightly with ropes, and affixed a roller. A strong bucket was then attached to a stout coil, this was placed over the roller, and the bucket was thus lowered down the well. Two ponies were hitched to the rope, and pulled up the bucket. Brother and I did the digging. Every day we removed some feet of earth, but still no water appeared. More than once we had to dig through the sandstone with a hatchet. We continued to dig until we reached a depth of 200 feet, where we struck water.

After digging the well, the two Jesuits undertook the even more arduous task of restructuring, completing, and augmenting the mission building so it could serve as a boarding school and residence. Constructed on pillars of cedar wood, the two-story, light-green structure was ninety-six feet long by forty feet wide. As it stood, however, it was little more than a shell with an unfinished interior that provided insufficient living quarters for the religious and children. Jutz and Nunlist ripped out and redesigned entire sections of the building as they saw fit, with little regard for the integrity of the original drawings.

It is quite clear that Jutz had little respect for Stephan, whom he lampooned in his reminiscences as "the Rev. Director of the Catholic Indian Mission Bureau, who had approved erecting our mission house on [a] waterless site." He probably did not ingratiate himself with Stephan when he shipped him a flask of water from the successfully completed well. He most certainly incurred Stephan's wrath when the "Rev. Director" discovered that the priest had sent Katherine Drexel a letter filled with disparaging remarks about the mission's locale and design. Filled with the wisdom of hindsight, Jutz wrote, "He [Stephan] it was who had selected the site, and had most likely approved of the plans for the building. The Reverend gentleman was very angry with me in consequence, and severely reproached me for my spirit of faultfinding and criticism, when my attitude should have been one of sincere gratitude. The letter likewise probably produced this other result, that I was removed from the superiorship of the Mission."

Jutz paid the price for his impudence late in March when Stephan returned to Saint Francis with the first party of missionaries, which included Fr. Emil Perrig, Br. Henry Billings, and Srs. Kostka Schlaghecken (the Franciscan mother superior), Rosalia Lampe, and Alcantara Fallon. In a move calculated to mollify Stephan, the German Province had appointed Perrig as the mission's new superior. Despite being relieved of his command, Jutz remained at Saint Francis until the summer, when he and Nunlist were transferred to the Pine Ridge Reservation to begin readying the opening of Holy Rosary Mission.

During their remaining months at Saint Francis, Jutz and Nunlist helped the newcomers complete the additional alterations needed to render the mission and boarding school operational. These changes included constructing a pair of temporary two-story buildings on the east and south sides of the original building. One of these structures was set aside for the boys' dormitory, and the second contained space for the Jesuits' refectory and a girls' quarters. The priests and brothers then raised a third structure to serve as the sisters' quarters. Large areas of the original building retained their original functions, including the spaces that had been set aside for a kitchen, pantry, and large dining hall. A porch that skirted the entire west side of the structure was transformed into a small refectory and sleeping room for the priests.

By mid-June 1886 the missionaries had made sufficient progress to open their school on "a trial basis" with sufficient space to educate and lodge up to eighty students. After a month, this experiment ground to a halt when the well's pump malfunctioned and one of the sisters fell ill.[6] When the school reopened in September, it had increased the number of boys and girls it could accommodate to one hundred. Its staff had also grown to two Jesuit priests, four Jesuit brothers, and six Franciscan sisters. Among these additional personnel was Florentine Digmann, who would spend most of the remaining forty-five years of his life as Saint Francis Mission's superior.

Meeting the Indians

The first company of religious to follow Jutz and Nunlist began their travels from Buffalo to Saint Francis on March 22, 1886. Father Stephan joined them in Chicago for the remaining journey to the mission. After two and a half days the party detrained at Valentine, Nebraska, at 12:30 A.M. Upon discovering that there was no room in the town's only hotel, they returned to the station, where they sat up until 9:30 the following morning, when Father Jutz arrived in the wagon that carried them the remaining thirty-two miles to Saint Francis. They finally reached their destination at dusk on March 25, the Feast of the Annunciation.

Having become accustomed to the urban environment of Buffalo, the religious were little prepared for the immense, treeless expanses of the Dakota plains. One of the sisters later confessed that it appeared as if they had been deposited "at the end of the world."[7] The Franciscan house chronicles for 1886 described the sisters' reaction to their new surroundings and their "first prairie ride" in horse and wagon: "The rough conveyance jolted over the uneven ground. As far as they could see there stretched miles and miles of somber, frozen grass. . . . not a tree loomed up against the sky. The monotony of the scene might have enticed sleep especially after a sleepless night, but the frequent jolts caused by clods over which the wheels had to pass banished any possibility of rest. It was nearly five o'clock . . . when Father, pointing to a dark speck in the distance, announced that this was their future home."[8]

As deep an impression as the Dakota landscape made on the newcomers, it was their first encounters with the Sicangus that convinced them how great a distance they were from Buffalo. Braving the frigid temperatures of the early spring night, a large party of Sicangus had gathered in front of the mission's entrance to witness the arrival of the religious. Few if any of them had ever seen a Catholic sister before, so they were particularly interested in catching a glimpse of the *winyan wakan*, or "holy women." In the words of one of the Franciscans, "We returned their wonder-filled glances with friendly greetings."[9]

The next morning Stephan called the missionaries into the priests' quarters, where they found a party of approximately twenty "long-haired Indians" seated around the perimeter of the room. If the partial roster provided by Franciscan historian Liguori Mason is to be believed, the group included a virtual "who's who" of Sicangu leadership. Among them were Roast, Big Turkey, Hollow Horn Bear, Two Strike, Course Voice, He Dog, Two Tail, Walking Eagle, Bad Feather, Bad Omaha, Good Word, and Yellow Blanket. Mason wrote that these "redskins were delighted that the Sisters said 'hau-hau' to each of them."[10]

According to a report by one of the sisters at the gathering, an interpreter (who knew very little English) informed the religious that the visitors had come to smoke a pipe with the missionaries as a sign of goodwill. After the calumet had completed its circuit, filling the room with smoke, three of the leaders gave speeches that the other Indians repeatedly interrupted with "grunts of approval." When the last speaker had finished, the fathers told the visitors that all those who planned to enroll their children in the Saint Francis boarding school should bring them to the mission the following day.[11] Continuing her account, the sister reported that at ten o'clock the next morning a long "gypsy caravan" of Sicangus that included forty-one prospective students had arrived at the mission. These "children of the wilderness" came sporting their finest attire, whose rich bead and metal work she described in admiring detail. On the other hand, she also noted that the Sicangus exhibited markedly different standards of cleanliness from her own. Remarking on the designs the women had painted on their forehead and cheeks, she observed that it appeared as if the undecorated portions of these faces had seldom been washed.[12]

To celebrate this first meeting, the Jesuits requested the Franciscans to prepare a meal for their guests. The sisters immediately set to work baking two hundred buns, which they served to the Sicangus with meat, cheese, crackers, and coffee. After the meal and several speeches, the Indians shook hands with the missionaries and departed for their camps.

With only one sister's report and Mason's subsequent retelling of the event to rely on, it is exceedingly difficult to interpret what the Sicangus made of these newcomers. Even such scanty evidence, however, supports the idea that they considered the arrival of the religious a matter of some importance. There is first the fact that so large a numbers of Sicangus journeyed to the mission to greet the Jesuits and Franciscans. The event's significance is also suggested by the celebratory attire the Indians wore for the occasion as well as the number of important headmen who took part in the gathering. Yet the most striking indicator of the gravity that the Sicangus assigned to the occasion was their insistence on commemorating it with a pipe ceremony. The ritualized smoking of the pipe was the central observance of Lakota spirituality and imbued all associated ceremonies and activities with special meaning and power. By hosting this ritual, the Sicangus at once demonstrated their respect for the missionaries and the significance they attributed to founding their relationship on spiritually solid ground.

This first encounter between the Sicangus and missionaries was not without humor, unintended though it might have been. According to Mason, the Sicangus appeared "delighted" with the sisters' first attempts at speaking Lakota by greeting each of them with a "hau-hau." Although this interpretation has its merits, it is equally likely that the Sicangus were amused by the sisters' use of a form of address reserved exclusively for males. By their modest attempt to bridge the cultural chasm between themselves and the Sicangus, the sisters only accentuated how great was this separation.

The Growth of the Mission

During spring 1886 the Saint Francis religious devoted considerable time attempting to persuade Sicangu parents to register their children in the new boarding school. The duties of publicizing and recruiting students for the school fell primarily on the Jesuits, whose ministries brought them into the camps and into contact with the steady flow of Sicangus who visited the mission. In an attempt to maximize the results of their efforts, the priests targeted the leaders of the various *tiyospaye* on the assumption that, if they could be convinced to send their children or grandchildren to Saint Francis, the other members of their camps would follow suit.

Although the priests claimed to have gathered fifty registrants when the school opened on June 15, only one girl and two boys showed up at the mission. During the next month, however, children continued to trickle in, so that by the end of the school's aborted trial run its enrollment had grown to thirty-six. In the years that followed the number of students would continue to swell, from sixty-five during the 1886–87 academic year to 221 for 1900–1901. By 1916 enrollment had ballooned to 310.

This steady increase of students over the mission's first thirty years demanded parallel expansions of its staff, facilities, and instructional organization. As early as the end of the experimental school term in 1886, the Jesuits' house historian observed that it had become "lucidly clear that more workers were necessary."[13] Whereas in 1886 a tiny company of two priests, four brothers, and six sisters could adequately perform the duties associated with civilizing and Christianizing Sicangu children and adults, by 1900 the same work required a force of four priests, eight brothers, and twelve sisters. In 1916 the number of religious had grown to four priests, eleven brothers, and sixteen sisters.

There are at least two reasons why the increase of brother and sisters far outstripped that of the priests during the mission's first thirty years of existence. Unlike the sisters and brothers, the priests worked primarily with the adults in the camps, except for their role of teaching catechism to the older boys. As a consequence, the steady increase in students did little to affect the nature and scope of their work. The sole exception was for the Jesuit superior, who, as the school's executive director, was responsible for its operation and for all correspondence on educational matters with the reservation agent, Office of Indian Affairs, and BCIM. The time superiors dedicated to these matters understandably had to keep apace with the growth of the school.

The appearance of two new forms of ministerial assistants beginning in the early twentieth century also helped to alleviate the need for additional priests. The first of these aids was the Jesuit scholastics whom the province assigned to the mission as part of their formation. Although not yet invested with the full powers of priesthood, scholastics could nevertheless assist priests with their sacramental duties at the mission and in the camps. Their major responsibilities, however, lay in the school, where they served as prefects for the boys' dormitory and taught the catechism classes that would have otherwise been assigned to the priests.

The training of the first Indian catechists also helps to explain how the mission was able to operate with so few priests. As their title suggests, the primary role of these native lay helpers was to teach Catholic doctrine to the unconverted members of their own and other *tiyospaye*. In addition, however, they organized and led nonsacramental church rites such as community rosaries and prayer meetings. The success of catechists in maintaining and promoting Catholicism permitted the mission's few priests to establish circuit ministries among the camps, visiting each site to perform Mass and other sacraments once a month on average. By 1916 the number of Indian catechists at Saint Francis had climbed to twelve.

In addition to prompting a steady increase in the mission's staff, the school's burgeoning enrollment also demanded that sizeable investments be made to enlarge its campus. In his report as mission superior to Agent Wright for 1890, Digmann stated that the mission had spent most of the school's contract money for 1887 on new buildings, including a house for the sisters and a boys' dormitory. These projects were followed during the next two years by a new dormitory for girls in 1888 and a "dwelling house" for the Jesuits in 1889.

The construction of additional school buildings and student and missionary residences continued through the remainder of the nineteenth and into the twentieth century. In 1893 a larger building was erected for the boys, though it almost immediately proved inadequate to meet the school's needs. As a temporary solution, a new Jesuit residence built the following year included additional classrooms, living space, and a play area for the boys. The old Jesuit house was converted into an infirmary and an ironing room. In an effort to provide the priests and brothers with more privacy, in 1909 the mission erected an independent three-story boys building. After only two years, however, it burned to the ground. The BCIM immediately initiated a successful appeal to construct a new boys' house. According to Father Goll, "In the rebuilding, appearances were now sacrificed to safety. A reinforced, all concrete, hollow wall structure was raised."[14]

The school's growing enrollment also required additional living and educational facilities for the sisters and girls. According to the Franciscans' house chronicles, in 1895 the school was forced to turn away many female applicants because of a shortage of space to house and educate them. "It was therefore decided that a new building 112 × 36 feet should be built. The building was to be made of tin-sheeting and wood and was to be used for dormitory, playhall and classroom." Within nine years, the number of female students had again grown so large that the mission was once more obliged to erect a new girls' building. Standing 112 × 50 feet, it housed classrooms, a sewing room, and dormitories.[15]

Running apace with its heavy investments in schoolrooms and residences were the large sums of money the mission poured into erecting facilities to meet the physical and spiritual needs of its students and staff. Between 1887 and 1906 the brothers constructed a carpentry and a blacksmith shop, a steam-fed laundry, a small bathing room, and a granary. During this nineteen-year period they also added a large drainage system, installed a huge cistern to supply the laundry with water, erected four large water tanks, dug additional wells equipped with windmills and pipes to irrigate the mission's fields, and erected a sawmill with a ten horsepower steam engine that supplied both the missionaries and the Indians with cheap cordwood and lumber for building.

Of all the mission's new additions, the religious took most pride in their church. For the first ten years a small chapel on the main building's second floor had served as the public sanctuary where the students, adult Sicangus, and other nonreligious were welcome to worship. At first Indian congregants appear to have experienced some difficulty mastering some of the basic elements of Catholic Church worship, as the following observations by one of the Franciscans concerning their struggles with kneeling demonstrates:

> Kneeling in the benches is still so strange to them that the first devotion is usually completed before they have learned enough, by watching and experimenting in all possible and impossible ways, so they can at least halfway kneel. However, they hold themselves so tight that you might think that they are glued on. But all this occurs with the greatest earnestness or timidness. Some sit between the benches on the ground and have their feet on the knee bench, so that you can hardly observe them and maintain the decorum of a sacred place. And yet, God must take great pleasure in the good will of the poor savages.[16]

Apparently these tribulations did not discourage large numbers of Sicangus from attending Mass. Records indicate that by 1888 Indian attendance at Sunday and holiday masses had grown to such an extent that, according to Digmann, on occasion from thirty-five to fifty Sicangus were required to stand throughout the liturgies for want of seats.[17] Such overflow crowds underscored the need for a new sanctuary. In addition to increasing seating capacity, the missionaries believed that a new church would serve as a weapon in their war with the Episcopalians for Indian souls. Writing BCIM director Stephan on April 7, 1890, Digmann stated, "Shall we stay back to the White gowns who build churches all over and brag that in [the] future all [the] Dakotas will be theirs. . . . The Evil One has servants enough around here. Why should not God have them who has bought them so dearly."[18]

When the Jesuits approached their provincial, Henry Behrens, in 1888 for permission to build a new church, he ordered that they first erect new quarters for their community. Once this new Jesuit building was completed in 1889, he gave his consent for one of the mission's brothers, Henry Wissing, to begin drawing up plans for the structure. Behrens was evidently shocked when he reviewed the brother's plans. Instead of the modest country church he had expected, Wissing had designed a veritable cathedral "in pure gothic style, with arches, height forty feet, floor 50 × 100, plus a ten feet steeple on the west end."[19] Anxious over the potential costs of the project, Behrens demanded that for economy's sake the brother architect redesign the church with a flat instead of vaulted ceiling. The cornerstone for the now flat-roofed house of worship was laid on October 19, 1890. On February 9 of the following year the Jesuits celebrated its inaugural Mass, not waiting for the oil paintings that would decorate its interior wall to be completed. The brothers immediately went to work recycling the old church into an assembly hall and additional playrooms.

The pride the religious took in the mission's new church is reflected in the ceremony with which they installed its bells, weighing 800 and 1,000 pounds. They arrived on April 8 but remained in storage until shortly before June 2, when Bishop Marty baptized them "Gabriel" and "Joseph." They were then hoisted up to the steeple and sounded for the first time on June 4. According to the sisters' house chronicler, this "first ringing of the bells made a profound impression. The boys who were in church preparing for confession rushed out to see what was going on. Many began to pray, others knelt down. The Angelus that night was a spectacle to behold."[20]

In spite of the care that the Jesuits had lavished on designing and building the church, by 1901 softening plaster in its ceiling posed a danger to worshippers. Generous contributions from Katherine Drexel, John Creighton, and other benefactors allowed the mission to install the vaulted ceiling of Brother Wissing's original design. During a tour of the renovated structure, Bishop Stariha of Lead is said to have remarked that he would have liked to have it for his cathedral.[21] It was the second-largest church in the state.[22] In 1903 a hot-air heating plant was put into the church; the rest of the mission remained heated with coal stoves.

Because of the great distances between the new church and their camps, many Catholic Sicangus were required to fulfill their religious obligations in far less lavish surroundings. Describing the twenty-five outlying stations in which the Jesuits generally said Mass, Fr. Henry Westropp stated:

> In some . . . Mass is said in a private house, in others, a cabin made of logs and mud forms the parsonage and church, or holy house. Often indeed the house is hole-y. . . . When it rains, the missionary finds it advisable to take an umbrella to bed with him and happy is he if the floor, the bare ground, is not a lake in the morning. In such cabins, the missionary has to say Holy Mass on an old box or stove, a dog or cat running around his heels, or perhaps a little papoose tugging at his alb.[23]

Despite the overall accuracy of Westropp's description, some of his picturesque prose may be attributed to the goal of raising money to build chapels for the outlying camps. In addition to written appeals and sizeable contributions from Mother Drexel's treasury, the priests occasionally took Catholic

Indians to meetings of the Federation of Catholic Societies as a means of eliciting contributions.[24] The effectiveness of their efforts is demonstrated by the relatively rapid growth in the number of camp chapels. Between 1900 and 1915, their number had increased from one to twenty-four.

During the period from 1886 to 1916, Saint Francis Mission and boarding school's significant success in recruiting converts and students gradually transformed its campus from a desolate landscape with one poorly designed multipurpose building and a half-finished well into an expansive, efficiently designed campus that was well equipped to meet the educational, spiritual, and practical needs of its students and Sicangu adults. At its center stood a commodious church where the Jesuit priests conducted daily Mass and other ceremonies for the pastoral staff, school children, and Indian Catholics who lived close enough to make the trip by horse and wagon.

Behind this transformed landscape lay thirty years of investments of capital, time, and labor on the part of the mission's religious, their respective orders, and the BCIM. Above and beyond this, however, stood the missionaries' faith that God had willed them to remake the savage and heathen Sicangus into civilized Catholics no matter what difficulties they encountered pursuing this end.

CHAPTER EIGHT

The Paradigm of Mission at Saint Francis

Civilizing and Christianizing the Sicangus

In common with other Catholic and Protestant Indian missionaries of their day, the Saint Francis religious viewed their civilizing efforts among the Sicangus through the skein of developmentalist thought that cast American Indians in the role of contemporary savages in need of the kind of helping hand that the Indian Office was extending them through its reform policy. Where Catholics and Protestants tended to part company was over both the speed with which the transformation from savagery to civilization could be expected to occur and whether reservations and reservation boarding schools aided or hampered this process (see chapter 2). In opposition to their Protestant counterparts, the Saint Francis missionaries fiercely defended their superiors' position that civilizing primitives was by its very nature a gradual process and that reservation-based boarding schools such as their own offered the best way to advance Sicangus in their social development.

Commonalities and differences also marked the way in which Protestant and Catholic missionaries viewed the relationship between their roles as "civilizers" and "Christianizers." The fact that both were able to participate in government Indian policy signified that they assumed that simultaneously civilizing and Christianizing was not only theologically permissible but desirable. On the other hand, Protestants and Catholics tended to base the theological rationale for their common position on different sources. Just as the Armenian proclivities of the liberal Protestant missionaries led them to understand salvation as a cooperative act between God (the supernatural) and man (the natural), they likewise interpreted "true" civilization as an inspired interaction between the human and divine. Shorn of this supernatural essence, the works of civilization lacked the substance and power that rendered them pleasing to God.

Though not opposed to this Protestant reconciliation of the natural and supernatural, the Saint Francis missionaries came equipped with a uniquely Catholic source for accommodating the sacred and secular arms of their work. In line with the Thomist credo that "faith builds upon nature," they took for granted that the seeds of faith must be sown on receptive cultural soil in order for them to take root. This, of course, did not mean that conversion needed to await progress in civilization. Rather, it underscored the dialectical relationship presumed to exist between the two processes so that progress in one positively influenced the other.

Evidence for how the religious at Saint Francis incorporated this dialectic into their work may be glimpsed in the successive annual reports that mission superiors Digmann and Jutz submitted to the Rosebud agent. Writing in 1892, Digmann observed, "My view of the question for the past six years I am among the Indians ever has been that true Christianity never will take root in them unless we succeed in getting them used to judicious work." Describing the missionaries' religious efforts the following year, Jutz stated, "Two of the fathers were almost continually engaged in missionary work around the mission and out in the different camps, having religious services and instructing the old ones and the young ones in the truths of religion, being fully convinced that neither true civilization nor true morality is possible without true religion, as the history of mankind proves from the beginning of the very creation."[1]

Civilization and Christianization at Saint Francis Boarding School

Although the Saint Francis religious ministered to Sicangus of all ages, they lavished the greatest portion of their resources and labors on the secular and religious education of their boarding school students. This preoccupation with the youth was primarily based on the developmentalist/progressivist principle that each generation of Sicangus they trained would achieve a superior standard of civilization and Catholicism to that of its predecessor. And so this improvement would continue, they believed, until Catholic

Sicangus were sufficiently prepared to take control of their social and religious (parish) lives.

In conformity with the calendar established by the federal Indian office of education, the mission's academic year began in September and ended in mid to late June. Upon entering school, each child was bathed, groomed, and fitted with a new school uniform. The girls were required to pin their hair back and up and to wear dresses that the sisters fashioned from government-issued calico. They were additionally provided with woolen shawls, to use as weather demanded. The boys received mandatory haircuts and were each furnished with wardrobes (again compliments of the government) of two denim shirts, suit, and overcoat. The moccasins that most of the children arrived wearing were also immediately discarded and replaced with leather shoes. For the missionaries, this makeover provided the children with their initial experience in civilized standards of dress and hygiene. For many of the students, however, it constituted an unwelcome departure from their customary lifestyle at home, where, as one Franciscan stated, "they lived a wild, careless, and unwashed life."[2] The most odious of these changes, for students and their parents alike, appears to have been the shearing of the boys' hair. As Digmann wrote, "It was quite a ceremony, when boys of ten or twelve years were taken to school and had to get their hair cut. It cost often tears to both boys and parents, the latter would wrap them [the hair] up and take them home as a keepsake." The Sicangus' emotional outbursts over this visit to the barber is cleared of its mystery once considered within the context of the pride that the Sicangus took in grooming and decorating their hair as well as the association they made between cutting one's braids and mourning a deceased relation.[3]

The culture shock that the children experienced from their initial confrontation with missionary standards of personal hygiene and appearance extended to their first encounters with other aspects of their new physical environment. Since most if not all of the students had lived their entire lives in one-story structures—tipis, frame tents, or log cabins—few if any of them had ever attempted to climb stairs. Nevertheless, because both the boys' and girls' dormitories were invariably located on the second floors of their respective buildings, it was absolutely necessary that they quickly master this art. Once upstairs, most of the children were faced with the additional novelty of sleeping in beds with cornhusk ticks. Though the government had distributed bed frames and mattresses to Sicangus as part of its "civilization" program, many of them ended up in the homes of neighboring non-Indians. Digmann reported that Agent Spencer once confided to him that when spending the night with a local Nebraska family he "had the honor to sleep . . . on a government bed [he] had issued to the Indians."[4]

The children were also expected to adapt quickly to Euro-American patterns of diet and mealtime etiquette, which differed markedly from those found at their homes and camps. So, in sharp contrast to the rather relaxed, individually determined Sicangu eating schedule, the students were required to take their meals in groups at specified times in the morning, at midday, and evening. The missionaries also insisted that forks, knifes, and spoons replace fingers as the proper conveyances for transporting food from plate to mouth, and that students perform this maneuver while seated on chairs at tables instead of on the ground. Finally, the mission's diet itself included more and different varieties of fruits and vegetables than was typical of the Lakotas' traditional meat and wild plant diet.[5] It is of interest that aspects of the school's mealtime fare had a distinctly Germanic character. Consider the following description by Father Goll of some of the girls' first encounter with sauerkraut. According to the priest, the girls "watched it in the pot on the stove; saw the piece of bacon with it enlarging in size, then dwindling down again. It was all a mystery." When the sauerkraut was ready to sample, "one girl mustered up courage and found the dish tasty; then the rest followed. In the dining room, the same timidity had to be overcome. But when the boys saw that the girls were not afraid of the sauerkraut, they were ready to take a chance."[6]

There is evidence that at least some of the students learned not only to tolerate but actually to enjoy these foreign delicacies, perhaps to a degree surpassing the missionaries' expectations and desires. In an article published in the German extension magazine *Die Katholischen Missionen*, Father Perrig observed that the students "have a voracious appetite that causes them to confiscate everything edible that they can lay hands on without any pangs of guilt. Good Brother Gardener," he continued, "has much to tell about that. In spite of careful guarding, many turnips, cucumbers and pumpkins have disappeared on him. Sometimes they used the following ruse: they acted as though they were playing tag, ran through the melons trampling the best ones. Then they came with innocent demeanor and asked Brother if he would allow them to eat the shards so that they wouldn't go to waste."[7]

While attending school, students were expected to comport themselves according to the following behavioral code that the Jesuits initially devised for the boys but soon adapted for the girls:

All must know that they are not here at school merely to learn the English language, reading, writing, arithmetic, and similar things; but they are here in order to be educated and brought up as good Catholic boys, who will afterwards be good Catholic men, and useful citizens.

Therefore, all must learn the Catechism, and live according to the Commandments of God; all must learn to say their prayers and must join in the common prayers in the Chapel, school-room and dining-room.

Pupils must go from one room to another in ranks and in silence.

Silence must also be kept (a) in Chapel, (b) in the dining-room, (c) in the classroom, (d) in the dormitory, when all are in bed.

Every Saturday the reading of notes will take place. Notes are given for:

Conduct, including obedience towards teacher and prefects, peace and charity among one another, truthfulness, etc. Bad notes are given for disobedience, disrespect, quarreling, lying, stealing, destroying property, etc.

Piety. Bad notes for want of reverence at prayer, or for using bad language.

Discipline. Observance of these rules, faithful discharge of office, etc.

Deportment, cleanliness of body and clothing, politeness in speech, in the dining room, with strangers.

On one Sunday in the month, those who have had their good notes will be allowed to go home; to those who have had bad notes, this privilege will not be granted

Those who have made their first confession will go once every month; those who have made their First Communion will receive after their monthly confession. Three times a week, Monday, Wednesday and Friday, English must be spoken at recreation.[8]

Though exacting in its expectations and tone, the code, it should be noted, was not totally lacking in concessions and rewards. As we see here, the religious initially permitted students to converse in Lakota during some of their recreation periods.[9] Soon, however, they rescinded this privilege, instituting a monolingual policy that they hoped would accelerate the students' acquisition of English. This new regime included both incentives and penalties to induce the children's cooperation.

By 1890 the missionaries were prepared to drop the carrots for additional sticks in order to improve results. In his report to Agent Wright for that year, Digmann stated that though the students "were never allowed to speak freely in Dakota among themselves . . . they did much so anyway as we could not grasp them as tight as one can outside the Reservation. We have tried," he continued, "kindness and encouragement by rewards, but may resort to more efficient means another year."[10]

The permission the code granted students with "good notes" to visit their families one Sunday afternoon each month also soon fell by the wayside. In an attempt to prevent homesickness, the missionaries had initially allowed all children whose parents lived near the school to visit their camps each Sunday after Mass. But this strategy backfired when many of the children failed to report back to Saint Francis in the evening. As the Franciscan house historian for 1887 wrote, "The results were somewhat disappointing as some stayed away for a whole week at a time. The condition," she continued, "was some what bettered when the Indian police took the responsibility of bringing back the missing children."[11] To further improve matters, the missionaries instituted the preventive measures of reducing the number of these leaves to once a month and dispensing them only as a reward for students with "good notes." When these steps failed to eliminate truancy, they decided to rescind such home visits altogether, keeping all of their brood inside the coop.

With the elimination of these furloughs, the sole opportunities remaining for students to visit their homes were a three-day Christmas holiday and a summer "recess" of approximately two months during which the children were expected to serve as little missionaries of civilization and Christianization to their unenlightened kinfolk.[12] Some students demonstrated their dissatisfaction with this scarcity of sanctioned leaves by refusing to return to Saint Francis at summer's end or, once back at school, by finding opportune moments to stage breakouts. The missionaries again fell into the pattern of appealing to the reservation police to retrieve the runaways, or they attempted to round them up on their own. Describing the difficulty the religious sometimes encountered in reclaiming fugitive scholars, the Franciscan house historian for 1894 reported that when a sister visited the home of one missing child "and insisted that she come along the girl crept under the bed and cried there for an hour. At last she decided to come along. Hardly had she again entered the school when she once more yielded to her old impulse and fled." According to the historian, the problem was resolved "after some months when she [the student] sent a letter in which she humbly asked to be again received at the school [and her] request was granted."[13]

Attributing the motive for these truancies to homesickness, Bishop Marty encouraged the religious to provide the students with a homey and loving environment so they would desire to remain at school. In response, the missionaries arranged for various sorts of "entertainments" on feast days and introduced assorted sports and other activities for the students to amuse themselves during their recesses.[14] Not totally satisfied with Marty's explanation for the children's penchant for fleeing from the mission, Digmann adduced an additional reason of his own. The boys, he stated,

> have a strong inclination to run away: not because they don't like it with us but rather because they love roaming about. The most dangerous [periods] for running away are the so-called "beef-days," those day on which the Indians receive the biweekly meat-rations. . . . Such "beef-days" are now naturally big holidays. The Indians come in full state, face and hands painted red, yellow and green to the agency. The feasting starts, and when the drums and pipes from the village announce that it's beef-day and that they're living high on the hog, dancing and singing, our children get the urge to participate.

Regarding both boy and girl runaways, on another occasion he wrote, "Strictness in making them do their duty, a scolding or slight punishment is enough for a certain sort of boys or girls to skip."[15]

For whatever reasons, when children continued to sneak away from Saint Francis the staff contemplated instituting harsher measures to deal with the problem. Writing to BCIM director Stephan, Digmann observed that the "runaways . . . have been periodically an annoyance. The Agent has supported us the best he could, but we have no prison yet on the premises to receive some desperados properly." Apparently the religious had no compunction against using the agency prison as a temporary expedient. In 1903, Digmann reported that a girl who had run away from school was caught by the police and tossed in jail.[16]

The missionaries' apprehension over home visits, whether licit or not, was spurred by their assumption that educating Indian children was best achieved by isolating them from the "primitive" conditions of their natal camps for as long as possible. Contrasting the advantages that boarding schools offered over day schools in this respect, Fr. Louis Goll wrote that the "most important consideration in choosing between a day school and a boarding school is the duration of the influence the school can exercise. . . . A boarding school . . . can exert a beneficial influence sixteen waking hours of the day, seven days of the week. . . . On Saturdays and Sundays the day school pupil is at home or in the tent, as free as a bird, and surrounded by an atmosphere hostile to the white man's way."[17]

The educational "process" at Saint Francis followed two tracks, one directed toward "natural" and the other toward "supernatural" ends. The former course of study sought to replace the children's traditional Lakota customs with the intellectual, social, and economic patterns of Euro-America civilization. Once beyond kindergarten, pupils received instruction in reading, composition, and math, and those who had attained sufficient intellectual and physical maturity were additionally required to spend three to four hours of their day learning gender-specific trades of "civilized" economy.[18] Jesuit brothers instructed boys in the essentials of agriculture, animal husbandry, smithing, shoe repair, carpentry, and painting. Franciscan sisters trained girls in the milking of cows, sewing, cooking, laundering, and other branches of "domestic science."

In theory such "industrial" training played an essential role in elevating Sicangu children from savagery to civilization, preparing them for the economic life and realities they would encounter once leaving school as well as providing them with object lessons regarding the fruits bought by healthy and wholesome labor. In practice, however, these courses performed an economic function upon which the missionaries seldom commented. It would have been simply impossible for the mission to survive without the inexpensive labor pool, goods, and services the students provided. In addition to the government rations and clothing that the mission received in the name of their students, the latter's plowing, herding, milking, and sewing quite literally kept the missionaries and their charges fed and dressed. Digmann's inventory of goods produced in the girls' sewing room and tailor shop during 1896–97 provides a striking example of the extent of the mission's dependence on its students' labor: "Aprons, different kinds, 324; comforters, 40; chemises,

38; drawers, assorted, 150; dresses, 389; Lace, thread and woolen, 225 yards; pillowcases, worked and plain, 130; skirts, 155; shirts, 50; sheets, 200; stockings, knitted, 20 pairs; bedspreads, crochet work, 3; scarfs, 10; ticks, 41; towels, 75; etc. . . . In the tailor shop, besides all the mending and sewing for the boys, 16 large boys' suits were made." The boys were kept no less busy. According to Digmann, "Besides the necessary house chores in the boys' quarters, the latter were occupied in gardening, farming, care of stock, and in the different working shops, viz. 9 in the carpenter shop, 4 in the blacksmith shop, 4 in the bakery, and 8 in the shoemaker shop. The carpenter boys," he continued "have helped and learned a good deal in erecting a new barn for the cattle and a henhouse, and during the winter months in helping to make tables, cupboards, and the like."[19]

Despite this impressive-appearing output of goods and services, the missionaries sometimes expressed dissatisfaction with the children's work ethic. This was especially true of their appraisal of the boys' commitment to their duties. In an article Fr. Aloysius Bosch published in *Die Katholischen Missionen*, he observed that the "greatest problem among our boys is to overcome their inborn dislike for work. You have to know, these are children of born beggars, who receive clothing and food from the government and thus never saw the example of a hard working father or brother. However, as long as you have the boys under your watchful eyes and work with them, they are hard working. But when you leave them on their own the Indian nature comes to light."[20]

To counteract sloth and other disciplinary problems, the religious instituted a system of rewards and punishments. Cooperative students earned "good notes" that eventually entitled them to various sorts of prizes and privileges. Describing the origins and earliest results of this effort at behavior modification, Digmann wrote: "To break them in and encourage them Father Perrig had a 'distribution of prices' after six weeks for those who never had run away, and had been diligent in school and in manual work. The first time there were only six of the whole crowd and they were mostly halfbloods. Mouth organs, handkerchiefs, knives and toys were given as rewards."[21]

Students who committed minor infractions of school rules received "bad notes" which, when accumulated, could result in their loss of such privileges as attending "magic lantern" shows or other entertainments. Those guilty of major transgressions, such as running away and stealing, were disciplined on the spot, usually by means of corporal punishment. For many Sicangus, whose norms of parenting strictly proscribed striking children, the mission-aries' recourse to physical "correctives" was deeply offensive and required retribution.[22] As Father Westropp once observed, "Punishment, especially with a whip, was a dangerous medicine to administer, as the parents are fond of their children to the greatest excess. Even in later years the Fathers have been struck, had their beards torn out, and been threatened by the infuriated parents for daring to give their children much-needed chastisement. An old and feeble father came once and offered to take his son's punishment."[23]

The missionaries publicized the achievements of their students, and by extension their school, through various means. One of the most important of these venues was a yearly round of assemblies and community gatherings. During these festivities, the religious would put the children through their paces with singing, concerts, poetry recitations, and dramatic tableaux performances that were intended to edify the local Indian and non-Indian spectators. Apparently the Sicangus, who were unfamiliar with Western theatrical conventions, initially experienced some difficulty understanding their expected role as audience. Apropos of this cultural "lacuna," the Franciscan house historian for 1887 wrote that the "children were to give an entertainment about the Christmas tree and all were invited. After the entertainment a supper was to be served. . . . At four o'clock pity was taken on the patiently waiting guests and supper was served. Thereafter the children were to perform. After good portions of meat and apples had been consumed all hurried home in great haste forgetting all about the Christmas entertainment. Luckily some of the Sisters succeeded in procuring the services of four Indians to play the part of an audience.[24]

It did not take long for mission-sponsored events to become an important part of the reservation social calendar. Probably the most popular of these galas were the annual graduation festivities that concluded the school year. Describing the 1912 commencement celebration, the Franciscan house historian recorded that the "children presented a beautiful play."

> The hass [house] was filled to the last place with spectators. The parents of children, government officials, and white settlers were present in great numbers. In the large sewing room there was an exhibition of the work of the girls. On both ends were located the needle and art handi-work of the girls; along the sides, the school work of the different classes; a little hand-carved altar, picture frames, and stands,

building plans, harness, and wagon seats all made by the larger boys. In the center was a long table with all kinds of bakery goods, bread, cake, pastry, pretzels etc., all made by the culinary workers. These latter had done everything to the best of their ability as they would be permitted to take everything away with them.[25]

Granted the importance that the religious attributed to nurturing literate, vocationally trained Sicangus, as Catholic missionaries they considered it the more important portion of their vocation to transform their students into members of a self-sufficient Sicangu church. It was absolutely essential, they believed, to "civilize" Indians, to save them from the aggressions of white Americans, and to promote their cultural progress. These "natural" ends, however, paled in comparison with civilization's role in preparing the ground for Indians to receive baptism and thus gain access to the Catholic sacraments that were essential to their salvation. Once Catholic faith and morals had gained a foothold among Sicangus, they would, in turn, serve to elevate and ennoble the tribe's newly acquired social and cultural lifeways, producing "true" civilization.

Given the priority on religious vocation, it is not surprising that the missionaries dedicated a major portion of the school year to instilling in their students the beliefs and practices that they considered necessary to their formation as devout Catholics. Though formal, catechetical instruction and retreats constituted the backbone of this training,[26] a virtually unbroken succession of daily, seasonal, and situational Catholic rituals and observances reinforced these lessons.

The daily religious obligations commenced each morning with attendance at Mass. Scholastics, sisters, and brothers proctored the liturgy to ensure that the children maintained decorum and stood, knelt, and offered correct responsorials at appropriate times. In addition, the sisters and priests encouraged those students who had celebrated their First Communion and had attended confession prior to Mass to receive the host. Mission policy required that all eligible students go to confession and receive communion at least once a month. After Mass, the children were led to the school's dining hall for breakfast, which, like all meals, was preceded by a thanksgiving prayer. Finally, at the conclusion of each day, dormitory proctors led the children in bedtime prayers.[27]

In addition to these daily religious practices the students participated in a yearly round of Catholic holy day observances. In general these ceremonies included the performance of one or more of the sacraments. The first of these celebrations occurred close to the Feast of the Immaculate Conception in early December with a four-day retreat at which one of the priests would guide the children through an appropriately tailored version of the Ignatian Spiritual Exercises. Reporting on the first such retreat in 1895, Digmann wrote, "Seventy-four made it. They kept silence better than our pupils in colleges. . . . Most made a general confession, many even a life's confession."[28]

Shortly after the retreat the missionaries hosted an elaborate Christmas to which they invited the students' relatives. After a Mass and entertainments they released those children whose parents' camps were sufficiently close to Saint Francis or who had set up their tents on the outskirts of the mission for a brief visit. Describing the celebration of 1911, the Franciscan house historian wrote: "On Christmas Eve after the devotion the distribution of presents for the children took place in the refectory. The Rev. Fathers, the Brothers and many of the parents of the children were present and rejoiced in the happiness of the little ones. During midnight mass 17 boys and 15 girls received their first Holy Communion. Very many Indians who in spite of the bitter cold had come to celebrate at the Mission, also received Holy Communion. On the second Christmas Day the girls gave a Christmas play (very creditably) for entertainment."[29]

Three more celebrations occurred during Holy Week. The first took place on Maunday, or Holy Thursday, when some of the children received their First Communion. Two days later, on Holy Saturday, the priests baptized non-Catholic students who had expressed their desire to join the church. According to the Franciscan house historian, this tradition continued until 1912, when "for the first time, there were no baptisms, since the Indians have their little ones baptized immediately after birth. Hence all are Christian when they come to school."[30] Then, on Easter Sunday the missionaries invited the students' parents to join them in a day of prayer, entertainments, and feasting. The holiday also served as an occasion for the priests to baptize adult Sicangus who had been sufficiently tutored in church dogma and practices. On Easter 1910, for example, 175 adults were received into the church. It was also the time when the bishop concelebrated the rites of First Communion and Confirmation during High Mass. On occasion the results proved less than exemplary, as the following report by Digmann from 1908 suggests: "Father Grothe went in raining to Crookston to fetch Bishop Stariha for Confirmation. . . . At 9:20 they arrived in the best of sunshine. Eighty-three were confirmed. The Bishop held a solemn pontifical mass but said later he would never do it again unless we would study better the ceremonies."[31]

The first major celebration after Holy Week occurred on Whit Sunday, or Pentecost, when students who wished so had another opportunity to receive their First Communion. Recounting the festivities of 1912, the Franciscan house historian wrote:

> On the 14th of April, Whit Sunday, 15 girls and 34 boys solemnly received their First Communion. The children had prepared for this reception by a two day retreat and all present were impressed by their quiet and devout behaviour. After the services the children betook themselves to the gymnasium where their families congratulated them. The old Indians were so touched that glistening tears rolled down their cheeks. In the afternoon there was a sermon and a solemn renewal of the Baptismal vows, and the reception into the Confraternity of the Scapular, followed by Benediction and a Te Deum.[32]

The last of the major calendric celebrations took place on the Feast of Corpus Christi. When weather permitted, the religious led the children in procession through the mission gardens, pausing for benediction at three altars that had been erected at various points of the march. During inclement weather the rite was held inside the church.[33]

Interspersed among these annual celebrations were a nearly ceaseless succession of impromptu or specially arranged religious observances in which the missionaries expected the students to take part. Some of these ceremonies were organized to commemorate events that the Jesuits and Franciscans considered of particular significance to the Saint Francis community, its staff, or the universal church. Examples of such celebrations included those held on the feast of the patronage of Saint Joseph to initiate the building of a new church in 1890, followed two years later by the blessing of the church bells;[34] the ceremonial laying of the cornerstone for the new boys' building in September 1908 and its subsequent dedication;[35] the blessing of a statue of Saint Francis in the sisters' garden on the Feast of the Holy Wounds;[36] festivities commemorating the golden jubilee of the proclamation of the dogma of the Immaculate Conception;[37] the seven-hundredth anniversary of the founding of the Franciscan Order and the twenty-fifth anniversary of the mission;[38] celebrations for visiting Jesuit, Franciscan, and church dignitaries;[39] those in honor of the silver and golden jubilees of staff members' religious professions; and the ordinations and first masses of priests belonging to the community.[40]

Students at Saint Francis were also expected to participate in rituals and observances that sought God's assistance during the mission's many crises or to thank him for the assistance he had rendered. One of the first such thanksgiving ceremonies followed the news that some Jesuits laboring on a mission well had finally struck water. Describing the monumental character of this event, the Franciscan house historian wrote, "Very great difficulty was experienced in digging a well to supply drinking water to the inhabitants of the Mission. The very existence of the Mission hung in the balance. . . . Finally, on the last Saturday in April, the glad news spread through the house. . . . On the following day (Sunday) a feast of thanksgiving was held in honor of Our Lady of Lourdes, to whom the affair had been entrusted from the beginning."[41]

The missionaries' almost perpetual worry over droughts commonly prompted them to exhort the students to pray for rain. In 1908, Digmann reported that he told the little girls in catechism class, "'If you do not want to peal potatoes of marble size, you have to pray for rain; let each say a Hail Mary.' Whether or not they have done it in their heart, I do not know but before half an hour had passed, a soaking rain came." On the other hand, when the missionaries desired clear weather—for example, when they were planning an outdoor celebration—they would again ask the students to pray toward this end. Digmann stated that for confirmation exercises the same year he told the children to pray for sunshine, and "we got it."[42]

The children also took part in memorial services and funerals for members of the religious communities and for their fellow students. In 1899, for example, they collected a dollar to offer a Mass for a classmate who had died during an epidemic of measles. After the funeral Mass held for one of the Franciscans, the "community of Sisters, priests, and brothers, and all the children accompanied the body to the grave." At the conclusion of the burial service the school orchestra played "a beautiful funeral march."[43]

Outside their involvement in religious ceremonies and observances, most of the students were encouraged to join one of a number of school-based confraternities. Among the largest of these associations were the Sodality of the Blessed Virgin, begun in 1895; the Aloysius Society, founded in 1897 (whose boys and girls pledged to observe the Six Sundays in honor of that saint); the Holy Family Society for the older girls organized in 1908; and the Scapular Society started in 1910. Aside from their specific practices and objectives, these organizations shared the goal of deepening their students' commitment to Catholic social and spiritual values and creating bonds of mutual edification and support that they would carry into adulthood. Associates of the Holy Family Society, for example, "were made to" sign a pledge stating that they would never marry outside the church. According to Digmann, this requirement "bore fruit."[44]

On occasion the religious memorialized the abbreviated lives of departed sodality members to edify their schoolmates. In one such case a seriously ill girl requested to be received into the Sodality of the Blessed Virgin. According to the Franciscan house historian for that year, "Her petition was granted and on the following day after receiving Holy Communion she passed into eternity. Her last words to her mother who was called to her bed side were, 'Mother receive the sacrament of Baptism and after that attend the Catholic Religion.' Her mother promised and kept it in spite of all the difficulties that her husband made. Shortly afterwards he also was received into the Church and both died a happy death."[45]

By virtue of an educational policy that confined students each school year within an environment saturated with Catholic beliefs, practices, and values, the children attending Saint Francis boarding school led "cloistered" lives not markedly different from those followed by members of Catholic religious orders. All activities at the school, in one way or another, were directed toward the missionaries' primary goal of creating a Sicangu Catholic church. By inculcating their pupils with American economic and cultural institutions, they hoped to transform them not only into good citizens but, more important, into members of a stable sacramental community that would allow for the transition from mission to church.

Civilization and Christianization in the Sicangu Camps

From their arrival the religious serving at Saint Francis took for granted that their work civilizing and Christianizing Sicangu adults would require a radically different form of pedagogy than the one practiced in their boarding school. This assumption was for the most part based on their recognition that much of the work evangelizing and assimilating grown Indians would necessarily take place within *tiyospaye* camps, and almost exclusively in the

Lakota language. The original company of religious, therefore, arrived at Saint Francis armed with copies of Father Ravoux's Dakota hymnal, catechism, and Bible history. More important, the priests successfully petitioned Standing Rock's veteran Benedictine missionary, Jerome Hunt, to take up residence at Saint Francis from October through November 1886 to tutor them in Lakota and to preach native-language sermons to the Indians on Sundays. Digmann recalled that immediately after Father Hunt's departure mission superior Emil Perrig directed him to prepare a homily on the sign of the cross for the following Sunday. "Writing my little address first in English, I translated it with the help of a mixed-blood into Sioux and read it to the assembled congregation." The priest further commented that "it helped not a little to attach the Indians to us when they saw how hard we tried to understand them, and make ourselves understood in their own language."[46]

In line with their developmentalist assumptions regarding the childlike state of Lakota mentality, the missionaries tried to attract the Sicangus' interest by use of catechetical techniques designed for children and racial and ethnic groups that were presumed to be incapable of abstract thought.[47] One of these devices, a "magic lantern," which projected colorful pictures of key events in Jewish scripture, the life of Christ, and the sacrifice of Christian martyrs, was used to entice Lakotas to church on Sundays. Sicangus who attended Mass were given a ticket that would admit them to the show that followed. According to Digmann, this "scheme worked well for both the Indians and the Missionaries. The latter feeling urged to learn Sioux, to be able to explain the pictures, and the Indians grasping the truth easier, entering the soul by both ear and eye."[48]

The missionaries also made frequent use of another form of visual instruction known as the Canku Numpa, or "Two Roads." Describing this picture-catechism, Fr. Louis Goll wrote: "On a strip of paper one foot wide and five feet long, practically everything of which a catechism treats is contained in Roads. Beginning with the Blessed Trinity and Creation at the bottom of the strip, the student follows the connected pictures to God in heaven at the top. The Apostles creed, the life and death of Christ, the Church, the sacraments, the theological virtues, the capital sins—all are there between two roads, a golden road leading to heaven and a black one ending in hell."[49]

George D. Rogers Sr., a mixed-blood Sicangu who witnessed the arrival of the first Catholic priest in the early 1880s when he was eight years old, described instruction by means of the Two Roads in the following colloquial manner:

> He [the priest] had a picture was made showing the Haven and the Hell and there a road or path layed starting in then branch of[f] to Right and one to Left—right lead to haven and left to hell. This pictures is big and long he has it in a Roll so it makes to carry so he get in tipi he unroll it out show to the family or all that are in this tipi then he explained by a hand motion best he knows how and in hand signs is naturally all the tribe knows so he work this way and got most of the people.[50]

To replace their dependence on sign language, the Jesuits quickly developed bilingual instructional scripts for the Two Roads to lead Sicangus from one illustration to another. Among the subjects covered in these lessons were an outline of salvation history (with the years before Christ colored in black and those after in red), the Ten Commandments, the seven sacraments, the seven deadly sins, faith, hope, love, the Catholic Church, the meaning of purgatory, and the communion of saints.[51]

Although the priests originally used the Two Roads during their own ministerial rounds, they soon discovered that it was a more powerful teaching device in the hands of their catechists and other reliable converts. Describing the work of these native missionaries, Father Goll observed that the "oratorical ability of converts proved a great help to the missionaries."

Indian converts acted as catechists to explain the *Two Roads* picture catechism. A catechist would go to a pagan neighbor's hut or tent. Friends who saw him going there would soon follow, and within an hour quite a few would smoke the pipe. Then the host would ask the follower of the New Prayer to tell them something about it. The convert was prepared for the request. . . . He was one who had not merely "caught on" to the bare facts of Catholic doctrine, but had entered into the very spirit of the new religion.[52]

In addition to instructing fellow Sicangus on the basics of Catholic dogma, catechists also aided the priests in performing other calls for service that might otherwise go unanswered. According to Father Westropp: "For every little sickness the priest, prayer-man or holy-man, has to be called and the Indians are highly indignant if he does not come, even for a sick baby. . . . so in each county there has to be a Catechist or Helper. . . . He has to hold lay services on Sunday, help the priest pray over the sick, teach hymns, baptize in case of necessity. His territory is often very large. They are very apostolic and zealous men and try to bring in as many converts as they can."[53]

After their conversion, Sicangu men and women were encouraged to become members of the Saint Joseph and Saint Mary Societies, respectively. Imported from the Benedictine missions in North Dakota, these lay organizations had been organized to foster informal instruction among their members, hold lay services, provide venues for addressing practical questions, and rally native opposition to government policies the missionaries believed to be injurious to Catholic interests on the Rosebud. The societies were also the major sponsors and participants at the annual Catholic Sioux Indian Congress.[54]

Aside from their religious functions, the Saint Joseph and Saint Mary Societies served as the major instruments through which the missionaries promoted their efforts to replace traditional Lakota customs with the institutions and mores of Western civilization.[55] In his report to the Rosebud agent for 1895–96, Digmann commented, "All the members [of the Saint Joseph and Saint Mary Societies] have declared to take allotment, facing boldly and not yielding to a strong opposition on part of old-fashioned Indians who tried hard to pull them back on the old track."[56] Elaborating on the societies' contest with "non-progressive" Sicangus, Goll observed that the "fight against old Indian customs and superstitions kept the meetings of the St. Joseph and St. Mary Societies animated. The members realized that the individual man and woman was helpless against traditional practices, that power lay in numbers. But knowing that Catholics were still a small minority, they bethought themselves of appealing to the Government." Commenting on the role that these societies played in helping the government uproot harmful Lakota practices, Goll pointed to their determination to end the "give-away," a traditional Lakota custom in which members of a *tiyospaye* give most of their possessions to guests attending a ceremony in honor of one of their relatives. In particular, the Catholic Indians wanted the help of the Indian Office in their fight against the give-away practice. "No one could doubt the bad effects of this ruinous custom. The missionaries knew very well that police regulations cannot of themselves bring a change of heart and interior renunciation of old habits. On the other hand, an organized minority protected by law and a watchful police is a powerful factor in swaying public opinion."[57]

One cannot fully appreciate the importance of the Saint Joseph and Saint Mary Societies and native catechists to the theory and practice of Catholic missionization on the Rosebud without understanding their relationship to the pedagogical presuppositions of the Saint Francis religious. Among the most important of these premises was the centrality of "word" and "example" in the secular and religious education of Indians. In his annual report on Saint Francis to the Indian commissioner for 1896–97, Father Digmann submitted: "As to our missionary work I would say that different camps have been visited pretty regularly. Our main endeavor has been to encourage them by word and example to work, improve their homes, and to take good care of their families and their property."[58] The fact remained, however, that unlike the school, where the religious were able to exercise direct and continuous control over discourse and conduct, the camps remained relatively sequestered from their instructions. Excluding the priests' monthly visits to hear confessions and celebrate Mass, or their ad hoc calls to baptize newborns and anoint those in danger of death, they saw little of the priests.

One of the ways the religious sought to compensate for their minimal contact with the camps was to encourage their Catholic residents to attend Catholic religious and social gatherings held at Saint Francis. They especially urged those with children at the mission school to attend Christmas, Easter, and other festivities with their families. Though the Sicangus relished such invitations for the opportunity they provided to see their children, the missionaries regarded them as occasions for the visitors' spiritual uplift. On occasion missionaries also hosted special convocations and religious gatherings intended to edify and strengthen the faith of church members. The most popular of such assemblies by far was the annual Omniciye Tanka ("Big Meeting"), or Catholic Sioux Congress, which attracted Lakotas and Dakotas from different reservations in the Dakotas (see chapter 13). Less grandiose and usually less successful events included the meetings that the mission sponsored for adult Sicangu Catholics from the different camps. One especially dismal effort, one never repeated, was the 1913 retreat for former students. That year's Franciscan house historian reported: "From the 4 to 7 of September a retreat was held for the former pupils. This was the first time anything like that was attempted. Over a hundred invitations were send out and thirty came to make it, but only 6 remained to complete it."[59]

Even when successful, such gatherings were too sporadic and ephemeral to counterbalance the extended periods when most Sicangu Catholics remained out of contact with the priests, brothers, and sisters. It was under these circumstances that the religious came to rely increasingly on catechists and members of the Saint Joseph and Saint Mary Societies to serve as their camp surrogates, propping up the resolve of fellow Catholics to adhere to church doctrine and to the progressivist agenda set by the mission and government. Although the missionaries believed that such Sicangu converts were still in a primitive stage of Christianization and civilization, they nevertheless considered them the leaven out of which a Sicangu church would one day arise.

CHAPTER NINE

"Always Crosses, but Never Unhappy"

Sicangu Obstacles to Missionization

D uring Holy Week of 1887, Bishop Marty offered the mission's Franciscan
sisters the following words of spiritual consolation to shepherd them
though a particularly trying period in their labors: "We never realize more fully
the happiness of being allowed to work and to suffer with Jesus for the salvation
of souls, than during Holy Week, and there can be no greater consolation for
us in the seeming want of success in our undertakings, than to hear our Divine
Lord close His years of preaching and of miracles with the words: 'Father,
forgive them for they know not what they do.'" Comparing their situation
with others who had toiled in the fields of the Lord, he encouraged them to
consider that "the Dakota Indians are not so bad as the Jews, nor as those
heathens who torture and kill their Missionaries. Therefore, it is my daily
prayer that the Lord may not only send labourers into His vineyard, but that
He may preserve, strengthen, guide and bless those who are already labouring
there. He that perseveres will in time see and taste the fruits of his labour."[1]

Tailoring his admonition with an eye to the season, Marty hoped that
its allusions to Christ crucified would bolster the sisters' resolve to continue
their mission. While acknowledging that the Franciscans' work among the
Sicangus was fraught with tribulations, he enjoined them to welcome them
as crosses and so imitate Christ's own humble obedience to his mission. In
recognition for their perseverance, the bishop assured the community that
God would allow them to witness the success of their efforts.

As an exhortation to faith, Marty's message scrupulously avoided the question of when the sisters could expect their reward. Both the bishop and the Franciscans understood that it was not within his purview or powers to second-guess the Lord's timing on such matters. The intent of his note was, rather, to remind the community of the missionaries' obligation and privilege to struggle against all manner of obstacles, always trusting that God would set things right in the end.

As decades passed and the prospects for founding a self-sustaining Sicangu church remained resolutely dim, the Franciscans periodically lapsed into despair over the underwhelming results of their labors. Reporting on a visit by their mother general in 1907, the sisters' house historian halfheartedly noted that "in her short stay here Reverend Mother saw that her daughters by their efforts among the Indians had really accomplished something, although one might at times think that there was but little progress."[2]

The sisters were not alone in occasionally stumbling under the weight of their crosses. In a diary entry from 1897, Father Digmann reported that on the eve of the Feast of the Patronage of Saint Joseph he dreamed that he was on the prairie while "the whole sky above was covered with white clouds, and all around dark colored crosses of the size of my Novitiate cross. At the same time I had a queer mixture of joy and desire and pain in my soul." The priest went on to state, "If any dream of mine ever has been realized, it is this: always crosses, but never unhappy and ever St. Joseph kind protection."[3]

In contrast, another entry in his journal from the same year suggests that on occasion the pain in his soul was accompanied by unhappiness and despair. After the Catholic Sicangus of one camp refused to volunteer to haul stones and lumber for their new church, the priest indignantly wrote: "The infidelity, laziness, etc. of our Indians—all for money, nothing for God—caused me such loath that I felt sometimes like 'giving up.' I offered it up," he confessed, "to our Savior in union with the loath I had caused Him in the Garden of Olives in His agony."[4]

A decade later Digmann's periodic outbursts had coalesced into forebodings of a more fundamental order. In a letter to BCIM director Ketcham, he brooded that "sometimes the thought looms up before my soul: should the All knowing have doomed our poor Indians, because—as a whole—they do not take to Christianity, as we might expect. But again, it is not so much their fault, under the circumstances, not in their control."[5]

Some of these "circumstances" were, evidently, beyond the control of not only the Indians but the missionaries as well. In his report to the commissioner of Indian affairs for 1901–1902, Digmann observed, "Our missionary work of the past year I may compare to a race with obstacles put in the road. All the missionary can do is to comply with the command of his Divine Master: 'Go and teach them all that I have told you.' This command contains the boundary of both his duty and his power."[6]

The Catholic religious identified two varieties of obstacles as the main impediments to their work among the Sicangus. One group were those difficulties that they attributed to Sicangu psychology, culture, and religion. Although the missionaries were frequently dismayed by the tenacity with which many Indians clung to their traditional modes of thought and behavior, they nevertheless considered their struggle to eradicate Indian savagery and paganism to be part and parcel of their missionary vocation. The religious, however, were not nearly so sanguine regarding obstacles that they attributed to non-Sicangu sources. Heading the list of these non-Indian impediments were the barriers that Rosebud's Episcopal missionaries and federal Indian Office employees erected in their path. The Catholic missionaries considered obstacles of this order far more menacing than those posed by Sicangu savagery and heathenism—the subject of this chapter, for they were the products of enemies of their church who were always in search of ways to subvert their work—as we see in chapter 10.

Sicangu Psychology and Character

In a survey of early Catholic missionary work on the Rosebud, Fr. Louis Goll reported that it did not take the Jesuits and Franciscans long to realize that there were "many good qualities beneath the blanket" of the savage Sicangus.[7] The religious believed that to elevate these virtues they needed to cast off the blanket of primitive psychology, customs, and heathenism and expose them to the light of American Catholic lifeways and religion.

In keeping with the assumptions of developmentalist thought, the missionaries assumed that Sicangu lifeways and heathenism were both the cause and consequence of a primitive psychology typical of persons in the lowest stage of social and cultural growth. One hallmark of this primitive mentality, they held, was the tendency of men and women to think and behave in a childish manner. In an essay published in an 1893 issue of *Die Katholischen Missionen*, Fr. Aloysius Bosch commented, "The most accurate understanding I can give you of our adult population is if I say that they are grown up children with all the personality faults this entails and only patience and more patience is the valuable medicine that a missionary must ever possess. Oh how often must I reach for this medicine!"[8]

Father Digmann similarly insisted on the need for patience when dealing with Sicangus. Toward the end of his nearly fifty-year career on the Rosebud, he characterized the Indians as "overgrown children, wards of the Government, and as such must be treated with patience and firmness."[9]

From the missionaries' perspective, one of the most frustrating characteristics of these "overgrown children" was their penchant for avoiding work for play. Not long after the missionaries arrived at Saint Francis, the Franciscan house historian recorded that, "while the poor Dakotas sit idly in their tents, the fathers are wearing themselves out hammering and carpentering the whole day to prepare the abode in which the children and the Indians themselves are supposed to become acquainted with God; and if they had the slightest realization of what it means to be raised a Catholic, they would take the tools out of the fathers' hands, instead of, as now, lying idly on the ground with their large, white sheets and watching the priests." All but despairing that anything short of a miracle from the Almighty could wrest the Sicangus from their indolence, the sister concluded: "Considering the laziness and unpredictability of the savages, we expect help only from God, who has power over all hearts. It is going to be very difficult for a people habituated since childhood to laziness to get used to an orderly life."[10]

Although the missionaries were sometimes angered by the Sicangus' unwillingness to help those who were helping them, they were limited in terms of where to locate the blame for this and other Indian character flaws. Given the essentially universalist and nonracist assumptions of developmentalist thought, their only logical option was to trace these problems to the primitive nature of Lakota culture and mentality. Accordingly, these Indians were incarcerated nomads and buffalo hunters who as yet lacked the intellectual and emotional maturity to appreciate the superiority of the white people's industries and Catholicism. The missionaries, moreover, insisted that it would require many years of reservation-based education and training to transform them into civilized men and women. Responding to the racist accusations of some whites that Indians were naturally lazy, Father Westropp declared that if there were any truth to these claims they should nevertheless be presented differently. He reminded his readers that their traditional lifeways had hardened Lakotas and other Indians to a variety of hardships, including those associated with war and hunting. What they were not used to was being "thrown out of a job and there is none to replace it." Replying to the rhetorical question, "But why does he not take to tilling the soil?" Westropp claimed that there was as much sense in this as "ask[ing] the carpenter who is thrown out of work why he does not take to tilling the soil or why he does not take to book keeping or the fine arts." The carpenter would justifiably answer, the priest stated, "that those are not his trades." Drawing upon his developmentalist agenda for his argument's climax, he claimed, "Why then can we expect more of this uncivilized tribes than we do of those far advanced in civilized life? Still he is hard at work learning trades, unknown to his forefathers, and if he is not adept at them, it can form no matter of surprise that a civilization, that has taken us two thousand years to acquire, cannot be conferred upon him as easy as a diploma upon a college student. It is not the work of one or two years but of a couple generations.[11]

The missionaries' understanding of the struggles Sicangus experienced in adopting Euro-American lifeways is further indicated by the following passage in which Digmann related one Indian's attempt to master plowing. The latter stated, "I had my summer blanket (bed sheet) on but the wind blew it off; I then held it with the hand on the plow handle but the wind kept on blowing so I finally through [threw] it off and dressed like white-men, took pants and coat."[12] Although the priest reported that the Sicangu told this story to amuse his companions, the narrative's subtext, of which Digmann was certainly aware, was that the lifeways of a culture constituted an integrated system so that changing one of its elements necessarily brought with it changes to others. Although the missionaries were enthusiastic proponents of this sort of wholesale culture change, they harbored no illusions concerning the difficulties that the process entailed for both its agents and subjects. This is precisely the reason that they believed that civilizing the Sicangus and other Indian tribes would take many generations to accomplish.

In addition to the hurdles they confronted in inducing Sicangus to adopt "civilized" trades, the missionaries considered their hair-trigger emotionality and vindictiveness to present major obstacles to missionization. Once again, the missionaries made sense of these traits in terms of the Sicangus' lack of psycho-social development. After describing one parent's violent outburst upon hearing of the death of his child, the sisters' house chronicler for

1915 observed, "The Indians are like children who follow their immediate instincts." The sister went on to report the Indians' position: "Naturally the mission is guilty of everything and therefore pay[s] for its misdeeds. It is even said that the entire mission will be burned down."[13]

As the historian's entry suggests, the missionaries expected angry Sicangus to lash out against their enemies with stealth and violence. Such vindictiveness, according to Father Westropp, was part of a savage code of conduct that differed radically from that of civilized persons; if Indians "could succeed in playing a mean trick, striking in the back, as it were, when one was not looking, even in cowardly attacking a single person with a numerous troop, they boasted of it and received the compliments of their fellow warriors."[14] In another allusion to this "code," Westropp wrote that Indians "are very harmless when they threaten. An Indian tells not before what he is going to do afterwards. He strikes one unware and from behind. The blow is no sooner delivered that he is off."[15]

The missionaries also believed that the undeveloped state of Sicangu character was responsible for the Indians' constant recourse to prevarication. In his report to the commissioner of Indian affairs for 1900, Father Digmann minced no words regarding the great roadblock he considered that this character flaw posed to Indian advancement: "This seems to me the hardest point in Christianizing these Indians—to educate them to truthfulness. An Indian will make any amount of promises, if by so doing he may hope to induce one to help him out of a scrape or lend him financial aid. On account of any arising difficulty, he will hold himself excused from keeping his promise."[16]

Obstacles Posed by Sicangu Culture

In addition to obstacles they faced from Sicangu psychology, the Saint Francis religious deemed certain Lakota customs to pose particular difficulties to their work of civilization and Christianization. Among the Sicangu traditions that they attacked with unrelenting ferocity were traditional Lakota forms of marriage. Of these polygyny—the polygamous union of a man with two or more women—received the greatest portion of their indictments.

Part of the missionaries' antipathy toward polygyny can be traced to Western society's traditional prohibition of plural marriage. Of greater significance, however, were the proscriptions and penalties that Catholic law imposed against such unions. Polygynous Sicangus were routinely barred from baptism until they had renounced their marriage ties to all but one of their spouses. Meanwhile, those Indians taking up the practice after joining the church were subject to various forms of discipline, including exclusion from the Eucharist and other sacraments.

The Saint Francis religious were not the first to cite polygamy as a significant stumbling block to Indian missionary work. On one of his first visits out west in 1839, Fr. Pierre-Jean De Smet had identified plural marriage as a significant roadblock to Indian conversion. "Frequently, after they have followed and relished our instructions for a long time, as soon as we touch upon this article they go away, like the disciples of the Lord, saying, '*Durus est hic sermo, et quis potest eum audire?*' ['This is a hard saying, who can hear it'] and we have the grief of seeing persons escape who, in all other respects, were giving us great hope."[17]

The Saint Francis Jesuits' refusal to baptize members of polygynous households even if it meant losing prospective converts is illustrated in the following entry in Digmann's diary. On August 19, 1907, the priest wrote:

> Old SF had three wives and had lived with them about thirty years. His second wife was sick and had wished long ago to be baptized. I told her it could not be done unless she promised not to live with him anymore as man and wife. . . . But he refused stoutly to divorce from the two and live with them only as with his sisters. . . . He first joined the Congregationalists who "left him in peace with his consorts" and it took him thirteen years until seventy-seven years of age that he joined the Catholic Church.[18]

Perhaps the most revealing gauge of the missionaries' enmity toward Sicangu polygyny was their frequent use of the term "bigamy" to refer to this custom. Unlike the value-neutral terms "polygamy" and "polygyny," "bigamy" connotes an immoral and illegal act. It was with this understanding that Father Digmann referred to multiwived chief Two Strike as "yet a bigamist."[19]

The federal statutes proscribing plural marriages among Indians and non-Indians alike provided legal grounds for the missionaries' identity of polygyny and bigamy. And yet the extent to which the government considered it worth their employees' time and energy to prosecute Indian polygynists was quite another matter. As we see in the next chapter, the Catholic missionaries at Saint Francis and elsewhere complained bitterly and often regarding the government's apparent laxity in punishing Lakota men with multiple spouses.

Sicangu "Stealing-a-Woman," Divorce, and Remarriage

Aside from polygyny, the missionaries considered the Sicangu marriage custom of "stealing-a-woman" to be a major impediment to their civilization and conversion. Sicangu "wife-stealing" took two forms. In one of these an unmarried man and a woman wedded without first receiving the sanction of their respective families. Although Lakotas did not celebrate elopement, it nonetheless was an exceedingly common practice and generally led to socially accepted unions once the groom had come to terms with his spouse's family over a satisfactory bride "price."

The Saint Francis religious were not, however, so easily mollified, especially when a Catholic "stole" or was "stolen by" a Protestant or pagan Indian. As part of their religious instruction in the camps and at school, the missionaries constantly exhorted Sicangu Catholics to marry within their faith and before a priest. In spite of their efforts, they were unable to eliminate such "mixed marriages," especially among the young. With the end of each school year, concern arose among the missionaries that some of their "big girls" would be "stolen" while home for the summer in their camps. That their apprehension was well founded is indicated in the following entry from August 29, 1892, in Digmann's diary: "Sad experience with three of our large girls, 'stolen' by lads in vacation—eloping!"[20]

Cases in which men lured women away from their husbands constituted the second form of "stealing-a-woman." Describing these unions to the readers of *Die Katholischen Missionen*, Father Perrig stated, "To steal the woman of another in broad daylight is considered an act of heroism. However, it happens infrequently because they are cowardly, deceitful fellows. For this reason they carry their theft at night and in the absence of the husband. And if a conflict arises afterward the perpetrator compensates for it with some wool blanket or a horse that the injured party receives."[21]

For Perrig and his fellow religious, the relative ease with which "wronged" husbands could be persuaded to dissolve their connubial bonds was symptomatic of the Indians' casual attitude toward marriage and divorce. Regarding this indifference, Digmann noted that marriage among the Sicangus "meant by time-honored custom only, that they could live together for a while on trial, to see how they would get along. If a man got tired of her, he would 'pay her off'; give ponies or money and send her home. Their dance hall was their court house. Before the chiefs and judges, the case was proposed, and if the alleged reason were found sufficient, a vigorous stroke of the big drum declared their union severed."[22]

Contending that the development of stable, monogamous households was a prerequisite for Sicangu civilization and Christianization, the missionaries appealed to federal lawmakers to enact statutes that would make it more difficult for Indians to obtain divorces and to remarry. As with their fight against polygyny, however, their efforts to enlist government support failed. The religious were consequently left to rely almost exclusively on church instruction and punishments to convince the Sicangus that their centuries-old practices were both uncivilized and sinful.

Try as the missionaries might, many Sicangus apparently remained genuinely bewildered concerning why "till death do us part" should constitute a sacred obligation rather than a personal or *tiyospaye* matter, and why the Catholic priests and sisters should consider remarriage so grievous a misdeed as to warrant ostracism from the church and its sacraments. Reflecting on his many years of dealing with Sicangu confusion on these "sins," Father Goll wrote:

> I have just to look at my confession register to know how many grown-up people were at Mass that day. I can easily add, a couple whose marriage cannot be fixed up. Half the number of such cases of divorced remarried people will come to church and work for the church doings. Such people will be most anxious to have their children raised Catholic, and work and pray for the day when they can be admitted again to the sacraments. Queer logic you may think! Yes, but . . . they do not see the greatness of their sin.[23]

In an attempt to reclaim the souls of some remarried Sicangu Catholics, Father Digmann sought interpretations of canon law, first from Bishop Marty and then from his successor Thomas O'Gorman, which would render their prior marriages invalid in the eyes of the church. Summarizing the results of his efforts, Digmann wrote that, when he referred the issue to Bishop Marty, he was of the opinion we could "consider them non binding for lifetime, unless contracted 'in facie ecclesiae,' because of their immemorial custom to take them first only on trial, not for lifetime. To be sure, however, and quiet in conscience we asked the Bishop to lay the case before the Holy See." The pope's ruling on this issue was "that they must have exteriorly manifested their will before the marriage contract, not to bind themselves for lifetime."[24]

This stern decree was hardly the ruling that Digmann had desired. Regardless of church teachings on divorce and remarriage, however, the missionaries suspected that God dealt with Indians according to a different standard than for whites. Echoing the sentiments of his fellow missionaries, Digmann thus stated, "God must have another measure of judgment for Indians."[25] Father Goll provided the following example to demonstrate God's compassion in dealing with "the souls of his straying sheep": "Here is a man, divorced with or without his fault. I warn him not to get married again. He makes an effort for a while, but then succumbs; he will live that way for some years; he gets sick. I can be sure that before he dies things will turn out in such a way that I can give him the sacraments. I am sure from my past experience." Puzzled by God's beneficence in such cases, Goll related, "Sometimes I say to the Lord: 'Why do You not protect Your own law. If I were You, I would give him the grace an act of contrition and let him die without the sacraments, to shake up others and get some sorrow into them.' But the Lord will not follow my suggestion."[26]

Social Dances, Roving, and the "Give-Away"

In common with most American Indian peoples, Sicangus considered social dancing to be one of their chief forms of recreation. By contrast, Catholic missionaries deemed these traditional entertainments to be a waste of time that Indians could more profitably direct toward tending to their homesteads and participating in church-sanctioned activities.

In a pastoral letter addressed to Sicangus and other Indians of his diocese, Bishop Joseph F. Busch of Lead decried the continued practice of social dancing and other uncivilized traditions. He cautioned that these customs were "used by the devil to put what is bad into the mind and the heart of him who takes part in [them]." Voicing regret that there were many in the diocese who saw no harm in these customs, the bishop went on to warn the Indians to "give them all up or [they] may be sorry in Hell forever."[27]

In his report to the commissioner of Indian affairs for 1900–1901, Digmann eschewed all references to the devil and hell when discussing the topic of Indian social dances. In fact, in seeming opposition to Bishop Busch, he declared that Indian dances "were not immoral themselves." The difference between the two priests on this matter, however, was more apparent than real, for Digmann immediately went on to characterize dancing as "the greatest obstacle in the way of civilizing and Christianizing these people." Clarifying his position on this matter, Digmann stated that the dances "are and remain the living tradition, keeping alive the old habits. . . . Besides, dancing starts late in the evening and lasts most of the time all night. The young folks, not being allowed to be present, are left to themselves at home. . . . Especially the Fourth of July celebration, as it was kept for the last five years, has resulted more in a revival of the old Indian habits than in a teaching of patriotism as was intended."[28]

One of the troublesome "old habits" that social dancing and other amusements kept alive was the Sicangus' roving disposition. During pre-reservation days Lakotas, in common with the majority of other Plains Indians, had traveled freely throughout their territories in search of buffalo to hunt and enemy tribes to fight and raid. The first generation of reformers believed that, once confined to reservations and "permanent" camps, Indians would rapidly abandon their wanderlust for the settled existence that was necessary to turn them into farmers and establish schools. Most Sicangus, however, demonstrated very little interest in remaining at home, especially during the summer when social dances occurred with great frequency both on and off their reservation. Commiserating with Father Digmann on his frustrated efforts to contain his vagabond fold, BCIM director Ketcham advised, "It is of course most unfortunate that the Indians must indulge in the many attractions that lure them away from the reservations for lengthy periods, and thereby impede their progress and delay the entry of their children into the schools; but there seems to be no help for it, and all we can do is to accept the situation with as much philosophy as possible and make the best of it."[29]

Of all the "old habits" that social dancing fostered, however, it was the *wihpeyapi*, or "give-away," that caused the Catholic missionaries the greatest concern. As Digmann put it, "The custom of giving away all kinds of property in the way of presents exercises its tyrannical force mainly on account of the publicity at dances. One who does not do it is decried as 'a dog,' and no Indian."[30]

To appreciate the missionaries' dim view of this custom, it is important to recall that one of the chief objectives of their government-mandated paradigm was to transform the Sicangus into self-sufficient yeoman farmers. They believed that a necessary prerequisite for achieving this goal was to convince the Indians to abandon their tribal institutions for the individualistic lifeways of Western society. The key to this transformation lay in replacing the *tiyospaye* with economically independent nuclear families in which each family was responsible for accumulating the capital necessary for supporting its members and homestead.

The magnitude of the hindrance that the missionaries believed the "give-away" posed to transforming Sicangu society is suggested in the following description by Digmann: "The customary 'giving away' at their dances is a draw back to civilization. It is their pride to beat their neighbor in generosity, and not seldom leave the dance hall . . . poor or broke, stripping themselves of what they would need for their own family. If one makes a considerable gift, his name is called out and with a vigorous strike on the big drum, carried up to the sky. They never heard: 'Let your left hand not know what your right hand gives.'"[31]

The missionaries not only discouraged Catholic Indians from hosting or participating in give-aways but also attempted to enlist their services to induce the Indian Office to do more to suppress the custom. They therefore encouraged members of the Saint Joseph and Saint Mary Societies to sign petitions urging the commissioner of Indian affairs to enact a policy outlawing the custom. After one such campaign in 1899, Father Digmann reported that he "gathered subscriptions" for an appeal against the give-away and it "found favor with all progressive Indians."[32]

Sicangu Religion

As men and women of the cloth, the Catholic missionaries at Saint Francis were particularly attentive to the obstacles that traditional Lakota religion posed to their work. Chapter 12, on Lakota Catholicism, provides an extended treatment of some of the Sicangus' assumptions regarding Catholic beliefs and practices. The present section deals exclusively with those aspects of Lakota religion that the missionaries found particularly daunting to their efforts to Christianize and civilize the Rosebud Sioux. Commenting on the difficulty of their efforts, Father Westropp remarked, "Faith, much like civilization, has to percolate through a goodly stretch of savage stratum before it reaches the fertile soil beneath."[33]

In keeping with the Catholic theology of their day, the religious of Saint Francis assumed that the sacred truths necessary for human salvation were contained exclusively in Jewish and Christian scriptures and traditions as interpreted, practiced, and promulgated by their church. Although the missionaries acknowledged that pagan religions might contain some spiritual insights and truths, they regarded them as quagmires of superstition, delusion, and idolatry through which the devil—the "Father of Lies"—blinded their devotees to the saving power of Christ.

One of the first "delusions" the Saint Francis missionaries encountered was the belief of many Sicangus that baptism killed rather than "saved" its recipients. Father Westropp provides an example of the difficulty this belief sometimes posed to performing the rite and a strategy the religious devised to circumvent it: Although parents sometimes barred the missionaries from baptizing their dying children, "charity commanded the [latter] to see that [they were] regenerated by the saving waters." Concerning such ruses, he wrote that "most refractory cases were visited by the sisters, who had or were supposed to have some knowledge of medicine. These then privately baptized the dying children. When this plan was not feasible," Westropp added, "the missionary [i.e., priest] himself would at times rub a little peppermint water on the forehead of the child to cool the fever and then baptize the child. Father Bosch had a method of his own. 'If the child gets worse,' he said to the mother, 'Will you baptize it, provided I show you how?' The woman assented, perhaps to get rid of him, and when he showed her how, he took care to perform a real baptism."[34]

For the Saint Francis missionaries, the *wicasa wakan,* or medicine men, constituted the greatest obstacle to breaking the devil's hold on the Sicangus. Although the religious accorded these traditional healers a certain knowledge of herbs, roots, and other natural medicines, they believed that their "baneful influence" was a consequence of the frightening deceptions and tricks that they performed during *lowanpi* (curing ceremonies) and other rituals.[35] In a brief biographical portrait of Nicholas Black Elk, the celebrated Lakota medicine man who eventually became a noted Catholic catechist, Father Westropp wrote, "During many a year, [he] fooled the people with his *wakan* or remedies, supposed to possess magical efficacy." The missionaries, though, "had not paid much attention to him, for the 'medicine men' are the last class of Indians whom we impress."[36]

That the missionaries did, in fact, pay a great deal of attention to medicine men is vividly portrayed in an entry from Father Digmann's diary. In July 1887 the priest agreed to baptize a terminally ill baby at the home of a non-Christian Indian family. After performing the baptism, he hurried back to the mission to seek the services of the Franciscan's mother superior,

Kostka Schlaghecken, who had training as a nurse. Upon arriving back at camp, Digmann reported:

G.K. met us saying, "The medicine men are conjuring the sick child, I do not want to be present." Arriving at the door, we heard their singing, beating the drum and without any compliments I opened. What a spectacle! In a corner of the room the father was sitting with the naked child in his arms. Along the wall four conjurors were crouching with their faces painted red and yellow. One of them had returned from an Eastern school, understood English fairly well, and spoke it tolerably. Him I address first. "George, you here?" He had asked me already to baptize him. Then I continued in Sioux the best I could do at the time, "Give up your Devil's work, the child is baptized and belongs to the Great Spirit." George said "Do you want that one of us shall die? You will not die, get out of here." They, however, continued their powwow singing and ringing pumpkin shells [gourd rattles]. On my repeated begging they finally kept quiet. Mo. Kostka examined the little patient and wanted to make hot poultices. . . . George flung the satchel of the sister out of the door. The scared mother took the baby outside[;] the Sr. followed. George, angry, grasped my arm to put me out but I stood my ground. In the presence of them, I told the father of the child not to allow them to continue their conjuration, and not to let their leader to take the sick child to his house. . . . George became cool. He said that he himself did not believe in this powwow but there was money in it. My experience in this first encounter with them was a good lesson, teaching 1st, they themselves don't believe in their charlantry, 2nd, that they are cowards (owing to their own bad conscience like all evil doers) and 3rd, that "money" is at the bottom of their superstitious practices.[37]

The missionaries' hostility toward Lakota spirituality and its medicine men is nowhere more evident than in their response to the Ghost Dance and its tragic aftermath at Wounded Knee.[38] During the final years of the 1880s, the Lakotas were swept up in a pantribal religious movement that originated from the visions of a Northern Paiute Indian named Wovoka (Jack Wilson). Known as the Ghost Dance, the Lakota version of this revitalistic religion promised adherents that by faithfully practicing its rituals and prayers they would usher back their traditional lifeways and conditions, including the return of the ancestors and buffalo and the removal or destruction of whites.

At approximately the same time that the Ghost Dance was reaching its climax on the Pine Ridge Reservation, agency police on the Standing Rock Reservation killed Sitting Bull when he reputedly resisted arrest. Fearing that the influential headman's murder signaled a stepped-up campaign to eliminate Indian leaders and culture, Miniconjou chief Big Foot and his band fled from the adjacent Cheyenne River Reservation toward the Pine Ridge Reservation, where they intended to rendezvous with a large contingent of Oglala Ghost Dancers in the Dakota Badlands. As the Miniconjous approached their destination on December 28, 1890, they were intercepted by troops of the Seventh Cavalry and escorted under armed guard to an army encampment on Wounded Knee Creek. The following morning Gen. James W. Forsythe posted soldiers armed with Hotchkiss cannons on a rise overlooking the Indian camp and then ordered other members of the company to search the tipis for weapons. In the midst of the search a scuffle erupted and a shot rang out that served as a signal for the troops to begin firing on the camp. Many of the estimated three hundred Lakota men, women, and children who were killed during the massacre that followed fell as they stood defenseless near their tents. Others were ridden down and slain by mounted soldiers as they fled from the camp. On New Year's Day a burial party gathered the bodies and piled them into a mass grave near the scene of the slaughter.

Nearly four years after the massacre, Fathers Bosch and Perrig (now at Holy Rosary Mission) camped near the site of the massacre on the first night of their journey to the Catholic Sioux Congress on the Cheyenne River Reservation. As part of an article about the Congress for the *Messenger of the Sacred Heart*, Bosch described his reflections while surveying the spot "where Almighty God had passed judgment on several hundred . . . poor Dakotas." Discerning "the all-watching providence of God in this event," the priest submitted that "the tribe was swept away from the face of the earth, with their ghost dances, their medicine-men and squaws so deaf and so blind to the word and work of God, preached to them so long and shown to them in such a clear light." And the priest's ruminations on the tragedy did not end there. He went on to relate that the "wretched grave of the poor Indians" brought to mind a lesson concerning the cruelty the devil metes out to those in his service. "What heart does not bleed for those wretched victims of ignorance and delusion? . . . all ages and sexes [thrown] in one common pit, piled upon one another; and now their grave looks like a cowyard guarded by posts and fence wire. Such is the monument on the Dakota braves, such is the end of the Dakota life! Would to God the survivors might profit by the lesson!"[39]

From Bosch's perspective this "lesson" was both compelling and clear. By participating in the Ghost Dance, the victims of the massacre had reaped the bitter harvest of their stubborn adherence to heathenism. Survivors of the tragedy would be wise to benefit from the folly of their less fortunate tribesmen and women by renouncing deviltry and savagery for Catholicism and American civilization, for the death knell sounded at Wounded Knee marked the passing not only of several hundred Indians but of the whole of Lakota culture.[40]

CHAPTER TEN

"We Indians Do Not Want Such Strife"

Non-Sicangu Obstacles to Catholic Missionization

In addition to the obstructions posed by Indian psychology, culture, and religion, the Jesuits and Franciscans at Saint Francis Mission attributed the slow progress of their work among the Sicangus to non-Indian impediments. Chief among this class of obstacles were the mission's contentious relationships with Rosebud's Episcopal church and the federal Indian Office. In addition, the religious ascribed the Sicangus' sluggish advancements in civilization and religion to selected natural and supernatural agents.

The Episcopal Church and Saint Francis Mission

It was the Catholic Church that mounted the earliest and most powerful challenge to Episcopal monopoly over Sicangu Christianization and civilization.[1] This contest began modestly in 1883 when Bishop Marty dispatched three diocesan priests—Frs. Francis Craft, Joseph Bushman, and Casper Hospenthal—to commence the work of establishing a Rosebud Catholic church. With the founding of Saint Francis Mission the number of Catholic religious swelled rapidly—from an initial company of eight in 1886 to twenty-four by 1916—and bred ever-increasing hostility between the two denominations. That this animosity was not lost on the Indians is revealed in the following blunt assessment of interdenominational bickering a Sicangu Ghost Dancer shared with Father Digmann: "You quarrel with each saying that the other was not right. You bite each other," the dancer told the priest. "We Indians do not want such strife. Let us alon[e] . . . and let us worship the Great Spirit in our own way. Now we have our own prayer; we do not want to resist anymore, but want to be left alone."[2]

Three areas of missionization generated the most truculent episodes of "biting." The foremost of these, as is not surprising, was the missionaries' rivalry over potential converts. All of the Rosebud's churches adopted the missionary strategy of proselytizing the leaders of the various *tiyospaye* in the hope that their conversion would influence other camp members to follow their example. Next to the denominations' contest over Spotted Tail, their battle to win the soul of Chief Hollow Horn Bear inspired the fiercest competition. In fact the denominations' competition for this great leader followed him beyond the grave. According to the Franciscan sisters' house historian, "While in Washington, the chief contracted pneumonia, was taken to a Catholic hospital by Fr. Ketcham, strengthened by the sacraments and died. . . . The Protestants did all they could. Father Digmann insisted on his Catholic burial. He had been a Catholic for six years."[3]

Simply because a Sicangu was a member of one of the reservation's denominations did not necessarily place him or her off-limits to the proselytizing efforts of other churches. The Saint Francis religious complained bitterly and often of attempts by "white coats" (Ogle Ska, or Episcopalians) and "short coats" (Ogle Ptecela, or Congregationalists) to lure Catholic Indians away from their fold. At times the strategies that were used to entice prospective defectors could be highly inventive. According to Father Digmann, the "Protestants . . . tried to catch the women folks by inviting them to join their sewing society." The priest countered this Protestant "invitation" by urging the women to "start [a society] of their own and [he] would help them get a machine and calico."[4]

Describing the efforts of one Congregationalist helper to woo Indians from other churches in 1907, Digmann reported: "He went around the camps and told them: 'You have been so far with the Black Robes and White Gowns, now try the Short Coats. They are, after all, one and the same. The Black Robes do not keep you, but we will make a collection for you and help you farming.' Our Catholic Indians came reporting." Digmann related that he "finally called the old Chief of the Camp (Ring Thunder). 'Yes,' he said, 'for the last three Sundays a Shortcoat came, and went to N.N. house, but nobody went there.' N.N. was a practically apostatized Catholic, having taken another one's wife."[5]

Ring Thunder's report so incensed Digmann that the priest wrote a letter to Rosebud's Congregationalist minister, Robert Hall, protesting the actions of the helper. Digmann informed Hall, "Your helper either believes himself what he tells the people, that all religions are one and the same or not. If he believes it, why does he go around pulling them away from their former belief? If he himself does not believe it, and speaks so anyhow he is a liar."[6]

It is only fair to note that the Rosebud Catholic church not only suffered from membership raids but launched them as well. The Jesuit priests often set their sights on Sicangus who claimed that they had been baptized Protestant without their desire or permission. Digmann recounted that in 1892 he converted three Episcopalian Indians in Two Kettle's camp who contended that they had received baptism against their wills.[7]

Passions really flared, however, when Catholic priests baptized defecting members of Protestant churches. In one such case, Digmann acceded to an ailing Episcopal woman's request that he baptize her so she could "die a Catholic." When her daughter voiced concern over the spiritual consequences of rebaptism, Digmann explained that he had actually performed a "conditional" baptism that "was no (second) baptism at all if the first had been valid." "Conditional" or not, Rosebud's Protestant churchmen considered these rites an added insult to the injury they suffered from lost membership. According to Digmann, they "felt quite sore about it that we [the Catholics] did not acknowledge their baptisms . . . [and the] Reverend A. B. C[lark] wrote quite an article about it in the Chilocoo Indian Magazine calling us Rebaptists." Soon after the appearance of this article, a Sicangu who had been raised Congregationalist, but who had joined the Episcopalians and was ordained a priest, confronted Digmann on the subject. Defending the Catholic position on "conditional baptisms," Digmann argued, "We believe in only one baptism, no one can be born again for the supernatural life, as little as for our natural life. The Church has been severe in punishments on the crime of rebaptizing." The priest, nevertheless, went on to assert that "conditional baptism . . . may not only be allowed, but necessary if a former baptism's validity is doubtful. One reason of making it doubtful," he continued, "is the [loss] of intention on the part of the minister to do what Jesus wanted when ordering baptism. Some of their own Bishops . . . called baptism a relic of popish superstition. I would not feel sure to be validly baptized by such. Sweep before your own door, before you blame us for conditional baptism, to make sure of this necessary Sacrament."[8]

At times missionary responses to defecting Sicangus could be rather uncharitable. On May 6, 1896, Digmann wrote, "There is a movement towards the Church in many camps. The Episcopalians are angry about it and told such that had left them, 'Take also your dead ones along.' Some have done so and started a cemetery of their own, first on Oak Creek. I gave them a large cross with a painted corpus on it."[9]

Sicangus possessed a variety of motives for changing their church membership (discussed in chapter 11). For the present it is sufficient to note that, although the Catholic religious benefited from this practice, they also considered it an obstacle to establishing a stable Catholic church on the Rosebud.

A second source for antagonism between Rosebud's Catholic and Protestant missionaries was the Blackrobes' use of the Two Roads picture-catechism. It did not take long for Episcopal missionaries to accuse the Catholic religious of sowing seeds of discord by teaching that all Protestant Indians were marching down the road to hell. Considering what this catechism said concerning non-Catholic churches, it is not difficult to understand why they believed this to be the case. "We must know the four reasons of the Saviour's Church: Because it is, One, Universal, Holy, *it came and passed down from the days of our Apostles.* Some of the so-called church have not yet reached the age of 400 years, they are not steady, they are not universal, they are not holy; those churches cannot bring us to heaven; hence we should not follow them. If we follow the Holy Catholic Church rightfully we will reach and enter into the Home of God. Therefore let us strongly pledge ourselves to follow this and do it."[10]

Despite the Episcopalians' complaints and a brief ban that the Rosebud agent imposed on the use of the Two Roads in 1886, the missionaries continued to use this picture-catechism for their work in the camps, with the understanding of agency officials that they disavowed the teaching of mass Protestant damnation to their catechumens.[11]

Competition for church members and the use of the Two Roads provided ample grounds for interdenominational conflict, but the issue of federal support for the Saint Francis boarding school generated the fiercest episodes of "biting." After the Supreme Court's decision in 1906 that allowed tribal funds to be used to support sectarian Indian schools, the Indian Office instituted a policy requiring that church schools periodically gather sufficient signatures from tribal members to warrant the federal contracts they had been awarded. During the weeks preceding the first signing, Protestant and Catholic clergy and their associates scurried about the Sicangu camps presenting their respective cases regarding federal support for Saint Francis school. Reporting to Ketcham on one such Episcopal-sponsored gathering, Digmann wrote that church helpers and catechists had asserted that "we [the priests at Saint Francis Mission] were not Blackrobes, we were Jesuits who had caused trouble in Europe and were turned out to the U.S. to cause trouble to the Government here and ask [for] the Government's money. They have their men all over the Reserve," he continued, "exciting and scaring the poor ignorant Indians out of their wits."[12]

The issue that was supposedly panicking the "benighted" Indians was whether the monies issued to Saint Francis boarding school would be deducted from the annual per-capita payments that they received from their federally administered trust funds. This subject was of no small concern to the Sicangus, with hunger and poverty stalking the Rosebud on the eve of the first signing in winter 1906. Digmann detected the hand of bigotry in this scheduling: "Very cleverly managed that they come out with this petition just now, when they are all starving. In the camps they had heard of it, and I found them in great consternation."[13]

In fact there was much confusion on what impact, if any, the petitions would have on Sicangus' per-capita payments. In a letter to Anthony Maitre of the American Federation of Catholic Societies, Digmann wrote that the "Pine Ridge Agent says, that the per capita money was not affected by it [the petition]; our Rosebud (new) Agent maintains it was. Our Rosebud Indians would get about $8.00 to $9.00 [per capita] for 'grassing,' 'hides' and interest on Sioux funds; and he thinks that it would take about $5.45 of each Indian, to make up for our Contract." Expressing concern over the effect this kind of talk was having on Indians with children enrolled at the Saint Francis Mission school, Digmann observed, "Mr. Clark's 'helpers' went around telling the Indians, 'Don't be so foolish to sign, do you want to starve right quick?' The Agent himself told me, 'The Indians bother me every day, to allow them 'coupon-books,' to buy on credit in stores on their issue-money, but I cannot allow it, before I know what each wants to sign for you.' It is especially this that scared our Indians."[14]

BCIM secretary Charles S. Lusk provided the clearest explanation for the tangled policy relating to petitions and Sioux funds. Responding in 1908 to a series of questions Digmann had addressed to the BCIM on this matter, the secretary explained that "the money that is to be used [for] the contract for your school may be taken from three funds of the Sioux Indians, to wit: the Education Fund, the Support and Civilization Fund, and the 'Education' part of the trust funds. It is impossible to say just what part of each of these funds will be used for this purpose." He nevertheless surmised that "only the Education Fund will be used, tho as to this, of course. . . . The only fund that was used for your contract of 1906 was the Education Fund, because of this fact I am inclined to think that is the fund that will be used this year." With regard to the question of the effect that this apportionment had on the amount of the Sicangus' per-capita payments, Lusk observed, "No part of the Education Fund or of the Support and Civilization Fund is ever paid directly to the Indians. The first fund is used exclusively for educational purposes and the second partly for education and partly for furnishing subsistence to the Indians and in other ways that will assist in their civilization." He further explained, "The interest on the Trust Fund is $150,000 per year, of this $75,000 is used exclusively for educational purposes, and the other $75,000 is paid to the Indians per capita. Not a dollar of the interest that is distributed has ever been used, or will be used, for educational purposes and, as I have said not a dollar of the other two funds has ever been paid directly to the Indians, and there is no reason to believe that it ever will be." Lusk concluded by assuring Digmann, "I think, that the Indians who sign the petition for the use of their money for the education of their children in your school will suffer no pecuniary loss by such signing, and it seems to me that if you can make this clear you should have little or no difficulty in securing the necessary signers."[15]

The battles that the Rosebud's Episcopal and Catholic churches waged over the petitions commonly took the form of a war between personalities, specifically between Digmann and Episcopal priest Aaron B. Clark. Assessing the obstacle that Clark posed to the Rosebud Catholic missionary work, Digmann informed Ketcham, "As long as that man is allowed to remain on the Reservation, we will have no peace. Under the last administration he had been suggested, to keep 'quiet,' or he would have to leave the Reservation; but he kept on all the while on the 'quiet' warpath. One imagines, what impression it must make on the Indians, if the 'leaders of the Prayer' are fighting against one another."[16]

The depths to which these personal attacks could sink is revealed in the following notice by Clark that appeared in the *Public Opinion Telegraph*:

A Message
from the Sioux Indaian [*sic*] country.
Sicangu Makoce, Feb. 1906.

An agent of Katch'em & Co., known as Friar Spademan, is out with his "double-entente" spade digging in the people's affections for sympathy and aid in placing his borrowed petition-trap among the Indian trust funds. While he fills the air with clouds of alkali dust showers of and, clods of gumbo and other chunks of wisdom (?) the Indian students who object to the trapping game might be heard tuning up thusly:

Dig, man, dig! Dig, man, dig!
Dig by night and by day!
Dig with will! Dig with might!
But take that trap away!
Take that trap away.[17]

It would be misleading to close this discussion of the battle over school funding without mentioning that the Catholic missionaries were not averse to using scare tactics of their own to induce Sicangus to sign the petitions. The religious were well aware that many Sicangu parents were terrified that the government would register their children in off-reservation government schools. Commenting on the Indian Office's desire to augment the meager enrollments of these institutions, Digmann stated, "That's what the Indians fear. . . . That our school being close[d], they will send their children to Non Reservation Schools."[18] We further examine how missionaries exploited this fear in chapter 12.

Local Indian Office Personnel

As mentioned earlier, Saint Francis Mission was founded during a period of relative tranquility in the relationship between the federal government and the Catholic Indian missions. Five years had already passed since the abrogation of the Grant Peace Policy, and the great tumult that would erupt over Commissioner Morgan's attempt to do away with sectarian Indian schools was still a decade away. Yet the atmosphere on the Rosebud was anything but peaceful as the first Jesuits and Franciscans arrived at the mission in 1886. Much of this tension could be traced to the continuing tenure of the agent, James G. Wright, whose frequent clashes with the reservation's initial company of diocesan missionaries had culminated in Father Craft's expulsion from the Rosebud. As far as the Catholics were concerned, the agent was a bigot who was willing to do everything in his power to make life difficult for their fledgling mission.

The missionaries appear to have had just cause for this judgment. When they opened their boarding school for its trial run in the summer of 1886, Wright refused to supply its three students their full share of federal rations guaranteed by the Treaty of 1868 and the BCIM's contract with the Indian Office. Notifying Indian commissioner J. D. C. Atkins of this situation, Stephan wrote, "It is the Bishop's [Marty's] intention to furnish tuition and school books as may attend the school free of cost, but they should be clothed and subsisted from the annuities and rations issued them in pursuance of treaty stipulations." Stephan advised the commissioner that "the Superintendent of said school informs me that the 3 pupils were in attendance, but owing to the insufficient rations furnished the children by the Agent it would be impossible to keep the school any longer." He then politely but firmly alerted Atkins that "in order that it may not become necessary to dismiss the pupils, I would respectfully ask that the Agent at the Rosebud Agency be instructed to issue to pupils now attending and that may hereafter attend the school the full ration of clothing and subsistence guaranteed them by treaty stipulations and provided by the regulations of your office."[19]

The commissioner quickly let Wright know that he was to cease fleecing the school's students of their rightful supply of rations. He bluntly informed the agent that, "as this school has been erected at great expense, without cost to the government, and will largely benefit the Indians in whose interests it has been established, it is the desire of this Office to foster and encourage it and to cooperate with its founders, in insuring its success by extending the limited aid it asks—food and clothing for the pupils." In order that there be no ambiguity on this matter, Atkins directed Wright "to issue to [the school's] Indian scholars, weekly in advance, on the usual requisition of the Superintendent or principal teacher, the full school ration, as provided under Sec 513, Regulations, 1884, or such variations in the ration as while affording ample nourishment will not exceed the money value of the established table."

He additionally ordered Wright to supply the school with those materials that its superintendent determined were "required to furnish a complete and comfortable outfit for each pupil includ[ing] bed-clothing, toweling, etc., and the thread, buttons, and necessary articles for the making up of the clothing. Shoes, stockings, hats, thimbles, and needles are also to form part of the issue."[20]

Atkins evidently harbored serious doubts concerning Wright's commitment to the success of the school, since he added two additional conditions to ensure that the agent would carry out his instructions. The commissioner ordered him to send the Indian Office a list of required materials "so that the deficiency may be supplied" and to transmit a detailed invoice for this issuance that was "witnessed by the Interpreter and two disinterested witnesses."[21]

Despite Atkins's actions, Stephan and the Saint Francis religious remained deeply suspicious of the Rosebud agent. The magnitude of their mistrust is witnessed in the BCIM director's response to the school's first federal inspection. Of the school's site the inspector wrote, "Had this been located properly and the money expended judiciously, this school would have been more beneficial to all concerned." Turning to its staff and administration, the inspector again complained that, "unless the present management places some man of common sense at the head of this school, they will waste money and accomplish nothing."[22]

As with all significant correspondence between individual missions and the federal government, the director of the BCIM took responsibility for replying to the report. Abandoning all pretense of diplomacy, Father Stephan countered the inspector's criticisms point by point, adding caustically that "this so-called Inspector did not stay 5 minutes, all told—at the house examined nothing and therefore does Know-nothing." He then turned his attention to the real intent of his letter—to identify the mastermind behind the report as none other than Agent Wright. According to Stephen, Wright had engineered the report to avenge the missionaries' recent complaint about school rations and Stephan's refusal to support his reappointment. He went on to pose the following rhetorical question: "But why this report made against us?"—to which he answered, "Major Wright did spit out his anger and Insp. Pierce picked it up as bill of fare for the Department, because Major Wright asked me to help him to get re-appointed and I did not do it, as I consider him a bigot of the first class and secondly: Fr. Perrig complaint about the rations and we brought the complaint before the Hon. Com. of Indian affairs which offended that bull headed english-man and therefore he calls Fr. Perrig 'senseless' in order to get revenge."[23]

In 1887, L. F. Spencer replaced Wright as Rosebud agent. In stark contrast with his predecessor, Spencer seems to have taken a largely hands-off approach to the mission and its school. Given the tribulations the missionaries had recently experienced under the highly interventionist Wright, one might think that Spencer's attitude of benign neglect would have suited them just fine. Nevertheless, Digmann complained that "the mission's success could have been greater if we had had an agent taking more interest in our school."[24]

In the spring of 1889 news began circulating around Rosebud that Spencer's days as agent were numbered. On the chance that Stephan could peddle his influence in Washington to help choose his replacement, Digmann reminded the BCIM director of the importance of finding someone sympathetic with Catholic missionary work: "Now, Rev. Dear Father," he wrote, "you know how much depends on it for our school, to get an Agent who is willing and able to support us by his authority, and not to keep us down as close as possible." Lest Stephan be at a loss for a suitable candidate, Digmann suggested that the reservation's present freight agent, who, "though no-Catholic," might fill the bill as he was not "preoccupied by prejudice against our Church."[25]

Digmann's counsel notwithstanding, by July the Indian Office had selected Spencer's successor. The news must have sent shock waves through the Saint Francis missionary community, for the new agent was none other than J. George Wright, the son of former agent James Wright. "Some have already told me two years ago," Digmann fretted, "that he hated every brick and board of our school, being a strong Episcopalian."[26]

Contrary to their expectations, the Catholic missionaries found the younger Wright to be generally genial and fair in his treatment of their school. Writing of the agent's retirement in 1896, the Franciscan house historian commented that "Major Wright had been very friendly to the Mission. . . . a farewell party was given for him." A deep and abiding friendship also quickly developed between the missionaries and Wright's replacement, Charles McChesney. By 1897 the new agent had won the confidence of the missionaries by obtaining an increased enrollment for their school from the Indian Office, in spite of the recent opening of the government's own boarding facility. Concerning this increase, the Franciscan historian appreciatively noted that "during the course of this year the large boarding school at Rosebud was opened by the Government, but instead of decreasing the number of students at our school it only helped to increase it and the number rose above 200. After God we owe this increase to our new Agent, who although not Catholic is very kindly disposed towards the Mission."[27]

In spite of such friendships, conflicts between local Indian Office personnel and the missionaries continued to punctuate the history of federal-Catholic relations on the Rosebud. One of the most serious of these battles erupted over the Jesuit priests' access to Catholic students attending the government boarding school. In September 1898, Father Digmann requested permission from its new superintendent, John B. Tripp, to continue celebrating a monthly 6 A.M. Mass for the Catholic students. When Tripp insisted that Digmann hold his service at 10:30 A.M., the same time as the Congregationalists and Episcopal clergy performed their services, the priest protested that the new time might prove a hardship for the students, since church law forbade them from eating before receiving communion. Though expressing sympathy for Digmann's position, Tripp refused to reconsider his decision on the grounds that he was prohibited by federal law from demonstrating favoritism toward any denomination.

By the time Digmann next visited the school in October, Tripp had further hardened his position on the kind of religious service the priest could perform. He now insisted that he dispense with Mass altogether and instead perform a nonsectarian service appropriate for all Christians. Believing that the superintendent's new ruling infringed on the religious liberty of the school's Catholic students, Digmann protested, "Does the rule mean to rob the children of their faith or make heathens of them again?" Weighing Digmann's challenge, Tripp decided to allow him to celebrate Mass that day and then let the Indian commissioner rule on the case.[28]

Early in the controversy, Tripp had invited the Saint Francis Mission to build a chapel in the vicinity of the school where the Catholic students could fulfill their religious obligations. Although the superintendent's proposal seemed to offer a reasonable solution to the standoff, Digmann suspected that it might lead to the further erosion of Catholic presence within the school. When Digmann asked South Dakota bishop Thomas O'Gorman whether or not he should proceed with the chapel, the prelate tersely responded, "Drop building."[29]

In December 1898 the commissioner of Indian affairs affirmed Tripp's ruling prohibiting all sectarian services at the Rosebud boarding school. In protest Digmann declared, "Either I go [to the school] as a priest or not at all" and remained true to his pledge until 1903, when Archbishop Ireland secured permission from the federal Indian Office for Catholic priests to "have Mass, Confessions, Communion Service, Retreats" at government boarding schools.[30]

The missionaries' mistrust of local federal employees also characterized their attitude toward the constant parade of visiting Indian Office officials and representatives of Protestant-dominated, government-affiliated Indian welfare organizations, especially the Indian Rights Association. The religious feared that anti-Catholic forces within the Indian Office might exploit criticisms by these visitors to frustrate their work, such as challenging their periodic requests for increases in Saint Francis's enrollment or, worse yet, reducing the number of students already attending the school. When possible, the religious thus carefully prepared the school facilities and children to make a good impression on these guests.[31]

Such impression management was in full action when Commissioner Browning, author of the regulation limiting the authority of Indian parents to choose schools for their children, visited the mission in 1894. According to the Franciscans' historian, Father Digmann coaxed the sisters to be "as friendly and talkative as possible" to the commissioner and his entourage. She wrote, "At about half past one the whole force appeared, 30 or so in all. The children were all lined up in front of the buildings. . . . The visitors were generously greeted and feasted. The children entertained well. Mr. Browning was very well pleased and promised to do his best in Washington for St. Francis Mission."[32]

Regular visits by Indian Office school inspectors also caused the missionaries considerable anxiety. Memories of the debacle that resulted from Inspector Pierce's initial, critical evaluation of the school in 1886 no doubt fueled their concerns. Tensions ran especially high, however, in the spring of 1890 as the religious prepared for Elaine Goodale's visit. Goodale was no ordinary inspector but the supervisor of Indian education for the Catholics' archenemy, commissioner Thomas J. Morgan. She also spoke fluent Dakota and thus was capable of engaging monolingual Lakota speakers in unmediated and uncensored conversations regarding the missionaries and their work. Finally, and probably the missionaries' greatest concern, was Goodale's close ties with the Eastern Dakota Protestant missions, where she had spent several years as a teacher. They thus feared that her evaluations and recommendations regarding their work might bear the imprint of not only nativism but Protestant pedagogy as well.

Considering all their reasons for concern, the Saint Francis staff must have been pleasantly surprised by Goodale's generally favorable (if not ecstatic) evaluation of their school.[33] Among her chief criticisms were the facility's want of recreational and assembly rooms and the children's "free" use of Lakota on campus. She also recommended that Saint Francis adopt the Appleton Company's "Appletonic Readers" for English instruction. Since following Goodale's advice would have required substituting texts from the Catholic Benzinger Brother press with a series by a secular publishing house, Digmann sought to determine if there was anything in the Appletonic lessons that might be "injurious to a Catholic education." After about a month's investigation, he concluded that the Appleton series was "the most innocuous [of all such publications] as far as religious training is concerned."[34]

The missionaries' wariness of visitors is probably nowhere more evident than in Digmann's report on Herbert Welsh's tour of the mission in 1899. The Indian Rights Association secretary's visit occurred approximately two years after Congress had enacted the phase-out of federal tuition for sectarian boarding schools, and Digmann chafed at playing host to someone he deemed to be one of the prime instigators of this law. Despite his loathing of Welsh, the mission superior was apparently able to maintain his composure until the secretary began heaping praise on the school and staff. Dismissing Welsh's accolades as hypocrisy, the mission superior lashed back, "In good faith, invited by the government we have entered the field, erected these large buildings, saved the government yearly thousands of dollars and after all it seems to say: 'Darkey has done his services, darkey can go.'" Digmann went on to blame Protestant bigotry and the American Protective Association for the government's policy, evidently stunning Welsh to such an extent that he "suddenly broke off and said nothing more."[35]

As a general rule, the Saint Francis religious maintained a wary eye toward all Indian Office employees and Protestant reformers until they had actively demonstrated their goodwill toward their mission and school. They required that each incoming Indian commissioner, Rosebud agent, government school superintendent, visiting school inspector, and "friend of the Indian" win their trust and confidence. This already daunting task was, at times, rendered even more difficult by rumors concerning a particular official's character or appointment, such as when the former agent of Standing Rock Reservation, James McLaughlin, notified Digmann that the newly assigned agent, Edward Kelly (1905–9), had been chosen to "work against" the Saint Francis petition drive.[36] Even the behavior of long-trusted officials, such as the younger Wright, was subject to reappraisal if they gave the missionaries any reason the doubt their friendship.

In spite of the missionaries' deep-seated mistrust of the Indian Office, they were able to maintain cordial, even friendly relations with most of Rosebud's government personnel. Sometimes this harmonious spirit manifested itself in small, symbolic gestures, such as when agency officials and missionaries attended functions held at each other's schools; or when Agent Tripp's successor at the government boarding school proposed that he and Digmann exchange sacks of onions for bran as a sign of their mutual desire to "work together and help out without jealousy and envy." At other times this desire for cooperation was exhibited in more substantial ways, such as in the attempts by particularly friendly agents, such as the younger Wright and Charles McChesney, to look after the mission's economic and political interests when and where possible. When introducing McChesney to the missionaries Wright announced, "He will also take care of you, perhaps better than I but he could not take a greater interest in you than I." McChesney, in fact, made good on Wright's pledge—or example, when he hired a Jesuit brother to refurbish some of the agency's cottages or when he used $2,000 for "civilizing purposes" to have wells dug close to Saint Francis.[37]

The mission reciprocated such favors in numerous ways, including defending the reputations of friendly agents from attacks launched from both within and without the reservation. For example, in 1890 when the Indian Office suspended Wright the younger for supposedly "overfeeding" the Sicangus with government rations, Digmann appealed to BCIM director Stephan to use his influence to have the agent reinstated. "If it be true that Mr. Wright should have 'overfed' the Indians as 'they' say," Digmann declared, "I would be thankful to him because what 'they' call overfeeding is about what the Indians absolutely need to live."[38] On another occasion, when several Sicangu headmen told Digmann that they had ordered Wright to leave the Rosebud because he had reduced their pay for freighting goods, the priest not only sided with the agent but warned Wright that the Indians were "planning a kind of conjuration" against him. Often, this sort of support did not come without a price. For example, with the aforementioned "conjuration" occurring during the height of the mission's struggles with the Browning rule, Digmann put the agent on notice during a subsequent visit that "we [the Catholic missionaries] would always stand by [his] authority but could not yield an inch in principles and right of parents to their children."[39]

Despite the mutual desire and effort of most of the missionaries and Rosebud's federal employees to cooperate with each other, their institutionally defined roles and objectives often set them on a collision course. Though both religious and government personnel had (at least in principle) the interest of Sicangu civilization and Christianization at heart, differences in what their respective organizations defined as the appropriate means to these ends often drew battle lines between them. It was such differences of policy, rather than those of individual character and attitudes, that the Saint Francis religious considered the greatest obstacles to their work.

Indian Office Policies

During the decades after the Catholic Church's decision to participate in reform Indian policy, ripples from battles waged on high between the federal government and the BCIM often trickled down to individual missions, including Saint Francis. It should come as no surprise that the Saint Francis religious were especially concerned with the outcome of those conflicts that affected federal support for their school.

To appreciate the responses of mission superior Digmann and other Jesuits and Franciscans in the Saint Francis trenches, it is necessary to remember that most of the first generation of Saint Francis religious had fled Germany as a result of the staunchly Protestant Otto von Bismarck's Kulturkampf. With the horrors of state-sponsored persecution permanently etched in their memories, it is understandable that they would fear that American nativism could usher in similar results in their adopted country. Verbalizing this fear to fellow Jesuit Aloysius Bosch during one of the school's funding crises, Digmann wrote, "We talked over the school question and children. Unless God steps in we will have a 'Kulturkampf.' We are on the open road to it."[40]

One of the first such crises was Commissioner Browning's 1896 ruling on school assignments. The missionaries interpreted this order both as a Protestant-inspired attempt to upend the constitutional right of Catholic Indian parents to send their children to a parochial school and as an Indian Office ploy to drain their school's enrollment. Fr. Louis Goll wrote, "When a day school was not filled to its capacity, a policeman would come and take the child away from the mission where their parents had placed it, and force it to attend the day school." He added that "Indians complained just: 'They treat us like dogs whose pups you take away.'"[41]

Dangers to Saint Francis's enrollment came from both inside and outside the reservation. In 1896 an exasperated Digmann wrote, "It is remarkable how the fight for children is renewed every year. Agent McChesney showed himself fair and well meaning but his predecessor [Wright] had built so many day schools and they had to be filled and kept up running."[42] In addition to making a priority of filling the Rosebud's day schools, the Browning rule also permitted the Rosebud agent to transfer students from Saint Francis to off-reservation schools such as Genoa and Carlisle without first receiving their parents' permission.

As a result of lobbying efforts by the Catholic Church in 1902, Commissioner Jones rescinded or, more accurately, recast the Browning rule so that it no longer endangered the enrollments at Saint Francis and other sectarian Catholic Indian boarding schools. And though the modified ruling prohibited agents from transferring students from mission to government schools, it continued to permit such transfers from one government school to another. As Jones explained to BCIM director Ketcham:

> The abrogation of the "Browning Ruling" has been carried out in good faith, and the wishes of the parents relative to the enrollment of their children in the mission schools adhered to. . . . however . . . so far as the transfer of children from one government school to another government school, the abrogation of the "Browning Ruling" cuts no figure. The purpose of the ruling was in relation to mission schools, but, so far as day schools on the Rosebud Reservation are concerned, or, in fact, other reservations, the proper authorities of the government, in my judgment are the ones to decide which government school children shall attend.[43]

The Indian Office's modifications of Browning's original ruling succeeded, as intended, in silencing its Catholic critics, even though the revised policy still granted reservation agents the power to transfer children enrolled in government educational facilities at will. Given a surfeit of charity, it is possible to attribute the church's silence on this disparity to its fear that any further agitation on the matter might endanger the concessions it had won. A more likely explanation is that it resulted from the church's recognition of certain advantages it afforded Saint Francis and other Catholic Indian schools (see below).

At about the same time that Commissioner Jones was amending the Browning rule in favor of religious schools, he was pushing ahead with a revision of the 1896 law withdrawing federal tuitions from church-operated Indian schools, which would exacerbate the economic havoc of the original act. In 1901 he convinced Congress to terminate the distribution of government rations and clothing to schools covered by this measure, arguing that, even if this action were not part of the letter of the original law, it was certainly in its "spirit." Accordingly, when Saint Francis Mission sent a wagon to the Rosebud agency to collect its usual supply of student foodstuffs and clothing shortly before the start of the 1901–2 school year, it returned empty.

Reporting the withdrawal of government goods, the Franciscan house historian for 1901 nonchalantly recorded, "The Government has now stopped all rations and therefore our care of the children is without government assistance." Her dispassionate tone stands in sharp contrast to the mood of desperation found in mission treasurer E. M. Perrig's description of the situation to BCIM director Stephan: "Mr. Jones cut off all the rations for the children of St. Francis. . . . the attendance at St. Francis promises to be far in excess of former years, probably not much short of 240. . . . It is surely a puzzle to me how we should feed and clothe 240 children. . . . It took a great deal more money last year, when we received still the Indian rations. What will it be this year?"[44]

The government's termination of tuitions and goods required the missionaries to direct all their available resources to the support of the school. Even with the introduction of severe belt tightening, the survival of the school remained in doubt. "I [Digmann] had saved some money to build a little house for our own Community [Jesuits]. . . . But I have thrown up this money to keep up the school so far. Besides we have taken steps to sell some cattle. If we succeed, we may run the school till Christmas. But then, we have exhausted our resources—and in case we should have to close, must see, how to get traveling money for the Brothers and Sisters. I hope, however, that it will not come so far."[45]

Although prepared for the worst, Digmann clung to the hope that at their upcoming meeting on the Indian school crisis the American archbishops would rally the will and resources to save Saint Francis. "If the archbishops only take earnest action," he insisted, "a way can be found to maintain our schools at least till the end of the year. Within a year our real situation will be more known to the Catholics at large, and if systematically taken in hand they will respond." If, on the other hand, the archbishops voted to abandon the schools, Digmann believed that would sound the death knell for preserving and propagating Catholicism among the Lakotas and other American Indians. Contemplating the worst-case scenario, Digmann wrote, "If they [the archbishops] decide to drop the schools, and if the Church joins hands with the politicians instead of fighting for our Lord's least brethren's rights, the Indians of the U.S. will be doomed to fall back to their old, or be swallowed up by modern, heathenism. With our schools we would let slip out of our hands the most powerful lever to Christianize them and if we let it slip now, there is no hope that we will never get hold of them again."[46]

To Digmann's relief, the archbishops ultimately voted in favor of continuing Catholic Indian education, incorporating the Society for the Preservation of the Faith among Indian Children to supplement Mother Katherine Drexel's donations to the schools with contributions from the laity. It was through these gifts, augmented by money the priests collected from their "begging tours" to parishes in the eastern United States, that Saint Francis was able to stay open until 1907, when the federal government renewed tuitions for the school.

Although the missionaries were most vocal about federal initiatives that threatened the survival of their school, they also poured out their frustrations over policies that they believed stymied their efforts to civilize adult Sicangus. Among those impediments they found the most aggravating was the Indian Office's supposed tolerance, even encouragement, of savage customs. During a meeting with the agent in April 1900, Digmann reported that one of his Sicangu assistants complained, "Dress like an Indian and dance with them and you'll have them all at your feet." Glossing this comment, the priest explained that "it was bitter sarcasm; he meant to say, the Agent should use a stronger hand and abolish the old customs, hampering their progress. But what can the Agent do when the Commissioner does not back him."[47]

Only a week earlier, Digmann himself had expressed a similar complaint to Inspector McLaughlin during a meeting of Catholic Sicangus. Digmann speculated: "It would seem to me as if those in Washington do not want to civilize but to ex[t]irpate the Indians, so they let them go on with their old customs, dancing, giving away, feasting, etc. They do not abolish it by authority though the progressive ones themselves wish it." According to the priest, one Sicangu attending the gathering amplified his grievances, complaining that "the Commissioner and the Agent should push us forward; we so want it, but they favor the old customs." Far from defending the Indian Office against this accusation, McLaughlin acknowledged its general validity. At the same time, he completely exonerated the Rosebud's own Agent McChesney from any culpability, placing all the blame on Washington: "There is much truth in what he says, but the Commissioner never wanted to give an order to abolish dancing, not even when the Agency is for it. When I was Agent in Standing Rock, the Indians owned eighteen thousand head of cattle, now they are down to about only eight thousand. It is a pity that we have no second McChesney."[48]

Aside from accusing Indian Office officials of conspiring to kill off the Indians, the missionaries entertained the equally cynical notion that government employees obstructed Indian assimilation to safeguard their jobs. Tormented by the continuing withdrawal of federal money from the mission's school, Digmann related that "the old official interpreter of Captain Penny in Pine Ridge told me that the Agent had told him: 'The Indian Office does not want the Indians civilized and self-supporting because then many white people would lose their position and salary. There was too much money in it yet.'"[49]

Digmann demonstrated no qualms in identifying no less than Commissioner Morgan as the chief conspirator in the federal government's war against Indian progress. Citing the commissioner's directive ordering reservation agents to promote July Fourth celebrations to foster Indian patriotism, Digmann sarcastically remarked: "Years ago nobody thought of it that the Indians should celebrate the Fourth of July. Then, of course the Protestant Agents had to do something and whilst the government before with pharisaicle [z]eal tried to abolish the old heathen customs, it now revives them on the celebration of the fourth. Commissioner Morgan had issued a circular to the Indian Agents to instill patriotism in the Indians and have them celebrate the legal holidays especially the Fourth of July."[50]

In a report on his recent visit to a Sicangu camp for the 1894 edition of *Die Katholischen Missionen*, Father Hillig similarly depicted the impediment the Fourth of July celebration posed for Indian civilization. On that day one could see how clearly the reservation was between two factions: on one side the nonprogressives who "driven by their heathen instincts hike for miles to amuse themselves with their tribal comrades with the ridiculous remnants of a dying paganism"; on the other side those who, "led by mercy, come together under the shade of the mission, to rouse blossoming Christian belief in their hearts through reciprocal edification and advice . . . casting off their splendid hair accessories for their festivities, dress in European clothing; there is barely anything that reminds of the wild native, besides the darker skin color and other racial features."[51]

Evidently the so-called nonprogressives were not alone in their desire to honor Independence Day, for in August 1896 Catholic Sicangus in one community asked Digmann whether they should contribute to the collections for the next year's celebration. Bristling at this suggestion, the priest snapped, "The sooner you bury your old unprofitable customs of dancing and giving away, the better for you." When one Sicangu proposed that they begin the celebration with an opening prayer, Digmann dismissed this compromise, retorting, "A new patch on an old coat will not hold."[52]

As the years passed, the missionaries' stringent opposition to the celebration faded to the point of near nonexistence. Realizing that Sicangu Catholics would take part in the festivities despite their reproaches, the missionaries admonished them to refrain from dancing, giving away, and other "harmful" practices while there. During the opening years of the twentieth century, the priests moved beyond the Sicangus' earlier suggestion that they say an opening prayer by offering Mass at the fairgrounds for Catholic participants on Sunday mornings. By 1911 their resistance to the celebration had so softened that they allowed the school's brass band to perform at the gathering.[53]

In addition to their initial opposition to the Indian Office's Fourth of July policy, the missionaries vehemently attacked the permission it granted Buffalo Bill Cody and other "wild west show" impresarios to hire Sicangus to join their troupes. They believed that the Indians' participation in such spectacles not only fostered the survival of primitive traditions but, worse yet, enticed participants away from their primary obligations to their families, farms, and church. Digmann was so adamantly opposed to such shows that, while undergoing treatments at a spa near the Jesuit provincial house in Saint Louis, he refused to visit a group of Rosebud and Pine Ridge Lakotas who were performing at the Pan American Exposition in that city. "The Indians going to shows," he told the superior, "were not worth to be preached at."[54] Complying with his vow of obedience, Digmann soon yielded to his superior's request and agreed to "preach at" the Lakota performers.

In view of these attacks on the government for fostering Sicangu "savagery," it is ironic that the missionaries demonstrated no compunction about asking Lakotas to "play Indian" when it served their own purposes. Thus, when the Franciscans' mother general, Camilla Lutz, visited the mission in 1902, the fathers allowed the boys to wear native dress and perform Lakota dances. On another occasion, Digmann attempted to pressure deacons Eugene Little and Joseph Horncloud to let loose with a war whoop to please one of the bishops at a conference they were attending. According to the priest, in spite of his encouragement both refused, stating "We did not come here to play Indians; let them go to Buffalo [Bill's] west to hear it."[55]

The Catholic missionaries also criticized the federal government for failing to prosecute Sicangus who were living together without benefit of wedlock or were in polygamous unions. They considered both forms of cohabitation illegal as well as immoral, often referring to the former as adultery and the latter, as already discussed, bigamy. In his reports to the commissioner for 1900 and 1902, Digmann took the federal government to task for requiring monogamy for Sicangus but then failing to impose sanctions against those who refused to abide by this regulation. He later observed, "With carnal people only spiritual weapons will not work; persuasion alone will not be effectual for the long run. On the other hand, our Indians have great accommodating qualities to the inevitable, they will bend under a strong hand of the law."[56]

The missionaries considered the government's unwillingness to punish "adulterers" and "bigamists" as symptomatic of its laxity in routing out Indian savagery. In 1905 a nearly dispirited Digmann bewailed the disastrous effects that this permissiveness was having on Sicangu missionization: "Whiskey and women stealing, breaking into houses, quarrelling and even killing and licentiousness seem to be on the increase and authorities 'let it go.' Our preaching is not minded but laughed at. Sometimes the thought steals upon me 'God has abandoned this people.' But no! Try again!"[57]

The missionaries reserved their harshest criticisms of government ineptitude for what they deemed the Indian Office's ineffective strategies for rendering Sicangus self-supporting. Almost all of these methods were rooted in the policy of allotment, which was initiated on the Rosebud in 1889. Although the Saint Francis religious were passionate supporters of individualizing reservation lands and advised their church members to file their applications early in order to receive the choicest tracts, they harbored strong misgivings about how the program was administered. Their most serious objection concerned the Indian Office's continued distribution of per-capita payments, rations, and supplies to able-bodied Sicangus, which they believed undercut their incentive for requesting allotments. Why would Indians take up the plow, the religious pondered, when the government fed and clothed them without their lifting a finger?[58]

Given the missionaries' criticism of government largess, one might assume that they would have celebrated Commissioner Morgan's 1890 directive that cut rations to Indians in order to force them to work. In fact, however, they complained that this order was not only ineffectual but also cruel because of the Indian Office's failure to provide sufficient equipment for all those Sicangus who wished to farm. In September of that year, Digmann sent Stephan a translation of a statement by Chief Big Turkey describing the great suffering caused by the government's "starvation" rations. In an accompanying letter, the priest transmitted the headman's accusation that he and his camp "did not get wagons, plows, yokes of oxen, cow and etc enough." Continuing in his own words, the priest wrote, "There are plenty young men that now would work, if they had a possibility to start. But how shall they earn money on the Reservation, with their fellow Indians, to buy them a wagon etc. The hunger," he conceded, "has to help to civilize them and make them work: that is all right. To see them, however, willing to work and no chance to do so, on account of want of implements in sufficient quantity, is a great pity."[59]

By October 2 the combination of inadequate rations and insufficient equipment had forced many Sicangus to resort to desperate measures. Assessing the situation for Stephan, Digmann wrote: "All I wish is they would get plenty of wagons, plows, etc. issued so as to enable them to make a living for themselves. But what is 50 wagons to be issued this fall among 45 bands! The other trouble is the stubbornness of some bands that have got up a new kind of sacred dance and prayer [the Ghost Dance] and refused the Agent [Wright] obedience, to quit. . . . When I asked them to submit, they said they could not do it just then, because it would need a full counsel." In less than a month, the situation had so deteriorated that Digmann again wrote the BCIM director warning of a new Indian war: "At present, the rations being cut down so awfully, it is indeed no easy task for a poor agent to keep them quiet. All over the Sioux agencies they are now excited, have their Ghost Spirit-dance and sing war songs. When the grass is getting green again, they want to go on the warpath. Hunger is an awful power, sharpening or conjuring up again the warlike spirit of the Sioux. It seems the Minnesota massacre has been forgotten. The circumstances then were very much the same as now."[60]

In the immediate aftermath of the Ghost Dance and Wounded Knee massacre on December 29, 1890, the Indian Office increased both rations and its delivery of farm equipment to the Rosebud. As years passed, however, both the missionaries and government officials began to entertain the idea that many Sicangus' aversion to farming was based on economic wisdom rather than savage stubbornness.[61] "No one can blame them for not taking to agriculture, after their efforts in that line proved failures, owing to the scarcity of seasonable rain," Digmann wrote to Ketcham in 1902. "Even cattle-raising," he continued, "is impossible for those who have their allotments on tableland, without any running water or even wells for 30 or more miles."[62]

Although finally acknowledging that the Rosebud was climatically unsuited for agriculture, neither the Indian Office nor the Catholic mission completely curtailed preaching the gospel of farming on the reservation.[63] By 1902, however, the repugnance that most Sicangus continued to demonstrate to tilling the soil had at last compelled the government to supplement its efforts at agricultural training with a program of community wage work, similar to the one that would be developed in the 1930s under Franklin Roosevelt. Digmann had, in fact, advocated such an initiative as early as 1900, advising Agent McChesney that the government should use the money it saved by cutting rations "to give [the Sicangus] work and wages on the Reservation: to make good roads, work towards irrigations. This," he had argued, "would improve their country and work doubly so towards making them self-supporting."[64]

There is little wonder why Digmann was thrilled when news of the government's plan to institute a mandatory wage program on the Rosebud reached him in 1902. On March 16 the priest notified Ketcham that from

the 1st of May work and wages are promised to all able-bodied Indians of our reserve. Upon the whole the measure has been hailed with joy by them. Had the government adopted this plan some 10 or 15 years ago they would be more advanced. All our preaching by word and example that they should earn their bread in the sweat of their face, has surely achieved much in this time, but it has not the proper and desired effect, as long as they are fed, without moving a finger for it: "they have to be pinched into it," as our agent says.[65]

On June 16, Digmann similarly wrote that the "working scheme of one dollar and twenty-five cents works better than expected. In a short time now more work is done than all the time since the Reservation existed. It proves," he concluded, "that the Indian is not lazy when he sees ready cash but only shirks work 'for nothing,' failure of crops even white people left their homesteads before they had 'proved up.'"[66]

Despite Digmann's initial enthusiasm for the government's works project, within a few years his support had flagged when the program proved to be rife with problems all its own. In his report to the commissioner for 1905 he wrote that "the system upon the whole has worked blessings for them. Still the missionary has often occasion to remind them of it—that receiving wages without doing the expected amount of work is equal to stealing." He complained that, "again, not a few spent the surplus of their earnings in liquor instead of laying it up for wintertime. Their homes and stock necessarily suffer by their being absent for a long time, and unscrupulous individuals take advantage of it. . . . We should never forget these Indians are now in a stage of transition, and many of the evils they are now going through by other barbarous tribes in their efforts to become civilized."[67]

Added to the aforementioned problems, the project also created difficulties for the missionaries' practice of their various ministries. In the same report Digmann notified the agent, "Our missionary work has been somewhat hampered by the way the Indians are employed in the different work camps spread all over the reserve." The priests were obliged to incorporate journeys to these workstations in their normal round of ministerial visits to the far-flung *tiyospaye*. Not only did these new assignments add days of travel to the priests' already exhausting schedules, but they presented difficulties of a material nature that they had not encountered since the earliest days of the mission. Describing his recent visit to a work camp on White Thunder Creek, Digmann observed, "No table [was] to be found on the wide prairie; some cracker boxes put on a trunk served as [a] table to put on the portable altar."[68]

The World and the Devil

In addition to the difficulties stemming from government policies and inter-denominational hostilities, the Saint Francis religious considered setbacks arising from the destructive forces of nature as major impediments to their goals of Sicangu Christianization and civilization. To the periodic droughts that devastated missionary attempts to induce the Rosebud's Lakotas to farm must be added the economic losses that the mission sustained owing to these dry spells. The missionaries were frequently forced to take out loans from the BCIM, their religious orders, or financial institutions to buy the produce needed to feed themselves and their students. Informing BCIM director Stephan of the mission's crop failure of 1890, Digmann stated, "As our crop in potatoes was very poor, and turnips, carrots also were a complete failure, you will understand that my purse had to make up for all this."[69]

When moisture did arrive, it sometimes took forms that were more of a curse than a blessing. During the summer and fall, hailstorms often descended upon the mission, leaving smashed windows and decimated crops in their wake. Describing the aftermath of one such tempest, the Franciscan house historian for 1892 wrote:

> The Sisters were at recreation when suddenly an uncanny stillness pervaded the house and everything became very dark. Within a few minutes the storm raged furiously. Hailstones fell as big as hen's eggs. Any moment it seemed the roof would be torn off. One window pane after another was broken. The Sisters made their way to the chapel and prayed with outstretched arms. There they found the superior Father Florentine Digman, S.J., before the Blessed Sacrament. Over 500 window panes were broken in this storm. The garden was greatly damaged.[70]

Though welcomed for their rain, thunderstorms also brought lightning that occasionally destroyed mission property. The Franciscan house history of 1911 noted: "The new school year began with a little cross. On the first Friday of September during morning prayers a storm arose during which the lightning struck the hay pile and set it burning. About 150 tons of hay were burned up representing a damage of two to three hundred dollars."[71] Since a bountiful supply of hay was generally needed as winter feed for the mission's herds of cattle and horses, the religious found it necessary to compensate for such losses by purchasing silage from Indians or non-Indians in the vicinity.

Besides destroying haystacks, lightning sometimes ignited grass fires that swept across the prairies surrounding the mission. News of such fires terrified the religious. After a few years' exposure to Dakota's blazing summer heat, the mission's wood frame buildings had been transformed into tinder. What is more, unless immediately contained, prairie fires could spread in a rapid and unpredictable fashion, especially with the presence of strong Dakota winds intensifying the fury and scope of their flames.

Though generally ignited by lightning, prairie fires were at times the product of human rather than natural agency. In 1908 a woman scattered hot coals on the grass near their camp, starting a fire that spread through a large portion of the surrounding area. The following year, government workers who were attempting to create a fireguard lost control of the burn; the ensuing fire consumed 750 tons of the mission's hay.[72]

Whatever their origins, news of prairie fires in the vicinity of Saint Francis filled the missionaries with terror. This fear is vividly displayed in the following excerpt from the Franciscan house history for 1912:

> On the 22nd of November about 2 o'clock of the afternoon, we heard that a prairie fire had broken out several miles from the Mission. . . . Soon we were convinced of the approaching danger by the rising clouds of smoke. A strong wind arose which added to the difficulty of combating the flames. It spread with such voracious rapidity that toward five o'clock the whole mission was ringed in with fire. It was a terrible sight to behold the fiery serpents leap up on the horizon and whipped by the storm with lightning speed; coming nearer and nearer to the Mission.[73]

All prairie fires were a source of great anxiety for the Saint Francis religious, but the fires over which they agonized the most were those that disgruntled students occasionally set within the mission compound. The most destructive case of arson, which occurred in 1916, is the subject of the final chapter. The earliest such incident took place in April 1893, only seven years after the opening of the mission. The Franciscan house historian for that year identified two girls who had been denied permission to attend a dance in the village as the arsonists. "While the children were filing in for Mass," she wrote, "two sneaked back to the dormitory. There a sack of straw was opened and a match put to the straw. The two then went back to Mass. No disturbance was noted during Mass or during breakfast. But when the children returned to the dormitory to set things in order the news of fire spread about the house. One bed that was burning was after some difficulty removed, and the fire was easily gotten under control."[74]

The fire that destroyed the new boys' building in 1911 was a much more costly and alarming affair. Recounting the event, Digmann wrote, "We [the missionaries] tried first pails and engine but the smoke was so thick and choking and the fire spread with such rapidity that it could not be saved. Bedding and desks were thrown out of the windows but all new clothing and blankets fell prey to the flames. Nothing insured. Loss about thirty thousand dollars. A 'cry for help' in the papers and in letters brought nearly five thousand dollars." Equally disturbing were the missionaries' initial and lingering suspicions that some students intentionally set the building afire. Concerning these suspicions Digmann stated:

> Whether it started through a defective chimney or stovepipe or was set we never found out. For the latter there were some reasons; already some weeks ago there was a fire detected in a closet where the brooms were kept but it was found out in time. Mr. D. told me that of late L.M., Jr. had said some boys wanted to set fire to the house. The more probable opinion is that it started through a chimney and that had settled and had a rupture and the rafters in the roof caught fire. Mr. P. who had rheumatism and had his stove red hot was at the time not in his room but in the classroom.[75]

Saint Francis was not the only mission on the Rosebud to be beset by fires. In August 1910, Saint Mary's Episcopalian boarding school burned to the ground. Digmann reported that he first heard of this event when testing the new phone system the government had installed at all schools on the reservation. Although inspectors quickly attributed the blaze to a gasoline explosion, the priest traced its origins to another, higher source. "One or two of our girls," he stated, "had expressed their wish to go to that school. I had told their parents: 'If you allow it, you need not come to confession and the Sacraments. Divine Providence showed her hand.'"[76]

The Saint Francis religious at times also ascribed their own tribulations to divine providence. Unlike the trials that plagued the Protestants and their other adversaries, however, they seldom interpreted such "crosses" as signs of God's displeasure with their work. Rather, they believed them to be the Lord's way of testing their fidelity to him and their mission exactly the way he had tested Job.[77]

This sort of theodicy did not always suffice to keep the missionaries from capitulating to despair or to questioning why God permitted the "evil one" such free reign to frustrate their work. Writing to Bishop Busch of Lead in 1913, Digmann observed that "the devil is loose in S.D. Murder, attempt of suicide, adultery, civil marriages first to try how they would get along, live in sin, etc.," to which the latter responded, "We have to work our salvation in fear and trembling."[78]

Notwithstanding the seemingly endless succession of their trials, the missionaries continued to believe that they would prove no match for God's plan to establish a Sicangu Catholic church. Though acknowledging that they might, on occasion, stumble under the weight of these crosses, the religious held fast to the conviction that God would eventually reward their fidelity to his work with success.

When attempting to understand the early Catholic mission on the Rosebud, the importance of the missionaries' assumption that the obstacles they encountered originated from outside their paradigm and were God's way of testing their resolve cannot be overestimated. They believed that questioning this paradigm's methods and goals constituted an act of disobedience not only toward their superiors but also against God's plan for Sicangu salvation. And so, despite the lackluster results of their work on the Rosebud, they continued to struggle on with unflagging dedication to the missionary status quo.

CHAPTER ELEVEN

Pre-reservation Lakota Religion and the Reception of Early Catholic Mission

Lakotas conceived, organized, and celebrated their spirituality according to a set of categories that was at once logically coherent and fluid. The existential core of this system was their wonderment at a profoundly mysterious universe. Any object, being, process, or idea capable of generating this experience they referred to as *wakan*, with the term "Wakan Tanka"— literally "Great Wonder"—reserved for the most unfathomable and awesome of these marvels.

Lakotas traced the *wakan* characteristics and powers of various phenomena to the potency (*ton*) of their spiritual essences (*sicun*). According to Oglala holy man Sword, "Every object in the world has a spirit and this spirit is *wakan*. Thus the spirit of the tree or things of that kind, while not the spirit of man, are also *wakan*."[1]

For Lakotas the most wondrous of all beings were those spiritual powers— the Wakanpi or Wakan kin—whom they considered as the source of all *ton*. They were, accordingly, Wakan Tanka or Taku Wakan, terms which, when understood at their most abstract, encompassed all that was at once divine and mysterious.[2]

The Structure and Power of the of Lakota Cosmos
Notwithstanding the fundamental inscrutability of the Wakanpi, Lakotas advanced many tenets concerning their collective and individual nature.

Among these beliefs was that the Wakanpi created and sustained everything on earth, including mankind, whose circumstances and behavior they scrupulously surveyed. According to Sword, the Wakanpi were all things that were above mankind and "greater than mankind in the same way that mankind is greater than animals."[3]

Lakotas also held certain convictions concerning the moral proclivities and attributes of the Wakanpi. Though many of these beings were believed to be benevolent and nurturing, others were thought of as merciless and wicked. Regarding this divergence Little Wound once observed that "mankind should think about the *Wakanpi* and do what will please them. They should think of them as they think of their fathers and mothers. But the evil *Wakanpi* they should think of as an enemy."[4] From the Lakota perspective, the ethical character of a Wakan being inevitably influenced the *wakan*, spiritual power, it generated and dispensed. The assumption shared by many anthropologists that *wakan* was an ethically neutral force, comparable to electricity, thus appears to be in fundamental variance with the Lakota concept. As Raymond DeMallie has observed, the *wakan* that was produced and inhered in Wakan kin was, like them, predisposed for good or evil.[5] What is more, the power of the good Wakanpi was regarded as more potent than that of the bad Wakan beings.

Lakota holy men addressed the good Wakanpi as the Tobtob kin—the "Four times Four." This esoteric designation reflected the belief that they were sixteen in number, constituting four hierarchical divisions of four gods each. In order of rank these divisions were Wakan Akantu (the Superior Wakan) to which belonged Wi (Sun), Skan (Energy), Maka (Earth), and Inyan (Rock); the Wakan Kolaya (the associates or kindred of the Superior Wakan), namely, Han Wi (Moon), Tate (Wind), Wohpe (the Beautiful One/ White Buffalo Calf Maiden), and Wakinyan (Thunder Beings); the Wakan Kuya (the lower or subordinate gods), comprising Tatanka (Buffalo Bull), Hunumpa (Two Leggeds), Tate Tob (Four Winds), and Yumni (Whirlwind); and the Wakanlapi (spirit kind or Wakan-like), Nagi (Spirit), Niya (Ghost; Life), Nagila (Spirit-like), and Sicun (the Potency of a Wakan being).[6]

According to Sword, the good Wakanpi could also be divided into two classes: Wakan Tanka, which comprised the four Superior Wakan and all of their kindred, and Taku Wakan, which together embraced the subordinate Wakan and the Wakanlapi. He and other holy men further believed that half of the good Wakanpi were *ton ton* (possessed physical attributes), whereas the other half were *ton ton sni* (possessed no physical attributes). Half of those deities with physical form were thought to be *ton ton yan* (visible) and half *ton ton yan sni* (invisible).[7]

In addition to the language of hierarchy, holy men also drew upon the terminology and concepts of kinship when discussing the Tobtob kin. They therefore spoke of these gods as constituting an extended family with the same statuses and roles as the members of a Lakota *tiyospaye*. Whether the holy men intended such discussions to be understood literally or metaphorically is not certain. What is clear, however, is that they served as a warrant for the moral dialectic that Lakotas believed existed between their own and sacred society. Thus, on the one hand, the notion that the Tobtob kin participated in a kinship system, comprising complementary rights and obligations much like their own, served to affirm the ethical character of these gods. On the other hand, it functioned to confirm and sanction the norms and values of Lakota society.

From the testimony available, it is not entirely clear how the evil Wakanpi fit into this system. As previously noted, the Lakotas took for granted the existence of many malevolent gods. However, as Sword once observed, unlike the gods of the Tobtob kin, they were not united as a family and they were unclassified. Their leader was Iya, a monster of enormous magnitude who was the third being created after the sky and the earth. Sword and other holy men held that, despite his constant harassment of humanity, Iya was one of the Wakan Tanka. However, neither he nor his evil associates were members of the Tobtob kin. "Tobtob," Lone Bear stated, "is all kinds of good spirits. It is Four-times-four. . . . The bad spirits are not of the Tobtob." With specific reference to Iya, Short Feather asserted, "Iya is a Great Spirit [Wakan Tanka]. He is a bad spirit. He does not take part in the council of the Great Spirits. He is jealous of the Sioux and tries to do them harm all the time."[8]

The exclusion of the evil Wakanpi from the company of the Tobtob kin begins to make sense once one remembers that the Lakotas thought of the latter as an extended family. The disharmony and anguish the malefactors spawned would have certainly constituted grounds for exiling them from this sacred family.[9] Bereft of kinship ties, the ultimate horror for a Lakota, the evil Wakanpi descended into a state of chaos, reflected in their "unclassified" status.

The Lakotas' well-populated pantheon has often been used as a basis for categorizing them as polytheists. Notwithstanding the general problems plaguing this classification, the manner in which Lakotas subsumed their manifold gods under ever widening rings of ontological identity separately and collectively referred to as Wakan Tanka renders it an especially unfit label for their religion. The following exchange, taken from a conversation between James R. Walker and the Oglala holy man Finger on the Pine Ridge Reservation in 1914, offers an excellent portal through which to view the metaphysical intricacies of Wakan Tanka:

> [Walker]: Is *Skan, Wakan Tanka?*
> [Finger]: Yes.
> [Walker]: Are *Wi* and *Skan* one and the same?
> [Finger]: No.
> [Walker]: Are they both *Wakan Tanka?*
> [Finger]: Yes.
> [Walker]: Are there any other [*W*]*akan* that are *Wakan Tanka?*
> [Finger]: Yes. *Han Wi*, the Moon; *Tate*, the Wind; *Wakiyan*, the Winged; and *Wohpe*, the Beautiful Woman.
> [Walker]: Are there any others that are *Wakan Tanka?*
> [Finger]: No.
> [Walker]: Then there are eight *Wakan Tanka*, are there?
> [Finger]: No, there is but one.
> [Walker]: You have named eight and say there is but one. How can that be?
> [Finger]: That is right. I have named eight. There are four, *Wi, Skan, Inyan*, and *Maka*. These are the *Wakan Tanka.*
> [Walker]: You named four others, the Moon, the Wind, Winged, and the Beautiful Woman and said they were *Wakan Tanka*, did you not?
> [Finger]: Yes. But these four are the same as the *Wakan Tanka*. The Sun and the Moon are the same, the *Skan* and the Wind are the same, Earth and the Beautiful Woman are the same. These eight are only one. The shamans know how this is, but the people do not know. It is *wakan* (a mystery).[10]

Although Finger clearly indicated that Wakan Tanka is composed of the eight-in-four-in-one, Sword conferred that designation on *all* the good Wakanpi who constitute the Tobtob kin: "Mankind is permitted to pray to the *Wakan* beings. If their prayer is directed to all the good *Wakan* beings they should pray to *Wakan Tanka*; but if the prayer is offered only to one of these beings, then the one addressed should be named. . . . When a Lakota prays to *Wakan Tanka* he prays to the earth and to the rock and all the other good *Wakan* beings."[11]

In an attempt to clarify his testimony, Sword suggested that although "*Wakan Tanka* is like sixteen different persons . . . each person is *kan*. Therefore they are all only the same as one." Here Sword employed the word *kan* to signify "strange," "wonderful," "incomprehensible," or "sacred." When joined with the prefix *wa* to form *wa-kan*, the term acquired additional and complex meanings. It could be used as an adjective to describe something with sacred or mysterious potency. Alternatively, one could employ the term as a proper noun, as in Wakan Kin or the plural Wakanpi. In this nominative sense, it signified those spiritual beings who, by their very nature, *were* or *did kan*. To the extent that the being and actions of all gods classed as Tobtob kin possessed this character, they were Wakan Tanka.[12]

One additional patch must be added to the already complex quilt. From the perspective of Lakota epistemology, anything that defied human explanation was considered Wakan Tanka. As Good Seat observed, "When anyone did something that no one understood, this was *wakan*. If the thing done was what no one could understand, it was *Wakan Tanka*. How the world was made is *Wakan Tanka*. How the sun was made is *Wakan Tanka*. How men used to talk to the animals and birds was *Wakan Tanka*. Where the spirits and ghosts are is *Wakan Tanka*."[13]

The polysemy associated with the term Wakan Tanka also typified many other categories of Lakota cosmology. For example, the designation Taku Wakan, like Wakan Tanka, was applied to various groupings of gods and potencies that Lakotas believed to be simultaneously identical and different. What is more, in many instances the terms Wakan Tanka and Taku Wakan were interchangeable.

As the preceding analysis makes clear, this fluidity of theological terminology was by no means the result of conceptual sloppiness on the part of Lakota holy men. Rather, it was a reflection of an ontology in which "the one" and "the many" were two faces of the same conceptual coin. Because Lakotas posited that each of the Wakanpi possessed a distinct personality and attributes yet constituted a single embodiment of a greater, intangible unity, they could speak of it as both the same as and different from the others.

The capacity to be at once singular and plural was among the many marvels that rendered the Wakanpi incomprehensible, or *kan*. Yet, though the Lakotas took the "otherness" of their gods for granted, they nonetheless assumed that their relationship with them operated according to a rationally ordered set of rights and responsibilities. This set was based on two fundamental presuppositions. One was the Lakotas' belief that the mysterious life force *ton* that linked them to all worldly creatures also united them to their gods. The ontological chasm between God and creation in Jewish and Christian theologies was thus completely absent in Lakota religious thought. The *ton* was the basic property of the one or multiple Sicunpi possessed by all material and immaterial phenomena. Enouncing a basic tenet of Lakota anthropology, One Star stated, "A *Sicun* is like a spirit. It is the *ton ton sni*, that is, it is immortal and cannot die. A Lakota may have many *Sicunpi*, but he always has one. It is *Wakan*, that is, it is like *Wakan Tanka*."[14] Sword meanwhile noted that Sicun

> signifies the spirit of man. This spirit is given to him at birth to guard him against the evil spirits and at death it conducts him to the land of the spirits, but does not go there itself. In the course of his life a man may choose other *Sicun*. He may choose as many as he wishes but such *Sicun* do not accompany him after death; if he has led an evil life no *Sicun* will accompany him. . . . When the Lakota chooses a *Sicun* such as the *Ton* of a *Wakan* or it may be the *Ton* of anything. . . . One's *Sicun* may be in any object as in a weapon or even in things to gamble with or in a medicine. But the *Sicun* that a man receives at birth is never found in anything but his body. This *Sicun* is like one's shadow.[15]

The Lakotas also assumed that their relationship with the Wakanpi was founded upon the values and norms of kinship. One major source for this assumption was the sacred narrative of Pte San Win (White Buffalo Calf Woman). According to this account, many years ago when the Sans Arc Lakotas were on the brink of starvation, the Wakanpi took pity on them and sent Wohpe in the form of Pte San Win with the gift of a sacred pipe. Meeting in council with a representative camp, Pte San Win addressed them as follows:

> My relatives, brothers and sisters: *Wakan Tanka* has looked down, and smiles upon us this day because we have met as belonging to one family. The best thing in a family is good feeling toward every member of the family. I am proud to become a member of your family—a sister to you all. The sun is your grandfather, and he is the same to me. Your

tribe has the distinction of being always very faithful to promises, and of possessing great respect and reverence toward sacred things. It is known also that nothing but good feelings prevails in the tribe, and that whenever any member has been found guilty of committing any wrong, that member has been cast out and not allowed to mingle with the other members of the tribe. For all these good qualities in the tribe you have been chosen as worthy and deserving of all good gifts. I represent the Buffalo tribe, who has sent you this pipe. You are to receive this pipe in the name of all the common people [Lakotas]. Take it and use it according to my directions.[16]

Through this act of *hunkaye*, or adoption, the entire Lakota people were made relatives of the Buffalo people and, by extension, the family of all the Tobtob Kin. As DeMallie and Lavenda have observed, "What is important here were the moral obligations of mutual respect and support that this relationship automatically prescribed. Significantly the term *cekiya*, 'to pray,' or call out, also means 'to address by kinship term.' Thus, the method of prayer was the invocation of relationship."[17]

The Lakotas' fundamental duty to the good Wakanpi was to perform acts that were to their liking. According to Little Wound, "Mankind should please [the good Wakanpi] in all things. . . . They should be pleased by songs and ceremonies. Gifts should be made to them. . . . Mankind should think about the *Wakanpi* and do what will please them. They should think of them as they think of their fathers and mothers."[18] As befitting good relatives, the Wakanpi were obligated to reciprocate these favors by answering the Lakotas' petitions for food and health.

Lakotas believed that one of the principal means through which gods transmitted knowledge or made their desires known to humans was visions. Visionary experiences might be solicited, as in the case of *hanbleceya* (vision quest), or might be unsought and freely given. In either case it was thought that Wakan beings generally delegated one of their *akicita* (messengers or soldiers) to transmit the vision to its appointed recipient. This vision usually took a form similar to a dream.[19] Some visions were interpreted as warnings of potential crises. Others notified individuals of duties, usually of a socially beneficial nature, which a god expected them to undertake. If these responsibilities entailed talents of an extraordinary nature, the god or its messenger would impart the necessary *ton* to the "dreamer" at the time of the vision or during a ceremony held shortly thereafter. This transfer of spiritual essence rendered its recipient an especially esteemed and useful member of Lakota society. He or she was considered *wakan*.

Among the most important of these powerful individuals were the *wicasa wakan*, Lakota shamans or holy men. It was the special function of *wicasa wakan* to serve as the representatives of the good Wakanpi, a responsibility that carried with it several vital roles.[20] They served as the custodians of the sacred esoteric language of the Wakan Tanka. In this capacity they were obliged to *yuiyeska*, or translate, the will of the gods to the rest of a camp's members. Since remaining on good terms with the Wakanpi required observing their dictates, it was necessary for those who had received visions to consult a shaman in order to know precisely what was expected of them.

In addition to their custodianship of the sacred language, shamans also acted as the stewards of all the major ceremonies. Their source for this obligation is found in several Lakota narratives, most of which concern Tokahe, the First or Wise One. According to these accounts, when the Lakotas' ancestors, the Ikce Wicasa, first emerged from beneath the earth, they were ignorant of ways pleasing to the gods. In their mercy, the Wakanpi sent Tokahe—like Pte San Win a member of the Buffalo Nation—to provide them with customs befitting their new status as Wicasa Akantula, or "people on the surface." After helping the Ikce establish these usages, Tokahe trained two young men—Sunk (Dog) and Pahin (Porcupine)—to administer those ceremonies that were especially *wakan*. He taught them also how to interpret and speak the will of the gods, urging them to share this holy knowledge only with worthy and upright individuals. As the recipients of this wisdom, Sunk and Pahin became the first Lakota holy men.

An example of the pivotal role shamans played in Lakota religious life is found in the process through which an individual chose a *sicun*. According to Sword, "A shaman should direct a person in the choice of his *Sicun*. . . . When one chooses a *Sicun* he should give a feast and have a shaman to conduct the ceremony, for no one can have the knowledge necessary to conduct a ceremony unless he has learned it in a vision."[21] So great, in fact, was the shamans' control over ceremonies that they might prohibit or change any of them if such a deviation were presented as the will of Wakan Tanka.

Perhaps the most dramatic marker for the great power that Lakotas attributed to shamans was their belief that they could impart the *sicun* and its associated *ton* of their spiritual helpers to others (*yuwakanpi*), thereby making them *wakan*. It was through this transmission of power that most shamans acquired the capacity and tools necessary to perform their functions. According to Sword:

> [A] *Wicasa wakan* . . . is made by other shamans by ceremony and teaching that which a shaman should know. He is made holy by the ceremony so that he can communicate with *Wakan Tanka*, and the ceremony also prepares his outfit and gives to it supernatural powers. This outfit may be anything that has a spirit imparted to it so that it will have all the powers of the spirit and all to cover and keep it in. This outfit is his *wasicun* . . . and it is very holy, and should be considered as a God. It must be prayed (over) for its power.[22]

Lakotas believed that many shamans obtained their power, knowledge, and tools to doctor through this sort of initiatory rite. The mysterious force—the *ton*—contained in their *wasicun* played a key role in the ceremonies of these curers. They were thereby distinguished from *pejuta wicasa* (medicine men), whose treatments entailed administering substances that had to be swallowed, smoked, or steamed. Sword, who was both a shaman and a medicine man, was greatly offended by the tendency of whites to refer to the curing performed by holy men as "making medicine." He thus explained, "Often when a shaman is performing a ceremony with his *wasicun* the interpreters say he is a medicine man making medicine. This is very foolish. It is the same as if when the minister is giving communion it was said he is a physician making medicine for the communicants."[23]

Both because of and despite the shamans' extraordinary powers, other members of the camp sometimes feared as well as respected them. They believed such holy men to be subject to the same foibles and temptations that plagued other people and, as such, might use (or rather misuse) their gift for their own ends. In the worst of all cases, they feared shamans might choose to align themselves with Iya or one or another malignant force of the cosmos. According to Short Feather, "A shaman who has *Iya* for his councilor is a bad shaman. The people fear such a shaman. He can make people into animals. He can kill people by incantations. He can make bad medicines." If discovered, such Wicasa Hmunga (sorcerers) and Wakan Skan Wicasa (magicians) not only forfeited their status as holy men but also were punished to the extent that their community judged proper. Execution by the camp *akicita* was often the price exacted for such crimes.[24]

In spite of occasional aberrations, most shamans utilized their powers for the benefit of their communities. As representatives of the Wakanpi they, more than any other individuals, were responsible for maintaining the ties of kinship and goodwill between the Lakotas and their gods.

The Lakota Sun Dance

Among all the Wakan Tanka, Lakotas most revered Wi, the Sun. They ranked him first among the superior gods and chief of the Tobtob kin. His color was red, a belief that Lakotas associated with the special love he evinced for the Lakotas. According to Tyon and other Lakota holy men, "Red is the color that belongs to the Sun. . . . This color is evoked by shamans, and represents the coming and the going of the Sun. When one wears red the Sun is pleased and will listen to such a one. The Indians are red, so they are the favorite people of the Sun. The Sun provides everything for them."[25]

Because of the Sun's special love for Lakotas, they celebrated their greatest ceremony, the Wiwayang wacipi, or Sun Dance (literally, Sun Gaze Dance), in his honor. Describing the complex nature of the ritual to Walker, several Lakota holy men concurred that the "ceremony of the Sun Dance may embrace all the ceremonies of any kind that are relative to the Gods."[26] Apart from the added benefits that these supplementary rituals might confer, the Tetons performed the Sun Dance to accomplish three important functions. It was a means for Lakotas to thank the Sun and the other Wakanpi for favors granted the preceding year. A warrior thus might take part in the Sun Dance to acknowledge the spiritual aid he had received in killing enemies, stealing horses, or surviving a battle. Additionally, participation in the ceremony served as a way of petitioning aid, perhaps for the recovery of a loved one, a successful buffalo hunt, or a year free of pestilence. Finally, undertaking the Sun Dance was an important means for securing spiritual power from the Wakanpi.[27]

The Sun Dance, like most Lakota ceremonies, was divided into four parts. According to Tyon, the reason for this was that, since "the Great Spirit caused everything to be in fours, mankind should do everything possible in fours." These four divisions took the following order: first, a period of preparation for the dance; second, the time set aside for people to assemble at the dance site; third, the interval allotted for establishing the camp and performing required pre-dance ceremonies; and fourth, the two days given over to the dance itself.[28]

During the period of preparation, those who had declared themselves candidates for the dance selected mentors to perform several required rituals including helping them ready their regalia and instructing them in all the ceremonial knowledge necessary for their participation in the ceremony. A special intimacy characterized the relationship between candidates and mentors, about which Sword observed, "One who instructs a candidate to dance the Sun Dance is the *tunkasila*. This means more than a grandfather. The candidate then becomes like a babe. His instructor governs him in everything. The instructor thinks for him and speaks for him and tells him how to think and how to speak. . . . The instructor becomes the candidate's other self. He is like the candidate's spirit."[29]

It was also during the preparatory phase that the candidates sent out messengers inviting members of other bands and Lakota tribes to be their guests at the Sun Dance. The invitations, which took the form of wands made from the sprouts of plum trees, were delivered to their recipients in a ceremony that included the presentation of tobacco and the smoking of a pipe.[30]

Although the location of the Sun Dance changed from year to year, it was typically held in late June or early July—the period when the plants required for the ceremony performance had reached maturity. This conventionalized timing made it possible for those planning to attend to pace their journey so that they would arrive no later than the four days before the ceremonial camp was to be established. According to Walker, this period began "when the Moon [was] four hands' breadth above the edge of the world, when the Sun [went] down out of sight." While en route to the site, the magistrate of each group would begin each day by offering smoke to the Tatuye Topa (Four Directions) for good weather. At the completion of every quarter leg of the day's journey, he would again pray while the other members of the band rested. During the trek, candidates attempted to abstain as much as possible from the levities and entertainments enjoyed by his or her fellow travelers.[31]

The arrival of all participants signaled the beginning of an eight-day period of preparation. This period was divided into two phases. The first four days, known as the "preliminary camp," provided the opportunity for socializing and conviviality. But it was also a time for performing many essential tasks, the most important of these being the selection of the shaman who was to act as the Sun Dance leader, the choice of a "scout" to locate the Sun Dance tree, and the appointment of those men and women who would ritually fell and hew the tree.[32]

During the next four days, the phase of the "ceremonial camp," officials directed the final preparations for the dance. On the first day, the Sun Dance leader chose the site for the ceremonial camp and, with the help of the mentors and candidates, cleansed it of malevolent spirits. Once the area had thus been purified, the people pitched their lodges in a great circle so that the sacred spot was its center and the camp's doorway faced east. Short Bull informed Walker that only circular tipis or lodges were permitted in the camp circle and, although they could be adorned with designs, the decoration of each tipi was supposed to "indicate something of note relative to the occupant."[33]

After the circle was completed, work was immediately begun on the Tent of Preparation, which was constructed with new hides and tipi poles and contained a bed of sage for each candidate. With the exception of the dance circle, this tent was the only place that the Sun Dancers were allowed during the ceremony.[34]

While work was proceeding on the ceremonial camp and Tent of Preparation, a scout was chosen to find a cottonwood tree that would serve as the sacred pole. His designation as "scout" was no mere happenstance, for the Lakotas considered the tree that he sought an enemy to be captured and brought back to camp.[35] The tree's actual seizure, based on the scout's reconnaissance, took place the following day.[36] One by one the four men who had been chosen to cut the tree took their positions, each first informing the onlookers of the great deeds he had performed that entitled him to this honor. Then, wielding an ax, each in turn feigned three blows before actually striking the cottonwood with his fourth swing.[37] This rite was believed to subdue the *nagila* of the tree and make it subordinate to the people.[38] A chaste woman was then handed an ax to complete the felling and, as the tree dropped earthward, a group of men broke its fall before it touched the ground. Poised in this manner, all its branches were pruned, excluding the forks on top. Answering why the upper forks were spared, Bad Heart Bull stated: "These [the upper forks] must not be trimmed because this is the head of the tree and its spirit-like [*nagila*] is there. The leaves must not be taken from the top, for these leaves are like the scalp of mankind and they control the spirit-like of the tree. The tree is captured and if its scalp is left on it, it will serve those who have captured it."[39]

From this point forward the tree, with its *nagila* now subdued but fully intact, was considered a "captive" who would serve the Lakotas as the sacred pole in their Sun Dance. Placing the prisoner onto a litter, four teams took turns hauling it back to the ceremonial camp. The return journey was punctuated by four stops during which teams were changed and a ceremony was performed in which all of the carriers howled like wolves, "for this is the cry of returning warriors who come bringing a captive." After the last team had taken its place, those carriers who had been relieved of their burden raced toward the camp, again howling like wolves.[40]

When the crew bearing the sacred pole finally returned, they moved slowly through the camp circle until they reached its center. There they carefully lowered their sacred hostage to the ground so that its head faced east and its stump touched the lip of a hole in which it would stand. As the crowd that had gathered to greet the captors looked on, the Sun Dance leader and mentors performed the rituals required to raise the pole. They first painted its west side red, north side blue, east side green, and south side yellow. They next attached offerings to a crossbar that had earlier been placed in a crotch located near the pole's crest. These gifts included rawhide effigies of a buffalo and a human enemy, symbolizing that the Lakotas' continued success in the hunt and war depended on the goodwill of the Wakanpi.[41] The ropes by which the candidates who had chosen to be tethered to or suspended from the tree were then attached to the crossbar. Finally, the leader and mentors prepared an amulet to which they imparted the potency (ton) of the Buffalo God. This was done so that, when the offering was tied to the fork of the pole, the Buffalo God, considered the special friend (kola) of the Sun, would prevail in the camp.[42]

Once these ceremonies had been completed, it was time for the pole to be raised. At the leader's command a team of respected men hoisted it in four intervals until it stood completely erect. They then secured it so that it would be able to withstand the exertions of the dancers as they struggled to break themselves free of their ropes.[43]

After the planting of the pole, work was begun on an enclosure of about fifty feet in diameter that would serve as the Sun Dance bower, which was divided into two parts—a central area exposed to the sun that served as a dancing space, and a protected perimeter covered top and back with newly cut pine boughs. The shaded area was, in turn, composed of two sections—a dedicated section, opposite the doorway, reserved for the Sun Dance officials and other key participants; and a common section where anyone could sit.

As soon as the bower was completed, men of distinction from the various *tiyospaye* streamed inside and performed the "Smoothing out the Floor with Their Feet Dance." This was done for the pragmatic end of protecting the bare feet of the Sun Dancers. During this time, some of these dancers performed a ritual intended to ensure their success in hunt and war.[44] Regarding this rite James O. Dorsey wrote, "The aged men and the chief men of the camp kick off their leggings and moccasins, and as many as have pistols take them to the dancing lodge, around the interior of which they perform a dance. As they pass around the sun pole, all shoot at once at the objects suspended from the pole, knocking them aside suddenly."[45] Once these observances were finished, all returned quietly to their tents, except for the candidates, who filed into the Tent of Preparation.

After all the candidates had assembled in the tent, each donned the outfit he would wear throughout the dance. The mandatory regalia included a skirt of tanned deerskin, an otter skin cape, a buffalo hair armlet, a rabbit skin anklet, an eagle bone whistle, and a willow hoop. The candidates wore their hair loose to the shoulders "after the manner of men who had recently killed an enemy."[46] Each mentor painted the upper torso, arms, and face of his apprentice in a manner in keeping with ceremonial prescriptions.[47]

When all the candidates had been duly prepared, the Sun Dance leader led them in single file to the dance lodge, which they circled four times before entering. After the procession was inside the lodge, the singers took their designated places. Using a large piece of rawhide for a drum, they commenced a series of songs to which the candidates danced all night.

Although the dancers were to observe a strict fast while in the lodge, officials averted their eyes when young women snuck up to the tent just before daylight and slid mixtures of cottonwood bark and water under the tent base where their sweethearts sat. According to Deloria's informants, this "service seems to be something that they are proud of. And the young men are made very happy by it and share the water with their friends."[48]

During the morning of the fourth day, while the dancers were resting, the leader prepared the sacred area or altar (*owanka wakan*) between them and the pole. Motioning three times toward the ground with a hatchet, he finally dealt it a blow on the fourth swing. He next chopped out a suitably large square of soil, pulverized it with a knife, and repacked it in the hole. In the center of the square he then fashioned a star and sprinkled it with red paint and tobacco that had been blended with the kinnikinick (*canshasha*).[49] With the area thus consecrated, the leader placed a loaded pipe atop a buffalo chip at its center. Next to these he positioned a buffalo skull that he proceeded to paint with sacred designs and whose eye sockets and snout he stuffed with crushed sage. The painted buffalo skull signified that the Buffalo God prevailed in the camp, and the sage that protruded from its orifices banished evil from the dance lodge.[50]

The remaining dancing and ceremonies of that day were performed in fulfillment of the vows the candidates had made, for a man could pledge to take part in the Sun Dance in a variety of ways. Some confined their participation to dancing, along with the fast stipulated for all dancers. Others added to their ordeal lacerations or offerings of their flesh. Finally, there were those who had promised the Wakanpi that they break loose from skewers that had been implanted in their skin. This last sacrifice might be performed in four different ways. According to Densmore, the "two most common forms of this treatment consisted in the piercing of the flesh over the chest with skewers attached by cords to the crossbar of the sacred pole, and the fastening of buffalo skulls to the flesh of the back and arms. The two more severe and less common forms were the suspending of the entire body by the flesh of the back and the fastening of the flesh of both back and chest to four poles at some distance from the body, the poles being placed at the corners of a square."[51]

No matter what mode of sacrifice they had chosen, the dancers attempted to lock their gaze onto the sun as they blew into their eagle bone whistles and kept pace with the tempo of the drums. Most important, they prayed in thanksgiving or in request for help from the Wakanpi. Many of these prayers took the form of songs. As Tyon observed, "If they wish for many buffalo, they will sing of them; if victory, sing of it; and if they wish to bring good weather, they will sing of it."[52]

Overcome by the grueling physical and emotional demands of the ceremony, many dancers collapsed in a faint and had to be carried into the shade. While unconscious, some of the fallen dancers experienced visions. Such was the case for Red Bird, one of the chief contributors to Frances Densmore's classic description of the Sun Dance. Densmore wrote that Red Bird had told her that "on the second day, as he was dancing, he noticed that the Intercessor [Sun Dance leader] held a small mirror in his hand, and that he threw the light reflected from this mirror into the face of one dancer after another, each man falling to the ground when it flashed into his eyes." He told Densmore that he then fell unconscious and while in this state "he saw something in the sun; it was a man's face, painted, and as he looked at it he saw that the man in the sun was the Intercessor. It was said that this vision was sufficient to entitle Red Bird to act as an Intercessor, after he had received the proper instruction concerning the duties of the office."[53]

It is important to note that participation in the Sun Dance was not limited to men. Women and children were allowed to take part as well, although performing sacrifices different from those of the adult males. Women were permitted to offer pieces of flesh.[54] Little Wound, American Horse, and Lone Star concurred that neither women nor children were "attached to the stakes or poles as men [were]." They also concurred that women "nearly always dance[d] in the name of some absent one."[55] Regarding the custom of women proxies, Dorsey wrote that it "is customary, when a man is too poor to take part himself in the sun dance, for a female relation to take his place, if such a woman pities him. She suffers as the male candidates do, except in one respect—her flesh is not scarified." Also, women were allowed to dance alongside a family member who was fulfilling a pledge.[56]

The sacrifice offered by children was limited to ear piercing. According to Rocky Bear, those Tetons who had their ears pierced were obliged to "live according to the Lakota customs and obey their laws." Even though the operation could take place at any time, Sun Dances were the most popular time for parents to have their children's ears pierced.[57] Such occasions were accompanied by much gift giving. Deloria has written that the exit of parents from the dance lodge "empty handed, with only their child in their arms . . . was considered a mark of great love for the child."[58]

The ceremony lasted as long as it took all the participants to complete their vows. At the same time, it was prescribed that camp should be broken before the end of the second day of dancing (i.e., the dawn of the following day).[59] This requirement allowed relatives and friends of dancers who were having trouble pulling themselves free from the buffalo skulls or pole to come to their aid in a manner that demonstrated both their compassion and generosity. In his firsthand account of the Sun Dance held at the Red Cloud Agency in 1881, Capt. John G. Bourke, U.S. Army, described one young man fainting four times and still unable to pull himself loose from the tree after "an hour and seven minutes." While the dancer was on the ground, the Sun Dance leader put dulcamara seeds in his mouth and women piled heavy robes and other valuables on the rope in hopes that the additional weight would allow him to break free. "The articles thus attached to the rope," Bourke wrote, "were taken away by the poor for whom they were given. 'So and so has done well. He is not afraid to look the poor women and children in the face!'"[60]

Despite such efforts, it sometimes happened that one or more dancers were still attached to the pole as the dawn marking the end of the ceremony approached. Walker reported that in such cases fellow participants rescued these "captives" by removing the sticks from their wounds. This liberation was deemed "as meritorious as an escape [i.e., pulling oneself free]."[61] When all had escaped, the dancers circled the arena four times before exiting and then walked in single file to the Tent of Preparation, which they again circled four rounds before entering.[62] After leaving the tent, each of the dancers was taken back to his family's lodge, where he was given four sips of water and a small amount of food. When he had regained sufficient strength, he joined the other dancers for a sweat bath.[63] With the completion of this ritual, the Sun Dance itself was at an end. The bands then quickly dispersed, abandoning the pole and its offerings to the Wakan Tanka.

Pierre Jean De Smet and an
Early Lakota Encounter with Catholic Mission

With few exceptions, the Lakotas' initial impressions of Christian missionaries are lost to history. However, the frequent reference to religious emissaries in Teton sacred traditions suggests that they possessed an indigenous missiology that prepared them for these encounters.

The preeminent examples of such pre-Christian missionaries are Tokahe (First One) and Pte San Win (White Buffalo Calf Woman), who brought the Lakotas many of their most cherished customs. One should, however, also include among their number the many spiritual messengers through whom the Wakan Tanka communicated visions of new knowledge and sacred power. If the concepts of *wakan*, the *sicun*, and *ton* as we have seen constituted the abiding theological core of the Lakota spiritual universe, missionaries were its primary agents of change.

Although we cannot be certain, it is reasonable to believe that Lakotas interpreted their early contacts with Christian missionaries through the skein of this indigenous missiology. They would, accordingly, have welcomed these visitors as envoys from Wakan Tanka and listened respectfully to their words and counsel. Pierre-Jean De Smet's account of his encounter with a band of Sihasapa (Blackfeet) Lakotas in 1840 provides important documentary support for this thesis.[64] The priest wrote that while en route to Fort Pierre he and several traveling companions were intercepted by a party of Sihasapa warriors. Bewildered by the Jesuit's long black robe and missionary's cross, the war party's leader exclaimed, "I have never seen such a man in my life. Who is he?" to which an interpreter accompanying De Smet responded, "It is the man who talks to the Great Spirit. It is a chief or Black-gown of the Frenchmen." De Smet reported that upon hearing these words the leader's "fierce look at once changed; he ordered his warriors to put away their weapons and they all shook hands with me. I made them a present," the priest continued, "of a big twist of tobacco, and everybody sat down in a circle and smoked the pipe of peace and friendship. He [the leader] then besought me to accompany him and to pass the night in his village, which was at no great distance."

De Smet interpreted this meeting as a providentially arranged opportunity to evangelize Lakotas. Detailing his journey and visit to the village, he wrote that shortly after he had been provided with a lodge twelve warriors arrived at its door and spread a large buffalo robe before it. "The head chief took me by the arm and leading me to the skin made me a sign to be seated." Having no idea of the meaning of the event taking place, De Smet remarked on his surprise when the warriors lifted the robe off the ground and carried it throughout the village so that everyone could see him. Finally arriving at the head chief's lodge, the priest reported that he was assigned the most honorable place in the tent, and the chief "surrounded by forty of his principal warriors harangued me in these terms: 'Black-robe, this is the happiest day of our lives. To-day for the first time we see among us a man who comes so near to the Great Spirit. Here are the principal braves of my tribe. I have bidden them to the feast that I have prepared for you, that they may never lose the memory of so happy a day.'" After this greeting the chief requested that De Smet pray to the Great Spirit before the feast commenced. "All the time it lasted, all the savage company, following their chief's example, held their hands raised toward heaven; the moment it was ended, they lowered their right hands to the ground."

Encouraged by this display of "primitive" piety, De Smet seized the opportunity to instruct the Sihasapas on some basic Catholic tenets. However, the interpreter's inability to render the priest's catechesis into Lakota quickly dampened his enthusiasm. By contrast, this language barrier was apparently of little concern to the Sihasapas, for according to De Smet the "next day, though we were still five days' journey from the fort [the leader] had his son and two other young men go with me, praying me to instruct them. He desired absolutely to know the words I had to impart to them in behalf of the Great Spirit; and at the same time these young men would be a safeguard for me against evil-disposed savages."

Despite its propagandist subtext and pervasive ethnocentrism, De Smet's description of his visit among the Sihasapas contains some valuable information on Lakota religious attitudes and behavior. Having accepted De Smet as "one who talks with the Great Spirit," the members of the *tiyospaye* welcomed him with the pomp and generosity befitting a delegate of the Wakanpi. Given their understanding of mission, they probably expected him to reciprocate their hospitality by teaching them some of his ceremonies and prayers. When he decided to depart without completing that work, the Sihasapa leader improvised the ingenious scheme of sending a few "bodyguards" on a five-day tutorial with the priest.

De Smet considered the kind of religious instruction that the Sihasapas desired to be fraught with dangers. He believed that, as long as they and other Lakotas adhered to their "superstitious" beliefs and practices, they could not help but debase Catholic media of grace into instruments of idolatry. The Sihasapas' desire to acquire Catholic prayers without concern for their meaning could have only bolstered his suspicions that they considered their power to adhere in the words themselves, rather than in God alone.

To avoid this corruption, De Smet advised itinerant missionaries to exercise utmost caution in evangelizing the Lakotas. He was especially insistent that they refrain from distributing religious objects during their visits. De Smet believed that effective Lakota evangelization would have to await the founding of missions whose work it would be to supplant Lakota spirituality with approved forms of Catholic ritual and prayer. In the contest for Lakota souls there could be no compromise between Christ Jesus and heathenism. Rather, salvation required the Lakotas' total capitulation to Roman Catholic standards of faith and morals, as well as to the civilized institutions that allowed them to thrive.

CHAPTER TWELVE

Pragmatism and Sicangu Catholicism

Whatever the good father De Smet might have considered necessary for the Lakotas' conversion to Catholicism, it is safe to assume that the Lakotas saw matters quite differently. In fact nothing in their worldview could have prepared them for the demands of missionaries and federal agents that they forsake their traditional lifeways and religion for those of the white Christian mainstream. In accord with the basic tenets of their missiology, they were quite happy to incorporate the ceremonies that De Smet and other agents of Wakan Tanka into their existing beliefs and practices. Nevertheless, the requirement that they abandon their Wakanpi for the ways and teachings of a *wanikiye* (lifegiver) named Jesus must have struck them as both unacceptable and absurd.

This certainly appears to have been the prevailing sentiment among the Sicangus as they arrived at Whetstone Agency in 1868. Embittered by their forced confinement, they were in no mood to take up the cross. Commenting on the indifference with which they greeted calls for their conversion, agent Dewitt Poole observed that, "so far as the church and ministers were concerned, the Indians were not anxious. They were already provided with a religion of their own, under whose tenets they constantly preached and practiced; the medicine man being their minister, the blue sky and high bluffs their church edifice."[1]

To illustrate the Sicangus' apathy toward Christianity, Poole recounted their response to a speech by William Welsh during his tour of Whetstone in 1869. Beginning with events leading up to the influential reformer's speech, the agent wrote:

In a council he [Welsh] spoke at considerable length of the efforts being made to procure, from this time on, the best of blankets and provisions for the use of the Indians, and his remarks met with constant expressions of approbation and approval from his hearers; but when he went on to tell of his great desire to establish schools and churches among them, and to have them become Christians, I was constrained to notice that his eloquence elicited no "hows," and was listened to with the most stolid indifference by those whom he wished to benefit.[2]

Though Poole did not mention any of the councilmen by name, it is known that Chief Spotted Tail was not among them, for he was visiting Washington at the time. Nevertheless, Poole's description of the Indians' indifference to Christianity is consistent with Spotted Tail's own attitude toward the religion. Throughout the remaining years of his life, the headman would rebuff every effort by Episcopal and Catholic missionaries to gain him for their flocks. Important evidence for Spotted Tail's religious conservatism is found in Col. Richard Dodge's 1882 publication *Our Wild Indians*. Dodge recounted that at the conclusion of a treaty negotiation in 1878 the headman engaged a young army captain whom the Lakotas had named "Black Beard" in the following theological discourse—one amusing enough to quote in full:

"I have a serious question to ask you about religion. Can you answer it?" "I am not a very good authority on religious matters," replied Black Beard, "and I don't know whether I can answer it or not. But put your question, and I will give you my honest opinion."

"Well," said Spotted Tail, "I am bothered what to believe. Some years ago a good man, as I think, came to us. He talked me out of all my old faith; and after a while, thinking that he must know more of these matters than an ignorant Indian, I joined his church, and became a Methodist. After a while he went away; another man came and talked, and I became a Baptist; then another came and talked, and I became a Presbyterian. Now another one has come, and wants me to be an Episcopalian. What do you think of it?"

"I was brought up an Episcopalian," said Black Beard, "but I can't give you any advice in this matter. I think that religion must be a matter of conscience, and that sect has little to do with it."

"That," said Spotted Tail, "is just what I am beginning to think. All these people tell different stories, and each wants me to believe that his special way is the only way to be good and save my soul. I have about made up my mind that either they all lie, or that they don't know any more about it than I did at first. I have always believed in the Great Spirit, and worshipped him in my own way. These people don't seem to want to change my belief in the Great Spirit, but to change my way of talking to him. White men have education and books, and ought to know exactly what to do, but hardly any two of them agree on what should be done.[3]

It is George Hyde's supposition that the headman's views on Christianity were not generally so irenic. According to Hyde, "A priest came to Spotted Tail to scout the ground. . . . Through an interpreter he kept asking Spotted Tail about the children De Smet had sprinkled water on. . . . At this time it was very rainy. 'Tell him,' he [Spotted Tail] said to the interpreter, 'that I do not know anything about Brule babies that [a] Black Robe threw water on at the old treaty council, but recently God Almighty has been throwing a great deal too much water on all of us, and I wish someone would ask him to please let up on us.'"[4]

The best evidence for Spotted Tail's religious conservatism is gleaned not from secondhand reports of his words but from his actions. Most compelling of all was his decision to sponsor a Sun Dance the summer after the Sicangus' relocation to the Rosebud. During spring 1879 the Sicangu leader began notifying Lakotas on his own and other agencies of the time and location of the upcoming ceremony. In the instance of the Lakotas of the Lower Brule Reservation he is known to have delivered his invitation in person, reportedly leaving the policy of civilization and Christianization a shambles in his wake. Describing the disastrous effects that Spotted Tail's visit to the Lower Brule was having on its populace, agent Col. E. J. Dougherty informed Rosebud agent Cicero E. Newell,

About a month ago Chief Spotted Tail came into this Agency and induced nearly the whole tribe to follow him back to Rosebud to attend the sundance and a council to be held at the full moon just past. I learn that the [dance] has been postponed until the next full moon. Meantime their fields are overgrown with weeds, broken into by stock and their whole domestic establishment entirely abandoned and disorganized in consequence of their absence, they have nearly taken all their stock with them, and without doubt consume a great deal of it if not all before their return.[5]

Conceding that it would be impossible for Newell to induce his errant charges to return home, Dougherty nevertheless implored him to punish them for their disobedience by "withold[ing] . . . any substantial encouragement in the case of supplies." The colonel would have foregone making even this modest request had he been aware of Newell's veritable sponsorship of the upcoming dance. In what was, arguably, the capstone of Spotted Tail's illustrious career of wheeling and dealing, the headman had not only persuaded Newell to sanction his Sun Dance but convinced him to write letters to other agents requesting that they allow the Lakotas on their reservations to attend to ceremony.

Unfortunately for Newell, one of these letters found its way to the desk of the acting Indian commissioner, E. J. Brooks. Seething with anger, Brooks fired off a communiqué admonishing the agent for abetting the Sun Dance. "I am surprised," Brooks fumed, "that an Agent who is expected to use his best efforts to promote the material interests and civilization of the Indians under his charge should send a notice of this character on their behalf to Indians of a neighboring reservation and I can only attribute the act to thoughtlessness or ignorance of the real nature and tendency of the heathenish ceremony referred to." Equating the "real nature" of the Sun Dance with its negative effects on Indian civilization, Brooks noted that the ritual "is directly antagonistic to all efforts made and influences exerted to promote the highest good of the Indians. It keeps alive their barbarous practices, incites to hostilities, to crimes and cruelties, and fosters a spirit of hatred . . . especially in the young men of the tribe, and the Agent is not only expected but required to employ all the means and instrumentalities at his command to break up this barbarous custom. To this end," he warned Newell, "you will advise Spotted Tail at once of the views of the office respecting this proposed 'Dance' and endeavor to induce him and other leading members of the tribe to cooperate with you in every effort possible to prevent the Indians from engaging in such demoralizing practices."[6]

There remains some question as to exactly why Newell permitted Spotted Tail to hold his Sun Dance. Hyde has argued that the chief merely bullied the young agent into cooperation. There is, however, some evidence to suggest that Newell was sympathetic to the Lakotas' continued practice of their religion and during his stay among the Sicangus may have "gone native." In a small pamphlet written many years after his tenure on the Rosebud, the former agent offered a stirring defense of Lakota culture, religion, and medicine men. On the subject of Lakota curers he stated, "They have many ways unknown to white people," and went on to predict that the "time will come when the world will understand and appreciate it [Lakota medicine]."[7]

Whatever Newell's motives for permitting the Sun Dance, it should come as no surprise that as a result of his actions his days as Rosebud agent were numbered.[8] In the end, Spotted Tail had achieved his goal of bringing Lakotas from widely dispersed reservations together to celebrate and honor the Wakan Tanka.

The Pragmatism of Sicangu Catholicism

Spotted Tail's rejection of Christianity should not be taken to mean that he saw no value in the churches and their workers. Rather, with a pragmatism that characterized all his dealings with whites, he assessed the value of these various forms of the "white man's prayer" in purely utilitarian terms. Once convinced that one denomination or another would be assigned to the Rosebud, he determined that it should at least provide some practical service for his people.

For Spotted Tail the most valuable assistance missionaries could render the Sicangus was to assist their children in achieving literacy in English. As a member of the Lakota and Arapaho delegation that visited Washington in 1877, he had advised the president, "My children, all of them, would like to learn how to talk English. They would like to learn how to read and write." He went on to inform the chief executive, "We have teachers there, but all they teach us is to talk and write Sioux, and that is not necessary. I would like to get Catholic priests. Those who wear black dresses. These men will teach us how to read and write English."[9]

Why Spotted Tail's insistence on Blackrobe teachers? And why, for that matter, did he place such great emphasis on training Sicangu children to read and write English? Both decisions were based on practical considerations. As Hyde has stated, "Spotted Tail and his chiefs were annoyed with the

Episcopalians, who had a missionary at the old agency as far back as 1875. The chiefs said the White Robes had not taught one Sioux child to speak or write English. As for the teaching of Christianity, that did not interest most of the chiefs. All they desired was to have some full-blood Sioux boys taught to read and write English, so that they might act as interpreters and also write letters from the chiefs to Washington."[10]

In addition to the varying capacities of the Christian churches to supply competent teachers, there is evidence that Spotted Tail assessed their worth in terms of the political clout that he believed they exercised over the Indian Office. In a diary entry dated March 28, 1899, Father Digmann reported that, when a daughter of Spotted Tail was asked why she was an Episcopal in spite of her father's desire for Catholic priests, she replied that when he wanted to bring her home from Carlisle Industrial School it was Episcopal bishop William Hare, not the Catholics, who were able to pull the right strings. She related that when Spotted Tail returned home he confessed, "I always thought that the Black Robes had great influence but found out now that this is not so but the White Robes have greater influence." He had let his daughter be educated by Protestants.[11]

A story found in Hyde's *Spotted Tail's Folk* indicates that some Catholic religious were willing to employ highly unorthodox means to gain the headman's favor. According to Hyde, a nun from Kansas City appeared one day at the Spotted Tail Agency to recruit students for her order's school. The wives of one of the agency's officials, who took an interest in her work, arranged for a meeting between the sister and the leader. At this meeting "lemonade was served, and the nun (who appeared to have been a lively lady) sprang up laughing, holding out her glass toward Spotted Tail and dancing toward him." Not one known to resist the charms of the opposite sex, the "chief instantly jumped up and began dancing toward her, holding out his glass. In the center of the room the two met, clinked glasses and stood laughing and drinking. Presently the nun had a promise from the chief that he would give her one of his daughters to take to the Kansas City convent to be educated." Despite this auspicious beginning, Hyde reported, Spotted Tail's candidate for the convent, Canku Luta Win (Red Road Woman), had no intention of "going to sacrifice to the white men's god called education." As soon as the opportunity arose, she eloped with a young warrior and settled in a camp distant enough from her father's influence to frustrate the nun's machinations.[12]

Spotted Tail was far from alone in drawing upon the services and resources of Christian missionaries. Many Sicangus found their Jesuit overseers particularly useful as lobbyists against selected aspects of government policy. The Sicangus' ability to recruit the Catholic religious as allies in their struggles with the government may at first appear odd, especially in view of the missionaries' frequent critique of federal personnel for their supposed indifference in pushing forward its policy of civilization and Christianization. But the Indians were quick to detect the fissures in the relationship between missionaries and government resulting from nativism or differences in approach and, when possible, used them to their advantage.

The Integrity of Reservation Lands

During the three decades covered by this study, the Sicangus were most successful in rallying support of the Saint Francis missionaries on two issues: dangers to the integrity of Sicangu lands, especially the periodic threats to relocate their reservation; and the kinds of schools their children should attend.

After relocating the Sicangus to four different agencies between 1868 and 1878, the federal government finally submitted to Spotted Tail's appeals that it designate the area surrounding the Little White River in present-day south-central South Dakota as the tribe's permanent homeland. The decade-long experience of wandering taught them that the federal government's notion of "permanent" actually meant for however long an arrangement suited its purposes. What is more, the Indian Office's willingness to pour enormous amounts of money and resources into establishing an agency at a given location was no guarantee that it would not suddenly decide to transfer its Indian population to another site.

The Sicangus therefore could not have been caught completely by surprise when in 1885 word began circulating around the Rosebud that the Indian Office was once again contemplating relocating the agency. The rumor quickly proved a disaster for the government's attempts to coax Sicangus to take up the plow. In September, Inspector Pearson informed Commissioner Upshaw that the "Indians are all in an unsettled state on this account, and when asked to open up land and commence farming, their answer is that the Agency may be removed or changed." Upshaw considered Pearson's assessment serious enough to notify Agent Wright "to advise the Indians that it is not the intention of the Department to remove the Agency."[13]

In fact, it appears that at the time the Indian Office had no plans to relocate the reservation. To underscore this point Upshaw informed Wright of the government's refusal to set aside the funds for the transfer.[14] By 1889, however, the public's hunger for land had compelled Congress to allocate sufficient monies to establish a "Peace Commission" charged with inducing the Lakotas to sell large portions of the Great Sioux Reservation.

News of this commission spawned fresh rumors among the Sicangus that the Indian Office was planning to remove them from the Little White River valley. The sites the Office was reputedly considering for their new agency were Oak Creek and Keya Paha (Turtle Mountain), both located on the eastern fringes of the reserve and reportedly rich in water, wood, and arable lands. These rumors were of sufficient gravity for Digmann to pass them along to BCIM director Stephan, glossed with his own speculations concerning the "actual" motives prompting the transfer. The priest recounted that "for ten miles and more around our Mission, east, south and west there is the best farming found, as one hardly can find better on the Reserve. But I know, there has been a scheme since several years to cut off about ten miles of the southern boundaries and hand it over to the Whites. At least such is the talk."[15]

Whatever the validity of Digmann's conjectures, there are good reasons to suspect that Agent Wright was manipulating this "talk" to extort the Sicangus' cooperation with his policies. After a meeting with the agent, Digmann informed Stephan, "When I told Mr. Wright of the uneasiness of our Indians, and their fear to be located elsewhere, he answered: 'I want them to set to work for this year. I don't care where they farm. So I urged them to start farming, so they would probably not be moved.'"[16]

Digmann's report of the meeting is fascinating on several counts. For one thing, it quoted Wright as intending to remove only individual recalcitrant Indians while brushing the subject of the government's plans to establish a new agency off to the side. This repurposing of relocation as a punishment for uncooperative Sicangus would have fit marvelously with the agent's efforts to persuade the Sicangus to farm. He was undoubtedly aware that previous threats to move the agency had left many Sicangus in an "unsettled state" and unwilling to begin farming. He may thus have determined that a strategy that allowed cooperative Sicangus to remain near the Little White River while threatening recalcitrant Indians with deportation had a good chance of goading the majority of Sicangus into taking up the plow.

Digmann's account also suggests that it was the agent's strategy to strong-arm the missionaries, as well as the Sicangus, into submitting to his dictates. Having invested thousands of dollars on the mission school and infrastructure, the Saint Francis missionaries would have been understandably terrified by any policy that significantly altered Indian-white demographics. Wright was well aware of this fact and might have used it to prod the missionaries into serving as his go-betweens with the Indians. That this strategy achieved its intended end is evidenced by Digmann's statement that after the meeting he urged the Indians to farm so that they "probably" would not be moved.

Aside from the Catholic missionaries' vested interests in maintaining the demographic status quo, another factor may have served the Sicangus' efforts to win them as allies. In spite of the missionaries' excellent relationship with the younger Wright, they maintained a deep mistrust of the Protestant-controlled Indian Office. As a result, little evidence was required to convince them that, though cooperative, his sympathies ultimately lay on the other side of the religious divide. Writing to Stephan about the agency's rumored relocation, Digmann speculated that the "plan . . . seems to have been to move [the Sicangus] later, and to move also the whole agency to the Butte Creek country. Inspector Jenkins, who visited Rosebud was in favor of this plan. The Protestant Episcopalian Mission was there, on the Antelope or Keya Paha Creek, and the Agent was planning possibly now already to have later also a government boarding school there so St. Francis could have been without Indians."[17]

It should be stressed that such suspicions were based on more than mere rumor and speculation. As a further incentive to enlist the missionaries' support, Sicangus from various camps notified the religious of their desire to establish homesteads near Saint Francis. Wright, however, promptly rejected these petitions, arguing that allowing Indians to move so far from their home camps would only encourage their "roving dispositions."[18]

Wright's decision both surprised and incensed Digmann, who considered it a betrayal of the agent's formerly amicable dealings with the mission.[19] He requested Stephan to send him a copy of the 1868 treaty in order to determine whether it was legal for Wright to prevent Sicangus from settling where they pleased within the reservation. Digmann advised the monsignor, "I do not wish, in any way to oppose him [Wright] and never did, I always have stood by his side." He nevertheless insisted, "I wish to have clear notions about this question. In my opinion an Indian can take his land wherever he pleases on the Reserve; especially now, when they have to settle for good taking their land with a mind to stay there."[20]

Some Sicangus were not content to sit idly by and place the fate of their reservation in the hands of the missionaries. Digmann reported that, in a meeting at the agency during which he was explaining the Indians' opposition to relocation, "suddenly the door of the office room was flung open and all policemen were ordered to come. A band of dissatisfied Indians in their Indian costume, with red painted faces and their long butcher knives in their belt, were opposed to the proposal of the 'Big Cat' or 'Tiger Man' as they called inspectors." The Sicangus profited little from this show of force for, as Digmann described, "the police disarmed them and put handcuffs on their wrists."[21]

Such acts of defiance were, however, exceedingly rare. Based on their knowledge of the mission's desire to maintain the status quo, most Sicangus were confident that the Saint Francis religious would fight the good fight against any attempt to move the agency. It is indicative of this confidence that Digmann should observe that the "more the enemies of the Church want to keep us down, the more the Indians draw near the Blackrobes."[22] It is equally true that the battle drew the missionaries near to the Indians.

The Education of Sicangu Children

In accord with the goals of reform Indian policy, the federal government built or sponsored the operation a variety of educational institutions to civilize and Christianize Indian children. This diversity was a direct consequence of competing philosophies of Indian education. Though all parties agreed that the goal of Indian schools was to assimilate native youngsters, they disagreed on the type of school best suited for this purpose. Those who supported reservation day schools and those who advocated boarding schools were the major parties in this dispute. The advocates of boarding schools were themselves divided over whether these institutions should be located on or off reservations.

Patterned after the rural one-room schoolhouse, reservation day schools were simple and economical to construct, maintain, and staff. Their proponents chiefly celebrated their capacity to civilize children and grownups alike. They argued that, by returning home each day, day-school students served as little agents of civilization by transmitting their lessons to the adults in their camp.

The critics of day schools had little difficulty in countering this argument. They maintained that sending students home at the end of each day often resulted in their relapse into savagery. To prevent this regression, they recommended sequestering Indian children in boarding schools so that the lessons of civilization could take root. Only then could they be safely returned to their communities to lead civilized lives and inspire others to progress.

All the supporters of boarding schools agreed on the necessity of separating Indian students from their families, but they broke rank over the question of where these institutions should be located. One side presented arguments in favor of establishing them on the students' home reservations. They observed that this proximity to their natal camps made it possible to return them home in case of family emergencies or death. It also permitted administrators to invite family members to a school for brief, tightly monitored visits. Often taking the form of "entertainments," or school fairs, such occasions allowed parents to check on the well-being and progress of their youngsters while being exposed to the school's "civilized" environment. These occasions also served to quell the homesickness that often made students rebellious or prompted them to run away. Finally, the supporters of these schools argued that by remaining on the reservation students could return home during summers to help on their families' farms, thereby reinforcing the agricultural training they had received at school and allowing them to pass this knowledge on to their parents.

Many opponents of on-reservation schools considered their proximity to Indian communities a major detriment to civilizing Indian children. They argued that parental visits, emergency leaves, and summer vacations all served to reindoctrinate children into savage practices and thus undermine all they had learned. What troubled these critics the most about reservation-based boarding schools was what troubled them about reservation policy as a whole. They believed that secluding Indian children and adults from whites deprived them of the opportunity to learn from the nation's civilized mainstream. This practice, more than any other aspect of federal Indian relations, they insisted, kept Indians in their backward state.

These critics by and large advocated replacing on-reservation schools with off-reservation facilities such as Hampton and Carlisle, at which students lived in the vicinity of white urban areas for five years or longer. While at these institutions most students had the opportunity to participate in the "outing system"—that is, to be hired as domestics or laborers in homes and businesses of whites, thus putting their domestic training into practice. According to their advocates, off-reservation schools boasted the further advantage of mixing students from tribally diverse backgrounds, thereby encouraging them to abandon their native languages and customs for English and Euro-American institutions.

During the late nineteenth and early twentieth centuries, Sicangu youth could be found in all the aforementioned types of schools. By 1915 there were twenty-one day schools operating within the reservation's seven districts. In addition to Saint Francis, there were two other boarding schools—Saint Mary's, run by the Episcopal Church, and a government facility built in 1892. As well, some Sicangu children found their way into off-reservation boarding schools, including Genoa, Hampton, and Carlisle.

Whereas whites debated the relative value of these schools primarily on the basis of their effectiveness in civilizing and Christianizing Indian children, Sicangu parents measured their merits according to very different standards and concerns. Topping their list was the capacity of a school to maintain the health and well-being of their children. The large number of Rosebud day schools strongly suggests that Sicangu parents overwhelmingly believed that their children's welfare was best served by educating them close to home.[23] There are at least two reasons why some parents who would have preferred to enroll their children in these schools did not. One is that not all families lived within commuting distance to such facilities, despite their prevalence. This condition became increasingly common as greater numbers of Sicangus began accepting allotments in the early twentieth century. Evidence that some parents attempted to circumvent this problem illegally is found in the following letter from Indian school supervisor H. B. Pearis to Agent Woods: "The Normal Instructor intimates that in some instances the attendance of the children at the day schools interferes with parents living on their allotments. She speaks of one or two cases in which she noticed parents living in camps near the schools in order that their children might attend." Entirely misconstruing the motives behind these actions, Pearis went on to observe, "It is very commendable on the part of the parents to be enough interested in having their children get an education to be willing to move into the vicinity of the school and live in camp. However," he concluded, "the advisability of such action is very doubtful."[24]

The parents of some children who lived within walking or horseback distance to day schools at times choose to send their children to one or another type of boarding school, often based on economic considerations. In 1900, Digmann wrote that the "hunger of the Indians is greater than ten years ago before the outbreak. Our hired men refectory is filled two or three times every day by starving Indians and they carry home whatever they can get; they ask for work, offer hay, etc. Mr. House, Day School Inspector, said that Mr. Barnes, Teacher of a day school had reported children at his school went to the barrel of weillings (hog wash) to still their hunger."[25]

The persistent difficulty government agents encountered in recruiting students for off-reservation schools underscores the hostility of most Sicangus to sending their children off the Rosebud to be educated. One reason for their aversion was the government's stipulation that the children enrolled at these campuses remain away from their families for many years at a time. In a letter ordering Agent Wright to select thirty boys and girls to be sent to Carlisle, Commissioner Price informed him that "these children should be surrendered by their parents on the understanding that they shall remain at Carlisle for five years. Experience has shown that a three years course is not long enough to fortify the students sufficiently against the surroundings which they must encounter on their return homes." That this same policy precluded students at Genoa from spending their summer recesses on the Rosebud is found in Commissioner Atkins's order that Wright "disabuse [his] Indians" that children attending Genoa boarding school in Nebraska would be returned home during the summer. "When they have completed their course at Genoa and learned enough to be of some use to themselves and their friends they can return home and then their parents and friends will see the wisdom of their having remained at school without interruption."[26]

The anguish that many Sicangu parents experienced sending their children to off-reservation schools is revealed in the following diary entry by Digmann: "An Indian woman first standing opposite [from me] walked up and down the main street, singing and mourning like they do over their dead. Asking one why she cried he said: 'They are taking her boy off to a non-reservation school far off, that's why.'"[27]

Anxious about their children's welfare, parents of students in off-reservation schools appealed to the Indian Office for permission and funds to visit their children.[28] Almost without exception, the Office rejected such requests. One reason for its opposition was the desire to avoid any repetition of the calamitous fallout from Spotted Tail's visit to Carlisle in June 1880. Writing to Rosebud agent Cook shortly after the chief's departure from the school,

Commissioner Brooks described the uproar he had caused during his stay and its potentially disastrous consequences for recruiting future Carlisle students from the Rosebud. Concerning the specifics of the tumult, Brooks wrote that Spotted Tail "demanded that his son in law, Charles Tackett should be retained by Captain Pratt as interpreter for the Carlisle School (after discharge for cause) and that his salary should be increased, threatening to remove his (Spotted Tail's) children from said school unless his demands were complied with." Regarding the outcome of these demands, he wrote that "the Secretary telegraphed him that Captain Pratt and not he must govern the Carlisle School, where-upon he took his own children and two grandchildren and they are now returning with them." In view of this incident, Brooks advised Cook to

> watch his movements carefully as it is possible that he will oppose sending any more children to the school. . . . Withdraw your confidence from him so far as it can be done safely and endeavor to get the support of the more progressive men of the bands under your charge. I am convinced that too much deference has been shown him and that he has been the recipient of too many favors, this of course evidently has led him to so magnify his importance that at present his influence instead of being of service to the Department, and as a result thereof, of benefit to his people, is calculated to embarrass and obstruct the plans of their improvement.[29]

A more general reason for the Indian Office's unwillingness to sanction parental visits was that they were at odds with the educational philosophy of off-reservation schools. The fundamental reason for the existence of such institutions lay in the presumed need of Indian children to be isolated from their "savage" relatives and brought into increasing contact with whites.

The paramount motive for the Indian Office's opposition to parental visits, however, lay neither in prior experience nor philosophy. Rather, it was simply a matter of dollars and cents. With so many students from different reservations enrolled in schools far from their homes, the Office balked at the enormous costs of paying for, arranging, and monitoring these trips. The ingenious attempt of Rosebud headmen Standing Bear and Red Fish to gain the permission and funds to visit their children at Carlisle by offering to piggyback this journey with an official trip to the Indian Office fared no better than other appeals. Upon being apprised of this proposal, Commissioner

Price notified Wright to inform the two headmen that there was "no money available which can be used by this office to assist either of these Indians in paying any portion of the expenses connected with the trip." Knowing full well of the impoverished state of most Sicangus, Price disingenuously added, "But if they can and will pay their own expenses you can grant their permission to make the visit and assure them that I will be pleased to see them and converse with them on matters pertaining to their interests."[30]

Not only was the Indian Office unwilling to pay for parental visits to off-reservation schools, it also refused to cover the expense of transporting the bodies of deceased students to their reservations for interment. The grief that parents experienced from being separated from their dead or dying children was thus exacerbated by their inability to bury and mourn them in a Lakota fashion. In response to White Thunder's and Swift Bear's pleas that the remains of their children be returned from Carlisle, on January 27, 1881, Commissioner Edward Marble informed Agent Cook that, although this request was "of course only natural and proper . . . [it] would establish a precedent not only among the Sioux but among the tribes who have sent children to Carlisle and Hampton and it does not seem to me practicable to establish the practice of returning to their distant homes (some live in Arizona) the bodies of all pupils who may die at those schools." Marble therefore inquired of Crook, "Will it not be possible for you by kind and sympathetic conversation with these chiefs to assure them of the desire of the Department to accede to this request if it could be done without establishing an unwise precedent and to persuade them to withdraw it and to reconcile them to the thought of leaving their children among the white men who were their friends during life and cared for them tenderly after the life had departed."[31]

The callousness with which the Indian Office notified parents of the death of their children is exhibited in a note dated September 8, 1883, in which Price informed Wright of the death of one of Carlisle's Sicangu students. In what may have passed in the commissioner's mind as an expression of condolence, he ordered the agent to inform her parents that "skilled physicians were in attendance during her sickness and everything was done to administer to her wants and alleviate her sufferings."[32]

Given their painful experience with off-reservation boarding schools, it is little wonder that Sicangus welcomed the building of reservation-based educational institutions, be they day or residential. The Sicangus' loathing of remote schools was hardly unique; it was part of a widespread pattern among Indians communities that periodically threatened the existence of these institutions. Addressing this danger in an 1892 circular distributed to reservation agents, Commissioner Morgan thus advised that the "great difficulty in filling the non-reservation schools [which] lies in the objection of parents to separation from their children . . . must be overcome, if possible, by kindness, by persuasion, and by holding out the advantages, both to the child and the parent, to be derived from a course of training at the industrial school." Aware that some of the problem lay with those in charge of on-reservation facilities, he then added, "In a few instances, I am sorry to say, the difficulty has been increased by the indifference or active opposition of agency and school employees. I need hardly say that the Office wishes and expects the hearty co-operation of every employee."[33]

The desire of Rosebud parents to educate their children on their reservation found a natural ally in the Catholic missionaries' eagerness to keep their boarding school filled to capacity. Parents would sometimes ask one of the priests to baptize their children so that they would have a better chance of being admitted to Saint Francis. In 1904, Digmann reported that the "Indians of Cutmeat complained that they were treated like animals with regard to their offsprings and asked our assistance in the fight. Many children were offered for baptism." It appears that the priest was not above using the desperation of some Protestant parents to keep their children on the reservation as a tool for enlarging Rosebud's Catholic fold. His diary entry for August 30, 1903, related: "These last days especially today children dropped in already. Even Protestants wanted to have theirs here. I told them: 'Our school is a Catholic school and if your children must remain Protestants, I have no room for them.'"[34]

In addition to its relative proximity to their homes, Saint Francis offered the children of impoverished families food, clothing, and protection. An unusual example of how some parents utilized the school as a haven for their children is found in the sisters' house history during the period of the Ghost Dance movement: "An Indian named *Cahanpa* (shoes) brought his child to stay at the Mission during his absence at the sacred dance. The child was much at home and soon became the favorite of everyone. It was decided that she stay. Some days later the Indian came to claim the child. As sudden as was the arrival, so also was the abduction. One Sister insisted in running after the father and prevailed upon him to leave the child at the Mission."[35]

The fact that Saint Francis was located on the Rosebud obviously did not guarantee the health or safety of the mission's students. In common with similar facilities located on other reservations, its boarding school's early history was marked by the death of many of its pupils. According to the Franciscan house historian for 1890, "On the feast of Corpus Christi an Indian child, one of the earliest arrivals, lay dying. When the father appeared on the scene, he was distracted with grief. He forced his way into the sick room, tore the patient from the bed and threw the girl on his wagon. One of the sisters finally succeeded in bringing the sufferer back. After the death of the child the father was quieted."[36]

The opportunity of this father to be close to his daughter at her death highlights one of the major reasons why many Sicangus preferred enrolling their children at Saint Francis rather than an off-reservation school. Though denied daily contact with their offspring, the parents of the mission's students were nevertheless near enough to reach them in event of emergency and transport them home in case of death. To further decrease the distance between the school and their camps during crises, such as epidemics, large numbers of parents established temporary villages on the mission's perimeter.[37]

At times missionaries were unable to restrain worried relatives from entering the mission compound. "Old Mrs. B.W.," Digmann wrote, "had stolen her sick granddaughter from the infirmary, carrying her off on her back. I went for her," the priest continued, "but she drew her knife and I thought it was wiser not to insist for the present."[38]

In addition to feeding, clothing, and boarding their children in relative proximity to their camps, enrolling them at Saint Francis boarding school offered Sicangus a certain amount of power over the missionaries. They were keenly aware of the Catholic mission's need to achieve the enrollment quota set by the government. On June 25, 1890, BCIM director Stephan wrote Digmann of the Indian Office's criticism of the BCIM when its schools failed to "keep up the attendance to the number provided by the contract." This, he reminded Digmann, not only resulted in "many Indian children being deprived of Catholic education, but also in the loss of thousands of dollars annually." Worse yet, it gave "the Indian Office in many instances a good reason for reducing the number of pupils now provided by the contact." He thus advised Digmann "that a good way to induce an early and full attendance of pupils would be to provide a feast for the Indians shortly before the time for the opening [of] the school. This would necessitate but a comparatively small outlay of money, which would be more than made up to you by the increased attendance that would result therefrom."[39]

An example of Sicangus attempting to use school enrollment as a bargaining chip in their dealings with the missionaries is found in the following exchange in 1894 between Digmann and an angry Sicangu individual after the superior curbed the distribution of coffee to the elderly after Sunday Mass. Digmann chided the parishioner, "We feed you now already six years and preach to you . . . [but] it seems you only come to eat, that you can do also at home," to which his critic retorted, "Then we will also not send our children to your school." In 1897 the members of the Saint Joseph Society employed this same strategy in an attempt to coerce Digmann into ousting the sodality's president. "Some threatened," the priest reported, "they would leave the Church and go to the White Gowns, taking their children out of our school."[40]

Despite such threats, the missionaries knew very well that most Sicangu parents were desperate to keep their children from being placed in off-reservation schools and that enrolling them at Saint Francis offered one of their only means of securing this end. The missionaries' leverage on this matter increased, first, in 1902 with a revision of the Browning bill that prohibited reservation agents from transferring students from religious schools without their parents' permission while continuing this practice with children enrolled in government schools; and, second, in 1910 with the destruction of Saint Mary's Episcopal school, Rosebud's only other denominationally operated boarding facility.

The religious accepted as a matter of course the loss of some of their students to other schools. In fact, it was not unusual for the mission to request that a reservation or school agent assign one of its more troublesome students to another facility. Writing to Rosebud day school inspector J. F. House about one of the mission's habitual runaways, Digmann reported that "his uncle told me that he would bring him back, but could not." He therefore advised House, "You better send a Policeman and keep him at the agency or dispose of him as you think best. All I would hate is to let the boy have his own will in the end."[41]

What *did* frighten the religious was the threat of any widespread Sicangu disaffection with the mission that would lead them to withdraw their children en masse from the school. Such an eventuality might make it impossible for the school to meet its enrollment quota or require the mission to return a portion of government-paid tuitions. This sort of disaster scenario was one of the major reasons why the religious were so intent on countering Protestant claims that these tuitions were subtracted from the Indians' per-capita treaty benefits.

Employer and Provider of Material Support

In addition to utilizing the missionaries as political advocates and educators, many Sicangus came to rely on Saint Francis as a source of income. From the beginning the Jesuits hired Indians as laborers to supplement the work supplied by the mission's brothers, sisters, and students. For example, the religious regularly contracted Sicangus to cut and deliver cordwood to heat their residences and school, as well as to haul goods from the railroad depot in Valentine, Nebraska, or from the agency headquarters. When the mission needed new buildings, the religious hired Indians from the camps to help with the construction.

By and large both the religious and Indians were content with and mutually benefited from this system. Sicangus welcomed the money that working for Saint Francis brought into their generally cash-strapped households; the missionaries found that hiring Indians to perform menial tasks provided them the freedom to pursue more specialized activities at the school or in the field. At the same time, it is important to underscore that the missionaries' appreciation for the arrangement was based on their developmentalist social philosophy as well as pragmatism. Along with whatever practical advantages it yielded, the religious thus considered their practice of employing Sicangus to be an essential aspect of their role as civilizers. They believed that employing Sicangus would simultaneously teach them the value of work necessary for life in a civilized society and wean them from dependence on government assistance.

Circumstances, however, sometimes conspired to produce fissures in this otherwise mutually beneficial relationship. For example, at times the number of Sicangus seeking employment swelled beyond the mission's capacity to employ them. One such disjuncture between supply and demand occurred in 1890 when the federal government reduced Sicangu rations to compel them to work. The disastrous results of this reduction and the dilemma it posed for Indians and missionaries alike are witnessed in Digmann's letter to BCIM director Stephan on September 7, 1890: "First I gave them without asking anything in return," the priest wrote. "When it became too much, I made them work for it. Now many come already a few days after they have got their rations of beef and ask for *work* to eat. . . . The hunger has to help civilize them and make them work. To see them, however, willing to work and no chance to do so . . . is a great pity."[42]

During less economically trying times, Sicangus were able to utilize the competition among Rosebud's Christian denominations as leverage in bargaining for employment and other rewards. In the following passage from his journal, Digmann described one Catholic Indian's veiled threat to defect to the Episcopalians unless the Catholics matched their job offer as a lay helper. According to the priest the young man pled, "'I did not want to go back on my faith and my Church, but I have a family and wanted to make money,' 'So, for money you want to sell your soul? If you are convinced that the Episcopalians are the true Church, go to them, if not you cannot do it. . . . You shall not deceive them being Catholic in heart, and with your tongue helping them.'"[43]

Although the missionaries enthusiastically drew upon the Indian labor pool and considered employing Rosebud Lakotas an important contribution to Indian civilization, they occasionally expressed irritation with what they perceived as some Sicangus' ingratitude for all the goods and services the mission supplied to them gratis. In 1896, Digmann complained, "The Indians asked us then to pay for the little chores or work they had to do."[44] He later wrote: "The Indians wanted more pay for cordwood; as much as they received from the government. They had to haul it ten or more miles to the Agency or government schools. I told them: 'I will not pay more, and if you insist on it, you may also get your drinking water where you get the wood in the canyons. I did not expect to be treated by you this way. A child in the government schools costs nearly twice as much as in the mission, the teachers too get salarys. We and the sisters do not.'"[45]

As mentioned earlier (ch. 8), none of the religious ever acknowledge the mission's absolute dependence on the unpaid labor of its students for its survival, though on one occasion he recorded his scathing rejoinder to some Sicangu parents who dared to broach this subject. In an article on Saint Francis that appeared in an issue of the *Woodstock Letters*—a publication of the Jesuits' Maryland Province printed exclusively for Society members— the priest complained that for a time the "Indians came bothering us for *pay* for the work of their children—as had been promised them in the

Government school." The priest reported that his response to such pressure was, "'With whites the parents have to pay for teaching their children trades, the apprentices get nothing.' Nor did they pay them at the Government school, except a few 'officers' who had to help to maintain discipline."[46]

As Jesuits and Franciscans, the religious stationed at Saint Francis mission were obliged to take vows of poverty that prescribed that they divest themselves of all personal property and finances and depend solely upon the resources of their respective orders for their sustenance. Although totally in accord with the individualistic assumptions of Euro-American social economy, this notion of poverty may have proven somewhat bewildering for Sicangus, who reckoned such matters according to the well-being of a person's group. They may have wondered how members of such wealthy *tiyospaye* could reckon themselves as poor. The question of *why* they would wish to do such a thing was probably even more of a mystery to them. As this chapter demonstrates, many Sicangus sought to tap the economic, social, and political resources of these Catholic communities in their fight for individual and collective survival. In the next chapter I examine the understandings and motives of those Rosebud Lakotas who converted to Catholicism to gain access to the spiritual resources of the church.

CHAPTER THIRTEEN

Reception of Early Catholic Mission, Part Two

Catholicism and Sacred Power

For Spotted Tail and many other first-generation Rosebud Lakotas, interest in the Blackrobes' presence commenced and ended with the social, political, and economic benefits that the mission passed along to their tribe. Other Sicangus, however, converted to Catholicism in order to secure the spiritual assets, as they understood them, of church practices and paraphernalia. Complying with the admonitions of the mission's Jesuit and Franciscan religious, some of these converts ceased participating in Lakota rituals. Others, by contrast, continued these practices clandestinely and, if or where possible, refashioned Catholic ceremonies to reflect their traditional spiritual beliefs and practices.

What were some of the assumptions underlying these Sicangus' reception and interpretation of Catholicism that gave rise to their various ways of being Catholic? How did the first generation of Saint Francis missionaries often unwittingly abet this transference of Lakota meanings and values into Catholic sacramentalism?

Catholic Sacraments and *Wakan*

Notwithstanding the tenacious efforts of Catholic missionaries to inculcate Sicangu converts with the orthodox church dogma of their day, reports by Father Digmann and other Saint Francis missionaries suggest that many Rosebud Lakotas of the late nineteenth and early twentieth centuries continued to interpret Catholic doctrine and practice in terms of basic categories of traditional Lakota thought and ritual. Not being Catholic theologians, the Sicangus may have simply been oblivious to or unconcerned with the very real differences between Catholic and Lakota spiritualities. For example, it would have been exceedingly difficult for Sicangu Catholics, whose ontology did not distinguish between a natural and supernatural order, to grasp Catholicism's metaphysical separation between creator and creatures and the myriad theological and anthropological assumptions (including original sin, concupiscence, and salvation) associated with this distinction.

It is, however, equally likely that the missionaries' need to communicate in Lakota, either through interpreters or by acquiring the language, also encouraged the Sicangus' inclination to make sense of the beliefs and practices of the Blackrobes' "prayer" by resorting to their own traditional tenets. Instead of replacing the central ideas of Lakota spirituality with those of Catholic doctrines and dogmas, the missionaries' recourse to Lakota theological vocabulary for their instructions and homilies thus, ironically, served to reinforce the presuppositions of traditional Lakota religious thought. Of particular importance was their adoption of the term *wakan* to convey Catholic beliefs and categories related to the supernatural, such as their renderings of God and the devil/demons as Wakan Tanka and Wakan Sica, respectively. Not only were both expressions lexical derivatives of *wakan*, but they also referred to important pre-Christian, Lakota deities. As such they served as conduits for Lakota precepts regarding sacred practices and beings to enter into Rosebud Catholicism. In the case of Wakan Sica, the missionaries further encouraged this process by explicitly identifying the Lakotas' traditional gods as devils and demons, akin to those found in Jewish scriptures and the New Testament.

In addition to their use of Lakota loan words, the Saint Francis religious also created neologisms or employed those that had been invented by earlier Catholic and Protestant missionaries, including the noted Benedictine priest of the Standing Rock Reservation, Jerome Hunt, and the equally famous Congregationalist missionaries from the eastern Dakotas, Samuel and Gideon Pond, Stephen Return Riggs, and John Williamson. Among the most important of these innovations and borrowings were *wanikiye wakan* (sacred giver of life) for savior, Anpetu Wakan (sacred day) for Sunday, *ogligle wakan* (sacred messenger) for angel, and *wakan waste* (sacred good) for saint.[1]

Examples of such manufactured spiritual vocabulary may be multiplied many times. What is key to remember for the purposes of this study is their collective effect, which was to reinforce traditional Lakota conceptions of the nature and attributes of sacred power and to shape Sicangus' understanding of the new religion. Nowhere is this more evident than in missionary reports concerning Indian theory and practice of *wo'econ wakan* (sacred doings), the seven Catholic sacraments.

The missionaries' translation of the sacraments simply as *wo'econ wakan* reflects the primacy of these rites in Catholic theology, ecclesiology, and missiology. In contrast to Protestants' emphasis on "the Word," Catholic missionaries concentrated their efforts on educating their converts on the importance of the sacraments, both for the sake of their individual salvation and as the condition for establishing self-sufficient sacramental communities, or churches, among them. The missionaries undoubtedly borrowed the term *wakan* to express the holy character of these "doings," the most important being their capacity to convey supernatural gifts from God—grace in its various forms—to the souls of their recipients.[2] For the same reason, it is not surprising that the term appears in the missionaries' translations for six of the seven sacraments. These include *yutapi wakan* (sacred meal) for the Eucharist, *woglakapi wakan* (sacred testimony) for penance, *wicayustanpi wakan* (sacred completion) for confirmation, *wiyunpi wakan* (sacred application) for extreme unction, *wicasa wakan kagapi* (making of sacred men) for holy orders, and *wakankiciyuzapi* (sacred union) for matrimony. The sole exception was the Catholics' translation of baptism as *mni'akastanpi* (pour water upon). Nevertheless, as we see below, even here *wakan* was part of the Lakota translation for the water used in the sacrament. They also used it in their rendering for the rite of Viaticum, the special form of Eucharist dispensed to persons who are near or in danger of death, *onweya wakan* (sacred provisions).

If the missionaries' appropriation of *wakan* allowed them to impress upon Sicangus the holiness of the sacraments, it did so at a tremendous liability of which they were apparently unaware, for the term also carried with it the ontological assumptions underlying the idea and experience of sacred power as they had evolved in traditional Lakota individual and collective life. The transmission of these assumptions is most readily seen in the Sicangus' understanding of the sacraments of baptism, extreme unction, confession, and the Eucharist.

In chapter 9, I noted that the missionaries considered the terror with which a great number of Rosebud Lakotas regarded the sacrament of baptism as one of the greatest obstacles to their conversion. The priests were quick to realize that this response originated from their practice of ministerial "triage," according to which they placed top priority on baptizing the terminally and gravely ill whose souls they considered to be in immediate need of cleansing from original sin. Although the missionaries were open to the possibility that God in his mercy might spare the lives of some of these "deathbed" converts, their overriding concern lay with the latter's spiritual rather than corporeal salvation.

For Sicangus, whose anthropology was devoid of anything akin to original sin, the necessity of ceremonially cleansing souls in order to ensure their happy afterlives would have made little sense. As with other Lakotas, their preeminent ceremonies for ensuring a tranquil transit of individuals from this world to the next included tattooing and keeping of the soul, neither of which deemed a person's spirit tainted or polluted. Ceremonies for sick individuals were performed exclusively for the purpose of their physical recovery.

The priests' use of holy water in baptism may have further added to the Sicangus' confusion and fear of the rite. During *inikage* (sweatbath), the *ton* of the heated rocks and water mingled together in steam that both purified participants' bodies and reinvigorated their own spiritual principle. Here water was a key element in a ritual that was performed for the physical and spiritual welfare of band members. According to traditional Lakota spirituality, malevolent medicine men could ceremonially pervert the *ton* of material objects such as water so that contact with them caused sickness and death. When a high percentage of individuals died shortly after receiving baptism, many Sicangus attributed their passing to the evil power of the baptismal water that the priests had *yuwakan* (empowered) to kill their loved ones. It was thus fully in keeping with a Lakota perspective that Sicangus should fear the uninvited "sick-calls" by priests, whom they equated with their own evil medicine men. What is more, the Sicangus' horror of the priests and their rite is even more understandable when one considers that the missionaries' translation for the "holy water" used in baptism was *mniyuwakanpi*, water that had been made *wakan*, spiritually powerful. Interpreting this translation according to spiritual presuppositions and processes familiar to them, they assumed that the priests had empowered the water with the *ton* from their malevolent *sicun*.

Over time, as Sicangus discerned that the fatality rate of sick individuals who received baptism demonstrated no marked deviation from that of Lakotas who underwent curing ceremonies, their fear of the rite gradually abated. More and more Rosebud Lakotas therefore agreed, for one or a combination of social, economic, and spiritual motives, to allow the priests to "pour water" on them and their family members. Using the following interview with the relatives of a recently deceased unbaptized Indian to demonstrate this change, Digmann wrote: "'Did baptism kill him?' we [Digmann and a fellow priest] asked the Indians. 'No, because he did not want it and so could not be baptized.' 'Did your medicine men kill him? You will not admit that so it was the sickness that caused his death, as we all have to die.' A few similar cases set them rethinking that after all it was not baptism but the sickness that carried them off, especially as others who were hopelessly sick recovered after having received baptism."[3] By 1904, Digmann confidently declared that "the fact that our Indians are now anxious to have their babes baptized soon after their birth shows that their old fear 'The pouring on of water would kill them,' has disappeared."[4]

In spite of the Sicangus' growing acceptance that baptism did not kill its recipients and that its primary purpose was to prepare their spirits for a happy afterlife rather than cure them of illness, many converts came to believe that the prayers and waters were *pejuta*, or "medicine," that could heal. This belief was bolstered by the occasional recoveries of apparently terminally ill individuals after they had the blessed water "poured" on them. In one such case, Digmann administered the sacrament to an ailing woman who "had wished long ago to be baptized" but had not been able to attend the required catechetical meetings. She not only survived her illness but went on to live another twenty years. In a similar case, Digmann recorded that the great headman Two Strike "having reached eighty years . . . often got swoons. [Digmann] said to him: 'If you die unbaptized, I would feel sorry for you my life long.' He yielded and after we instructed him [he] received the sacrament. After this the swoons did not return anymore and he lived thirteen years longer ascribing it to baptism and often repeating: 'Baptism was good medicine.'" Digmann reported that on another occasion after being baptized an old woman exclaimed that the "medicine I had put in her mouth (salt) at baptism was very good. It made her feel so good." Another somewhat different case involved a young man who suffered from "fiery apparitions." He reported to Digmann that, after being "instructed in the Faith and baptized, these apparitions did not return anymore."[5]

It is of interest that Sicangu attitudes regarding the sacrament of extreme unction apparently underwent a transvaluation similar to that of baptism. In January 1901 an ailing Sicangu notified Digmann of his desire to receive this rite. The priest wrote that this individual "was the first one who asked for it. The effect," he continued, "was salutary for body and soul and did to overcome the prejudice as if it meant 'sealing for death.'" The Sicangus' diminishing fear of this sacrament is also revealed in the following report of yet another Indian's desire to receive the sacrament. Digmann wrote that when he and Father Westropp arrived at this individual's house they "heard already outside the powwows [curing songs] and the voice of the medicine men but they opened the door; the noise stopped at once; his [the ailing man's] father (pagan yet) himself, helped at the Extreme Unction, pulling off his shoes and stockings, turning him around etc." Although the recipient died, Digmann found in the happenings "some change for the better, comparing with their former fear and apathy."[6]

The belief that sacraments performed for the sick not only posed them no danger but occasionally had salutatory effects is found in statements by other Sicangus. Digmann reported that one grateful recipient of extreme unction informed him, "You have doctored me, I am much better." She went on to describe how she had "seen Jesus appearing to her and pointed to the place where He had stood." Consider also the comment by a woman who had requested that Digmann perform the rite on her daughter. When the priest asked the mother ("who was pagan yet") to help remove her child's moccasins, she responded, "You don't need to anoint her feet, she is very fast yet."[7]

Although Sicangus most commonly attributed healing properties to those sacraments performed over individuals who appeared to be on the verge of death, they ascribed medicinal qualities to other sacraments as well. They believed that the consecrated communion wafer, which they consumed during the Eucharist, possessed revitalizing powers akin to their traditional medicines. One Sicangu Catholic confided to Digmann, "When I did not receive Holy Communion for a long time, I don't feel good. After I received it, I feel fresh again." The experience of being empowered or cured also appears in statements regarding confession. Another church member told the priest that, when he recently contracted a severe cold, he rejected the offers of a medicine man to perform a doctoring ceremony and requested, instead, that the Little Father (Westropp) come to his house so he could "go to confession." Digmann reported that he did so and was well again the next day, "[ascribing] his bodily recovery to the Sacraments." On another occasion, a Sicangu who had suffered a stroke told Digmann that "after going to Confession, he felt better, could again talk and walk."[8]

Other Catholic Practices and *Wakan*

In addition to ascribing recuperative and energizing powers to selected sacraments, Sicangu Catholics attributed sacred powers to other Catholic rituals in a manner that was consistent with traditional Lakota notions of *wakan*. Once again, this mode of interpretation was encouraged by the Saint Francis religious, whose appropriations of Lakota spiritual terms served to highlight superficial similarities between Catholic and Lakota beliefs and practices while blurring the fundamentally different assumptions of the nature and source of the sacred informing them.

An intriguing example of such obfuscation is found in the missionaries' translation of the Catholic retreats as *hanbleceya*, the Lakota term for their vision quest. When performing this custom Lakotas fasted and prayed for four days away from camp to receive spiritual guidance and power from their spirit relations. Digmann stated that, when he used the term *hanbleceya* to notify parishioners that he was on retreat, Sicangu Catholics who encountered him "seemed to have a holy awe and did not dare address him."[9] Such respect for one undertaking the rite was thoroughly consistent with the Sicangus' appreciation of the sacred nature of the vision quest as well as traditional proscriptions that forbid interaction with vision seekers until they have been ceremonially reintroduced to the camp during the rite's closing public phases.

In November 1906 an Oglala medicine man turned Catholic catechist, Nicholas Black Elk, traveled from Pine Ridge to the Rosebud in order to make a retreat under Digmann's direction. Although one of the most noted and effective of the Lakota catechists, he was apparently sufficiently unclear about the theology and method of the Catholic tradition to ask, "How is it about eating during the Retreat? The Indians do not eat during their recesses."[10]

In spite of the missionaries' use of the term *hanbleceya* for Catholic retreats, most Sicangu converts understood that this appropriation did not signal any softening in the former's stern opposition to their performance of its Lakota namesake. Consider in this context Digmann's response to a

Sicangu Catholic who asked to borrow one of the mission's fur coats. "'What for?' [the priest asked]. He first did not want to come out. Finally he said bashfully: '*hamblemiciyinkte*' [I am going to perform a vision quest]. . . . He had taken a vow. 'First go to your Easter-duty' was my reply and leave those old customs."[11]

For Sicangus and other Lakotas, *hanbleceya* was part of a wider system of beliefs and practices that derived from fundamental assumptions regarding the nature and significance of dreams or visions (*woihanble*). Among the most important of these were that *woihanble* constituted the primary means through which spirits communicated information and knowledge to human beings and that it was the role of medicine people to elucidate their meanings.

The importance that Lakotas traditionally accorded dreams at times served as a conduit leading Sicangus to Catholicism. In 1894 one of Saint Francis's non-Catholic students informed Digmann that Jesus had prevented a ghost from carrying him off and then, before leaving his bedside, advised him that he "would be all right again" after the priest baptized him. The priest first questioned the boy to determine whether his vision was merely a product of his fever. Satisfied that it was not, he "examined him about the necessary truths of faith, prayed with him and baptised him." Obviously moved by the event, he wrote, "Never before the prayers of the Ritual made such impression on him. Never before the prayers of the Ritual made such impression on me. ("Whom Jesus Christ, Our Lord has called to the grace of baptism.") The next day I asked him again: 'Was any ghost with you?' 'Not today but last night.' Be it as it may, God can call also by dreams."[12] In yet another *woihanble*-inspired cure that eventually resulted in conversion, a Sicangu informed Digmann that he had experienced a vision in which an individual whom he identified as a bishop came in and prayed over him and said he would get better. According to the priest, "This came true. He never had seen a Bishop. He recognized Bishop Lawler as the one two days later."[13]

Once baptized, Sicangus sometimes enlisted the Jesuit priests to discern the meaning of visions and dreams, much as they had solicited medicine people to provide the same service. One convert informed Digmann that, while he was lying awake in bed, "a white robed man coming through the window had grasped him by the shoulder and said: 'Hurry up.' He asked me: 'What should that mean?'" After Digmann had satisfied himself that this vision was neither the product of drunkenness nor an unfulfilled promise, he inquired, "'Did you make your Easter duty?' 'No,' [he answered] 'So hurry up, go to Confession, bring your conscience . . . in order and then: Come what may.' He went and did it; and others had noticed that he prayed with great earnest."[14]

In addition to seeking the aid of medicine people to cure illnesses and to interpret visions and dreams, Lakotas frequently appealed to these religious specialists to draw upon the power of their spiritual helpers or paraphernalia to help them recover misplaced or stolen property. Sicangus appeared to have transferred Lakota assumptions concerning this application of sacred power to priests' custom of appealing to saints for these same purposes. Thus, for example, in 1908 Digmann wrote that he promised a "devout rosary" to Saint Anthony and Saint Expedit if they would aid in his recovery of a lost horse. "There at 10 A.M. a policeman brought [the] horse and rig back from the Agency. Breviary on the side like I had left it—Nothing lost and nothing broken." On another occasion, the priest suggested that one of the Jesuit brothers promise a rosary to Saint Anthony for the return of a gold watch that had apparently been stolen from the wall of the mission's bakery. Shortly thereafter one of boys confessed to the crime. "He had got it out with a long stick with an iron hook on it; all clean and good yet." In view of these examples, it is hardly surprising that Lakotas should identify the saints as spirit helpers to whom the priests appealed to help them recover their property. On one occasion the Sicangu chief Iron Shell asked Father Perrig for a rosary "to say it for himself when hunting for his horses on the prairie."[15]

Iron Shell's request for a rosary is reminiscent of the conundrum Fr. Pierre-Jean De Smet faced during his initial visits to bands of Lakotas in the mid-nineteenth century. Although he valued the place of material objects in the ceremonial life of the church, De Smet worried that the Indians would distort their meaning and purpose to accord with their traditional "idolatristic" practices. Echoing De Smet's misgivings from pre-mission days, Digmann wrote in 1900 of having to warn Sicangu Catholics about "put[ting] their faith in outward things." Yet in spite of such misgivings, missionaries continued to distribute blessed objects to Sicangu Catholics. Among the most popular of these with the sick and dying were crucifixes, medals, and scapulars. The priest related the following incident, in which he arrived at the home of a seriously ill Catholic elder just as a medicine man was about to begin a curing ceremony. "The medicine man made his powwow [and] did not open the door for a long time. . . . [I] could do nothing with the sick man. He only asked for a crucifix, had lost his. I gave him one, also a scapular he had been enrolled already and a medal of the Blessed Virgin saying: 'Call me if you want me again.'"[16]

Two final examples of the powers that Sicangus accorded to blessed objects involve the "medicinal" use of Saint Ignatius water. In one case Digmann presented a woman suffering from gallstones a bottle of the water to drink and apply over the infected area of her body. Her husband later told the priest that "after she had done so, she had vomited yellow stuff and felt much relieved. They ascribed it the St. Ignatius water." On another occasion, the priest gave the parents of a sick boy who had already received extreme unction Saint Ignatius water for him to drink and in which to bathe. The patient's mother later told Digmann that after she had done as he directed the boy broke out in a heavy sweat and ascribed it to the water.[17]

Sicangu Catholicism and "Wonder-Working"

Prior to their conversion, Sicangu Catholics' participation in Lakota spirituality had thoroughly familiarized them with the wondrous capacity of sacred power to benefit human beings. Encouraged by the missionaries' Lakota translation of key Catholic beliefs and ceremonies, they drew upon this experience to make sense of their new religion. In so doing, however, they replaced orthodox Catholic tenets concerning the supernatural character of sacred power and wonder-working with those founded on the significantly different metaphysical presuppositions informing the nature and operation of *wakan*.

Based on the ontological split it posits between the natural and supernatural realms, the Catholic Church maintains that supernatural abilities and works lie purely within the provenience of God. Thus, although God in his mercy and at his pleasure may employ some aspect of creation (e.g., images, shrines, relics from saints and martyrs) to perform miracles or wonders, the latter are never more than instruments of his wonder-working and remain without any inherent efficacy or power in relationship to these works. To attribute this virtue or capacity to any created phenomenon is to commit the mortal sin of idolatry. The same holds true for persons, places, or things that have been blessed or consecrated and are thereby set aside for a special purpose or service within the church. All remain part of the created order without any inherent supernatural capacity to perform supernatural works. Even the saints, whom God has endowed with the ability to hear the petitions of those in need, do not directly answer these requests but act as intermediaries, presenting them before God, who alone may or may not choose to answer them.

As mentioned earlier in this chapter, the Catholic distinction between natural and supernatural was entirely foreign to Lakota metaphysics. The latter instead posited a universe in which all reality was united by a spirit (*sicun*), with different phenomena boasting varying qualities and degrees of spiritual potency (*ton*) and, consequently, wonder-inducing effects (*wakan*). This assumption of a plentitude of spiritual power not only served to distinguish Lakota notions of wonder-working from those found in Catholicism but deeply influenced many Sicangu converts' understanding of the central practices of their adopted religion. For Lakotas it was a phenomenon's inherent or ceremonially imputed *ton* that determined the nature and extent of the wonders associated with it. Though *wicasa wakan* were at times necessary to activate and direct this power, the fact remains that the potency inhered in the phenomena itself. In this respect, De Smet was wrong in his assessment that the Lakotas did not attribute power to those items from their own or Euro-American society that they considered *wakan*. In fact, what made these objects the source of spiritual significance and awe for Lakotas was precisely their belief that they contained power that could do harm or provide help. Given the Lakotas' understanding of spiritual power and wonder-working, there should be no question why they considered Catholic rituals and ceremonial objects a source of "medicine." And though the missionaries may have considered this attribution a form of idolatry, they nonetheless abetted it by their use of *wakan* and other Lakota sacred terms in their translation of Catholic beliefs and practices.

The Plentitude of Power and Sicangu Responses to Catholicism

The Lakotas' identification of *wakan* with Catholic categories of the supernatural and grace not only facilitated their acceptance of the Blackrobes' prayer but constituted the major avenue through which they culturally reconstructed the meaning and purpose of Catholic doctrines and practices. It makes sense that Catholic beliefs, practices, and objects should possess their share of spiritual power, and that this power could be tapped for the benefit of themselves, their families, and the larger Lakota community. The Catholic missionaries unknowingly aided and abetted this process of appropriation and adaptation through their use of *wakan* and other Lakota spiritual categories in their translations of church doctrines and practices. The fact that Lakota and Catholic conceptions of sacred power were based on antithetical ontological assumptions concerning the source and operation of such power seldom if ever surfaced as a point of theological reflection, for either Sicangu Catholics or the missionaries.

Although remaining tacit, this difference between the two spiritualities was at the root of the majority of conflicts that occurred between Sicangus and their Catholic missionaries. One of the most significant of these clashes concerned the missionaries' demand that Rosebud converts eschew participation in the observances of all other religions, whether Lakota or Protestant forms of Christianity. This requirement quite likely appeared ludicrous to most Sicangus, whose basic assumption concerning the plentitude of sacred power not only ran contrary to the assumption that any one tradition held a monopoly on sacred power but also encouraged them to adopt and adapt the religious traditions of other peoples. For the Saint Francis religious, who believed that the Catholic Church was the sole repository and arbiter of sacred wisdom and power, Sicangus had to choose to be members of the one true communion, schismatics, or servants of the devil. Lecturing one convert who wished to continue participating in Lakota ceremonies, Digmann thus insisted, "If the Lord is God . . . Hold to Prayer; if Lakota customs are from the Great Spirit, stick to them, but you cannot serve two masters. Do not limp from one to the other." Discussing the need to maintain a strict adherence to the principle of church exclusivity, Digmann remarked to one school inspector, "If I were Protestant and believed [in] what they say of the Mass, I would never set foot into a Catholic Church."[18]

Based on traditional Lakota assumptions concerning power, Sicangus responded in various ways to the missionaries' insistence that Catholics refrain from participating in all other forms of religion. Adhering to a doctrine of religious pluralism strikingly similar to that espoused by contemporary ecumenists, some Sicangus chose to confront the missionaries directly on this point. Digmann reported that one Sicangu insisted that "God made three Prayers" (Lakota "prayer," Protestantism, and Catholicism). Unwilling to allow such blasphemy to go unchallenged, the priest sarcastically retorted, "Why not one hundred and forty. . . . The kings in Europe have established Churches for their respective countries, but God did not make them." After another Sicangu expressed the opinion that "'both Prayers, the Black robe and the White Robes come from the heart of the

Great Spirit," the priest reported that he struggled "to make him understand that the Great Spirit had not 'two tongues.'" Then, once he had depleted his arsenal of "rational" arguments, Digmann resorted to sternly accusing the Sicangu of "wholly sitting in darkness" and "not knowing anything." "That made an impression," Digmann continued, "All around laughed at him, he was ashamed, and laughed himself and was silent."[19]

Some Sicangus chose to put their pluralism into practice by participating in the religious gatherings of all of Rosebud's denominations but refusing to affiliate themselves officially with any. When Digmann asked one elderly Sicangu if he belonged to a church, the latter responded: "When the Short Coats [Congregationalists] have a meeting, I go there and pray: Great Spirit have mercy on me and sit down and eat with them. If the Blackrobes have a meeting, I also go there and pray and eat with them. And if the White Gowns [Protestant Episcopalians] have a meeting, I also go there and eat with them. They all believe in the same Great Spirit."[20]

To gain access to the sacraments, other Sicangus decided to convert to Catholicism while clandestinely attending rituals and services of other religions. The religious were apparently reluctant to believe that members of their flock could be guilty of such bad faith. When one of Rosebud's non-Indian residents—a "divorced woman"—informed Digmann that a Sicangu had told her that he was Episcopalian and Congregationalist as well as Catholic, the priest dismissed the report. "What you say seems to be impossible," he retorted, preferring to call into question the competency of her interpreter than to grant any credence to the shocking revelation.[21]

On those occasions when the religious decided to follow up on such information, Sicangu Catholics could resort to a strategy of plausible deniability. Aware of the fierce competition for members that existed among the Rosebud's Christian denominations, a suspected "pluralist" could cast blame on crafty Protestant ministers and their helpers. When Digmann asked one longtime Catholic whether she had joined the Protestants, she responded that when an Episcopalian or Congregationalist minister had asked her merely if he "could take her name down" she had agreed, having no idea that she was joining his church.[22]

From the information available, it seems clear that some Sicangus honored the missionaries' demand to disassociate themselves from all other religions as a precondition for their conversion. Digmann reported that when he exhorted one Wild West showman and traditionalist to join the church, the latter informed him, "I think it would be a mockery offered to the Great Spirit if I let you baptize me and still would keep the old Indian customs." Some Sicangus could make the decision to renounce Lakota religious practices with little or no hesitation. Describing his religious instruction to the members of one camp, Digmann noted that when a medicine man asked him about several points of "superstition" he "cleared him up about what was allowed and what not. Finally he said: 'I'll give it up.'"[23]

Other Sicangus apparently took their time before deciding to abandon the "old" ways. Some of these individuals adopted the strategy of delaying their conversion until concerns about impending death, from either disease or old age, finally prompted them to take action. When the daughter of an elderly medicine man asked Digmann to baptize her ailing father, the *wicasa wakan* told him: "I want to be baptized and will call you in time. . . . I have yet a medicine, I want to give my sons; after that I will be baptized." The priest went on to write that the following summer "he was on his wagon to go to the Agency for his 'per capita money.' He was very weak and sick. After finding it necessary, we finished the necessary instruction and acts, I baptized him on his wagon. The following day he died."[24]

In another case of "deathbed" conversion, an Episcopal woman in the last stages of consumption called for Digmann after Rev. Aaron B. Clark had sent a helper to "pray over her" in his place. According to the priest, "She wanted to die a Catholic." Digmann wrote that he bluntly informed the woman, "'If you want to become Catholic for spite against the Episcopal, I cannot receive you.' But she was in full earnest; all her family had joined before, and she was the only one left outside the fold."[25]

We thus see that Sicangus who wished to gain access to the *wakan* ceremonies and properties of the Catholic Church were able, within limits, to determine the timing and character of their Christianization. Yet other Sicangus, who likewise acknowledged the power of the Blackrobes' "prayer," steadfastly refused to convert to Catholicism under any circumstances. Their rejection was, in some cases, based on an aversion to one or more Catholic ceremonies. As noted, many Sicangus initially ran in terror from the priests because of the belief that they killed people by sprinkling baptismal waters on them. There is some evidence that Catholic burial practices may likewise have discouraged conversion. Lakotas traditionally disposed of their dead by placing them in the crotch of trees or on "burial" scaffolds, and the idea of entombing the departed underground may have simply repulsed some.[26]

Still other Sicangus refused to convert to Catholicism based on their belief that Wakan Tanka had provided whites and Indians with "prayers" appropriate to their respective lifeways and that it was best for each group to remain true to its own traditions. "The Great Spirit has raised us another way," one such individual observed. "We also pray to Him, but we grew up on the Buffalo hunt and you with the plow."[27] This line of reasoning was, apparently, especially common among older Sicangus. When Father Perrig asked a group of elders including Chief Swift Bear to consider receiving instruction in the Catholic faith, Swift Bear politely informed the priest that Christianity "was all right for the children at school, but that they were too old for it." A few years later Digmann stated, "The same excuse I have heard often. They have the idea, that to be baptized means to change their manners and live like whites."[28]

One cannot help but wonder what Digmann was thinking when he wrote these lines. Given the nexus between civilization and Christianity that lay at the heart of both reform Indian policy and the Catholic missionary paradigm, it would be hard to imagine him dismissing those Sicangus who harbored this idea as misguided. In fact, almost everything the missionaries said and did—both at the school as well as in the camps—reinforced the Sicangus' assumptions concerning the necessary linkage between religion and culture and that to be baptized meant to live like whites. Nowhere were these assumptions more potently played out than in the goals and activities of the Saint Joseph and Saint Mary Societies. Describing the "disposition" of Rosebud Catholics who organized these guilds, the priest stated that they "intended [them] to replace their old Indian league with its war dances and other childish entertainments." He went to state: "In their meetings they encourage one another to do away with their old habits and follow the white man's way. . . . The members oblige themselves to dress like white men, take good care of their families, not to admit the medicine men to the sick, and to help one another. The non-progressive Indians are now faced and opposed by a party in their own midst, which I hope will steadily grow, attract the sound element, and by making public opinion draw the rest."[29]

The missionaries theologized their unmasked antipathy toward all Lakota customs by classifying their practice as sins, which they translated into Lakota as *wicohan sica*, literally "bad deeds" or, more commonly, *wowahtani*. This second translation is exceedingly interesting, from both a semantic and pragmatic perspective. Semantically, it comprises three elements: the prefix *wo*, which transforms terms it precedes into collective nouns; the root *wahte*, signifying "good," or "worthy"; and *ni*, a marker that negates or denotes the antithesis of the character or essence of the term it modifies. That at least some Sicangus accepted this negative characterization of their traditions is suggested by the following confession of a recent convert. Asked whether he remembered any sin after his baptism, the penitent responded, "No, I only cried very much when a grandchild of mine had died. I have no other Indian habits."[30]

Sicangu Indigenization and the Catholic Sioux Congress

Though the Saint Francis religious may have considered Lakota "habits" sinful, not all Sicangu Catholics necessarily accepted this assessment. The preceding section shows the strategies certain Rosebud Lakotas employed to maximize their access to the spiritual resources of both forms of "prayer." In addition, some converts began the process of consciously or unconsciously recasting elements of Catholic belief and ritual so they reflected qualities and attributes of traditional Lakota spirituality. Their genius for transforming Catholic beliefs and rituals into conduits of cultural and religious continuity reached its heights with the Catholic Sioux Congress.

The brainchild of Bishop Marty, the Congress was inaugurated in 1890 as an annual opportunity for Lakota Catholics from throughout his diocese to assemble and encourage one another in their commitment to the Catholic Church and civilized life. Most of the participants in this four-day revival were delegates from reservation chapters of the Saint Joseph Society for men and Saint Mary Society for women. Among the rules governing these sodalities were that their members be Catholic and that they give a good example by taking care of their houses and homes; reject all bad habits of whites, including drunkenness and profane language; avoid participating in any Protestant services; abstain entirely from all superstitious Indian customs; and "strive to learn by heart the *Our Father, Hail Mary*, the *Apostles' Creed*, the *Ten Commandments, Commandments of the Church*, and an *Act of Contrition*." The bylaws also recommended that members of the Saint Mary Society "give special attention to needle work, as a help to the treasury and a good example to outsiders."[31]

Bishop Marty scheduled the first Catholic Sioux Congress for the second through fifth of July. Several factors determined his choice of these dates. He believed that overlapping the convention with the Fourth of July would provide Lakota Catholics with a wholesome alternative to Independence Day celebrations, at which agents turned a blind eye to traditional dancing, give-aways, and other practices that the missionaries thought revitalized Lakota "savagery." He was also aware that the Lakotas had traditionally assembled for their Sun Dance in late June and early July and thus hoped that a Congress held at that time would serve to "baptize" the period and provide Lakota Catholics with a powerful symbol of Christ's victory over devil-dominated paganism. As well, the bishop felt that a midsummer Congress would act as a pressure valve, releasing the pent-up wanderlust of the recently immobilized Lakotas in socially and spiritually constructive directions.

As a loyal son of his order, Bishop Marty chose the Benedictine mission of Saint Michael's in North Dakota as the location for the inaugural Congress. Thereafter, however, Congress delegates appropriated the role of selecting host missions, indigenizing the process in ways probably not imagined by the good bishop. A Jesuit priest who attended the 1919 convention provided a detailed account of the "picturesque and striking ceremony":

> It was the evening of the fourth day and the bower was in darkness except for the light of the moon and a feeble lamp. When all who were interested had gathered in the bower, three spokesmen in turn took their place in the midst of the assembly and in glowing terms described the advantages of the locality at which their people desired the next Congress to convene. A vote was called for by the president. Thereupon those in favor of a particular place came to the center to be plainly visible, and were counted by the secretary. When the vote for Holy Rosary Mission was demanded a peculiar yell resembling the oldtime war-hoop was raised and an overwhelming majority rushed to the center of the bower. So next year's Congress will be on the Pine Ridge Reservation.[32]

Sponsoring a Congress carried with it a formidable array of obligations for a mission's chapters of the Saint Joseph and Saint Mary Societies. Not only were the members of these locals required to construct the meeting places used for Congress sessions, but they also had to prepare a campground and meals for all who attended. One can only appreciate the great quantity of capital needed for these projects when one realizes that the number of Congress visitors sometimes ran into the thousands. In explaining the social and economic conditions that made such an undertaking possible, Fr. Goll wrote that the "guests one year will be hosts some other year. And if a locality cannot afford to be host,—well the congress cannot be held there." This principle of reciprocity, traditional among Lakota *tiyospaye* and bands, was merged with canons of hospitality. As Goll went on to state, "It would require a complete change of the law of hospitality among Sioux, if visitors had to provide board for themselves. The man who would have the courage to advocate such a plan has not yet appeared among the Sioux."[33]

In addition to a massive outlay of foodstuffs and other material resources, sponsoring a successful Congress entailed many hours of planning. That sodality members shaped this requirement in ways not necessarily congenial to their missionary mentors finds expression in the following report by Fr. Placidus Sialm of Holy Rosary Mission: "We are preparing for the next Indian Sioux Congress to be held at Holy Rosary Mission. The Indians wish to have meetings and more meetings where the talkers enjoy good days of plenty to eat, plenty to talk and plenty to smoke,—with the final resolution to meet again. And so the vicious circle has become congenial to their nature. It develops talkers and voters not seldom paupers." Despite his critique, Sialm ends the report in a conciliatory fashion, suggesting that these things are merely incidentals—that, in fact, the "solemnity of the meetings passes anything you see among meetings of white people."[34]

Until midcentury, when cars and pick-up trucks became common on Lakota reservations, most participants traveled to the Congress on horseback or by team and wagon. Since some participants lived several hundred miles from the convention, they needed to begin their trek as much as two weeks before opening day. In a fashion nearly identical with the pre-reservation era, members of one or more *tiyospaye* would journey together in long caravans. Certain individuals were assigned the role of *akicita*, or soldier, deciding where the party would stop and ensuring that decorum was maintained en route. After arriving at a campsite, the preparations for the evening took place according to the traditional Lakota sexual division of labor: women took charge of setting up the tent and prepared a meal, and men tended to the horses and gathered firewood. At sunset an *eyapaha*, or herald, announced news of interest as members of the party entertained themselves with conversations, games, and storytelling. With dawn, he would again make his rounds, standing before each tent and shouting "*Kikta po*" (Get up). Then, at the *akicita*'s pacing, the travelers prepared and consumed their morning meal, struck camp, and recommenced their journey. If a priest and catechist were part of the group, as was often the case, he would lead evening rosaries and perform Mass as part of the various camp activities. This offering of prayer while journeying to a Congress ran parallel with patterns of indigenous religious practice. James R. Walker related that, before beginning each leg of a band's journey to the Sun Dance, its magistrate would "offer smoke to the Four Winds and pray to Him for good weather; and to the Sky and pray for His care while the band was moving."[35]

Upon approaching the site of the Congress, the party was made welcome by customary expressions of Lakota etiquette. Officers from the host sodalities would ride out on horseback to greet their guests and escort them to a camp circle that contained, at times, up to six hundred tents. Although remarkable to the missionaries, camps of this size and larger were the routine when the Lakotas gathered for their Sun Dances. Alice Fletcher reported that in 1882, at the last Sun Dance celebrated before the government banned the ceremony, "over 9,000 [Lakotas] were so camped, the diameter of the circle being over three-quarters of a mile wide."[36] The welcoming committee would next assign the newcomers their proper place in the tribal circle, calculated based on their *tiyospaye* and districts. They then feasted and shared gossip at the tents of relatives or friends from other bands.

Positioned a short distance from the camp circle was the arbor that served as the Congress headquarters. An article in *Jesuit Missions* about the Congress held on the Pine Ridge Reservation in 1931 described this structure:

> The Indians enclose a large circle by a sort of bower and covered above and behind by pine branches thick enough to form a wall on the outside and a heavy top covering to keep off the heat of the sun. The inner side is open, facing the center of the circle in which the American Flag flies from a tall flagpole. The whole inner portion of the circle is open to the skies. At one side of the circle an entrance is left, and at the other end a stage is erected where the officers of the Congress take their places. Behind this is a large tent open on the side facing the circle.[37]

One cannot help but be struck by the similarity of the Congress bower and the enclosures Lakotas typically erected for their Sun Dance and Hunka ("making a relative," or adoption, ceremony). There is nothing in Catholic theology or in the structure of Congress rituals that dictated the bower's circular form. Rather, like all Lakota ceremonial lodges, it took its shape from the Lakota paradigm of *cangleska wakan* (the sacred hoop or circle) and the *tatuye topa* (the four cardinal directions). The internal divisions of Congress bowers likewise emanated from Lakota presuppositions of sacred form and space. In common with Sun Dance lodges, Congress enclosures were divided into two parts: a central area exposed to the sun and a protected perimeter covered with pine branches on its top and back. The shaded area, once again, like Lakota Sun Dance lodges, was partitioned into "reserved" and common sections. In the reserved part, or *catku*, located opposite the bower entrance, stood the stage and tent reserved for Congress officers and other key personnel. All of the arbor's remaining space was "common" and open to all.

The officers' platform and tent also served as the setting for the daily open-air masses celebrated at a Congress. On such occasions a temporary altar was set up at the back of the shelter. As Mass began, a procession of clerics would march into the bower and slowly wend its way to the altar. This association of *catku* and altar again had its precedents in the Sun Dance and Hunka.

At the center of the Congress bower stood a pole on which Congress officials would hoist and lower an American flag at the opening and conclusion of each day of the convocation. The prominent place accorded "Old Glory" was consistent with the important role that Catholic missionaries on the Pine Ridge and Rosebud Reservations granted the process of civilization in their work. Thus, although never forgetting that their primary obligation was to save Lakota souls, they nonetheless interpreted this obligation in line with the Thomistic maxim that "faith builds upon nature." In accord with this maxim, the religious viewed training the Lakotas in Western social and cultural institutions as a necessary, secular adjunct for planting the faith among them. As noted in chapter 2, one reason for the enthusiasm with which the Catholic Church greeted the government's reservation policy was that it forced the Lakotas to settle in communities that could serve as the bases for parishes.

Many progressives imbued the Congress flagpole with spiritual and political meanings quite distinct from the Christian civilization that it symbolized for the missionaries. Like the Sun Dance pole and the Hunka fireplace, the flagpole marked the center of the sacred hoop at which the six sacred directions, or "grandfathers," converged. It was, as such, an important manifestation of the sacred flowering tree of Nicholas Black Elk's famous vision that was "the center of the life of the nation."[38]

Because it was a church-sponsored celebration, the liturgical and ceremonial observances of the Congress necessarily fell comfortably within the parameters of orthodox belief and practice. Lakota Catholics, however, succeeded in molding many of these rites into forms strongly reminiscent of the traditional Sun Dance. Among the most striking of these adaptations was the procession of the Saint Joseph and Saint Mary Societies in which members of each sodality formed two separate lines as they marched from the bower to the church. In his monograph on the Sun Dance, Walker described a "procession of sex" for which participants similarly segregated themselves into gender-based groups. During other rites, such as the Eucharistic and Corpus Christi processions, participants circumambulated the Congress grounds while singing hymns, which again appear to have their basis in Sun Dance ceremonials. Walker reported, for example, that in the Buffalo Procession participants moved clockwise around the inside of the camp circle as they chanted in praise of the gods and shouted out sentiments appropriate to the occasion.[39]

At other times, Lakota traditions that the missionaries looked upon as savage or wasteful received a new Christian respectability when incorporated within the Congress. Such was the case with the *wihpeyaypi*, or "give-away," in which sizeable amounts of property were redistributed among members of one or more *tiyospaye*. When practiced outside a Congress, the missionaries considered this custom an impediment to the Lakotas' assimilation into a Western market economy. But as a "baptized" element of the Congress it became for them a pious expression of Christian charity. An account from an article on the 1910 Congress published in the BCIM's *Indian Sentinel* noted:

> The centre of the council bower was filled with trunks and boxes. The Indian women have sewing circles, and their work of the year was in these trunks and boxes, to be distributed to the poor and to their friends—all kinds of well-made clothing for the poor, all kinds of beautiful bead work for special friends. At the close of the meeting the distribution took place. . . . The Apostolic Delegate received a pair of beautiful moccasins and a pipe with a handsomely worked bag in

which to carry it. As His Excellency is not a smoker this Indian gift will be an attractive ornament in his Washington home. Father Ketcham received a pair of moccasins and beautifully ornamented saddlebags, to be used in his trips among the Indians.[40]

Perhaps the Lakotas' most intriguing subversion of the Congress's assimilationist agenda is found in the manner in which they utilized the celebration to continue the yearly reunions with friends and relations that the Sun Dance allowed in pre-reservation times. The extended period some Lakota Catholics wishing to attend a convocation had to spend traveling was equaled by the travel time required for their return home. Since the Congress was held during the summer, a long absence inevitably took a toll on the crops, which by government mandate Lakotas were required to plant. Government agents charged with the responsibility of transforming the formerly nomadic Sicangus and Oglalas into farmers often bitterly complained of the disastrous consequences of the timing of this religious celebration. For their part, Catholic missionaries found themselves caught on the horns of an exceedingly uncomfortable dilemma. On the one hand, they were staunch supporters of federal agricultural policy. On the other hand, they were not about to forsake any initiative that fostered the growth of a Lakota Catholic church.

In 1897, Bishop Marty attempted to resolve this dilemma by floating a proposal past the members of the Saint Joseph and Saint Mary Societies that the Congress be divided into two territorially defined sessions. Leaving the matter totally in the hands of the societies, the proposal met a resounding defeat.[41]

During one of his interviews with John Neihardt, amanuensis of *Black Elk Speaks*, Nicholas Black Elk remarked:

You will notice that everything the Indian does is in a circle. Everything that they do is the power from the sacred hoop, but you see today that his house is not in a circle. It is square. It is not the way we should live. . . . Everything is now too square. The sacred hoop is vanishing among the people. . . . Everything tries to be round—the world is round. We Indians have been put here [to be] like the wilds and cooperate with them. Their eggs of generations are in the sacred hoop to hatch out. Now the white man has taken away our nest and put us in a box and here they ask us to hatch our children, but we cannot do it. We are vanishing in this box.[42]

Forced to live on reservations, Sicangus and other Lakotas sought different means to keep from vanishing within the "box" of Western institutions and values. By selectively reconstituting elements of the Catholic Sioux Congress, they were able to round off its squared edges and imbue it with the power of their sacred hoop.

A Crisis in Mission

On January 20, 1916, a fire that originated in the attic of the girls' dormitory reduced nearly all of Saint Francis Mission to ashes. Only the concrete boys' building, a bathhouse, and several shops and utility buildings survived the flames. Recording the disaster for her community's house chronicles, the Franciscan house historian wrote, "The first we knew about the fire was when Sr. Juventia Hennecken, who was in charge of the dormitory saw a lamp fall that was fastened to the ceiling and she noticed that the rope was burning. She immediately ran up stairs, but the attic was so filed with smoke that no one could enter. The children's wardrobe was kept in the attic, but nothing could be saved." Within moments of the fire's discovery, "the alarm was given and the Brothers and many people from the town came running and tried to save all they could but since the buildings were all built of wood it didn't take long before they could not get near enough, on account of the terrific heat, the things that they had carried out started to burn out in the yard. It was soon realized that nothing could be saved and everything was carried out of the church. . . . In less than 4 hours the fruit of 30 years labor was destroyed."[1]

During its thirty-year history, the missionary community at Saint Francis had witnessed many fires. As recently as October 1911, the three-year-old frame boys' building had burned to the ground. The following year, the

Jesuits and Franciscans watched in horror as a prairie fire came within yards of engulfing the mission before the gusts propelling it forward suddenly abated.

On that cold January morning almost four years later, there would be no reprieve from the flames. "The day was a beautiful one for winter," wrote Rosebud agent Charles L. Davis, "the snow having begun to thaw. There was but little wind, but what there was was from such direction to carry the flames directly into the monastery and church. All these buildings were consumed in a very short time."[2]

Among the missionaries' few consolations was that no one had perished or been seriously injured in the fire. Nevertheless, from an economic standpoint the mission's losses were staggering. Although the Jesuits carried $52,000 in insurance on the mission buildings and properties, they estimated their damages at between $100,000 and $200,000. In his report to the Indian commissioner, Davis predicted that this shortfall would prove "a very severe blow to this institution, and even with the best [that] can be done, it will retard the work there for a year or two."[3]

The Dilemmas Surrounding Rebuilding the Mission

Despite Agent Davis's gloomy forecast concerning the mission's recovery, Father Goll reported that the religious made "plans for rebuilding . . . on the spot." Because their first priority was to prevent the school from closing, the brothers poured their efforts into fashioning a temporary campus to house and educate as many students as possible. To aid the brothers in their work, Digmann petitioned Davis to order the Saint Francis "carpenter boys" back to school by January 26. "I will allow them some compensation for work done," the priest wrote, "and they have a good chance to *learn* building."[4]

The primary motive behind the missionaries' rush to reopen the school was their dread of losing students to other educational institutions. Throughout most of its history Saint Francis had been required to compete for students with Rosebud's government day schools, Saint Mary's Episcopal boarding school, and, starting in 1897, a government boarding school. In addition, superintendents from such off-reservation boarding schools as Hampton, Carlisle, and Genoa regularly petitioned the Indian Office for large numbers of boys and girls from the Rosebud. For example, in 1911 the Franciscan house chronicler complained, "Of the larger boys and girls many registered in outside schools, for the Protestants and the Free-masons take pains to wean away the Mission children." The missionaries feared that the fire provided these competing institutions with the opportunity to raid the mission's enrollment under the cloak of charity. Evidence substantiating their anxiety is found in a telegram from the assistant Indian commissioner, E. B. Merritt to Davis, on the day after the fire advising that "Carlysle [Carlisle] could accommodate students "where advisable."[5]

The determination with which the missionaries worked to avert the alienation of large numbers of their students is exhibited in the following excerpt from the sisters' chronicles for 1916:

> [The] boys building was turned into living quarters for the Sisters and the Father and Brothers lived in a little house that was formerly used by the workmen. In the morning the boys' playroom was used as a Church and during the rest of the day as dining room and play hall. A temporary building was erected within a few days and by the end of three weeks it was completed. Classes were immediately resumed and things went on about the same as usual only that we had to get used to cramped quarters. On March 1, 150 children were again in class.[6]

The missionaries matched their resolve to reopen the school with their determination to discover the cause of the fire. From the outset they suspected that it had been set deliberately, a supposition that would be substantiated by the subsequent investigation. Writing to Davis on January 21, 1916, Digmann confided that after interviewing a student the preceding day he had "hardly any more doubt that the house ha[d] been set on fire." Nevertheless, he implored the agent to keep this conclusion confidential, for it "would throw a bad light not only on the present accident, but on the Reservation at large, where all three Boarding Schools have fires the past years."[7]

On January 26, Davis informed Digmann that one of Rosebud's store-keepers had provided him with a list containing the names of two girls who had allegedly started the fire and three others who had abetted or known of their plans. The merchant had urged the agent to "investigate this matter with a view of establishing proof of his allegations." Not wishing to usurp the mission's right to proceed as it saw fit, Davis went on to inform the priest:

> I feel that you, as the head of the St. Francis Mission, should be the one to suggest any investigation of this kind and I therefore submit the matter to you before taking action. If in your judgment there is

any probability that the buildings were set on fire by pupils or by other personas and if there [is] anything tangible on which investigation can be instituted, I will be pleased to take the matter up and interrogate any one whom may seem to have any information. I would request, however, that you or some other person delegated by you be present at such an investigation.[8]

Repeating his desire to avoid publicity, Digmann advised Davis on January 28 that before requesting an "official" investigation he would first launch a preliminary probe, calling the suspects and witnesses into the mission when weather permitted. "It would prove fatally for the name of the School and the resp. families," he wrote, "to make it more public, as it maybe already, by an 'official' investigation on the part of the office."[9]

While conducting interviews the next day, Digmann uncovered the alleged motive for the arson. Apprising Davis of his findings, he wrote: "[I have] investigated and found out that some of the larger girls have been in a bad mood because they had been punished for talking Indian and insubordination[;] they should have worked during recreation time." Before their punishment, Digmann observed, "the Sister asked one: 'have you deserved it and will take it?' to both she answered 'Yes.' I should hardly believed it possible that some went so far as to set the house on fire. Of course, juvenile lightmindedness, and Indian impetuosity that acts on the first impulse without reflecting do not exclude the possibility, but so far I have no tangible proof."[10]

To obtain such "tangible proof," Digmann requested that Davis "oblige" the girls rumored to have perpetrated or abetted the arson to appear at the mission for questioning. Their testimony convinced the priest that sufficient grounds existed for the agent to launch an official inquiry.

By this time the roster of suspects and witnesses had grown from five to eight students. Between February 8 and 16, Davis and his chief clerk, C. W. Rastall, cross-examined seven of the girls in Digmann's presence. The eighth girl, a resident of the Pine Ridge Reservation and one of the two suspected arsonists, initially refused to respond to Davis's requests that she appear at the inquest. She did, however, finally submit herself for questioning on March 2, after repeated visits to her home from the Pine Ridge police and the Indian commissioner's threat of "further action" should she continue her defiance.[11]

As evidence mounted against the suspects, Davis wrote to South Dakota's U.S. attorney, R. P. Stewart, to inquire whether the mission's case would be remanded to state or federal court should it decide to press charges against the girls. It is not difficult to understand the agent's confusion. Though the arson had occurred on land to which the mission held title and that lay within the borders of South Dakota's Todd County, this property was also part of the federally administered Rosebud Reservation.[12]

Stewart's response was quick and unequivocal. He informed Davis that should the case arise it would be remanded to the area's federal court. In explaining his decision, the state attorney omitted any mention of the tangled jurisdictional issues that had prompted the agent's letter and referred instead to the requirements, as he interpreted them, of the "Major Crimes Act" of 1885 (U.S. Stat. 62). According to Stewart, "The crime committed was that of arson and is one of the eight special crimes over which the United States has jurisdiction, if committed within the limits of an Indian Reservation."[13]

Whatever its legal merits, Stewart's interpretation would remain untested. Even before the investigation had run its course, Digmann and Davis had concurred on the wisdom of pursuing extralitigious avenues of redress. Writing to the Indian commissioner on February 25, 1886, Davis stated, "I feel that Father Digmann, like myself, hesitates to do anything that would mean prosecuting any of these girls criminally." Still, worrying about the signal that this course would send, he went on to confess, "We realize that if nothing is done it may result in similar fires in the future at St. Francis, the Government Boarding School, or in any school where children from this reservation may be attending."[14]

Davis considered the problem of how to sanction the witnesses to the arson particularly problematic. Though the agent acknowledged that they could have prevented the fire, he was reluctant to punish them for not intervening. Explaining his position, he wrote, "The standards of Indians in their stage of development are necessarily different from our standards. Whether we may approve or not," he reflected, "it is a fact that Indians do not regard themselves as in duty bound to report the evil intentions of others as we do and these children have been reared under these standards. Taking this into account I would not feel justified in recommending punishment for any except those who may have committed the overt act or induced some other girl to do so."[15]

Davis's arguments notwithstanding, Digmann had other, more practical motives for not wishing to press charges against the girls. In consultation with BCIM director Ketcham, the superior had determined that a mission attempt to take legal action would have dire consequences for its upcoming petition drive for students. Having gained leverage over the Sicangus with the revised Browning rule, which prohibited the government from transferring students in mission boarding schools without first gaining permission from their parents, the missionaries were not about to do anything that would compromise this advantage. Saint Francis therefore dropped the case without any action taken against the students.

A Failure of Mission?

As part of her entry on the fire of 1916, the Franciscans' house historian included the following assessment of the Sicangus' behavior during the crisis: "By this occasion the Indians showed that they were far from being civilized as yet. Things that had been placed out in the yard were picked up by the Indians and placed in their wagons and taken home with them. Everything was done to prevent them from taking these things, but nevertheless some of them got away with things."[16]

The sister's disgust over the Indians' "uncivilized" behavior was echoed later that year in a letter from Father Digmann to Director Ketcham. Responding to the director's despair over the lackluster results of Sioux and other Catholic Indian missions, Digmann advised: "Don't get heartsick; it is often sickening, I know, but let us hold out as long as we breathe and the Lord wants our cooperation. Yes, the devil seems to consider the Indians his own, and does not want to give them up, but let us try to snatch from his claws as many as want to be saved; one more soul weighs out the suffering."[17]

Digmann's explanation for the apparent failure of mission provides a fitting point of departure for a summary and some final thoughts on how the Saint Francis religious understood and evaluated the mission's three decades of work among the Sicangus and the Sicangus' response to these efforts. In accord with the Catholic paradigm of Indian missionization, the Saint Francis Jesuits and Franciscans envisioned the Rosebud as a controlled environment where they could systematically train the Sicangus in American civilization until they had obtained a stage of social and economic maturity that allowed them to take on the responsibilities of American citizenship and support a local church or parish. This paradigm was, as described, in part a derivative of the Thomist assumption that faith builds upon nature and its consequent requirement that missionaries teach Sicangus the "civilized" manners and customs that the church believed necessary for Catholicism to take root and thrive.

Although Catholic missionaries, unlike many of their Protestant counterparts, considered the work of "civilizing" and Christianizing Indians an arduous, multigenerational process, the Saint Francis religious occasionally despaired over the slow progress of their efforts. Instead of attributing these problems and setbacks to their approach to mission, they placed the blame on two classes of obstacles that lay outside their basic model of missionization. Constituting one of these classes were the difficulties posed by the Sicangus' "primitive" psychology, culture, and religion. The second class of impediments were of non-Indian origins, including the aggressions of Rosebud's Protestant missionaries; the ineptitude, corruption, and nativism of federal policy and employees; and natural disasters such as storms, drought, and fires. Lurking behind all these obstacles was the devil, whose evil machinations God used to test the missionaries' fidelity to their faith and vocation.

For their part, Sicangus strategized on how best to make use of this new religion. Some Rosebud Sioux eagerly drew upon the missionaries' economic, political, and social resources in their struggles for individual and corporate survival while resisting conversion to the Blackrobes' "prayer." Others, by contrast, welcomed the opportunity to gain access to the sacred powers flowing from Catholic observances and paraphernalia. However, they did so in ways that mitigated the missionaries' demand that they renounce all other forms of worship, especially Lakota spirituality and ceremonies. Some converts continued to take part in non-Catholic practices in secret; others delayed their conversions until threatened by death or until they could adhere to the requirement that they eschew all other religions with a clear conscious; still others attended the gatherings of all the religions, refusing to commit themselves exclusively to any one of them.

Informing all these strategies was a distinctly Sicangu understanding of Catholicism centered on the traditional Lakota concept of sacred power. The Catholic missionaries abetted this indigenized interpretation of church doctrine and ritual by incorporating the Lakota term for such power, *wakan*, and its lexical derivatives into their Lakota catechetical materials and homilies. Church rituals and paraphernalia thus became a source of "wonder-working" consistent with traditional Lakota concepts of sacred power but quite out of line with orthodox Catholic teachings on this matter. Sicangu and Lakota converts from other reservations also reworked selected features of their annual Catholic Indian Congress to reflect spatial and ceremonial traits of their traditional Sun Dance.

Set within the context of the Sicangus' wider social and political struggles to come to grips with their new identity as reservation "Sioux," the first three decades of Catholic mission on the Rosebud were fraught with difficulties for both the missionaries and Indians. Yet both groups were able to draw upon the spiritual resources of their respective traditions and instill these difficulties with meaning and purpose.

Notes

List of Abbreviations

ARCIA *Annual Report of the Commissioner of Indian Affairs*
BCIM Bureau of Catholic Indian Missions Archives
FHH-SFM Franciscan House History, Saint Francis Mission
NARA-DC National Archives and Records Administration, Washington, D.C.
NARA-KC National Archives and Records Administration, Kansas City, Mo.
SSF Sisters of St. Francis of Penance and Christian Charity. Provincial Archives, Stella Niagara, N.Y.

Preface

1. For comparative purposes, I had planned to include a chapter on late nineteenth- and early twentieth-century Protestant missionary work with the Sicangus, but the tension between following through on this goal and keeping the manuscript to a manageable size ultimately defeated my efforts. I can, nevertheless, refer those who are interested in pursuing this line of research to some important primary sources. The National Archives, Record Group 75, created by the Bureau of Indian Affairs, is the premiere provenance for correspondence and other documents on federal relations with both Catholic and Protestant missions. Information concerning Rosebud agency missions has been generally assigned to Record Group 75.19.96. The Papers of the Indian Rights Association, housed at the Historical Society of Pennsylvania in Philadelphia, is another invaluable repository for primary documents revealing Protestant perspectives on Indian missions, Indian boarding schools, and reform Indian policy. Of particular value

are its collections of the IRA's official correspondence with the federal Indian Office and the Board of Indian Commissioners. The archive of the American Missionary Association, Amistad Research Center, Tulane University, New Orleans, also contains some Protestant materials from the Dakotas and Nebraska. One of its most valuable holdings is its run of the *Iape Oaye*, a newspaper that Dakota missionaries John P. Williamson and Stephen R. Riggs began publishing in May 1871. Though originally printed in Dakota and intended mostly for its neighboring Santee readers, issues of the *Iape Oaye* often carried correspondence related to and stories about Lakota Protestant affairs. In 1884, the Santee Normal Training School began publishing an English version of the newspaper (*The Word Carrier*). As members of the Board of Commissioner for Foreign Missions, some of Williamson's and Riggs's correspondence and reports are also found among its papers. These may be found at the Houghton Library, Harvard University. Yet another important source for information on the Rosebud Reservation is the annual reports of the Board of Missions of the Protestant Episcopal Church, which includes information on the reservation under its Niobrara Deanery.

2. Of the sixteen Oceti Sakowin tribes, thirteen contain the term "Sioux" as part of their official government name. For an excellent overview of the history and present status of Oceti Sakowin peoples, see Center for American Indian Research and Native Studies, *Oceti Sakowin Origins*, 31.

Chapter 1

1. Andrew Jackson, "First Annual Message to Congress (December 8, 1829)." Miller Center. www.presidency.ucsb.edu.
2. There are many excellent treatments of the policy of Indian removal. Among the most noteworthy are Foreman, *Indian Removal*; Debo, *Road to Disappearance*; DeRosier, *Removal of the Choctaw Indians*; Van Every, *Disinherited*; Young, *Redskins, Ruffleshirts*; and Green, *Politics of Indian Removal*. For varying perspectives on Andrew Jackson's role in Indian removal, see Satz, *American Indian Policy*; Rogin, *Fathers and Children*; and Prucha, "Andrew Jackson's Indian Policy."
3. For an interesting entry in this debate, see Washburn, "Indian Removal Policy."
4. Luke Lea, *Annual Report of the Commissioner of Indian Affairs* [hereafter *ARCIA*], 27 November 1850.
5. *United States Statutes at Large* 38: 572–73.
6. U.S. Senate, "Condition of the Indian Tribes: Report of the Joint Special Committee Appointed under Joint Resolution of March 3, 1865," 39th Cong., 2nd sess., 1867.
7. For an excellent overview of the problems plaguing the Doolittle Report, see Kelsey, "Doolittle Report of 1867."

8. U.S. Congress, Senate, "The joint special committee of the two houses, appointed under the joint resolution of March 3, 1865." Senate Report no. 156, 39th Cong. 2d sess., serial 1279, 3–10, 3.

9. Ahlstrom, *Religious History*, 8.

10. Marsden, *Fundamentalism*, 12.

11. Marty, *Righteous Empire*, 48.

12. Mead, *Lively Experiment*, 141–42.

13. Hutchison, *Errand*, 91–124.

14. Ibid., 42.

15. Latourette, *Great Century*.

16. Mott, *Evangelization*.

17. Handy, *Christian America*, 104.

18. An informative discussion of developmentalism can be found in Bidney, *Theoretical Anthropology*. Though his analysis is primarily concerned with the so-called evolutionary anthropology of the late nineteenth and early twentieth centuries, it provides insight into developmentalist thought in the popular culture of that day.

19. *United States Statutes at Large*, 15:17–18.

20. Nathaniel G. Taylor, *ARCIA*, 1868, 18.

21. *United States Statutes at Large*, 16:40.

22. Useful overviews of Grant's Peace Policy and reform Indian policy include Priest, *Uncle Sam's Stepchildren*; Fritz, *Movement for Indian Assimilation*; Washburn, *Assault*; Hoxie, *Final Promise*; and McDonnell, *Dispossession*.

Chapter 2

1. For an excellent history of Catholic participation in the Peace Policy, see Rahill, *Catholic Indian Missions*.

2. Gibbons, "Petition of James Cardinal Gibbons," BCIM.

3. Ryan, "Appeal."

4. Girard, "Our New Indian Policy," 90, 100. For additional Catholic criticisms of the Peace Policy, see *Address of the Catholic Clergy*. Catholic critics commonly exempted Grant from direct responsibility for the anti-Roman bias they believed to be exhibited by the Peace Policy. In an overview of Catholic Indian missions presented to the Washington conference of the Catholic Missionary Union of 1905, William Ketcham, director of the BCIM, stated that it was "the unjust interpretation and application of President Grant's Peace Policy" that resulted in the formation of the Catholic Indian Office (Ketcham, "Missions among the Indians").

5. Ewing, *Circular*, 3. In addition to the BCIM, the Indian Office's alleged bias against Catholics spawned other organizations. Among these was the Ladies' Catholic Indian Missionary Association of Washington, D.C.

6. In a statement explaining the reasons for the founding of the BCIM to the Catholic public, Catholic Indian commissioner Charles Ewing stated:

   Such an office as the one just organized, if it has not been at all times necessary for the most successful prosecution of our missionary labors among the Indians, would certainly the last fifty years have been to them a most valuable auxiliary. But whatever it might have been in the past, there is no question but that its existence, since 1870, has been absolutely necessary, not only for the prosperity of our Missions, but in fact to save them from utter ruin. And when I remind you that we have, among the Indians, more than forty Mission Houses, with over three hundred stations, at which full 100,000 Indians are often visited and receive from our missionaries religious instruction and the sacraments of the Church; that the Government Agents, at the majority of these Agencies are now using all of their power to counteract the labors of our Priests in their efforts to convert and control the Indians, and at many stations have forbidden and prevented religious instruction and the administration of the sacraments. (ibid., 4–5)

7. Fletcher, "Appendix: Extracts," 152.
8. The Carlisle Institute was founded and managed by Capt. Richard Henry Pratt. For good summaries of the educational philosophy and regime found at Carlisle, see Eastman, *Pratt*; and Ludlow, *Captain Pratt*.
9. Gates, "Opening Address," 16, 14. Although Protestant reformers greeted the Dawes Act with enthusiasm, many of them were not blind to the potential impediments to its implementation. As part of a speech he delivered before the Society for Promoting Good Citizenship in 1892, Herbert Welsh, president of the Indian Rights Association, observed that the "dangers to which that operation [land allotment] is open are apparent; they are the pressure from white population contiguous to the reservations to urge the work of allotment with too great haste, so that settlers may obtain control of the Indians' surplus lands; a desire to secure the settlement of the Indians on poor land, and to have the good land thrown open to the whites; the inexperience, or ill intention, on the part of the special or resident Agents which will result in unwise selections of land for the Indians" (Welsh, "How to Bring the Indian to Citizenship").
10. Ganss, "Religious Work," 91.
11. Hughes, "Catholic Missions," 78.
12. Butler, "Glance at the Indian Question."
13. Marty, "Statement." Marty's most extended treatment of Indian development can be found in his "Indian Problem."
14. William H. Ketcham, "The Nation's Wards," c. 1912, typed manuscript, BCIM. The Catholic Church was not alone in its criticism of off-reservation Indian schools. In 1892, C. C. Painter of the Indian Rights Association found it necessary to defend such schools against a growing sentiment in the U.S. Congress that their students quickly reverted to savagery and paganism once back on the reservation (Painter, *Extravagance*, 4–22).

15. Ganss, *Present Status*, 19–20.
16. Ketcham, *What Shall Become*, 2–3. In their 1899 "Appeal on Behalf of the Negro and Indian Missions in the United States," the clerics of the Commission for the Catholic Missions among the Negroes and Indians—James Cardinal Gibbons, P. J. Ryan, and J. J. Kain—argued for the importance of mission schools among African Americans and Indians in the following manner: "From all quarters we learn that while some success in dealing with the adults of Negro—and so also Indian blood—the greatest and most enduring success follows from the proper care of the young of the race. Let but proper school facilities be afforded these children and they do more in their home circles than the missionary could accomplish, for they win within a short time the hearts of their parents to that faith which so carefully and sacrificingly through its priests and nuns, labors for these children" (Gibbons et al., "Appeal," 6).
17. Beaver, *Introduction*, 83.
18. J. A. Stephan to James Gibbons, 21 December 1894, BCIM.
19. Nativist fears generated a mass market for the peddlers of controversial literature. In one such tract, *Miss Columbia's Public School; Will It Blow Over*, A. Cosmopolitan apprised its readers of a Catholic plot—hatched primarily by the Irish and Jesuits—to conquer America for the Vatican. In the pamphlet's rousing conclusion Miss Columbia declares, "We acknowledge that among liberal Catholics there are many worthy and estimable ones, who never dream of intruding their religion into state affairs . . . but for those turbulent bigots, who are continually dragging their Church into national affairs, there is no course left us but to compel them to conform to our rules, or to go back where they came from. It is not *their* country, as they seem to think; it belongs equally to all of us."
20. For an early historical analysis of the APA, see Desmond, *APA Movement*. For Morgan's relation to the APA's agenda, see Kinzer, *Episode*, 74–77.
21. In fact, Morgan's military record ultimately proved more of a liability than an asset to his appointment as Indian commissioner. On the eve of the Senate hearings on Morgan's nomination, news that he had been arraigned and tried before a general court-martial at Chattanooga, Tennessee, in 1865 was leaked to the press. The charges against him had included violation of the Fifteenth Article of War, conduct unbecoming an officer, and conduct prejudicial to order and good discipline. Morgan's account proved sufficiently credible to save his nomination and win him approval, but not everyone found his explanation convincing. Both Morgan's defense and a counter-offense by one such critic are found in "Morgan's Military Record."
22. Sievers, "Catholic Indian School Issue," 133, 141. During his career as Indian commissioner, Morgan was forced to issue frequent disclaimers concerning his reputed intolerance of Catholics. "The purpose of discriminating against Catholics," he wrote in one such release, "has never entered my mind, and I do not intend to allow either religious or political prejudices to influence my action" ("No Enmity to Catholics"). On the other hand, the depth of his antipathy

toward the Catholic Church is on unmasked display in an address he presented as "ex-commissioner of Indian affairs" in April 1893 in the Music Hall, Boston, Massachusetts. In this speech Morgan maintained that the "Roman Catholics [had] assumed an attitude on the Indian School question that [was] un-American, unpatriotic, and a menace to our liberties." In succeeding sections he accused "Rome" of waging a relentless war against his policies, defeating the reelection bid of Harrison, and "betraying the republic." Toward the conclusion of his address, he characterized the Catholic Church as an "ecclesiastical imperialism modeled after the Roman Empire [that was] organized for conquest, and with an insatiable greed of power, arrogating to itself the divine right of sovereignty over temporal government, an alien transplanted from the Tiber, out of sympathy with American institutions . . . hating our public schools as her deadly foes [and] recruiting her ranks by myriads from the slums of Europe" (Morgan, *Roman Catholics*), 23.

23. Daniel Dorchester was already acting as superintendent of Indian schools when Morgan took office. His well-known bias against Catholics was no detriment to his working relationship with the new Indian commissioner. Superintendent Dorchester's hostility toward the Catholic schools may best be seen in his *Romanism versus the Public School System* and toward that church's Indian schools in his article "Government Schools and Contract Schools."

24. Morgan, "Indian Education," 5–11.

25. Reflecting on the speed with which many of the Protestant denominations divested their Indian schools of federal support, BCIM director Ketcham later wrote: "Blinded by bigotry, the Protestants voluntarily gave up government help in order to prevail upon Congress to withdraw all appropriations from Catholic Indian schools, hoping thereby to arrest the progress made by the Catholic Church among the Indians. In this, however, they failed signally, for they themselves have been the losers" (Ketcham, "Missions among the Indians," 185).

26. Ireland, "Why They Oppose Morgan."

27. Stephan to Archbishops Ireland, Ryan, and Corrigan, 21 December 1894, BCIM.

28. Ibid.

29. In 1904, Director Ketcham listed as first of the great obstacles that in later years plagued the advancement of Indian Christianization "the despotic and vacillating policy of the government, often administered by narrow minded men of anti-Catholic and anti-Indian prejudices, which reached its culmination in the second administration of President Cleveland, when, on the recommendation of the Secretary of the Interior, Mr. Hoke Smith, Congress abolished the contract system, and Indian Commissioner Browning promulgated his famous and infamous ruling, denying to Indian parents the right of choosing the school which their children should attend—that right being reserved to the Indian Agent" (Ketcham, "Missions among the Indians," 179–80).

30. Stephan to Sheridan, 3 February 1896, BCIM.
31. *United States Statutes at Large*, 30, sec. 79.
32. Gibbons et al., "Appeal," 3.
33. Ketcham, *Report, 1900–1901 and 1901–1902*, 13–19.
34. "From the Report of the Indian Rights Association for 1902," BCIM.
35. Stephan, *Report, 1899–1900*, 6.
36. Ibid., 3.
37. Ketcham, *Report, 1900–1901 and 1901–1902*, 2.
38. Ketcham, *Report, 1904–1905*, 26.
39. By this time, the proprietors of the Catholic Indian missions had good cause to believe that they had a friend in Roosevelt. In 1904, Ketcham stated that "President Roosevelt has proved himself to be pre-eminently the President of the *American people* with out regard to *race* or *creed*. . . . One thing is beyond question: President Roosevelt, in his official as well as private acts, has risen above unchristian racial and partisan prejudices, and has manifested a determination to mete out equal justice to all men. . . . In fact, it can now be truthfully stated the *Bureau has no grievance against the Administration*" (Ketcham, "Missions among the Indians," 180–81.
40. The reaction of the Protestant press to Roosevelt's actions was by and large unfavorable. The editors of *Outlook* saw the president's executive order as violating the spirit if not the letter of the Act of 1897 in which Congress declared as its "settled policy" to make no further appropriations to sectarian operated Indian schools. ("Indian Appropriations for Sectarian Schools," 222).
41. Reuben Quick Bear v. Leupp, 210 U.S. 50 (1907). Speaking for the Court, Chief Justice Melville Fuller stated:

It is contended that the spirit of the Constitution requires that the declaration of policy that the Government "shall make no appropriation whatever for education in any sectarian schools" should be treated as applicable, on the ground that the actions of the United States were to always be undenominational, and that, therefore, the Government can never act in a sectarian capacity, either in the use of its own funds or in that of the funds of others, in respect of which it is a trustee; hence, that even the Sioux trust fund can not be applied for education in Catholic schools, even though the owners of the fund so desire it. But we can not concede the proposition that Indians can not be allowed to use their own money to educate their children in the schools of their own choice because the Government is necessarily undenominational, as it can not make any law respecting an establishment of religion or prohibiting the free exercise thereof. The Court of Appeals well said: "The 'treaty' and 'trust' moneys are the only moneys that the Indians can lay claim to as a matter of right; the only sums on which they are entitled to rely as theirs for education; and while these moneys are not delivered to them in hand, yet the money must not only be provided, but be expended for their benefit and in part for their education; it seems inconceivable that Congress should have intended to prohibit them from receiving religious education at their own cost if they so desired it; such an intent would be one 'to prohibit the free exercise of religion' amongst the Indians, and such would be the effect of the construction for which the complainants contend."

42. Ketcham, *Report, 1905–1906*, 10.

43. Captain Pratt, creator of the Carlisle Institute, added fuel to these flames, as can be seen in the following excerpt from his article "The Indian Problem": The missionary goes to the Indian; he learns the language; he associates with him; he makes the Indian feel he is friendly and has great desire to help him; he even teaches the Indian English; but the fruits of his labor have been too often to strengthen and encourage the Indians to remain separate peoples. . . . The operation of these tribalizing missionary systems has been disastrous to any individual escape from the tribe, has vastly and unnecessarily prolonged the solution of the question and has needlessly cost the charitable people of this country large sums of money, to say nothing of the added cost to the Government, through prolonged supervision and the delay in accomplishing their civilization and citizenship. . . . The missionaries dictate what our policy shall be with the tribes, and their dictations are always along the lines of their colonies and church interests, never toward citizenship, and the Government must gauge its actions to suit the purposes of the missionary, or else the missionary influences are exerted to defeat the purposes of the Government. Thus, the Government in paying large sums of money to some churches to carry on schools among Indians only builds hindrances to Indian citizenship.

44. Ketcham, *Religious "Garb,"* 4. The controversy arose when the government purchased or leased formerly Catholic schools but retained the service of men and women with religious vocations. President Taft's "solution" to this matter was to permit nuns, priests, and brothers already on staff at such facilities to continue to wear their religious garb but to forbid this right to those hired after a school's "secularization." For an overview of the debate, consult "Indian Government Schools"; "Religious Garb in Indian Schools"; "Religious Garb in the Indian Schools"; "Critics of Catholic Garb"; and "Nun's Garb Question."

Chapter 3

1. The Commission was an unstable alliance of one congressman, five army officers, and two civilians: chairman of the Senate Committee on Indian Affairs J. B. Henderson, commissioner of Indian affairs Nathaniel G. Taylor, Samuel F. Tappan, and Gens. W. T. Sherman, Alfred H. Terry, William H. Harney, John B. Sanborn, and Christopher C. Augur.

2. For an excellent treatment of the central importance of Fort Laramie in Lakota-white relations, see Nadeau, *Fort Laramie.*

3. The fort was erected in 1834 by William Sublette and Robert Campbell, who sold it the following year to Fontenelle, Fitzpatrick, and Company (a fur trading firm comanaged by Lucien Fontenelle, Thomas Fitzpatrick, Jim Bridger, and Milton Sublette). The ownership of the fort again changed hands 1836, to the American Fur Company. The post was originally called Fort William after its principal owner, William Sublette, as well as William Anderson and William Patton. Robert W. Frazer reports that it was subsequently named Fort John, "presumably" in honor of John B. Sarpy (Frazer, *Forts,* 182).

4. An estimated 20,000 emigrants journeyed the Oregon Trail in 1853. In addition to disrupting the regular migrations of game, they brought with them diseases against which the Lakotas and other native peoples had no immunity (Berthrong, "Nomads," 31).

5. Beginning in the summer of 1849, Fort Laramie quartered two companies of mounted riflemen and one company of infantry, under the command Bvt. Maj. Winslow F. Sanderson. In terms of number, these troops were hardly sufficient to patrol and protect the Oregon Trail.

6. That not all the Lakotas were positively disposed toward being assigned a homeland is reflected in the following statement by the Oglala Black Hawk: "You have split the country and I don't like it. What we live upon we hunt for, and we hunt from the Platte to the Arkansas, and from here up to the Red But[t]e and the Sweet Water. . . . These lands once belonged to the Kiowas and Crows, but we [the Oglalas, Cheyennes, and Arapahos] whipped these nations out of them, and in this we do what the white men do when they want the lands of the Indian" (*Missouri Republican,* 9 November 1851, quoted in DeMallie, "Touching the Pen," 45).

7. For a complete transcript of the treaty, see Kapplar, *Indian Treaties,* 594–96.

8. Many discussions of the "Mormon cow" incident and its aftermath are available. Reliable treatments are found in Nadeau, *Fort Laramie*; and Cash, *Sioux People.*

9. Sometime prior to this assault, Harney had notified Lakotas to move south of the upper Platte River or otherwise face attack. Harney interpreted the presence of Little Thunder's camp on the Blue Water, located to the north of the river, as a sign of defiance and hostility. Why Little Thunder chose to remain on the Blue Water in the face of Harney's threats remains a mystery.

10. Able summaries of the Minnesota uprising are found in Carley, *Sioux Uprising*; Meyer, *History of the Santee Sioux*; and Andrist, *Long Death.* For Dakota perspectives on the war, see Holcombe, "Sioux Story"; and Anderson and Woolworth, *Through Dakota Eyes.*

11. Notes taken by Dr. William Folwell in 1909 based on the transcripts of the trial are available in Folwell et al., *Court Proceedings.*

12. One the best accounts of the Sand Creek massacre is Hoig, *Sand Creek Massacre.*

13. Svaldi, *Sand Creek,* provides an interesting analysis of the symbolic importance of the massacre for white conceptions of Indian relations and policy.

14. Joseph White Bull, a Miniconjou Lakota chief, told Stanley Vestal that the preeminence whites traditionally accorded Red Cloud in the "Sioux Wars" of the 1860s and 1870s more properly belonged to Crazy Horse and others; see Vestal, *Warpath*, 68, 71.

15. These posts included Fort Phil Kearny, located north of the present-day city of Buffalo, Wyoming; Fort Reno, constructed on the Powder River opposite Fort Connor, which it replaced; and Fort C. F. Smith, near the Big Horn River in southern Montana. For details on the construction and histories of these forts, see Frazer, *Forts*.

16. For a Lakota perspective on the Fetterman massacre, see Vestal, *Warpath*, 50–69.

17. The text of the 1868 Fort Laramie Treaty can be found in Kapplar, *Indian Treaties*, 998–1007.

18. On the other hand, John W. Bailey's contention that for the Sioux the councils of 1867 and 1868 merely "represented social occasions where they received presents and food" seems an unwarranted conclusion (Bailey, *Pacifying the Plains*, 70).

19. Hyde, *Spotted Tail's Folk*, 132; James C. Olson made the same point in *Red Cloud*, 37.

20. Poole, *Among the Sioux*, 64–66.

21. Robinson, "Tales of the Dakota," 491.

22. On July 30, 1878, Commissioner Hayt wrote Agent Pollock of the Spotted Tail Agency concerning the location and name of the new agency. For a summary of the history of the Rosebud Reservation from its origins to the years immediately preceding World War I, see Clow, *Rosebud Sioux*.

23. Pancoast, *Impression of the Sioux Tribes*, 22–23. Compare Pancoast's description with a later account by Fr. Florentine Digmann of the St. Francis Mission:

> Every two weeks over one hundred beef cattle were driven to a stockade on a plateau above the Agency. The Indians camped around; the men on horseback with their rifles ready, and the women with their large butcher knives. They were divided in bands of thirty head each. The name of a band's headman was called out by a government clerk, the gate of the stockade opened, an animal rushed out and the chase began. Most of them were right on the spot disemboweled, skinned, divided. . . . Returning to the Camp they were received by the youth with shouts of joy (ashiapi). The women handled the chunks of beef very dexterously, cutting them in thin slices, strewing salt over and hanging them up on horizontal tentpoles for drying, high enough that the dogs could not reach them. (Digmann, "History," 3, BCIM)

Chapter 4

1. Norton, "Catholic Missions," 163–65.

2. This decision was largely based on the advice of Pierre-Jean De Smet (Rahill, *Catholic Indian Missions*, 225). After visiting the Grand River Agency in 1868, the Jesuit had written to the commissioner of Indian affairs to explain why he favored it as a site for a Catholic mission. He informed the commissioner that a mission located there would "bring the missionaries in closer contact with a greater number of Indians, and give them more facility to visit the hitherto hostile bands in the interior" (Chittenden and Richardson, *Life, Letters and Travels*, 4.1297).

3. In his *Report of a Visit to the Sioux and Ponka Indians on the Missouri River*, William Welsh, of the Indian Board of Commissioners, provided some context for the negative responses that the two priests may have encountered. Welsh stated that the Sioux at Grand River and Cheyenne, the two upper Missouri agencies, were "points of the greatest interest and difficulty, as the roving hostile Indians come there to trade, and to procure food when suffering from hunger. Some few of these Indians that have recently come in are discourteous to their agents with the view of keeping up their standing with the wild roving Sioux." He went on to state, however, that "others, who were, until recently, leaders in the hostile camps, are already well advanced in agriculture and other civilizing occupations" (*Report of a Visit*, 7).

4. Burke to Ewing, 8 June 1875, BCIM.

5. Ewing's negotiations with the government hit a temporary snag in July over the type of school that would be erected on the reservation. To the government's offer to construct a day school for Catholic personnel to staff and maintain, Ewing replied, "Our church will not take any steps towards helping a day school which, as a rule, is a useless school towards Indian civilization. Whenever suitable buildings for a boarding school are provided by the Department at Standing Rock, our church will undertake to provide four teachers for the school at $2400 a year, with board and lodging" (Ewing to Edward P. Smith, 23 July 1875, BCIM). Father Brouillet's overview of the beginnings of Catholic education on Standing Rock are contained in Brouillet, "Plan for the Education."

6. Sherman to Brouillet, 9 April 1876, BCIM; Sherman to Brouillet, 18 May 1876, BCIM.

7. Brouillet to Marty, 11 May 1876, BCIM; Marty to Brouillet, 31 May 1876, BCIM; Brouillet to Marty, 10 June 1876, BCIM.

8. Marty to Brouillet, 7 August 1876, BCIM.

9. Kleber, *History of St. Meinrad Archabbey*, 267.

10. Marty to Brouillet, 7 August 1876, BCIM.

11. Ibid.

12. Marty to Ewing, 9 October 1878, BCIM.

13. Marty, "Extracts from Annals," 31.

14. Marty, "Abbot Martin Visits Sitting Bull," 8.

15. The transcript records Spotted Tail as stating: "My Great Father I would like to say something about a teacher. My children, all of them would like to learn

how to talk English. They would like to learn how to read and write. We have teachers there, but all they teach us is to talk Sioux and write Sioux, and that is not necessary. I would like to get Catholic priests. Those who wear black dresses. These men will teach us how to read and write English." (Report of the Council Held by the President of the United States and the Visiting Chiefs of the Sioux and Arapahoe Tribes of Indians, September 26, 1877, in Washington, D.C., in Ricker, Eli, "Transcripts of the Sioux and Arapahoe Delegation to Washington," 1877, Ricker Collection RG8, Tablet 37, Nebraska Historical Society, Lincoln, Neb. Concerning Spotted Tail's request for Blackrobes, George Hyde has written, "He [Spotted Tail] did not care a jot about white men's religion; but he had learned to value the ability to speak, read, and write English, and he claimed that the White Robes [Episcopalians], who had a school at his agency for the past four years, had not taught one Brule child to speak, read, or write in that tongue. He said if the Episcopalians kept school at the agency for one hundred years they would do no better and he wanted the Black Robes to start a school" (Hyde, *Spotted Tail's Folk*, 295).

16. Marty, "Abbot Martin Visits Sitting Bull," 10.

17. Marty to Brouillet, 28 December 1877, BCIM; Marty to Brouillet, 14 January 1878, BCIM.

18. Frederick to O'Connor, 15 March 1878, Diocese of Omaha, Chancery Archives, Omaha, Neb.

19. Ibid.

20. Hyde, *Sioux Chronicle*, 17.

21. In two letters to Prior Fintan of Conception Abbey, Marty suggested but did not explicate the severe transgressions that led to Father Frederick's dismissal from the Rosebud. In the first, written in late September, he stated:

> Rev. Frederick, from whom I hear that after leaving this place he went to visit you, unfortunately did not keep himself under control and can never again be employed in the care of souls. When I took leave of him, I advised him to go to St. Meinrad and gave him a letter addressed to Fr. Prior that he should take him in and put him to use in the school. However, his behavior in this region up to now has been so irreconcilable with faith and conscience that I must ask you, in case this letter arrives before his departure, to confiscate the letter to Fr. Prior and to inform him on my behalf that I absolutely and utterly will do without his further services in any capacity whatsoever. Not knowledge and talents alone, but piety and virtue are in no way less important for God's work to be accomplished with success: and his sin was less when he misused one person to gratify his passion than it subsequently became, whereby through him a large number of people will be contaminated in body and soul. (Marty to Fintan, 30 September 1878, Conception Abbey Archives, Conception, Mo.)

Less than two weeks later, Marty again wrote Fintan, stating, "I heard that Rev. Fr. [Frederick] went to St. Meinrad by way of St. Louis. His fall and so many things that went before are proof enough that we can't accomplish more than other people and eventually will lead us to the conclusion not to keep on trying something in which more clever minds have failed. I wrote to St. Meinrad's that he should not be accepted there" (Marty to Fintan, 10 October 1878, Conception Abbey Archives, Conception, Mo.). I am indebted to Fr. Quentin Kathol, O.S.B., archivist of Conception Abbey, for the translations of the letters, which are housed in the abbey's archives.

22. Marty, "Abbot Martin among the Sioux," 71, 74.
23. For an excellent summary of Marty's maneuvers to win Rosebud and Pine Ridge for the Catholic Church, see Rahill, *Catholic Church*, 221–72.
24. Frederick to Marty, 15 March 1878, Diocese of Omaha, Chancery Archive, Omaha, Neb. Frederick reported

> Today I had a long talk with the Agent, Major Lee, who, though belonging to no church seems highly to approve the idea of having that church amongst the Indians which they themselves are wanting. He said that he knew positively that the Episcopalians tried their utmost to have their church exclusively established amongst Spotted Tail Indians. Further, Mr. Clark in Washington told him that the President had positively promised Spotted Tail that he would have Catholic priests and that he (Mr. Clark) would speak to the Commissioner of Indian Affairs about the matter.

25. Rahill, *Catholic Church*, 247–48. Rahill reported that Hammond was an energetic booster for Catholic interests in his superintendency, advocating Catholic management of the Rosebud during one of his trips to Washington, D.C.
26. Kleber, *History of St. Meinrad*, 104.
27. For an excellent summary of this crisis, see Keller, *American Protestantism*, 181–84.
28. Schurz to Commissioner of Indian Affairs, 17 February 1881, BCIM.
29. Hiram Price, 13 October 1883, BCIM.

Chapter 5

1. Karolevitz, *Bishop Martin Marty*, 68.
2. Ibid., 83.
3. For a discussion of O'Connor's importance to Marty's elevation to bishop, see Rahill, *Catholic Church*, 267–69.
4. Kleber, *History of St. Meinrad Archabbey*, 320–21.
5. Scott, "'To Do Some Good," 31.
6. Marty, "Abbot Martin Visits Sitting Bull," 10.
7. Marty to Commissioner of Indian Affairs, 12 December 1883, NARA-DC.

8. Wright, *ARCIA, 1883,* 43. For an excellent analysis of Craft's battles with Agent Wright, see Foley, *Father Francis Craft.*
9. Craft to Brouillet, 3 November 1883, BCIM.
10. Dawson to Wright, 18 November 1883, NARA-KC.
11. Wright to Price, 16 January 1884, Outgoing letters, Rosebud Agency, Outgoing Correspondence Book 10, NARA-KC.
12. Price to Wright, 24 January and 30 January 1884, Rosebud Agency, Incoming Correspondence, Book 110, NARA-KC.
13. Wright to Craft, Rosebud Agency, 20 February 1884, Book 10, NARA-KC. In his report to the Indian commissioner for 1884, Wright included the following summary regarding Craft's banishment:

> It was my painful duty to report to the Department some of the teachings and sayings to the Indians of the Rev. Mr. Craft, wherein he held himself and his church above all civil law or the authority, wishes, or instructions of the President, honorable Secretary of the Interior, or any other constituted authority. Such pernicious doctrine inculcated into the minds of these people could not but be subversive of all law and authority of the agent. Reports of other acts of Rev. Mr. Craft had previously been made to the Department by parties in official position visiting the agency, stating wherein he had used his influence with the Indians to prevent them sending children to the Indian industrial schools. Upon these reports the order of the honorable Secretary of the Interior was received, through the Office of Indian Affairs, that he (Rev. Craf) should be expelled from the reservation and Indian country, which was executed, and Rev. Mr. Craft ordered away, leaving February 20 last. It is hoped his successor, should one be sent, will entertain different views of civil law, be possessed of that Christian virtue "charity," entertain and teach more catholic views on all subjects, religion included. This has been one of the most unpleasant duties of my experience at this agency, preferring to see and aid every effort in the direction of Christianity and advancement, and not even in appearance impede any effort from minister, priest, or layman, whose special duty this is or should be. (Wright, *ARCIA,* 1884, 48)

14. Craft's departure brought an end to the first Catholic school on the Rosebud, which had been in operation from January 1 to February 20, 1884. According to Wright's report to the Indian commissioner, 1884, the school serviced an aggregate of seventy-nine students with daily attendance averaging twenty-one. When the school closed, apparently none of the children were permitted to attend the agency school. Wright complained, "Certainly some corrective influence should be used to prevent a continuance of this practice; otherwise agency day school given entirely into this control" (Wright, *ARCIA,* 1884, 45).
15. Craft to Lusk, 12 March 1884, BCIM.
16. Lusk to Price, 24 May 1884, BCIM.

17. Craft to Lusk, 23 June 1884, BCIM.
18. Craft to Indian Commissioner, 10 July 1884, NARA-DC.
19. The copy of Tappan's notes of proceedings that found its way to Lusk gives equal support to both Wright's and the Craft's accounts. According to Tappan, Craft stated:

> I have told the Indians that if they sent their children away to school it was a good thing. If there was a school away among the whites, it would be good for them to send their children there. I told them if I ever heard of a good place to send their children I would advise them to send them there; that it was good for their children to come in contact with the whites and learn their ways. I told them if I heard of a bad place where their children would die if sent there, I would advise them not to send their children to that school. I told them I did not care what the President, Secretary or Agent said, I would tell them the truth. I told them I did not care any law of the Government—that I did not belong to any man, only God. I came to teach them to save their souls. I live among them, as one of themselves, with no object but to tell them the truth, fearing only God. Therefore, when they ask my advice I will always give it to them, and no man shall prevent me. The Agent asked me to come here and he asks me to speak to the Indians. He does not speak kindly to me, but I don't care if he does not speak kindly to me. I hear there is a gentleman here (Col. Tappan) after children for a place I know nothing about; this is the first time I have met him. I want to hear about that place—if it is a good place for you to send your children; I have told you to send your children where you could see them—that you were to say where you would send them. . . . Then "Turning Bear" made a speech, saying they would not send their children to school at Genoa, which was applauded by the Indians, who immediately went off. (Tappen, "Proceedings of Rosebud Council, 14 January, 1884," BCIM).

20. Craft to Indian Commissioner, 10 July 1884, NARA-DC.
21. Lusk to Price, 24 September 1884, BCIM.
22. Craft to Lusk, 14 October 1884. BCIM.
23. Hospenthal to Stephan, 4 April 1885, BCIM. The Catholic Hospenthal had in mind was the "Hon. T. O'Leary of Avoca, Minn," who "would no doubt make an excellent off-set for Wright's bigotry." Having informed O'Leary that he would write Stephan about his desire to be named the Rosebud agent, the priest continued: "The Episcopal Church will fight hard to have their man appointed. The present agent is a member of the Episcopal Church and very bigoted and unpopular. . . . The Indians at Rosebud and Pine Ridge are most anxious to have a change" (ibid.).
24. Ibid.
25. Standing Bear, *My People*, 194.

Chapter 6

1. My summary of Otto von Bismarck's policies toward the Catholic Church and the Kulturkampf is based primarily on the following sources: Aubert, *Church in the Industrial Age*; Craig, *Germany*; Eyck, *Bismarck*; Pulzer, *Germany*; Ross, *Failure of Bismarck's Kulturkampf*; and Taylor, *Bismarck*.
2. Francis X. Curran has provided several excellent historical overviews of the Jesuits' Buffalo (German) Province, including *Return*; "Buffalo Mission of the German Jesuits"; and "Buffalo Mission Centennial."
3. Curran, *Return*, 126.
4. Curran, "Buffalo Mission Centennial," 5.
5. Curran, "Buffalo Mission of the German Jesuits," 117–18.
6. Curran, *Return*, 140–45.
7. Ibid., 179, 144–45.
8. Treatments of the origin and early development of the Sisters of St. Francis of Penance and Christian Charity are found in Dunne, *Towers of Montabaur*; and Sr. Liguori Mason, "History of the American Foundation," Sisters of St. Francis of Penance and Christian Charity, Provincial Archives, Stella Niagara, N.Y.
9. Archer, *History*, 10–11.
10. Historian Sr. Mary Urban Archer has summarized the disastrous consequences of these changes for the German apostolate in the following manner: "The Congregation had twenty-one branch houses in Germany in 1870. Under the so-called May Laws the following educational institutions and orphanages were withdrawn from them: Zell, Polch, Loberich, Till, Wetzlar, Konitz, Zens, Sonbeck, Oberwesel, and Bruggen. In addition, the following boarding schools were forced to close: Freckenhorst, Cappellen, Munchen, Gladbach, Barthaus, Suchteln, Linz and Prum. The convent at Nonnenwerth was permitted to remain open; the school, however, was saved only by transferring pupils and teachers to Marienwerth in the Netherlands" (ibid., 11).
11. Ibid., 37–38.

Chapter 7

1. Upshaw to Wright, 9 October 1885, Rosebud Agency, Book 110, NARA-KC.
2. Digmann, "History," 1, BCIM.
3. Wright, *ARCIA*, 1885, 43.
4. Wright to Upshaw, 11 January 1886, Rosebud Agency, Outgoing 12, NARA-KC.
5. For the complete reminiscence, see Jutz, "Recollections," 143–49.
6. "Jesuit House History," St. Francis Mission, photostat copy, BCIM.
7. "Nordamerika," *Die Katholischen Missionen* 14 (1886), 198. Here, as in most other cases, no authorship is attributed to the letters that the sisters contributed to *Die Katholischen Missionen*.

8. Quoted in Mason, "History," 8, SSF. Sr. Liguori Mason, OSF, also produced verbatim English translations of both the *Chronik*, a yearly chronicle kept by the sisters at Saint Francis Mission, and their *Jahresberichte*, annual reports that contain only portions of the house history. Throughout the remainder of this book, I retain the term "Jahresbericht" for citations of the latter but cite the chronicles as "Franciscan House History, St. Francis Mission," abbreviated FHH-SFM.

9. "Nordamerika," *Die Katholischen Missionen* 14 (1886), 198.

10. Mason, "History," 10, SSF.

11. Ibid.

12. "Nordamerika," *Die Katholischen Missionen* 14 (1886), 199.

13. "Jesuit House History," St. Francis Mission, 1886, BCIM.

14. Goll, *Jesuit Missions*, 65.

15. FHH-SFM, 17, 26; *Indian Sentinel*, 1907, 25.

16. "Nordamerika," *Die Katholischen Missionen* 15 (1887), 22.

17. Digmann, "History," 20, BCIM.

18. Digmann to Stephan, 7 April 1890, BCIM.

19. Digmann, "History," 20, BCIM.

20. FHH-SFM, 9.

21. Digmann, "History," 20, BCIM.

22. FHH-SFM, 23.

23. Westropp, *Bits of Missionary Life.*, 4–5.

24. Goll, *Jesuit Missions*, 61.

Chapter 8

1. Digmann, *ARCIA*, 1892, 468; Jutz, *ARCIA*, 1893, 302.

2. FHH-SFM, 6.

3. Digmann, "History," 6, BCIM.

4. Ibid., 3.

5. Concerning the students' consumption of vegetables, Father Jutz informed Agent Wright in 1895, "Our children almost without exception 'learned' to eat lettuce. . . . Our hope is that these children will take along from school a liking for vegetables and future try at their homes what they had to do at school under the guidance of Brother Gardener, viz, plant and cultivate" (Jutz, *ARCIA*, 1895, 300).

6. Goll, *Jesuit Missions*, 48.

7. Perrig, "Nordamerika," 66.

8. Mason, "History," 470, SSF.

9. In her inspection of Saint Francis in 1890, federal supervisor of Indian education Elaine Goodale commented that "the school is not up to the standard in the matter of speaking only English. The children talk Dakota freely among themselves on the school grounds" (Goodale to Morgan, 29 May 1890, BCIM). Writing to Stephan, Digmann informed the BCIM director that he had responded to

Goodale's criticism: "None of us speaks Indian with the children, the school is entirely English, we check their speaking Dakota and encourage and urge them to speak and write English as much as we can" (Digmann to Stephan, 16 June 1890, BCIM).

10. Digmann to Wright, 23 August 1890, BCIM. Two years later, Digmann informed the agent that "to enforce the speaking of English among themselves a little bell was introduced, calling those that had spoken Sioux out of their plays to the classroom for English exercises" (Digmann, *ARCIA*, 1892, 468). However, it is of interest to note that in the mission's report to the agent for 1895, Father Jutz stated, "We do not entirely prohibit the use of their mother tongue" (Jutz, *ARCIA*, 1895, 300). Nevertheless, in his report for 1900, Digmann unequivocally stated, "Our insisting upon the exclusive use of English is backed now by the parents, who take pride in using their children as interpreters" (Digmann, *ARCIA*, 1900, pt. 1, 383).

11. FHH-SFM, 3.

12. According to the Franciscan house historian for 1912, starting that year Christmas leave was also eliminated. She wrote: "Since many toys and boxes full of gifts had been sent to [the] Mission during the year the children were recompensed in a great measure by the surprise of Santa Claus and in consequence they did not find the new regulation of remaining at the Mission during the vacation so very hard. In other ways and means the Fathers and the Sisters succeeded in making the vacation very pleasant for the children. On the second Christmas Day the girls gave an entertainment and on the Sunday following the boys presented a nice play" (ibid., 47).

13. Ibid., 16.

14. Among these sports were baseball and kickball. The missionaries also introduced social dances for the older boys and girls in 1909 to get them "more acquainted together in a good way for the future." According to Digmann, "Those that had received 'first note all through' in a week or a month were entitled for a dance. I would almost call it 'calisthenics.' Today [November 21] we had the first sample of it. Twenty-four were excluded, because they had not come up to the first mark. So it may work some good. Especially the girls were so crazy for dances that they had asked the Sisters' permission that some should wear boys' coats to distinguish them. Later they changed and let boys and girls play 'skat' together" (Digmann, "History," 183, BCIM).

15. Digmann, "Nordamerika: Indianer Mission," 258; Digmann to George Willard, 2 January 1890, BCIM.

16. Digmannn to Stephan, 22 June 1890, BCIM. The government boarding school was apparently no more successful in preventing runaways than Saint Francis. Digmann reported that in 1900 one policeman told him that "the boys at the [government] boarding school were mean; they run away by day and night, using their bedsheets as ropes to let themselves down" (Digmann, "History," 112, BCIM); ibid., 133. See also FHH-SFM, 4.

17. Goll, *Jesuit Missions*, 46. In a similar vein, Digmann wrote: "The Big Schools [boarding schools] have this advantage before Camp Schools that the children are taken out of their old fashioned customs, the dances, the sweat baths, the superstitious practices yet in vogue and are brought in contact with civilized habits and held to regular life" (Digmann, "History," 5, BCIM). In a letter to Rosebud agent Wright, the elder, in 1882, Indian commissioner Price offered the following very different assessment of day schools: "I shall be glad if you will endeavor to establish a system of day schools among your Indian settlements. . . . If the right sort of teacher is selected, he will not only teach the children, but will stimulate and direct the efforts of the parents toward civilized labor and modes of life and the teacher and the school will form a center of civilization whose influence will radiate among the Indians in its vicinity, in much the same way that the agent's influence should be felt by the Indians located near the agency" (Price to Wright, 3 October 1882, Box 109, Incoming, Rosebud Agency, NARA-KC).

18. Goll, *Jesuit Missions*, 48.

19. Digmann, *ARCIA*, 1897, 278.

20. Bosch, "Nordamerika," 133.

21. Digmann, "History," 6, BCIM.

22. Confronting the father of one sixteen-year-old student who had been whipped after repeatedly running away, Digmann admitted: "Yes, I have had him whipped, after all good words did not avail." In the son's defense, the father countered, "The boy is now sixteen years old; when the Lakota boys get in that age, they run after girls. They do not want to go to school anymore, to whip such big boys is considered a shame with us; people would say you are crazy to whip your own child" (Digmann, "History," 103, BCIM).

23. Westropp, "Letter of the Rev. H. I. Westropp," 140.

24. FHH-SFM, 5.

25. Ibid., 44. In his diary, Digmann also commented on the large crowd attending that year's commencement exercises. He stated that there were "so many visitors from Rosebud, Crookston, Valentine, etc. that there was no room for all our children." To discourage the number of non-Indian guests at the following year's graduation and yet turn a profit from those who attended, the missionaries charged admission to whites (Digmann, "History," 192, 195, BCIM).

26. The Franciscan house historian for 1913 mentions that the children who received their First Communion on Holy Thursday of that year had been "prepared well by careful instruction and a two day retreat" (FHH-SFM, 48).

27. Personal communication, Henry Horselooking, 7 October 1977.

28. Digmann, "History," 68, BCIM. The Ignatian Spiritual Exercises constitute the system of meditative prayers formulated around 1524 by the founder of the Society of Jesus, Ignatius of Loyola. They are generally given under the direction of Jesuit leader during retreats for both the clergy and laity alike.

29. FHH-SFM, 42.

30. Ibid.

31. Digmann, "History," 177, SSF.

32. FHH-SFM, 43. The house historian's account for the preceding year contributes additional information concerning the children's introduction to religious ceremony and obligations: "On Whitsunday, April 23, 35 girls and 46 boys of ten years and over received their first Holy Communion, after a retreat of three days. They were conducted in procession by the Rev. Fr. Superior and the mass servers from the girls' play room to the church. The first communicants and others thereafter daily received Holy Communion and made the Sundays in honor of St. Aloysius" (ibid., 39).

33. Ibid., 10. The Franciscan house historian for 1912 included a description of the ceremony when weather required that it be held indoors:

On the 9th of June we celebrated the Feast of Corpus Christi. Since the weather was inclement the whole celebration took place in the church, which was properly decorated for the occasion. After the solemn High Mass the procession moved through the aisles of the church. First came the Communicants carrying cymbals; after them came girls dressed in white strewing flowers. Immediately before the Blessed Sacrament was a long row of acolytes. During the procession were sung hymns to the Blessed Sacrament alternately accompanied by the organ and the band. On all three altars Solemn Benediction was given and the whole celebration was closed with a Te Deum. (ibid., 10)

34. Ibid., 7, 9.

35. Ibid., 33, 35. Describing the activities surrounding the laying of the cornerstone, the Franciscan house historian for 1908 wrote, "Reverend Father Florentine Digmann, S. J. the Superior, with acolytes, Brothers, Sisters, and all the children, marched in procession to the site of the new building. Here our Reverend Father gave a little talk after which the relic box was placed in the cornerstone" (ibid., 33).

36. Ibid.

37. "St. Francis Mission, Rosebud Agency, South Dakota," *Woodstock Letters* 34 (1905), 106–7. Reporting on the students' participation in activities associated with the anniversary, the author wrote:

Out of 270 children, which we have here, about 100 prepared themselves for the feast by a retreat of three days. Father Emil Perrig preached the retreat. The way some of the children observed silence and conducted themselves during the retreat was a consolation, as many would hardly expect them to understand what it was all about. One of the boys even refused to talk with the Father when asked a necessary question. Other when obliged to ask a question, rather than talk wrote the answer on a piece of paper. On Dec. 8th, they all went to Communion at early Mass. Later in the morning Solemn High Mass was sung by Father Digmann, whilst Father Spangemacher preached the sermon. The sisters of St. Francis, who are in charge of the girls' choir, prepared the singing. For the evening the boys got up a beautiful entertainment. It was a dram entitled "The Picture of the Madonna" composed in blank verse by Father Perrig. . . . The evening's entertainment was closed by the beautiful hymn "Virgin Mother, pure and stainless" written by Mr. Gottlemann, S.J. and set to music by Father Lessmann, S.J.

38. FHH-SFM, 36–40.
39. Ibid., 10, 16, 24–25, 39–40.
40. Ibid., 25, 50, 53.
41. Ibid., 3.
42. Digmann, "History," 177, BCIM.
43. FHH-SFM, 22, 38.
44. Digmann, "History," 176, BCIM.
45. FHH-SFM, 18–19. In her history of the sisters' work at Saint Francis, Liguori Mason offered the following hagiographic version of the incident:

In February 1895, the Sodality of the Blessed Virgin was established. A little girl . . . was lying ill in bed at the time, and expressed a great wish to be received into the Sodality. On the occasion of the Forty Hours' Devotion [she] had remarked to a little companion: "Sister Canisia said that any grace you ask for at Exposition of the Blessed Sacrament will be granted to you, so I am going to ask God to take me to Heaven, I want to die." And now the little petitioner was really at the point of death; so Father Superior received her into the Sodality to her great joy. The next day her pure soul took flight to heaven, but just before dying she said to her pagan mother: "Mother, be baptized and go to church." [Her] father was a heathen and had two wives of whom [the girl's] mother was the second; after her child's death, she resolved to become a Christian. She was instructed and baptized by Fr. Lindebner who, of course, told her that she must leave her husband as he had another wife. She was quite willing to do this and went back to her own people. . . . But [the child's] father . . . was highly incensed and . . . brought back by force [her] mother. When Father Lindebner heard this, small as he was, he strode into the wigwam with the courage of a lion, and confronting the angry Indian told him that he *must* give up his second wife. Then the valiant missionary placed the poor trembling woman in his wagon ad drove her to the Agency, placed her under the care of the Agent there, and made the latter promise to convey her back to her people. . . . But the poor woman had gone through so much mental agony that she sickened and died soon after. Father Digmann tried several times to persuade the father to be baptized, but all to no purpose. One day, however, [he] sent in hot haste for Father Superior. As soon as the latter entered, the old Indian exclaimed: "Father, baptize me quick, quick!"—"And why this haste?" asked the missionary. "You have so often refused when I asked you." "Blackrobe," said the sick man, "last night that man you have in the church, with the brown blanket and the flower in his hand (St. Joseph) came to me and said: ". . . you are on the wrong road, ask the Blackrobe to put you on the right one." The Father was deeply moved, for here was evidently the fruit of [the child's] prayer. The old man was instructed and baptized; he then prepared with great earnestness for death. Shortly after this his pagan wife came for instruction, and she too was baptized. [The child] had interceded for all of them. (Mason, "History," 41–42, SSF)

46. Digmann, "History," 7, 130, BCIM.

47. Goll, *Jesuit Missions*, 29.

48. Digmann, "History," 7, BCIM. Digmann went on, commenting on the "magic lantern's" utility for instructing the Sicangus: "How hard it is to bring home to these children of nature . . . and how great a help in the life pictures, are experience showed me."

49. Goll, *Jesuit Missions*, 30. In *Crusading*, Sr. Claudia Duratschek credited Father Lacombe as the originator of the "Two Roads": "Father Lacombe had labored with Fr. George Belcourt at Pembina in North Dakota. He discovered that by illustrating his instruction with pictures the Indians were able to grasp abstract truths. His crude pictures served as a guide to the Sisters of the Congregation, of Montreal who drew the 'Two Roads'" (Duratschek, *Crusading*, 133).

50. George D. Rogers Sr., unpublished manuscript, BCIM.

51. A brief excerpt from the portion summarizing salvation history suggests the synoptic character of their content:

God is the living Spirit. He has no body, and don't need to have any. God is very Great; can do all things, He knows everything, and is in Heaven and on earth. God made everything according to His will. First He created angels and made them good, but a part of them failed to adore god so He cast them away and made them to suffer. They will suffer for all eternity in the home of the devil. Those who were obedient to God are now in heaven. Then God created those things that could be seen: the earth and water, trees and flowers, the sun, the moon, and the stars, the fish in the water and the birds, then the animals and lastly He created man. The first man's name was Adam and the first woman's name was Eva. God created the first man and the first woman very perfectly, and made them to be rulers of the earth. Those are the only ones to know God and could adore and love Him, hence. He also made their descendents. They were to live on earth for a few winters but to love God and they were to enter Heaven without dying a death. So God placed Adam and Eva in a very good land and there they lived happily. But they did not stay long. Because they did not obey God. So then God drove them out of the good land, cast them away and for many years they lived in hardship, suffered, and hard labor then died. But God did not cast them away like he did the angels, he pitied them and promised them a Saviour and did give it to them, 4000 years later. In the meantime Adam and Eva had many children. Their oldest son was (Cain) and his brother (Abel) who was killed. Since that time the earth populated, but all [led] bad lives. They have committed sins. Therefore they were punished and died in a big flood; but eight in number lived (Noah and his family) were saved in a boat because they were good ("Instruction by Means of the Two Roads," 1–2, BCIM).

52. Goll, *Jesuit Missions*, 35.
53. Westropp, *Bits of Missionary Life*, 7–8.
54. Goll, *Jesuit Missions*, 36–37; Digmann, "History," 77, 81, BCIM. "Father Jerome's [Hunt, O.S.B.] Indians were the most progressive having for years been under Catholic influence. Father Jerome had started first with them the St. Joseph and St. Marys Societies. . . . Especially through these Societies the Benedictines for the past fifteen years had obtained wonderful results" (Digmann, "History," 33, BCIM). One striking example of the political function was the petition the societies started for the continuation of the mission's boarding school.
55. Digmann, "History," 33, 100, BCIM: "Bishop Marty's advice 'Gather the good elements into societies and before long the non-progressive party will go to the wall,' has proved to be the right motto, though we found how hard it is to go against the tide of old habits. Habit is a second nature, but is bound to yield to systematic and perseverant effort."
56. Digmann, *ARCIA, 1895–96*, 300.
57. Goll, *Jesuit Missions*, 37–38.
58. Digmann, *ARCIA, 1896–97*, 278.
59. FHH-SFM, 50.

Chapter 9

1. Mason, "History," 24, SSF.
2. FHH-SFM, 31.
3. Digmann, "History," 16, BCIM.
4. Ibid., 100.
5. Digmann to Ketcham, 3 May 1907, BCIM.
6. Digmann, *ARCIA*, 1902, part 1, 347.
7. Goll, *Jesuit Missions*, 36.
8. Bosch, "Nordamerika," 133.
9. Digmann, "Picture," 89.
10. "Nordamerika," *Die Katholischen Missionen* 15 (1887), 20.
11. Westropp, *Bits of Missionary Life*, 2–3. Three years after Westropp authored his defense of the Indian, Father Ketcham presented a similar repudiation of racist explanations for Indian "savagery" to a Washington, D.C., chapter of the

Knights of Columbus. Together, both reveal how wedded the Catholic Church remained to a developmentalist model of Indian "civilization" and the need to retain reservations. Ketcham stated:

> I look upon the Indian race precisely as I do the white race. I consider the Indian the equal of the white man—morally, mentally, physically. I think the apparent superiority of the one and inferiority of the other can be accounted for by the difference of opportunity and by the different stages of development of the two races. The pale face, having passed through a tutelage of many hundreds of years, and having had the guidance of Christianity[,] has arrived at a high plane of civilization, and is impatient because the red skin fails to reach the same plane in a few generations and under conditions which have been far from favorable to any development at all. Instead of fostering gradual change and development among these people we have kept them as the rolling stone in one section and forcing them to remove to another; we snatch their children from them and carry them into the full glare of our enlightenment and then seem to think it is strange that the poor creatures are dazzled and bewildered and that they feel more content in the simple life of the wigwam than in our complex mode of existence (Ketcham, "Nation's Wards," BCIM).

12. Digmann, "History," 121, BCIM.
13. Sisters of St. Francis of Penance and Christian Charity, Jahresbericht, St. Francis Mission, 1915, Provincial Archives, Stella Niagara, N.Y.
14. Westropp, "Indian Missions."
15. Westropp, *Bits of Missionary Life*, 3.
16. Digmann, *ARCIA*, 1900, 384.
17. Chittenden and Richardson, *Life, Letters and Travels*, 4.1213–14.
18. Digmann, "History," 173, BCIM. In another case, a dying girl coaxed a promise out of her father to dismiss one of his wives and be baptized. According to Digmann, "The poor old man one day told me so, adding: 'I know that I will not get to see my children in the future life,' but he could not make up his mind to dismiss the second wife or look upon her only as 'his sister'" (ibid., 154). The priest reported that shortly after this conversation the man died suddenly.
19. Ibid., 34.
20. Ibid., 40.
21. "Nordamerika," *Die Katholischen Missionen* 16 (1888), 258.
22. Digmann, "History," 16, BCIM.
23. Goll, "Shepherd," 83.
24. Digmann, "History," 22, BCIM.
25. Ibid., 94.
26. Goll, "Catholic Missions among the Sioux," 34.
27. Busch, undated letter addressed to the Catholic Indians of the Diocese of Lead, BCIM.
28. Digmann, *ARCIA*, 1901, pt. 1., 375.

29. Ketcham, 25 September 1913, BCIM.
30. Ibid.
31. Digmann, "History," 23, BCIM.
32. Ibid., 101.
33. Westropp, *Bits of Missionary Life*, 3–4.
34. Westropp, "Letter of the Rev. H. I. Westropp," 141. Father Digmann described the following incident that occurred when he tried to baptize a dying baby at No Water's camp on the Pine Ridge Sioux Reservation in 1893. When he arrived he found that the "mother held the dying child in her arms. His nose was already cold and death seemed approaching. Expressing my sympathy I asked the mother to let me baptize him. She said she had to ask his father. He had gone to water the ponies. I asked the child's grandfather. He said: 'You kill the children by pouring water over them, many have died of it. You better go back over the big water where you have come from and let us alone.' Finally the grandmother took the child and carried it in the brushes to hid it. Meanwhile the father came back. He flatly refused to have it baptized." The priest went on to recount that on the way back to the mission he reported his failure to an non-Indian Catholic who "promised to try again. He did and succeeded. He was well acquainted with the family, asked for a drink of water, and after having quenched his thirst, washed the forehead of the dying baby, pronouncing at the same time the words of baptism" (Digmann, "History," 46, BCIM).
35. Goll, *Jesuit Missions*, 15.
36. Westropp, "Catechists among the Sioux," 113.
37. Digmann, "History," 10–11, BCIM.
38. Mooney, "Ghost-Dance Religion," an extended history and analysis of the Ghost Dance and massacre at Wounded Knee, remains unsurpassed in terms of scope and detail.
39. Bosch, "Indians Again in Council," 394.
40. Westropp similarly noted, "The Wounded Knee massacre marks the end of a great nation. With this event the redman of the plains has passed away" (Westropp, "In the Land of the Wigwam: Children's Lecture on the Jesuit Missions in S. Dakota," undated ms., BCIM).

Chapter 10

1. In fact, a representative from the Dutch Reformed Church seems to have ministered on the Rosebud for so short a time that, unlike the Catholics and Episcopals, this church does not seem to have received a Lakota designation. Digmann estimates the minister's stay at one month (Digmann, "History," 8, BCIM).
2. Ibid., 27.
3. FHH-SFM, 23.
4. Digmann, "History," 42, BCIM. As the following example illustrates, the "theft" of souls occasionally transpired while converts were being readied for

baptism. Discussing his catechetical visits with an ailing Sicangu in spring 1906, Digmann stated: "He said he understood it all and had my words in his heart. When I visited him again June 5th, he was changed. 'Mr. Clark has been here and fixed me up and I got also the drink of wine (Episcopal Communion) and told me if I could come again, he should tell him (Clark) and he would tell the Agent about it.' I reminded him of his former words and said: 'You and God know whether you spoke the truth at the time' gave him the hand and left him. May god be merciful to him and Mr. Clark" (ibid., 168).

5. Ibid., 8–9.
6. Ibid.
7. Ibid., 42.
8. Ibid., 71, 72
9. Ibid., 70.
10. "Wankiye taokolakiciye taku topa on slolunyapi kta: *He* Wanjila, Owancaya, Wakan, *wakosyapi taanpetu kin u kin heon.* Okolakiciyapi umnaapi kin hena nahanr'ci waniyetu 400 ihun'nipi sni, owanjila najinpi sni, owancaye hecapi sni, wakan sni; heca mah'piya eta unkayapi okihipi sni; heon hena unkokapi unkokihipi sni. Sina Sapa Okolakiciya tanyan unopapi ehantans owotanla Wakantanka ti ekta unyanpi kta. Heon he econk'unpi kte na sutaya unkic'iconzapi kta" ("Instruction by Means of the Two Roads," 8, BCIM).
11. Digmann, "History," 7, BCIM. In fact, the instruction accompanying the Two Roads never explicitly stated that Protestants were doomed to hell. Instead, it asserted that these churches "cannot bring us to heaven," leaving the final destination of their members unspecified. However, it is hard to imagine the Rosebud's Protestant missionaries and Sicangus being appeased by this omission, having been told that their churches would not lead them to a heavenly reward. Nor was Digmann's summary of the picture-catechism any more conciliatory on this point. According to the priest, "The 'Road Pictures' were . . . a thorn in the eyes of our separated brethren, the Protestant Episcopalians, because Luther and other heresiarchs were on them, leaving the good road and walking over to the wrong one, and especially because on top of the right road, next to the gate of heaven, throned the successor of St. Peter, with the keyes of the Kingdom of Heaven, all had to pass by him to enter" (ibid.).
12. Digmann to Ketcham, 7 February 1906, BCIM.
13. Digmann to Ketcham, 31 January 1906, BCIM.
14. Digmann to Maitre, 8, 12, 13 March 1906, BCIM.
15. Lusk to Digmann, 10 January 1908, BCIM.
16. Digmann to Ketcham, 17 December 1913, BCIM.
17. This is marked as an enclosure to a letter sent perhaps to Ketcham by a resident of Rosebud town, W. Courtis. The letter is dated 15 March 1906. The letter states: "Mr. A. B. Clark the episcopal clergyman here who has been raising much a row over the proposed contract for the Indian schools left for Washington today where he expects to make things hot for you all. Here enclosed gentlemanly

and well bred literary production comes from the talented pen of Mr. Clark referrd to above." It is found, along with the doggerel, in the BCIM records from Saint Francis Mission to the BCIM for 1906 (Father William Ketcham was director by that time). It was printed in *Public Opinion Telegraph.*

18. Digmann, "History," 156, BCIM.

19. Stephan to Atkins, 21 July 1886, BCIM.

20. Atkins to Wright, 3 August 1886, Rosebud Agency, Book 110, Incoming, NARA-KC.

21. Ibid.

22. Stephan to Atkins, 28 September 1886, BCIM.

23. Ibid. Stephan's use of "Know-nothing" was an obvious reference to the vehemently anti-immigrant, anti-Catholic Know-Nothing Party, alternatively referred to as the Native American Party or American Party.

24. Digmann to George Willard, 20 July 1889, BCIM. That the missionaries had honest grounds for complaint is suggested by Spencer's report to the Indian commissioner for 1888. In his review of the educational achievements for that year, he merely mentioned in passing that there was "1 contract school (Roman Catholic)." Later, in his four-line summary of Sicangu missionization, he complained that the "missionary work of this agency has been seriously interfered with by reason of other than a native worker during most of the year" without alluding to the work of the Catholic priests in the camps. What is more, unlike the preceding report for the Pine Ridge Agency, Spencer's contribution is missing a firsthand account of Catholic initiatives on the reservation by the mission superior (Spencer, *ARCIA,* 1888, 54–56).

25. Digmann to Stephan, 8 May 1889, BCIM.

26. Digmann to Willard, 20 July 1889, BCIM. It is interesting to note that none other than Herbert Welsh of the Indian Rights Association also harbored misgivings concerning Wright's selection as agent, albeit based on the appointee's ties to the "spoils system" rather than his reputed anti-Catholicism. Welsh complained: "All appointments recently made have been of this character; in other words, appointees to positions of trust in the affairs of the Indians are chosen from communities whose interests are in many cases professedly antagonistic to those of the Indians. A more unjust policy, or one more likely to bring bad results, could scarcely be devised." In a letter to James Cardinal Gibbons, Welsh observed: "The Agent recently appointed at Rosebud is a young man, without that experience or those qualities of character which promise success in so responsible a post" (Welsh to Gibbons, 9 July 1889, BCIM).

27. FHH-SFM, 19, 20. Six years earlier, Digmann had written to Stephan about his change of heart concerning the agent: "Now Reverend Father, you may remember how much I was opposed last year this time to Mr. J. Geo. Wright's appointment because I feared we would be worse off with him than with the former agent Spencer. Yet I soon changed my opinion finding out that he was just and fair, took a true interest in the welfare of the Indians and especially in

the progress of the schools" (Digmann to Stephan, 14 October 1890, BCIM). It is significant to note that Martin Marty also wrote a letter in Wright's defense. The bishop characterized the agent as "a most competent and honest man and just now indispensable to the Indians here, who are going through a crisis here" (Marty to Stephan [?], 18 October 1890, BCIM).
In an article that appeared in *Catholic World*, Bishop Marty described the behavior of reservation agents who were not as kindly disposed as the younger Wright toward Catholic religious: "Not infrequently have agents seemed anxious to prove to the Indians that the priest is of no worth to them, and that his suggestions have little weight. . . . Thus, the civilizing efforts of the government and the Christianizing efforts of the missionaries are unhappily hindered and robbed of their proper effects, and the Indian remains . . . in a nondescript state of transition, which, unless speedily bettered, will soon prove itself a state of moral and physical corruption and decay" (Marty, "Indian Problem," 579).

28. Digmann, "History," 92–93, BCIM.

29. Ibid., 117.

30. Ibid., 125.

31. When rumors of Commissioner Morgan's impending visit to the Rosebud reached the mission, acting superior Aloysius Bosch appealed to BCIM director Stephan: "Would you be so kind and drop us a few lines before the man comes to our place. We could perhaps [pare?] off a blow" (Bosch to Stephan, 17 September 1890, BCIM).

32. FHH-SFM, 17.

33. Goodale's evaluations of the school's physical plant and academic achievements alternated between "fair" and "good." However, her overall impression was favorable enough for her to write, "The industry and perseverance which has been displayed here is highly commendable, and an excellent example to the Indians" (Goodale to Morgan, 29 May 1890, BCIM). Responding to Goodale's report, Digmann informed BCIM director Stephan: "I acknowledge the truth of her criticisms and have written her that no one feels the wants mentioned more keenly than we ourselves; but that St. Francis Mission could not be built in one year; that, after we would get the present chapel free, we would gain plenty of room for a brighter schoolroom and playrooms for both boys and girls" (Digmann to Stephan, 16 June 1890, BCIM).

34. Digmann to Stephan, 16 June, 21 July 1890, BCIM. In the latter letter, Digmann revealed an additional reason for his initial reluctance to change from Gilmour to Appletonic readers: "I myself have no objection surely to introduce any new books, but one: Last fall, I have bought a great number of Gilmours and obliged myself with Benzinger Bros to keep them for five years. I mentioned at the time to Messrs. Benzingers I had to risk Mr. [Commissioner] Morgan's good pleasure in the choice, but I risked it."

35. Digmann, "History," 98, BCIM.

36. Ibid., 152.

37. Ibid., 84, 71, 83, 87.
38. Digmann to Stephan, 14 October 1890, BCIM. In fact, Wright beat Digmann to the punch in asking the monsignor for assistance, albeit of a different order. At the conclusion of a "personal and confidential" letter to Stephan in which he presented his side of the story, the agent wrote, "As you kindly interested yourself in my behalf when I had the pleasure of meeting you in Washington and if consistent with your feelings will you quietly ascertain if possible who is persecuting me . . . and advise me in reference thereof" (Wright to Stephan, 26 September 1890, BCIM). Wright was exonerated of all charges in November 1890.
39. Digmann, "History," 68, BCIM.
40. Ibid., 77.
41. Goll, *Jesuit Missions*, 53.
42. Digmann, "History," 74, BCIM. It is of interest to note that off-reservation competitors for Rosebud students sometimes included Catholic schools as well. In 1888 the acting Indian commissioner, A. B. Upshaw, put agent Spencer on notice that the Indian Office had "entered into contract with the Bureau of Catholic Indian Missions for educating Indian pupils at the Immaculate Conception Mission School, Crow Creek Agency, Dakota." He went on to state that, "by the terms of the contract, the Bureau has the right to obtain children from the reservation under your charge. When the representative of the school arrives at the Agency, you will give the usual and necessary assistance in procuring pupils" (Upshaw to Spencer, 20 August 1888, BCIM).
43. Jones to Ketcham, 9 October 1903, BCIM
44. FHH-SFM, 23; Perrig to Stephan, 4 September 1901, BCIM.
45. Digmann to Ketcham, 11 November 1901, BCIM.
46. Ibid.
47. Digmann, "History," 105, BCIM.
48. Ibid., 104. Writing about the havoc caused by the Independence Day celebration to BCIM director Stephan, Digmann stated: "The old heathen Indian habits are revived in good style by the celebration of 4th of July, and I have it from good authority that, when our Agent asked for faculties to stop the dances, etc. he was refused again. [I]t makes the impression that they [the Bureau] want to keep the Indians on the old track; this being the sweetest and surest [way] to lead them to extirpation. How hard it is to work under the circumstances you will readily see" (Digmann to Stephan, 5 June 1900, BCIM).
49. Digmann, "History," 106, BCIM.
50. Ibid., 74. Not one to mince words, Digmann repeated his recriminations against Commissioner Morgan in several reports he submitted to the Rosebud's agent for publication in the annual report of the commissioner of Indian affairs.
51. Hillig, "Nordamerika," 212.
52. Digmann, "History," 73, BCIM. Nevertheless, in 1905 the missionaries tried reversing the "patch" and "coat" by including an Independence Day celebration

as part of the annual Catholic Indian Congress with, at least according to Digmann, successful results: "The celebration of the 4th came off so nicely, that they (the Indians) concluded to have it the same next year." Yet the priest's description of what was "not allowed" leaves one wondering what those attending the festivities found so appealing. He continued: "Indian dances, shows and old-time customs, especially the giving away of horses and property were excluded a priori. . . . I hope the ice was broke and will keep on breaking. The old timers that had gone to have their old way in another camp feel rather cheap now" (Digmann to Ketcham, 17 July 1905, BCIM).

53. Digmann, "History," 88, 118, 172, 204, 190, BCIM.

54. Ibid., 119. Permission for wild west show companies to include reservation Indians was generally granted or denied by the secretary of the interior, who left the matter of informing agents of his decision up to his commissioner of Indian affairs. Writing to Rosebud agent Wright in 1894 concerning the "casting" for Buffalo Bill Cody's show, Daniel Browning stated, "The Honorable Secretary of the Interior granted permission for Messrs. Cody and Salisbury to employ 125 Indians from reservations of North Dakota, South Dakota and Oklahoma to accompany their exhibition (Wild West) for the period of one year" (Browning to Wright, 26 March 1894, Rosebud Agency, Outgoing, NARA-KC).

55. Mason, "History," 35, SSF; Digmann, "History," 166, BCIM. Digmann also seems to have been rather inconsistent in his attitude toward wild west shows. While visiting the World Exposition in Saint Louis in 1904, Digmann had occasion to visit such a pageant operated by the Cummins family. Reporting on this visit, the priest stated, "They just performed the Custer battle. Mr. Cumings [Cummins] was very friendly, remembered me from Buffalo, let [us] in 'gratis.' Illumination was magnificent" (Digmann, "History," 145, BCIM).

56. Digmann to Ketcham, 5 March 1903, BCIM.

57. Digmann, "History," 152, BCIM.

58. Ibid., 150. This belief was apparently shared by persons in high places. Digmann reported that Commissioner Francis Leupp once confided to him that "the real civilizing of the Indians as a nation will begin after they have got the last cent due them by the U.S. and have more to expect but have to stand on their own feet and resources" (ibid.).

59. Digmann to Stephan, 7 September 1890, BCIM.

60. Digmann to Stephan, 2 October, 14 October 1890, BCIM.

61. In fact, misgivings concerning the government's attempts to turn the Rosebud's Sicangus into farmers were present almost from the origin of the reservation. In his annual report to the Indian commissioner for 1882–83, Agent James G. Wright acerbically observed: "Certainly this location could not have been selected for an Indian agency for its agricultural advantages. Surrounded by barren sand hills, far from what little timber there is, so little arable land to cultivate, where the same number of white men as Indians could not make a living if dependent on the product of the soil, why should or can Indians be expected

to self-sustaining by engaging in agriculture?" (Wright, *ARCIA*, 1883, 39).

Ten years later, Commissioner Morgan wrote Agent Wright, the younger, with news of possible relief from the pending Indian Appropriation Bill of 1893 that earmarked funds for irrigation projects and well sinking on reservations: "One of the most important questions to deal with in connection with the Pine Ridge and Rosebud Reservations is the water supply for agriculture, domestic and stock purposes, the scarcity of which is seriously felt. So it has been thought best to try the experiment of an artesian well and you will readily see the importance of having it sunk where it will be likely to do the most good to the greatest number and where the conditions are favorable for obtaining water through the means and with the money appropriated" (Morgan to Wright, 11 February 1893, Outgoing correspondence, Rosebud Agency, Archives, NARA-KC).

62. Digmann to Ketcham, 16 October 1902, BCIM. In the same letter Digmann went on to identify yet another obstacle to Sicangu cattle ranching: "Besides, these poor Indians should not be induced anymore, nor even allowed, to sell more of their country to the whites. If they shall be made self-supporting by cattle raising, they will need every square-inch they call yet their own, as public grazing land. You may know that in Nebraska they wanted two sections (1280 acres) for each family because one section is not sufficient to support one. How much less it would be so for the Indians."

63. In the mission's annual report to the Rosebud's agent for 1897, Digmann remarked: "The old Indians were overjoiced to hear that their country had been declared to be 'cattle country, not fit for farming.' This, of course, was more congenial to their nature and their old habits. We try, however, to encourage them to do a little farming and gardening" (Digmann, *ARCIA*, 1897, 278). In his report to the Indian commissioner for 1900, Agent McChesney reported: "Special Agent William A. Winder and his assistants have been engaged since my last reports in allotting these Indians. On June 30, 1899, 2,856 allotments had been increased to 4,064, making 1,208 allotments during the year." However, he went on to relate that "quite a number of the older and least progressive of these Indians have not taken their allotments and are strongly opposed to doing so. I have had several talks with them in regard to their action and pointed out to the best of my ability the advantage of taking their allotments, but thus far have not succeeded in inducing them to do so" (McChesney, *ARCIA*, 1900, 381).

64. Digmann to McChesney, 4 August 1900, BCIM.

65. Digmann to Ketcham, 16 March 1902, BCIM.

66. Digmann, "History," 122, BCIM.

67. Digmann, *ARCIA*, 1905, pt. 1., 346.

68. Digmann, "History," 133, BCIM.

69. Digmann to Stephan, 28 April 1891, BCIM.

70. FHH-SFM, 11.

71. Ibid.

72. Digmann, "History," 179–83, BCIM.
73. FHH-SFM, 45–46. The remainder of the entry reads:
    Only with the greatest difficulty could we keep the children quiet. They saw from the window of the playroom how buildings and haystacks went up in flames. Everyone was afraid it might be her own home. As a matter of fact, many of the children's parents lost all their property. About seven o'clock, when the children were at supper, an Indian woman rushed in with the cry "the haystack behind the house is in flames!" Screaming and pressing the 270 boys and girls pushed to the door, each trying to get out first. In a few moments all were in the open; but where could one turn? On every side was fire, bright leaping flames. God be praised that the cry of the Indian woman was not based on fact, else the whole mission would have been the prey of the flames. The work of the Sisters among the Indians would have been at an end. Finally we calmed the children enough to make them return with us to the house. And yet the Sisters had to watch the doors in police-fashion, for whenever they saw another house go up in flames they would scream and rush the door. The storm went on; always closer and closer came the devouring fury, finding rich nourishment in the dry prairie grass. We were prepared for the worst each sister had packed the most necessary articles of clothing so that in case of necessity we could leave at once. Those were nerve-racking hours. God only knows how it would have fared with us on the cold winter night. Yet where the need is greatest God's help is nearest. At ten o'clock when the danger was most imminent the storm suddenly stopped. Then it was possible for the fire fighters to gain the upper hand. Toward eleven o'clock the danger was practically over. We could send the children to bed. Throughout the night we beheld in the distance buildings and haystacks go in flame. Only in the morning when we saw how close the fire had come did we realize from what great danger God had spared us. Four of the cattle had to be sold. Much of the fodder and grain for the cattle was destroyed in the conflagration. For that reason much of the cattle had to be sold. The remainder about 400 cows and horses were brought to the Mission where they are now in the cold meadows.
74. FHH-SFM, 12.
75. Digmann, "History," 191, BCIM.
76. Ibid., 187.
77. In her history of Saint Francis Mission, Liguori Mason explicitly compares the trials of the Jesuits and Franciscans to those of Job. Writing of the festive mood surrounding the mission's twenty-fifth anniversary, she stated: "Every heart was stirred with gratitude to God for His past mercies, and full of trust in Him for the future, a trust which would not have been diminished even could all have foreseen the crosses destined for them. Indeed, when reading the history of St. Francis Mission, one is sometimes reminded of the passage in the Bible in

which the Lord said to the evil Spirit: 'Hast thou considered my servant, Job?' and then permitted Satan to test the faith and endurance of this holy man" (Mason, "History," 60, SSF).

78. Digmann, "History," 194, BCIM.

Chapter 11

1. Sword, "*Wakan.*"
2. Dorsey, *Study of Siouan Cults*, 433.
3. Little Wound, "*Wakan*," 69; see also Sword, "*Wakan.*"
4. Little Wound, "*Wakan*," 69.
5. DeMallie, "Lakota Belief and Ritual," 29.
6. DeMallie and Lavenda, "Wakan," 155–56; see also Walker, "Sun Dance," 160.
7. Sword et al., "Secret Knowledge of Shamans," 95.
8. Sword, "*Nagapi*," 99; Lone Bear, "Sacred Language"; Short Feather, "Spirits," 116.
9. See also the narrative of the White Buffalo Calf Woman, below.
10. Finger, "Conception of Energy."
11. Sword, "*Wakan*," 152, 153.
12. Sword et al., "Secret Knowledge of Shamans," 95–96.
13. Ibid., 70.
14. One Star, "*Sicun*," in Walker, "Sun Dance and Other Ceremonies," 158.
15. Sword, "*Sicun*," 158. The primary *sicun* of a Lakota was his or her guardian spirit. Of these James Owen Dorsey wrote: "Each Teton may have his special guardian spirit. If such spirits are remembered they confer great power on their favorites. The latter may be surrounded by foes and yet escape, either by receiving great strength, enabling them to scatter their enemies, or by being made invisible, disappearing like a ghost or the wind. Sometimes it is said that one is rescued by being turned into a small bird that flies off in safety" (Dorsey, "Teton Folk-Lore," 155).
16. Densmore, *Teton Sioux Music*, 65.
17. DeMallie and Lavenda, "*Wakan*," 156.
18. Little Wound, "*Wakan*," 69.
19. Sword, "Life and Visions," 84.
20. Regarding the source and functions of holy men, Oglala Lakota Flat Iron stated:
    To the Holy Man comes in youth the knowledge that he will be holy. The Great Mystery makes him to know this. Sometime it is the Spirits who tell him. The Spirits come not in sleep always, but also when man is awake. When a Spirit comes it would seem as though a man stood there but when this man has spoken and goes forth again, none may see whither he goes. Thus the Spirits. With the Spirits the Holy Man may commune always, and they teach him holy things. . . . The Holy Man goes apart to a lone tipi and fasts and prays. Or he goes into the hills in

solitude. When he returns to men, he teaches them and tells them what the Great Mystery has bidden him to tell. He counsels, he heals, and he makes holy charms to protect the people from all evil. Great is his power and greatly is he revered; his place in the tipi is an honored one. (Curtis, *Indians' Book*, 39)

21. Sword, "*Sicun*," 158.
22. Sword, "On Ceremonies," 81.
23. Sword, "Treating the Sick," 92; Sword, "Foundations," 80.
24. Short Feather, "Spirits," 116; Sword, "Foundations," 80.
25. Tyon, "Foundations," 108. It is interesting to note that the holy men continued their testimony by stating, "White is the favorite color of *Waziya* [the god of the north]. The white people are like *Waziya*. They have no mercy on the red people."
26. Little Wound et al., "Holy Men," 181–82. Luther Standing Bear concurred with this assessment, calling the Sun Dance "the greatest of all ceremonies with the Lakotas." Attributing its origin to "an earthly visit by the "Holy Woman [Pte San Win]," he characterized the ceremony as "form[ing] the Lakota decalogue" (Standing Bear, *Land of the Spotted Eagle*, 220).
27. Walker, "Sun Dance," 60.
28. Ibid., 159–60; Little Wound et al., "Holy Men," 181.
29. Sword, "Instructing the Sun Dance Candidate," 182. For additional information on the rights and duties of candidates and mentors, see Walker, "Sun Dance," 63–92.
30. Walker includes a thorough discussion of invitations in his "Sun Dance," 65–66.
31. Ibid., 95. Walker has written that the following conditions determined the timing of the Sun Dance: "1. When the buffalo are fat; 2. When new sprouts of sage are a span long; 3. When chokecherries are ripening; 4. When the Moon is rising as the Sun is going down" (Walker, "Sun Dance," 61).
32. Ibid., 96–100.
33. Walker, "Short Bull's Painting,"185; Walker, "Sun Dance," 100–121.
34. Although Walker stated that the tent should be entirely new (Walker, "Sun Dance," 102), Dorsey wrote that, "when the managers wish to set up the tent of preparation, they borrow tent skins here and there" (Dorsey, *Study of Siouan Cults*, 454).
35. According to Deloria a party of scouts searches for the tree. Concerning their capture of this "enemy," she stated:

They pretend to be cautious, as though in the neighborhood of an enemy. They stole up within site of the tree, and sneaked off without "letting him see them." The scene here is as follows: the scouts ride back in a bee-line towards camp and all the young men of the tribe ride out to meet them, bringing them home, but riding in circles around them as they come. Meantime someone has put up a cluster of boughs about the height of a man, near the place where the accompanists are seated. This is another effigy of the enemy. As soon as possible, the scouts break through the circling riders and charge towards the figure of boughs. The one first to arrive, strikes it from where he sits on his horse, with his whip as he dashes by. That is called "atayela kte, to kill directly," the first to count coup. The second, third and fourth would also be counted. After that, those arriving and striking the tree get no honors. And it is believed that the first four will be able to count coup in that order on the next warpath. For this reason they rush forth to arrive first. (Deloria, "Sun Dance," 395–96, note 3)

36. Walker stated that the capture of the tree took place on the second day of the ceremonial camp (Walker, "Sun Dance," 105). Deloria, however, contended that it occurred immediately after the scouts found the tree (Deloria, "Sun Dance," 396).

37. Short Bull told Walker that the four men chosen to deliver these blows were elders from the Silent Society (Walker, "Short Bull's Painting," 191).

38. Walker, "Sun Dance," 106.

39. Bad Heart Bull, "Sun Dance Pole."

40. Walker, "Sun Dance," 107. Capt. John G. Bourke, U.S. Army, who witnessed the Sun Dance held at the Red Cloud Agency, Dakota, in June 1881 stated: "In carrying the tree to the camp it was placed upon skis, no one being allowed to place a hand upon the tree itself. Upon reaching the summit of the knoll nearest the camp the tree was left in charge of its immediate attendants while the rest of the assemblage charged at full speed upon the camp itself" (quoted in Dorsey, *Study of Siouan Cults*, 465).

41. According to Short Bull's testimony, the rawhide effigy hung on the pole was that of Tatanka Gnaskiyan, or Crazy Buffalo (Walker, "Short Bull's Painting," 189). Holy men George Sword, Bad Wound, No Flesh, and Thomas Tyon told James Walker in an interview that he "is the most to be feared of the Evil Gods. He appears like the good Buffalo God and persuades the people to do all kinds of evil things. The *Hmugma Wicasa* (wizards) do his ceremonies" (Sword et al., "Secret Knowledge," 94). See also Densmore, *Teton Sioux Music*, 118.

42. Walker, "Sun Dance," 109. Regarding the special relationship between the Buffalo and the Sun, Walker stated, "He is the comrade of the Sun and in ceremonies pertaining to the Sun, his potency prevails" (ibid., 84).

43. Standing Bear provided the following description of the raising of the Sun Dance pole:

When the hole was ready, all the men from the different lodges got together to help erect the pole, which was sometimes sixty or seventy feet long. They tied two braided rawhide ropes about the middle of the pole, on which some brave was to hang. . . . When all was ready, some of the men used forked poles, some held on to the ropes, and others got hold of the pole. It required about forty men to do this work properly. The pole must be raised and dropped in the hole at one operation, and with no second lifting. Some pushed, others pulled, while the men with the forked sticks lifted. As the pole dropped into the hole, everybody cheered. . . . There was a strong superstition regarding this pole. It was believed that if the pole dropped before it was set into the hole, all our wishes and hopes would be shattered. There would be great thunder-storms and high winds; our shade or council hall would be blown away, and there would be no Sun Dance. On top of this, it was believed that the whole tribe would have a run of bad luck. (Standing Bear, *My People*, 117)

44. Deloria, "Sun Dance," 399.

45. Dorsey, *Study of Siouan Cults*, 458. Concerning the role the effigies of the enemy and the buffalo play in this ritual, Short Bull stated that these are "colored black, which gives to them the receptivity of an enemy and of the Demon Buffalo [Tatanka Gnaskinyan] so that whatsoever is done to these images occurs to the enemy and to the demon" (Walker, "Short Bull's Painting," 189).

46. Densmore, *Teton Sioux Music*, 125.

47. Different opinions can be found in the ethnographic literature concerning the painting of the candidates. In his interviews with Walker, Short Bull reported that all the dancers were prepared alike, "each with his body painted red, except his hands" (Walker, "Short Bull's Painting," 187). He additionally disclosed that the attendants chosen to wait on the candidates were "prepared and adorned like the candidates, except that their bodies, *including their hands* indicating that they can touch sacred things" (ibid., 188, emphasis added). In his monograph on the Sun Dance, however, Walker wrote that "each Mentor should paint his Candidate's feet and hands red," and afterward "he should paint on the person of the Candidate the design he devised to be the Candidate's totem" (Walker, "Sun Dance," 112). Dorsey's essay, which seems to confirm Short Bull's statement, suggests that the torsos of the Sun Dancers are painted red, except for their hands: "Meanwhile, the men [attendants] who have been selected for the purpose redden their entire hands, and it devolves on them [the Sun Dancers] to dance without touching anything, such as the withes connected with the sun dance pole or the buffalo skulls; all that they are required to do is to extend their hands towards the sun, with the palms turned from them" (Dorsey, *Study of Siouan Cults*, 460). Finally, Deloria's essay stated:
   They [the candidates] are not all painted alike, but each one is painted with minor differences. The traditional painting was like this: The entire face was given a vermilion base. Then a blue line, the breadth of a man's finger, was made around the face, complete. A straight line of the same width and color was made down the center of the forehead ending at the bridge of the nose. On each cheek, a similar line ran down; and also one down the chin, from the lower lip to the bottom of the chin. The whole body is always given a red base. And down the shoulders and outer arm, a blue line is made. The line divides down the back of the hand and extends along each finger, but the palm is left untouched. (Deloria, "Sun Dance," 402)

48. Deloria, "Sun Dance," 400.

49. *Canshasha*, a pluralized form of the term for "red wood," is the Lakotas' designation for the inner bark of the red willow tree that they pulverize and mix with tobacco for ceremonial use in their pipes. The term's pluralization probably denotes the fragmented state of the wood after it has been prepared for use.

50. Walker, "Short Bull's Painting," 188.

51. Densmore, *Teton Sioux Music*, 131. Speculating on the severity of the ordeal, Densmore noted that the sticks probably pierced the "subcutaneous fascia" as well as the skin (Densmore, *Teton Sioux Music*, 131). In spite of this, Deloria's informants told her that the piercing seldom caused infection or lasting injury:

> In terrible ways they dance with their chests pierced. And so long as they don't tear themselves away they continue to dance. But nobody ever got infected from the wounds nor were they permanently injured by the cuts. Only once a man by the name of Lone Man who had his chest pierced in two places pulled out not only the pegs from their pinnings, but the whole flesh off his chest, leaving a hideous, red circular wound. When this happened they took some pine charcoal and pulverized it and dusted the wound with it and healed it. Always that was what was used to heal a wound of that sort. (Deloria, "Sun Dance," 412)

According to Little Wound, American Horse, and Lone Star, "If one wishes to become a shaman of the highest order, he should dance the Sun Dance suspended from the pole so that his feet will not touch the ground" (Little Wound et al., "Holy Men," 181–82).

52. Tyon, "Thomas Tyon Tells," 180.

53. Densmore, *Teton Sioux Music*, 149. Concerning such visions, High Bear noted, "The men usually get faint on account of fasting and see all sorts of animals and birds" (High Bear, "Sun Dance").

54. Dorsey, *Study of Siouan Cults*, 462.

55. Little Wound et al., "Holy Men," 181. Their statement is given additional weight by Captain Bourke's account of the Red Cloud Sun Dance. He wrote, "The young woman, Pretty Enemy, was not tied up to the tree, but she danced with the others, and had her arms scarified from the shoulders to the elbows" (quoted in Dorsey, *Study of Siouan Cults*, 465).

56. Dorsey, *Study of Siouan Cults*, 460; Densmore, *Teton Sioux Music*, 133, 135.

57. Rocky Bear, "Piercing the Ears," 192.

58. Deloria has remarked that "the piercing of a child's ears was a great honor." "One of the meanest things one can say of another whose ears are not pierced is. . . . 'It is patent nobody loved him for look at his white ears'" (Deloria, "Sun Dance," 403, note 1).

59. Densmore, *Teton Sioux Music*, 150.

60. Bourke, quoted in Dorsey, *Study of Siouan Cults*, 466. Deloria described a varying form of this practice in her monograph:

> When the sufferer tried painfully to be free, and pulled in vain on the pierced places and yet could not tear out the ropes, a relative, generally

a woman but sometimes an old father, not being able to stand the sight, and caring more for the victim than his possession, gave him a stick and told him to throw it into the crowd. He did so, and the poor women, and the boys scrambled for it. The one who, according to the accompanists' decision, got it first, received a horse from the relative. After parting with so valuable a thing as a horse, the relative had the right to go to the one who pierced the victim, and ask him to free him. The piercer would then either go up and swing him a few times strenuously to free him, or else, he would take his knife and cut out the wounds, taking out the sticks with which he was pinned and to which the ropes holding him to the sacred pole were attached. (Deloria, "Sun Dance," 405, note 2)

61. Walker, "Sun Dance," 120. Walker's account offers an intriguing opportunity for structuralist analysis. The tree/pole, at once the captive of the Sun Dancers, is at the same time their captor.

62. Dorsey, *Study of Siouan Cults*, 463.

63. Densmore's description of the concluding phase of the Sun Dance differs somewhat from that of Dorsey:

Those who had taken part in the Sun dance returned to their respective lodges at the close of the dancing. Before partaking of food or water they spent some time in the vapor lodge. Their first sip of water was taken in the following manner: a large bowl was filled with water, and beside it was placed a bunch of sweet grass. Having dipped this into the water, the dancer placed it to his lips. He was then given a small piece of cooked buffalo meat, and later sat down to a meal which was spread in his own lodge. (Densmore, *Teton Sioux Music*, 149)

64. The following account is taken from Chittenden and Richardson, *Life, Letters, and Travels*, 1.252–54.

Chapter 12

1. Poole, *Among the Sioux*, 74.

2. Ibid., 212–13.

3. Dodge, *Our Wild Indians*, 111–12.

4. Hyde, *Spotted Tail's Folk*, 235.

5. Dougherty to Newell, 19 June 1879, Spotted Tail Agency, Book 108, Incoming, NARA-KC.

6. Brooks to Newell, 6 June 1879, Spotted Tail Agency, Book 108, Incoming, NARA-KC.

7. Newell, *Life among the Sioux*, 6.

8. Apparently the Indian Office was blessed with an institutional memory of astonishingly short duration. In spring 1883 the acting commissioner, E. S. Stevens, granted Newell permission to take a few of his "Indian friends" for a brief visit to his home in Iowa, which ended in a fiasco (Stevens to Wright, 22 May 1883,

NARA-KC). In August, Newell wrote Agent Wright to inform him of the well-being of his Sicangu guests and to assure him that he was "spending nearly all of [his] time showing them how white men grow crops and care for stock in winter." However, he almost immediately contradicted himself on both points, first by reporting that he had been forced to send the party's young Indian interpreter, Ralph, home due to illness and, second, that he gave "a lecture occasionally about the customs and habits of the Sioux which gives us money sufficient to pay our incidental expenses" (Newell to Wright, 29 August 1883, NARA-KC). News of these "lectures" soon reached Indian commissioner Hiram Price through a letter from Richard Pratt, headmaster of Carlisle Institute. Pratt informed the commissioner that during his recent visit to Rosebud "the agent received a copy of the Chicago Times containing a flaming advertisement of some museum in Chicago stating that Roaster and others . . . were on exhibition at their museum in full paint and feathers at ten cents a sight. The advertisement stated that they were 'the murderers of Custer's gallant band.'" As further incriminating evidence against Newell, Pratt attached a copy of a note from one of his former students begging him to do what he could to send his grandfather and the other members of Newell's party home because he didn't "want them going to dance or show business" (Pratt to Price, 27 November 1883, NARA-KC). The author of this appeal turned out to be none other than "Ralph" (Eagle Feather to Pratt, 21 November, 1883, NARA-KC), who evidently had decided to take leave of the group for reasons other than health, as reported by Newell. Outraged by these revelations, Price demanded that Wright immediately investigate the matter (Price to Wright, 6 December 1883, NARA-KC). This closed the book on the former agent's official relation with the Sicangus.

9. Eli S. Ricker Collection, RG8, Tablet 37, 16–17, Nebraska Historical Society, Lincoln, Neb.
10. Hyde, *Sioux Chronicle,* 16–17.
11. Digmann, "History," 95, BCIM.
12. Hyde, *Spotted Tail's Folk,* 236.
13. Upshaw to Wright, 14 October 1885, Rosebud Agency Book 110, Incoming, NARA-KC.
14. Ibid.
15. Digmann to Wright, 3 March 1890, BCIM.
16. Digmann, "History," 35, BCIM.
17. Digmann to Stephan, 1 April 1890, BCIM.
18. Digmann to Stephan, 1 May 1890, BCIM.
19. Digmann to Stephan, 7 April 1890, BCIM.
20. Digmann to Stephan, 16 April 1890, BCIM.
21. Digmann, "History," 25, BCIM.
22. Digmann to Stephan, 7 April 1890, BCIM.
23. Thus, in his report to the Indian commissioner for 1883–84, agent James G. Wright observed, "There is a decided reluctance to send away to school for

many reasons, sickness and death not the least, and the labor is great necessary to induce them to do so" (Wright, *ARCIA*, 1884, 45).

24. Pearis to Woods, 19 November 1910, NARA-KC.

25. Digmann, "History," 111, BCIM.

26. Price to Wright, 3 August 1882, Rosebud Agency, Book 109, Incoming, NARA-KC; Atkins to Wright, 29 April 1885, Rosebud Agency, Book 110, Incoming, NARA-KC.

27. Digmann, "History," 45, BCIM.

28. Apparently some parents sought neither Indian Office money nor permission before setting out to see their children. During summer 1884, Commissioner Stevens informed Wright of the disastrous unscheduled "visit" of a Sicangu named Making Blazes and his wife to the Genoa school in Nebraska. According to Stevens: "After remaining a few days, they suddenly left taking with them three of their own children, and two other pupils. The Superintendent immediately took the necessary steps to have the fugitives captured, and with the aid of the civil authorities, succeeded in bring back the children and 'Making Blazes' was sent to his home. The expense in connection with this affair will cost the government about $1215.00." The acting commissioner went on to write: "It also appears that the wife of 'Making Blazes' is a medicine woman and says she is going to make her daughter a 'Medicine Woman' and that the Catholic priest at the Agency had promised to educate the children and not require them to do any work. Further it is reported that there is to be a 'Sun Dance' on the Rosebud in July next." With regard to the Making Blazes case, Stevens warn Wright: "Such parties as 'Making Blazes' and his wife should not be permitted to leave the Reservation for the purpose of visiting the school referred to, and if they left without permission, you will see to it that they are properly punished for this violation of the rules." Concerning the rumored Sun Dance, he stated, "The orders in regard to the 'Sun Dance' must be obeyed even if you have to use force to compel obedience to the rules on this subject." Finally, with regard to the conduct of the Catholic priest, he ordered the agent to "inquire into and report the facts in the case to this office" (Stevens to Wright, 14 June 1884, Book 110, Incoming, NARA-KC). It is quite likely that the unnamed priest was none other than Father Craft, who by this incident gave Wright additional cause to seek his expulsion from the Rosebud.

29. Brooks to Cook, 24 June 1880, Spotted Tail Agency, Book 108, Incoming, NARA-KC.

30. Price to Wright, 20 December 1883, Rosebud Agency, Book 109, Incoming NARA-KC.

31. Marble to Cook, 27 January 1881, Rosebud Agency, Book 108, Incoming, NARA-KC.

32. Price to Wright, 8 September 1883, Rosebud Agency, Book 109, Incoming, NARA-KC.

33. Morgan, *ARCIA*, 1892, 176.

34. Digmann, "History," 81, 137, BCIM.
35. FHH-SFM, 7.
36. Ibid., 8.
37. Describing an epidemic of measles that swept the mission after Easter in 1915, the Franciscan house historian stated:

> The Holy Easter brought us a great number of guests who camped in the vicinity to celebrate this beautiful celebration at the mission. Our children had permission to visit their parents and relatives in their tents. Upon her return a little girl brought measles into the house. Necessary precautions were immediately enacted to prevent infection, but all efforts were to no avail. In a few days 110 girls and 90 boys had come down with the disease. The older ones were especially sick. . . . Then you should have heard the lamenting of the Indians. They all feared for the lives of their loved ones whom they were not permitted to visit. They looked wistful up at the windows in anticipation of spotting one or another of the children. But the little redskins were too sick to move and were glad to be left alone. Everyone was sufficiently restored to health after four weeks for the quarantine to be lifted, and we thanked God with happy hearts that he had spared us from worse. But the worst was still yet to come, as more children got bronchitis and pneumonia and one boy three girls died shortly one after another in the house. . . . *Missionblieben, kamen, um sie nach Hause zu holen.* (Sisters of St. Francis of Penance and Christian Charity, Jahresbericht, 1915, SSF)

38. Digmann, "History," 52, BCIM.
39. Stephan to Digmann, 25 June 1890, BCIM.
40. Digmann, "History," 57, 79, BCIM. It seems clear that the strategy of some Sicangus to use the school their children would attend as a bargaining chip in negotiations was neither new nor directed solely at the mission. In 1883, Carlisle's Richard Pratt thus informed Indian commissioner Hiram Price that "when at Rosebud Agency after children, Milk, one of the Chiefs, complained to me that he had been promised one of our wagons at the time he visited Washington in the Spring of 1880. . . . He states that three of our wagons were sent to Pine Ridge Chiefs, but only one had ever been sent to the Rosebud Chiefs." Pratt went on to report: "This appeared to rest heavily on his mind and was some excuse, if not the whole excuse, for his not aiding the agent and myself in getting children. He not only did not send his own children, but by his apathy in the matter, stood in the way of others" (Pratt to Price, 16 November 1883, NARA-KC). Price must have considered the situation of some weight, for in less than a week he had forwarded Agent Wright of Rosebud a copy of Pratt's letter, adding, "I desire to be informed by you, if you, if you recommend furnishing 'Milk' with spring wagon under the circumstances" (Price to Wright, 21 November 1883, NARA-KC).
41. Digmann to House, 3 February 1900, NARA-KC.

42. Digmann to Stephan, 7 September 1890, BCIM.
43. Digmann, "History," 82, BCIM.
44. Ibid., 27. There is a hint of similar irritation in the following comment by the Franciscan house historian for 1890: "The Indians were very willing workers, but they wanted their pay" (FHH-SFM, 7).
45. Digmann, "History," 34, BCIM.
46. Digmann, "Mission of Our German Fathers," 357.

Chapter 13

1. In the script for the "Two Roads," the Lakota rendering for the first commandment was "Wakantanka isnala ohounlapi kta; wowicala on, woape on, wowastelake on na wocekiye on. Ogligle wakan na wakan wastepi kin hena unyuonihanpi kte na wastewica;unlakkapi." ["We must honor God by Faith, by Hope, by Loving Him and by Prayer. We must respect the angels and Saints and we should love them."] ("Instruction by Means of the Two Roads," 4, BCIM).
2. Concerning the sacraments, the "Two Road" instrument stated "Wanikiya taku wakan (wicoh'an wakan) sakowin unk'upi, na hena un wakan unkagapi na [wakan] ounkiyapi, hecel Wakantanka woope tanyan unopapi kta na hecel mah'piya ekta wiconi kin he unkiglamnapi unkokihipi kte." ["The Saviours gift of the (holy sacraments) were seven in number, and with these it helps us to become holy, thus it will give us the divine strength to observe the commandments of God and thereby gain the heavenly reward and that we must gain by our own merits."] (Ibid., 5). A more literal translation of the Lakota is "The savior gave us seven sacred things (the sacraments) and by means of these we become sacred and they help us in order that we be able to participate in God's laws and in order that we will be rewarded with eternal life in heaven."
3. Digmann, "History," 14, BCIM.
4. Digmann, ARCIA, 1904, 337. Digmann reported that on one occasion a medicine men came to him for the rite. He wrote that one "pejuta wicasa [medicine man], had the courage to have his little sick baby baptized, and it got well." The priest continued, "Now I have the laugh: that I am going about killing their children by pouring the water over them, and he laughs with me."
5. Digmann, "History," 14 , 47, 15, BCIM.
6. Ibid., 116, 140.
7. Ibid., 149, 108.
8. Ibid., 197, 68, 140.
9. Ibid., 40.
10. Ibid., 168.
11. Ibid., 143.
12. Ibid. In another case of "God calling in dreams," Digmann reported that a group of Protestant Sicangus requested him to hear their confessions. When the priest informed them that they must first be instructed, one member of the company stated, "'Last night I was dreaming. Blackbeard [Digmann] stood in

the water and I on the bank, and I wanted to go with him to be baptized but he said, "You cannot as yet." My dream came true'" (ibid., 102).

13. Buechel, Diary, July 1919, BCIM.
14. Digmann, "History," 88, BCIM.
15. Ibid., 90, 131.
16. Ibid., 109, 77.
17. Ibid., 197.
18. Ibid., 75, 85.
19. Ibid., 85, 81.
20. Ibid., 122.
21. Ibid., 167.
22. Ibid.
23. Ibid., 97, 149.
24. Ibid., 154.
25. Ibid., 146.
26. Ibid., 31.
27. Ibid.
28. Perrig, Diary, 1894, BCIM; Digmann, "History," 47, BCIM. In a letter to *Die Katholischen Missionen*, Digmann similarly stated:

    You often get this answer for old Indians, men and women: "I am too old to get baptized." This, I later convinced myself, means for many of them: "I am too old to resign myself to the way of life of the whites"; because this, they think, is a necessary aspect of baptism. For others, of course, it is just an excuse. They just don't want to break with their heathen customs and all that is connected to it. As last summer a certain Big Rib, who was begging for food, told me when I asked: "Is then heaven only for the young and not for you old ones as well?" As he answered "yes" I responded: "Well, then go and have breakfast there as well." (Digmann, "Nordamerika," *Die Katholischen Missionen* 23 [1895], 163)

29. Digmann, *ARCIA*, 1892, 468–69.
30. Digmann, "History," 94, BCIM.
31. From bylaws I saw stamped on a metal plate, suitable for hanging, at the Saint Francis Mission.
32. C. M. Weisenhorn, "Great Catholic Sioux Congress," c. 1919, BCIM.
33. Goll, *Jesuit Missions*, 43.
34. Sialm, "American Indians."
35. Walker, "Sun Dance," 95.
36. Fletcher, "Sun Dance," 580.
37. Gschwend, "Catholic Sioux Indian Congress," 184.
38. Black Elk, *Sixth Grandfather*, 130.
39. Walker, "Sun Dance," 104.
40. "Great Catholic Congress of 1910."
41. Digmann, "History," 81, BCIM.
42. Black Elk, *Sixth Grandfather*, 290–91.

Conclusion

1. FHH-SFM, 54.
2. Davis to Commissioner of Indian Affairs, 21 January 1916, Rosebud Agency, Outgoing, NARA-KC.
3. Ibid.
4. Goll, *Jesuit Missions*, 65; Digmann to Davis, 23 January 1916, Rosebud Agency, Incoming, NARA-KC.
5. FHH-SFM, 55; Meritt to Davis, 21 January 1916, Rosebud Agency, Incoming, NARA-KC.
6. FHH-SFM, 55.
7. Digmann to Davis, 21 January 1916, Rosebud Agency, Incoming, NARA-KC.
8. Davis to Digmann, 26 January 1916, Rosebud Agency, Outgoing, NARA-KC.
9. Digmann to Davis, 28 January 1916, Rosebud Agency, Incoming, NARA-KC.
10. Ibid.
11. Transcripts of the interrogations are housed at NARA-KC.
12. Davis to Stewart, 9 February 1916, Rosebud Agency, Outgoing, NARA-KC.
13. Stewart to Davis, 10 February 1916, Rosebud Agency, Incoming, NARA-KC.
14. Davis to Commissioner of Indian Affairs, 25 February 1916, Outgoing, NARA-KC.
15. Ibid.
16. FHH-SFM, 54.
17. Digmann to Ketcham, 24 October 1916, BCIM. The Saint Francis missionaries' dismay over the unimpressive results of three decades of mission was apparently shared by the Jesuits and Franciscans stationed among the Oglala Lakotas at Holy Rosary Mission on the neighboring Pine Ridge Reservation. Reflecting on the mission's upcoming silver anniversary, Fr. Eugene Buechel stated: "We intend to celebrate the event before we dismiss the children at the end of June. It is true, we don't feel elated at the results of 25 years of missionary work—they are not such to make us feel proud—but we thought we would make a revival of it" (Buechel to Ketcham, 21 February 1913, BCIM).

Bibliography

Books and Articles

Address of the Catholic Clergy of the Province of Oregon, to the Catholics of the United States, on President Grant's Indian Policy, in Its Bearings upon Catholic Interests at Large. Portland, Or.: Catholic Sentinel, 1874.

Ahlstrom, Sydney E. *A Religious History of the American People.* New Haven, Conn.: Yale University Press, 1972.

Anderson, Gary C., and Alan R. Woolworth, eds. *Through Dakota Eyes: Narrative Accounts of the Minnesota Indian War of 1862.* St. Paul: Minnesota Historical Society, 1988.

Andrist, Ralph K. *The Long Death: The Last Days of the Plains Indians.* New York: Macmillian, 1964.

Archer, Mary Urban, O.S.F. *A History of Holy Name Province of the Sisters of Saint Francis of Penance and Christian Charity.* Stella Niagara, N.Y.: Sisters of Saint Francis of Penance and Christian Charity, 1987.

Aubert, Roger, et al. *The Church in the Industrial Age.* New York: Crossroad, 1981.

Bad Heart Bull. "The Sun Dance Pole." In James R. Walker, *Lakota Belief and Ritual,* ed. Raymond J. DeMallie and Elaine A. Jahner, 183. Lincoln: University of Nebraska Press, 1980.

Bailey, John W. *Pacifying the Plains: General Alfred Terry and the Decline of the Sioux, 1866–1890.* Westport, Conn.: Greenwood Press, 1979.

Bannon, John F. "The Blackrobes in the Americas." *Historical Bulletin* 18, no. 3 (March 1940): 53–54, 65–66.

Beaver, R. Pierce. *Church, State and the American Indians: Two and a Half Centuries of Partnership in Missions between Protestant Churches and the Government.* St. Louis, Mo.: Concordia, 1966.

———. *Introduction to Native American Church History.* Tempe, Ariz.: Cook Christian Training School, 1983.

Beckwith, Paul. *The Illustrated Catholic Missions*, vol. 5. London: J. Donovan, 1890–91.

Berkhoffer, Robert F., Jr. *The White Man's Indian: Images of the American Indian from Columbus to the Present.* New York: Knopf, 1978.

Berthrong, Donald J. "The Nomads: Cheyenne and Arapaho." *The First Voices, Nebraskaland Magazine* 62, no. 1 (1984): 31–35.

Bidney, David. *Theoretical Anthropology.* New York: Schocken Press, 1967.

Black Elk, Nicholas, with John G. Neihardt. *The Sixth Grandfather: Black Elk's Teachings Given to John G. Neihardt.* Edited by Raymond J. DeMallie. Lincoln: University of Nebraska Press, 1984.

Bosch, Aloysius. "Indians Again in Council." *Messenger of the Sacred Heart*, 1895.

———. "Nordamerika: Sud-Dakota." *Die Katholischen Missionen* 21 (1893): 132–33.

Brauer, Jerald C. *Protestantism in America: A Narrative History.* Philadelphia: Westminster Press, 1965.

Brouillet, J. B. A. *Management of the Catholic Indian Office at Washington.* Washington, D.C.: Bureau of Catholic Indian Missions, c. 1878.

———. "Plan for the Education of the Indians of the Sioux Nation," *Annals of the Catholic Indian Missions of America* 2 (January 1879): 65–70.

Bucko, Raymond A. *The Lakota Ritual of the Sweat Lodge: History and Contemporary Practice.* Lincoln: University of Nebraska Press, 1998.

Butler, E. "A Glance at the Indian Question." *Catholic World* 26 (November 1877): 202–3.

Butterfield, C. W. *History of the Discovery of the Northwest by John Nicolet in 1634 with a Sketch of His Life.* Cincinnati, Ohio: Robert Clarke, 1881.

Campbell, Henry Colin. *Pere Rene Menard.* Milwaukee, Wisc.: E. Keogh, 1897.

Campbell, T. J. *Pioneer Priests of North America, 1642–1710.* New York: American Press, 1911.

Carley, Kenneth. *The Sioux Uprising of 1862.* St. Paul: Minnesota Historical Society, 1976.

Casey, M. P. "Indian Contract Schools." *Catholic World* 71 (1901): 629–37.

Cash, Joseph H. *The Sioux People: Rosebud.* Phoenix, Ariz.: Indian Tribal Series, 1971.

Catholic Young Men's National Union. *Catholic Grievances in Relation to the Administration of Indian Affairs.* Richmond, Va.: Catholic Visitor Print, 1882.

Center for American Indian Research and Native Studies. *Oceti Sakowin Origins and Development: Foundational Resources for Educators.* Martin, S. Dak.: Center for American Indian Research and Native Studies, 2012.

Chaput, Donald. "Generals, Indian Agents, Politicians: The Doolittle Survey of 1865." *Western Historical Quarterly* 3, no. 3 (July 1972).

Chittenden, Hiram Martin, and Alfred Talbot Richardson, eds. *Life, Letters and Travels of Father Pierre-Jean de Smet, S.J., 1901–1873.* 4. vols. New York: F. P. Harper, 1905.

Clow, Richmond L. *The Rosebud Sioux: The Federal Government and the Reservation Years, 1878–1940.* Ann Arbor, Mich.: UMI Dissertation Services, 1991.

Cosmopolitan, A. *Miss Columbia's Public School: Will It Blow Over.* New York: Francis B. Felt, 1871.

Craig, Gordon A. *Germany, 1866–1945.* New York: Oxford University Press, 1978.

"Critics of Catholic Garb in Indian Schools." *Literary Digest* 44 (1912): 429.

Cross, Whitney R. *The Burned-Over District: The Social and Intellectual History of Enthusiastic Religion in Western New York, 1800–1850.* Ithaca, N.Y.: Cornell University Press, 1950.

Curran, Francis X, S.J. "Buffalo Mission Centennial." *Jesuit Bulletin* 48 (October 1969): 3–5.

———. "The Buffalo Mission of the German Jesuits, 1869–1907." *Historical Records and Studies* 43 (1955): 95–126.

———. *The Return of the Jesuits.* Chicago: Loyola University Press, 1966.

Curtis, Natalie, ed. *The Indians' Book.* New York: Harper and Brothers, 1935.

Danziger, Edmund J. "The Indian Office during the Civil War: Impotence in Indian Affairs." *South Dakota History* 5, no. 1 (Spring 1974): 52–72.

Debo, Angie. *The Road to Disappearance.* Norman: University of Oklahoma Press, 1941.

Deloria, Ella. *Speaking of Indians.* New York: Friendship Press, 1944.

———. "The Sun Dance of the Oglala Sioux." *Journal of American Folklore* 42 (1929): 354–413.

DeMallie, Raymond J. "Introduction." In James R. Walker, *Lakota Society*, ed. Raymond J. DeMallie, 3–12. Lincoln: University of Nebraska Press, 1982.

———. "Lakota Belief and Ritual." In *Sioux Indian Religion*, ed. Raymond J. DeMallie and Douglas Parks, 3–44. Norman: University of Oklahoma Press, 1981.

———. "Touching the Pen." In *Ethnohistory on the Great Plains*, ed. Frederick C. Luebke. Lincoln: University of Nebraska Press, 1980.

DeMallie, Raymond J., and Robert Lavenda. "Wakan: Plains Siouan Concepts of Power." In *The Anthropology of Power: Ethnographic Studies from Asia, Oceania and the New World*, ed. Richard Adams and Raymond D. Fogelson, 153–65. New York: Academic Press, 1977.

Densmore, Frances. *Teton Sioux Music.* Smithsonian Institution, Bureau of American Ethnology Bulletin 61. Washington, D.C.: Government Printing Office, 1918.

DeRosier, Arthur H. *The Removal of the Choctaw Indians.* Knoxville: University of Tennessee Press, 1970.

Desmond, Humphrey J. *The APA Movement: A Sketch*. Washington, D.C.: New Century Press, 1912.

Digmann, Florentine. "Mission of Our German Fathers among the Dakota Indians." *Woodstock Letters* 31 (1902): 352–59.

———. "Nordamerika." *Die Katholischen Missionen* 23 (1895): 163.

———. "Nordamerika: Indianer Mission in Dakota." *Die Katholischen Missionen* 16 (1888): 258.

———. "Picture from the German Sioux Missions." *Central Blatt and Social Justice* (June 1933): 89–90.

Dodge, Richard. *Our Wild Indians*. Williamstown, Mass.: Corner House, 1978.

Dorchester, Daniel. "Government Schools and Contract Schools." *Lend a Hand* 10 (1893): 118–26.

———. *Romanism versus the Public School System*. New York: Phillips and Hunt, 1888.

Dorsey, James O. A *Study of Siouan Cults*. Eleventh Annual Report of the Bureau of American Ethnology, 351–544. Washington, D.C.: Government Printing Office, 1894.

———. "Teton Folk-lore." *American Anthropologist* 1, no. 2 (April 1889): 143–58.

Dunne, Georgia. *Towers of Montabaur*. Derby, N.Y.: St. Paul, 1971.

Duratschek, Claudia. *Crusading along Sioux Trails*. Yankton, S.Dak.: Grail, 1947.

Eastman, Elaine Goodale. *Pratt, the Red Man's Moses*. Norman: University of Oklahoma Press, 1935.

Enoch, Ross. *The Jesuit Mission to the Lakota Sioux: A Study in Pastoral Ministry, 1886–1945*. Franklin, Wisc.: Sheed and Ward, 1996.

Ewers, John C. *Teton Dakota Ethnology and History*. Rev. ed. Berkeley: Western Museum Laboratories, United States Department of Interior, National Park Service, 1938.

Ewing, Charles. *Circular of the Catholic Commissioner for Indian Missions to the Catholics of the United States*. Baltimore: John Murphy, 1874.

Eyck, Erich. *Bismarck and the German Empire*. New York: W. W. Norton, 1964.

Feather on Head. "Preparing the Hunka Implements." In James R. Walker, *Lakota Belief and Ritual*, ed. Raymond J. DeMallie and Elaine A. Jahner, 215–17. Lincoln: University of Nebraska Press, 1980.

Finger. "Conception of Energy." In James R. Walker, "The Sun Dance and Other Ceremonies of the Oglala Division of the Teton Dakota." *Anthropological Papers of the American Museum of Natural History* 16, pt. 2 (1917): 154–55.

———. "Wohpe and the Gift of the Pipe." In James R. Walker, *Lakota Belief and Ritual*, ed. Raymond J. DeMallie and Elaine A. Jahner, 109–12. Lincoln: University of Nebraska Press, 1980.

Fletcher, Alice C. "Appendix: Extracts from Letter from Alice C. Fletcher." In *Proceedings of the Eighth Annual Meeting of the Lake Mohonk Conference of Friends of the Indians*, 1890, 152. Lake Mohonk, N.Y.: Lake Mohonk Conference, 1890.

Fletcher, Alice C. "The Sun Dance of the Ogallala Sioux." *Proceedings of the American Association for the Advancement of Science* 31 (1882): 580–84.

Foley, Thomas W. *Father Francis Craft, Missionary to the Sioux.* Lincoln: University of Nebraska Press, 2002.

Folwell, William Watts, et al. *The Court Proceedings in the Trail of Dakota Indians following the Massacre in Minnesota in August 1862.* Minneapolis: Saterlee Printing, 1927.

Foreman, Grant. *Indian Removal: The Emigration of the Five Civilized Tribes of Indians.* Norman: University of Oklahoma Press, 1932.

———. "J. George Wright: 1860–1941." *Chronicles of Oklahoma* 20 (June, 1942): 120–23.

Frazer, Robert W. *Forts of the West: Military Forts and Presidios and Posts Commonly Called Forts West of the Mississippi River to 1898.* Norman: University of Oklahoma Press, 1965.

Frelinghuysen, Theodore. "Speech of Mr. Frelinghuysen of New Jersey Delivered in the Senate of the United States, April 6, 1830." Washington, D.C.: National Journal. 1830.

Fritz, Henry E. *The Movement for Indian Assimilation, 1860–1890.* Philadelphia: University of Pennsylvania Press, 1963.

Ganss, H. G. *The Present Status of Catholic Missions among the American Indians.* New York: Marquette League, 1907.

———. "Religious Work among the Indians." In *Proceedings of the Twenty-First Annual Meeting of the Lake Mohonk Conference of the Friends of the Indian, 1903,* 90–93. Lake Mohonk, N.Y.: Lake Mohonk Conference, 1904.

Garraghan, Gilbert. *Jesuits in the Middle United States.* 3 vols. New York: America Press, 1938.

———. "The Society in America: 1566–1940." *Historical Bulletin* 18 (March 1940): 59–60.

Gates, Merrill E. "Opening Address." In *Proceedings of the Eighteenth Annual Meeting of the Lake Mohonk Conference of Friends of the Indian, 1900,* 10–21. Lake Mohonk, N.Y.: Lake Mohonk Conference, 1901.

Gibbons, James Cardinal. "An Appeal in Behalf of Catholic Indian Mission School." *Indian Sentinel,* 1902–3: 28.

Gibbons, James Cardinal, et al. "Appeal on Behalf of the Negro and Indian Missions in the United States." In *Mission Work among the Negroes and Indians, 1898.* Clayton, Del.: Press of St. Joseph's Industrial School, 1899.

Girard, P. "Our New Indian Policy and Religious Liberty." *Catholic World* 26 (October 1877): 90–108. [*Catholic Grievances in Relation to the Administration of Indian Affairs.* Richmond, Va.: Catholic Visitor Print, 1882, 21–22.]

Goll, Louis. *Jesuit Missions among the Sioux.* St. Francis, S.Dak.: St. Francis Mission, 1940.

———. "Shepherd of the Sioux." *Jesuit Missions* 7, no. 4 (1933): 82–94.

Good Seat. "Wakan Tanka." In James R. Walker, *Lakota Belief and Ritual*, ed. Raymond J. DeMallie and Elaine A. Jahner, 70–72. Lincoln: University of Nebraska Press, 1980.

Grant, Ulysses S. "Address to Congress, December 5, 1870." In *Documents of United States Indian Policy*, ed. Francis Paul Prucha, 135. 2nd ed. Lincoln: University of Nebraska Press, 1991.

"The Great Catholic Congress of 1910." *Indian Sentinel* (1911): 7.

Green, Michael D. *The Politics of Indian Removal*. Lincoln: University of Nebraska Press, 1982.

Griffin, Clifford S. *Their Brothers' Keepers: Moral Stewardship in the United States, 1800–1865*. New Brunswick, N.J.: Rutgers University Press, 1960.

Gschwend, Joseph. "Catholic Sioux Indian Congress." *Jesuit Missions* 5, no. 8 (September 1931): 184–85, 195.

Guilday, Peter. *A History of the Councils of Baltimore: 1791–1884*. New York: Macmillan, 1932.

Hagan, William T. *American Indians*. Chicago: University of Chicago Press, 1993.

Handy, Robert T. *A Christian America: Protestant Hopes and Historical Realities*. 2nd ed. Oxford: University of Oxford Press, 1984.

Hardman, Keith. *Charles Grandison Finney, 1792–1870: Revivalist and Reformer*. Syracuse, N.Y.: Syracuse University Press, 1987.

Hassrick, Royal. *The Sioux*. Norman: University of Oklahoma Press.

Herman, Antoine, and James R. Walker. "The Seven Council Fires." In James R. Walker, *Lakota Society*, ed. Raymond J. DeMallie, 14–18. Lincoln: University of Nebraska Press, 1982.

Hickerson, Harold. *Sioux Indians I*. New York: Garland Press, 1974.

High Bear. "The Sun Dance." In James R. Walker, *Lakota Society*, ed. Raymond J. DeMallie, 99. Lincoln: University of Nebraska Press, 1982.

Hilger, H. Inez. "The Narrative of Oscar One Bull." *Mid-America* 28, no. 3 (1946): 147–72.

Hillig, Frederick, "Nordamerika." *Die Katholischen Missionen* 22 (1894): 212.

Hodge, Frederick W. *Handbook of American Indians North of Mexico*. Washington, D.C.: U.S. Government Printing Office, 1912.

Hoig, Stan. *The Sand Creek Massacre*. Norman: University of Oklahoma Press, 1961.

Holcombe, Return I., ed. "A Sioux Story of the War: Chief Big Eagle's Story of the Sioux Outbreak of 1862." *Minnesota Historical Collections* 6 (1894): 382–400.

Holler, Clyde. "Black Elk's Relationship to Christianity." *American Indian Quarterly* 8 (Winter 1984): 37–49.

———, ed. *Black Elk's Religion: The Sun Dance and Lakota Catholicism*. Syracuse, N.Y.: Syracuse University Press, 1995.

Horsman, Reginald. "American Indian Policy and the Origins of Manifest Destiny." *University of Birmingham History Journal* 10 (December 1968): 128–40.

Hoxie, Frederick E. *A Final Promise: The Campaign to Assimilate the Indians, 1880–1924*. Lincoln: University of Nebraska Press, 1984.

Hughes, William. "Catholic Missions among the Indians." In *Proceedings of the Thirtieth Annual Lake Mohonk Conference of Friends of the Indians and Other Dependent People*, 76–80. Lake Mohonk, N.Y.: Lake Mohonk Conference, 1912.

Hurt, Wesley R. *Sioux Indians II*. New York: Garland Press, 1974.

Hutchison, William R. *Errand to the World: American Protestant Thought and Foreign Missions*. Chicago: University of Chicago Press, 1987.

———. *The Modernist Impulse in American Protestantism*. Oxford: Oxford University Press, 1976.

Hyde, George. *A Sioux Chronicle*. Norman: University of Oklahoma Press, 1956.

———. *Spotted Tail's Folk*. Norman: University of Oklahoma Press, 1974.

"Indian Appropriations for Sectarian Schools." *Outlook* 79 (January 28, 1905): 221–22.

"Indian Government Schools." *Outlook* 100 (March 30, 1912): 718–19.

Ireland, John. "Why They Oppose Morgan: Interview with Archbishop John Ireland." *Philadelphia Press*, December 14, 1889, 3.

Jacker, Edward. "Who Is to Blame for the Custer Massacre?" *American Catholic Quarterly* 1 (1876): 712–41.

Jutz, John. "Recollections of an Old Missionary," pts. 1–4. *Canisius Monthly* 5, nos. 1–4 (October 1918–January 1919).

Kapplar, Charles J. *Indian Treaties: 1778–1883*. New York: Interland, 1975 (searchable at *Indian Treaties* 2, http://digital library.okstate/kappler/vol2/ treaties/sio0594.htm).

Karolevitz, Robert F. *Bishop Martin Marty: "The Black Robe Lean Chief."* Yankton, S.Dak.: Sacred Heart Convent, 1980.

Keller, Robert. *American Protestantism and United States Indian Policy, 1869–82*. Lincoln: University of Nebraska Press, 1983.

Kellogg, Louise Phelps. "Fort Beauharnois." *Minnesota History Bulletin* 8 (September 1927): 232–46.

———. *The French Regime in Wisconsin and the Northwest*. New York: Cooper Square, 1968.

Kelsey, Harry. "The Doolittle Report of 1867: Its Preparation and Shortcomings." *Arizona and the West* 17, no. 2 (1975): 107–20.

Ketcham, William. "Missions among the Indians." *Missionary* 9 (1905): 178–88. (journal of the Catholic Missionary Union)

———. *Religious "Garb" and "Insignia" in Government Indian Schools*. Washington, D.C.: Bureau of Catholic Indian Missions, 1912.

———. *Report of the Bureau of Catholic Indian Missions for 1900–1901 and 1901–1902*. Washington, D.C.: Bureau of Catholic Indian Missions, 1902.

———. *Report of the Bureau of Catholic Indian Missions, 1904–1905*. Washington, D.C.: Bureau of Catholic Indian Missions, 1906.

———. *Report of the Bureau of Catholic Indian Missions, 1905–1906*. Washington, D.C.: Bureau of Catholic Indian Missions, 1907.

———. *What Shall Become of Our Catholic Indian Missions*. Washington, D.C.: Bureau of Catholic Indian Missions, n.d.

Kinzer, Donald L. *An Episode in Anti-Catholicism: The American Protective Association*. Seattle: University of Washington Press, 1964.

Kleber, Albert. *History of St. Meinrad Archabbey, 1854–1954*. Saint Meinrad, Ind.: Grail, 1954.

Kleber, Walter, ed. "Brown, Orlando." *Kentucky Encyclopedia*. Lexington: University of Kentucky Press, 1992.

Kuppens, Francis. "Extract from a Letter of Father F. X. Kuppens, S.J." *Woodstock Letters* 1 (1872): 106–10.

Kvasnicka, Robert M., and Herman J. Viola, eds. *The Commissioners of Indian Affairs, 1824–1977*. Lincoln: University of Nebraska Press, 1979.

Latourette, Kenneth S. *The Great Century, 1800–1914*. Vols. 4–6 of *A History of the Expansion of Christianity*. New York: Harper and Brothers, 1938–46.

Little Wound. "Wakan." In James R. Walker, *Lakota Belief and Ritual*, ed. Raymond J. DeMallie and Elaine A. Jahner, 68–70. Lincoln: University of Nebraska Press, 1980.

Little Wound et al. "The Holy Men Tell of the Sun Dance." In James R. Walker, *Lakota Belief and Ritual*, ed. Raymond J. DeMallie and Elaine A. Jahner, 181–82. Lincoln: University of Nebraska Press, 1980.

Lone Bear. "The Sacred Language." In James R. Walker, *Lakota Belief and Ritual*, ed. Raymond J. DeMallie and Elaine A. Jahner, 127–28. Lincoln: University of Nebraska Press, 1980.

Ludlow, Helen W. *Captain Pratt and His Work for Indian Education*. Philadelphia: Indian Rights Association, 1886.

Lyttle, Donald, and Vine Deloria Jr. *The Nations Within: The Past and Future of American Indian Sovereignty*. Austin: University of Texas Press, 1998.

Manual of Catholic Indian Missionary Associations: Appeal to the Catholic Ladies of the United States. Bureau of Catholic Indian Missions, c. 1875.

Mardock, Robert W. *The Reformers and the American Indian*. Columbia: University of Missouri Press, 1971.

Marsden, George M. *Fundamentalism and American Culture: The Shaping of Twentieth-Century Evangelicalism, 1870–1925*. Oxford: Oxford University Press, 1980.

Martin, Joel W. *Sacred Revolt: The Muskogee's Struggle for a New World*. Boston: Beacon Press, 1991.

Marty, Martin. "Abbot Martin among the Sioux at Red Cloud and Spotted Tail Agencies." *Annals of the Catholic Indian Missions of America* 2 (January 1879): 71.

———. "Abbott Martin Visits Sitting Bull." *Annals of the Catholic Indian Missions of America* 2, no. 1 (January 1878): 7–10.

———. "Abbott Martin Visits the Red Cloud and Spotted Tail Agencies." *Annals of the Catholic Indian Missions of America* 2, no. 1 (January 1878): 10.

———"Extracts from Annals of the Catholic Indian Missions—1877." *Indian Sentinel*, January 1920, 31.

———. "The Indian Problem and the Catholic Church." *Catholic World* 48 (February 1889): 577–84.

———. "Statement of the Right Reverend Bishop Martin Marty of the Roman Catholic Church." In *Report by the Indian Rights Association*, ed. C. C. Painter. Philadelphia: Indian Rights Association, 1892.

Marty, Martin E. *Righteous Empire: The Protestant Experience in America*. New York: Dial Press, 1970.

McDonnell, Janet A. *The Dispossession of the American Indian*. Bloomington, Ind.: University Press, 1991.

McLoughlin, William G. *Awakenings and Reform: An Essay in Religion and Social Change in America: 1607–1977*. Chicago: University of Chicago Press, 1978.

Mead, Sidney E. *The Lively Experiment: The Shaping of Christianity in America*. New York: Harper and Row, 1976.

Meyer, Roy W. *History of the Santee Sioux: United States Indian Policy on Trial*. Lincoln: University of Nebraska Press, 1967.

Mirsky, Jeanette. "The Dakota." In *Cooperation and Competition among Primitive Peoples*, ed. Margaret Mead, 382–427. New ed. Boston: Beacon Press, 1966 [1937].

Mooney, James "The Ghost-Dance Religion and the Sioux Outbreak of 1890." *Fourteenth Annual Report of the Bureau of Ethnology*, pt. 2. Washington, D.C.: U.S. Government Printing Office, 1894.

Morgan, Thomas J. "Indian Education." *U.S. Bureau of Indian Education*, Bulletin 1. Washington, D.C.: U.S. Government Printing Office, 1890.

———. "Reminiscences of Service with Colored Troops in the Army of the Cumberland, 1863–65." In *Soldiers and Sailors Historical Society of Rhode Island, Personal Narratives* 13. Providence: The Society, 1885.

———. *Roman Catholics and Indian Education*. Boston: American Citizen, 1893.

"Morgan's Military Record: Facts Which the Senate Should Consider." *Cincinnati Commercial Gazette*, July 10, 1889, 7–10.

Mott, John R. *The Evangelization of the World in This Generation*. New York: Student Volunteer Movement, 1905.

Nadeau, Remi. *Fort Laramie and the Sioux Indians*. Chicago: University of Chicago Press, 1967.

Neill, Edward D. *Dahkotah Land and Dahkotah Life, with the History of the Fur Traders of the Extreme Northwest during the French and British Dominions*. Philadelphia: J. B. Lippincott, 1859.

———. "Notes on Early Wisconsin Explorations, Forts and Trading Posts." *Report and Collections of the State Historical Society of Wisconsin* 10 (1883–85): 292–306.

Newell, Cicero. *Life among the Sioux Indians*. New York: New York Popular, ca. 1890–1900.

No Ears. "Men's and Women's Roles." In James R. Walker, *Lakota Society*, ed. Raymond J. DeMallie, 40. Lincoln: University of Nebraska Press, 1982.

"No Enmity to Catholics: General Morgan on the Indian School Appointments."
    Boston Post, September 13, 1889, 43.
"Nordamerika." *Die Katholischen Missionen* 14 (1886): 197–200.
"Nordamerika." *Die Katholischen Missionen* 15 (1887): 19–22.
Norton, Mary Aquinas. "Catholic Missions and Missionaries among the Indians
    of Dakota." *North Dakota Historical Quarterly* 5, no. 3 (April 1930): 149–65.
"The Nun's Garb Question." *Literary Digest* 45 (October 12, 1912): 626.
Old Horse. "Iktomi." In James R. Walker, *Lakota Belief and Ritual*, ed. Raymond
    J. DeMallie and Elaine A. Jahner, 128–29. Lincoln: University of Nebraska
    Press, 1980.
Olson, James C. *Red Cloud and the Sioux Problem*. Lincoln: University of Nebraska,
    1975.
One Star. "Sicun." In James R. Walker, "The Sun Dance and Other Ceremonies of
    the Oglala Division of the Teton Dakota." *Anthropological Papers of the American
    Museum of Natural History* 16, pt. 2 (1917): 158–59.
Painter, C. C. *Extravagance, Waste and Failure of Indian Education*. Philadelphia:
    Indian Rights Association, 1895.
Pancoast, Henry S. *Impression of the Sioux Tribes in 1882 with Some First Principles
    in the Indian Question*. Philadelphia: Franklin Printing House, 1883.
Perrig, Emil. "Nordamerika." *Die Katholischen Missionen* 15 (1887): 66–67.
———. "Nordamerika." *Die Katholischen Missionen* 16 (1888): 257–58.
Peterson, Susan C. "Holy Women" and Housekeepers: Women Teachers on South
    Dakota Reservations, 1885–1910." *South Dakota History* 13, no. 3 (Fall 1983):
    245–60.
Poole, Dewitt C. *Among the Sioux of Dakota: Eighteen Months' Experience as an
    Indian Agent, 1869–70*. St. Paul: Minnesota Historical Society, 1988.
Powers, William. *Oglala Religion*. Lincoln: University of Nebraska Press, 1977.
Pratt, Richard Henry. "The Indian Problem." *Missionary Review of the World* 33,
    no. 11 (1910): 855–56.
Priest, Loring B. *Uncle Sam's Stepchildren: The Reformation of United States Indian
    Policy, 1865–1887*. New Brunswick, N.J.: Rutgers University Press, 1942.
Prucha, Francis. *American Indian Policy in Crisis: Christian Reformers and the
    Indian, 1865–1900*. Norman: University of Oklahoma Press, 1976.
———. "Andrew Jackson's Indian Policy: A Reassessment." *Journal of American
    History* 56 (December 1969): 527–39.
———, ed. *Documents of United States Indian Policy*, 2nd ed. Lincoln: University
    of Nebraska Press, 1991.
———. *The Great Father*. Lincoln: University of Nebraska Press, 1984.
———. *United States Indian Policy in Its Formative Years*. Lincoln: University of
    Nebraska Press, 1962.
Pulzer, Peter. *Germany, 1870–1945: Politics, State Formation, and War*. New York:
    Oxford University Press, 1996.

Rahill, Peter J. *The Catholic Indian Missions and the Grant Peace Policy, 1870–1884.* Washington, D.C.: Catholic University of American, 1953.

Ravoux, Augustine. *The Labors of Mgr. A. Ravoux among the Sioux or Dakota Indians from the Fall of the Year 1841 to the Spring of 1844.* St. Paul, Minn.: Pioneer Press, 1897.

———. *Memoires, Reminiscences, et Conferrences de Monseigneur A. Ravoux, V. G.* St. Paul: Le doux et Le Vasseur, 1897.

———. "Missionary Excursion in Iowa—No. II." *U.S.C. Magazine,* February 1848, 84–86.

"Religious Garb in Indian Schools." *Independent* 72 (February 15, 1912): 374–75.

"Religious Garb in the Indian Schools." *Literary Digest* 44 (February 24, 1912): 379–80.

Remini, Robert V. *Andrew Jackson and His Indian Wars.* New York: Viking Adult, 2001.

Ring, Nancy. "The First Mission to the Sioux." *Mid-America* 3 (1932): 344.

Riggs, Stephen. "The Dakota Missions." *Collections of the Minnesota Historical Society* 3 (1880): 115–28.

———. *Mary and I: Forty Years with the Sioux.* Boston: Congregational Sunday-school and Publishing Society, 1887.

Robinson, Doane. *A History of the Dakota or Sioux Indians.* Minneapolis, Minn.: Ross and Haines, 1904.

———. "Tales of the Dakota: One Hundred Anecdotes Illustrative of Sioux Life and Thinking." *South Dakota Historical Collections* 14 (1928): 485–538.

Rocky Bear, "Piercing the Ears." In James R. Walker, *Lakota Belief and Ritual,* ed. Raymond J. DeMallie and Elaine A. Jahner, 191–93. Lincoln: University of Nebraska Press, 1980.

Rogin, Michael P. *Fathers and Children.* New York: Alfred A. Knopf, 1975.

Ross, Ronald N. *The Failure of Bismarck's Kulturkampf: Catholicism and State Power in Imperial Germany, 1871–1887.* Washington, D.C.: Catholic University of America, 1998.

Ryan, P. "An Appeal in Behalf of the Indian Schools." *Indian Sentinel,* 1902–3, 28.

Satz, Ronald N. *American Indian Policy in the Jacksonian Era.* Lincoln: University of Nebraska Press, 1975.

Scott, John C. "'To Do Some Good among the Indians': Nineteenth Century Benedictine Indian Missions." *Journal of the West* 23, no. 1 (January 1984): 26–36.

Severin, Timothy. *Explorers of the Mississippi.* New York: Alfred Knopf, 1968.

Shea, John Gilmary. *The History of the Catholic Missions among the Indian Tribes of the United States, 1529–1854.* New York: Edward Dunigan and Brother, 1857.

Short Feather. "Spirits." In James R. Walker, *Lakota Belief and Ritual,* ed. Raymond J. DeMallie and Elaine A. Jahner, 115–16. Lincoln: University of Nebraska Press, 1980.

Sialm, Placidus. "American Indians." *Jesuit Missions* 4, no. 5 (May 1930), 117.

Sievers, Harry J. "The Catholic Indian School Issue and the Presidential Election of 1892." *Catholic Historical Review* 38 (July 1952): 129–55.

Smith, Timothy L. *Revivalism and Social Reform in Mid-Nineteenth Century America*. Nashville, Tenn.: Abingdon Press, 1957.

Stahl, Robert. "Carrying the Word to the Sioux: The Williamson and Riggs Families." In *South Dakota Leaders from Pierre Chouteau, Jr. to Oscar Howe*, ed. Herbert T. Hoover and Larry Zimmerman, 65–79. Vermillion: University of South Dakota Press, 1989.

Standing Bear, Luther. *Land of the Spotted Eagle*. Boston: Houghton Mifflin, 1933.

———. *My People, the Sioux*. Boston: Houghton, Mifflin, 1928.

Stephan, J. A. *Report of the Bureau of Catholic Indian Missions, 1899–1900*. Washington, D.C.: Bureau of Catholic Indian Missions, 1900.

"St. Francis' Mission, Rosebud Agency, South Dakota." *Woodstock Letters* 34 (1905): 106–7.

Svaldi, David. *Sand Creek and the Rhetoric of Extermination*. Lincoln: University of Nebraska Press, 1989.

Sweet, William Warren. *Revivalism in America: Its Origin, Growth and Decline*. New York: C. Scribner's Sons, 1944.

Sword, George. "Foundations." In James R. Walker, *Lakota Belief and Ritual*, ed. Raymond J. DeMallie and Elaine A. Jahner, 74–81. Lincoln: University of Nebraska Press, 1980.

———. "Instructing the Sun Dance Candidate." In James R. Walker, *Lakota Belief and Ritual*, ed. Raymond J. DeMallie and Elaine A. Jahner, 182. Lincoln: University of Nebraska Press, 1980.

———. "Life and Visions." In James R. Walker, *Lakota Belief and Ritual*, ed. Raymond J. DeMallie and Elaine A. Jahner, 83–84. Lincoln: University of Nebraska Press, 1980.

———. "Nagipi." In James R. Walker, *Lakota Belief and Ritual*, ed. Raymond J. DeMallie and Elaine A. Jahner, 98–100. Lincoln: University of Nebraska Press, 1980.

———. "Ni, Ini, and Initi." In James R. Walker, *Lakota Belief and Ritual*, ed. Raymond J. DeMallie and Elaine A. Jahner, 100. Lincoln: University of Nebraska Press, 1980.

———. "On Ceremonies." In James R. Walker, *Lakota Belief and Ritual*, ed. Raymond J. DeMallie and Elaine A. Jahner, 81–82. Lincoln: University of Nebraska Press, 1980.

———. "Sicun." "The Sun Dance and Other Ceremonies of the Oglala Division of the Teton Dakota." *Anthropological Papers of the American Museum of Natural History* 16, pt. 2 (1917): 158.

———. "Treating the Sick." In James R. Walker, *Lakota Belief and Ritual*, ed. Raymond J. DeMallie and Elaine A. Jahner, 91–93. Lincoln: University of Nebraska Press, 1980.

———. "Wakan." In James R. Walker, "The Sun Dance and Other Ceremonies of the Oglala Division of the Teton Dakota." *Anthropological Papers of the American Museum of Natural History* 16, pt. 2 (1917): 152.

Sword, George, et al. "The Secret Knowledge of Shamans." In James R. Walker, *Lakota Belief and Ritual*, ed. Raymond J. DeMallie and Elaine A. Jahner, 93–96. Lincoln: University of Nebraska Press, 1980.

Tanner, Helen, ed. *Historical Atlas of Great Lakes Indians*. Norman: University of Oklahoma Press, 1987.

Taylor, Alan P. *Bismarck: The Man and the Statesman*. New York: Random House, 1955.

Thiel, Mark G. "Catholic Ladders and Native American Evangelization." *U.S. Catholic Historian* 7 (Winter 2009): 49–70.

———. "Catholic Sodalities among the Sioux, 1882–1910." *U.S. Catholic Historian* 16 (Spring 1998): 56–77.

Thomas, George M. *Revivalism and Cultural Change: Christianity, Nation Building, and the Market in the Nineteenth-Century United States*. Chicago: University of Chicago Press, 1989.

Trennert, Robert A. *Alternative to Extinction: Federal Indian Policy and the Beginnings of the Reservation System, 1846–51*. Philadelphia: Temple University Press, 1975.

———. "Orlando Brown." In *The Commissioners of Indian Affairs: 1824–1977*, ed. Robert Kvasnica and Herman J. Viola. Lincoln: University of Nebraska Press, 1979.

Truteau, Jean Baptiste. "Remarks on the Manners of the Indians Living High Up the Missouri." *Medical Repository* 6 (1808): 52–53.

Tyon, Thomas. "The Circle." In James R. Walker, "The Sun Dance and Other Ceremonies of the Oglala Division of the Teton Dakota." *Anthropological Papers of the American Museum of Natural History* 16, pt. 2 (1917): 160.

———. "Foundations." In James R. Walker, *Lakota Belief and Ritual*, ed. Raymond J. DeMallie and Elaine A. Jahner, 100–108: Lincoln: University of Nebraska Press, 1980.

———. "Thomas Tyon Tells about the Beginning of the Sun Dance." In James R. Walker, *Lakota Belief and Ritual*, ed. Raymond J. DeMallie and Elaine A. Jahner, 176–81. Lincoln: University of Nebraska Press, 1980.

Tyler, Lyman S. *A History of Indian Policy*. Washington, D.C: Department of the Interior, 1973.

Utley, Robert, and Barry Mackintosh. *The Department of Everything Else*. Washington, D.C.: Department of the Interior, 1988.

Van Every, Dale. *Disinherited: The Lost Birthright of the American Indian*. New York: William Morrow, 1966.

Verwyst, Fr. Chrysostom, O.S.F. *Missionary Labors of Fathers Marquette, Menard and Allouez in the Lake Superior Region*. Milwaukee, Wisc.: Hoffmann Brothers, 1886.

Vestal, Stanley. *Warpath: The True Story of the Fighting Sioux Told in a Biography of Chief White Bull*. Lincoln: University of Nebraska Press, 1984.

Walker, James R. "Communal Chase of the Buffalo." In James R. Walker, *Lakota Society*, ed. Raymond J. DeMallie, 74–94. Lincoln: University of Nebraska Press, 1982.

———. "Divisions of the Lakotas." In James R. Walker, *Lakota Society*, ed. Raymond J. DeMallie, 18–20. Lincoln: University of Nebraska Press, 1982.

———. "The Hunka Ceremony." In James R. Walker, *Lakota Belief and Ritual*, ed. Raymond J. DeMallie and Elaine A. Jahner, 216–39. Lincoln: University of Nebraska Press, 1980.

———. *Lakota Belief and Ritual*. Edited by Raymond J. DeMallie and Elaine A. Jahner. Lincoln: University of Nebraska Press, 1980.

———. *Lakota Myth*. Edited by Elaine A. Jahner. Lincoln: University of Nebraska Press, 1983.

———. *Lakota Society*. Edited by Raymond J. DeMallie. Lincoln: University of Nebraska Press, 1982.

———. "Marriage and Divorce." In James R. Walker, *Lakota Society*, ed. Raymond DeMallie, 41–44. Lincoln: University of Nebraska Press, 1982.

———. "Oglala Social Customs." In James R. Walker, *Lakota Society*, ed. Raymond J. DeMallie, 50–69. Lincoln: University of Nebraska Press, 1982.

———. "Short Bull's Painting of the Third Day of the Sun Dance." In James R. Walker, *Lakota Belief and Ritual*, ed. Raymond J. DeMallie and Elaine A. Jahner, 185–91. Lincoln: University of Nebraska Press, 1980.

———. "The Sun Dance and Other Ceremonies of the Oglala Division of the Teton Dakota." *Anthropological Papers of the American Museum of Natural History* 16, pt. 2 (1917): 51–221.

Wallace, Anthony F. C. *The Long, Bitter Trail: Andrew Jackson and the Indians*. New York: Hill and Wang, 1993.

Washburn, Wilcomb E. *The American Indian and the United States*. New York: Random House, 1973.

———. *The Assault on Indian Tribalism: The General Allotment Act (Dawes Act) of 1887*. Philadelphia: Lippencott, 1975.

———. *The Indian in America*. New York: Harper and Row, 1975.

———. "Indian Removal Policy: Administrative, Historical and Moral Criteria for Judging Its Success or Failure." *Ethnohistory* 12, no. 3 (1965).

Welsh, Herbert. "How to Bring the Indian to Citizenship, and Citizenship to the Indian." In *Office of the Indian Rights Association*. Philadelphia: Indian Rights Association, 1892.

Welsh, William. *Report of a Visit to the Sioux and Ponka Indians on the Missouri River*. Washington, D.C.: U.S. Government Printing Office, 1872.

Westropp, Henry Ignatius. *Bits of Missionary Life among the Sioux*. Pine Ridge Reservation, S.Dak.: Holy Rosary Mission, c. 1911.

———. "Catechists among the Sioux," *Catholic Missions* 2 (1908): 113–14.

———. "Indian Missions in South Dakota." *Annals of the Propagation of the Faith* 64 (1904): 140–41.

———. "Letter of the Rev. H. I. Westropp, S. J., to the Rev. Joseph Freri, D. C. L., Director of the Society for the Propagation of the Faith." In *Annals of the Propagation of the Faith* 67 (1904): 139–42.

Wissler, Clark. "Societies and Ceremonial Associations of the Oglala Division of the Teton-Dakota." In *Anthropological Papers of the American Museum of Natural History* 11, pt. 2 (1912): 1–110.

Yarrow, Henry C. "Some Superstitions of the Live Indians." *American Antiquarian and Oriental Journal* 4 (1882): 136–44.

Young, Mary E. *Redskins, Ruffleshirts and Rednecks: Indian Allotments in Alabama and Mississippi, 1830–1860*. Norman: University of Oklahoma Press, 1961.

Unpublished Documents

Buechel, Eugene. Diary. Bureau of Catholic Indian Missions Records, Marquette University Archives, Milwaukee, Wisc.

Digmann, Florentine. "History of the Saint Francis Mission: 1886–1924." Bureau of Catholic Indian Missions Records, Marquette University Archives, Milwaukee, Wisc.

Gibbons, James Cardinal. "Petition of James Cardinal Gibbons, Archbishop of Baltimore, for Himself and Behalf of Other Catholic Archbishops of the United States, Praying the Congress for a Reopening of the Indian Contract School Question; for an Inquiry Concerning the Whole Subject of Indian Education, and for an Investigation, by Committee, of the Schools Operated under both the Government and the Contract System," December 5, 1898. BCIM Records, Marquette University Archives, Milwaukee, Wisc.

"Instruction by Means of the Two Roads." Bureau of Catholic Indian Mission Records, Marquette University Archives, Milwaukee, Wisc.

Ketcham, William. "The Nation's Wards." c. 1912. Bureau of Catholic Indian Mission Records, Marquette University Archives, Milwaukee, Wisc.

Mason, Sr. Liguori. "History of the American Foundation." Sisters of St. Francis of Penance and Christian Charity. Provincial Archives. Stella Niagara, N.Y.

Perrig, Emil. Diary, vol. 1. Bureau of Catholic Indian Missions Records, Marquette University Archives, Milwaukee, Wisc.

Ricker, Eli S. "Transcripts from the Sioux and Arapaho Delegation to Washington, D.C.," 1878. Eli S. Ricker Collection, RG8, Tablet 37, Nebraska Historical Society, Lincoln, Neb.

Sisters of St. Francis of Penance and Christian Charity. House History, St. Francis Mission. Provincial Archives, Stella Niagara, N.Y.

———. Jahresberichte, St. Francis Mission. Provincial Archives, Stella Niagara, N.Y.

Society of Jesus, St. Francis Mission. "House History." Bureau of Catholic Indian Mission Records, Marquette University Archives, Milwaukee, Wisc.

Weisenhorn, C. M. "Great Catholic Sioux Congress," c. 1919. Bureau of Catholic Indian Mission Records, Marquette University Archives, Milwaukee, Wisc.

Westropp, Henry Ignatius. "In the Land of the Wigwam: Children's Lecture on the Jesuit Missions in S. Dakota" (n.d.). Bureau of Catholic Indian Mission Records, Marquette University Archives, Milwaukee, Wisc.

Index

Page numbers in italic type indicate illustrations.